Classical Modern Philosophy

A contemporary introduction

Jeffrey Tlumak

 Routledge
Taylor & Francis Group

LONDON AND NEW YORK

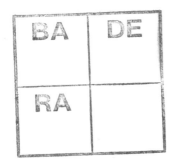

First published 2007
by Routledge
2 Park Square, Milton Park, Abingdon, Oxon OX14 4RN

Simultaneously published in the USA and Canada
by Routledge
270 Madison Ave, New York, NY 10016

Routledge is an imprint of the Taylor & Francis Group, *an informa business*

© 2007 Jeffrey Tlumak

Typeset in Garamond and Gill Sans by Taylor & Francis Books
Printed and bound in Great Britain by TJ International Ltd, Padstow, Cornwall

British Library Cataloguing in Publication Data
A catalogue record for this book is available from the British Library

Library of Congress Cataloging in Publication Data
A catalog record for this book has been requested

ISBN10: 0-415-27592-X
ISBN10: 0-415-27593-8
ISBN10: 0-203-64242-2

ISBN13: 978-0-415-27592-7 (hbk)
ISBN13: 978-0-415-27593-4 (pbk)
ISBN13: 978-0-203-64242-9 (ebk)

To my splendid daughter, Jennifer
My touchstone for what counts most
With my love and admiration

Contents

Preface

This is a guide through the systems of the seven brilliant seventeenth- and eighteenth-century European philosophers most regularly taught in college Modern Philosophy courses. I have taught Modern Philosophy at Vanderbilt University twenty-seven times, never quite the same way twice. I have taught graduate seminars on individual Moderns twenty-three times (as well as tutorials on more focused student concerns – twenty-two on Kant alone), also never mimicking an earlier outing. This is not because I am a glutton for gratuitously hard work, but because every time I restudy the magnificent contributions of these thinkers I see still more which convinces me that they are even better than I had judged, and so I both enthusiastically want and feel obliged to convey my improved understanding and evaluation. No doubt this means that I will believe I could represent these systems still more elegantly and forcibly by the time you read this. But we should not let the perfect be the enemy of the good, and I do think you will enjoy an unusually up-to-date, sympathetic appreciation of these great minds in the incarnation of my efforts now before you.

I struggled with overall format, and concluded I could serve you best by treating with special care the masterworks of each philosopher studied most often, and using that treatment as the skeleton around which all enrichments from other sources should be organized. I can assure you that even if you are not reading some selected masterwork, taking my journey will help you grapple with your text. The pivotal texts I will explore and interrelate are Descartes' *Meditations on First Philosophy*, Spinoza's *Ethics*, Locke's *An Essay Concerning Human Understanding*, Leibniz's *Discourse on Metaphysics* and *Monadology*, Berkeley's *A Treatise Concerning the Principles of Human Knowledge* and *Three Dialogues between Hylas and Philonous*, Hume's *An Enquiry Concerning Human Understanding*, *A Treatise of Human Nature*, and *Dialogues Concerning Natural Religion*, and Kant's *Critique of Pure Reason* and *Groundwork of the Metaphysics of Morals*.

I aim to give you well-informed guidance. I will do so by combining my own readings of these ingenious efforts with fair representations of serious, alternative interpretations. Since Modern Philosophy courses tend to concentrate on metaphysics, the study of the nature and structure of reality, and epistemology, the study of the nature, scope, and limits of knowledge and justified belief, I will highlight those concerns, but will also put those concerns in systematic context. Finally, because of their extraordinary influence on subsequent philosophy and especially prominent role in contemporary debates, and because discussion of a wider set of their concerns provides a significantly more complete understanding of our period, I devote notice-ably more space to Descartes, Hume, and Kant than our other innovators, but I hope my admiration for all seven shows throughout. If possible, read Chapter 1 before you study any of the others; minimally read section 1.10, a summary of Cartesian commitments which set the agenda for subsequent defenders and critics.

Acknowledgments

I thank the many fine students who have allowed me the joy to reread and rethink the masterpieces of modern philosophy. Among my graduate students, these include Paul Moser, Andy Cling, Daryl Hale, Tim McGrew, Dan Silber, John Lysaker, Jeff Tiel, Derek Turner, Brian Ribeiro, Tommy Crocker, Scott Aikin, James Bednar, Steve Hammontree, Toni Nicoletti, Diane Williamson, and my first, wonderful supervisee and friend, the late Scott Shuger. Among my own teachers, special thanks to Fred Feldman, who influenced me most; thanks also to Bruce Aune, Vere Chappell, Gareth Matthews, Robert Sleigh, Robert Paul Wolff, and the late Roderick Chisholm. Among my own graduate student classmates, fondest memories of Michael Hooker, who remained my closest friend until his untimely death. Gregg Horowitz and Rob Talisse embody what one seeks and admires in departmental colleagues; I appreciate their enriching friendship. Among those in the profession with whom I am not intimate, the most impactful on this book have been Robert Adams, Henry Allison, Annette Baier and Barry Stroud. Of course many others have informed and motivated me as well, including an anonymous referee who commented on my near-completed manuscript for Routledge. Finally, I most deeply appreciate my daughters, Jennifer and Zena, who have bolstered immeasurably the abiding sense of stability and meaningful commitment that frames life's various challenges and opportunities.

1 Descartes and the Rise of Modern Philosophy

Modern philosophy emerged in Europe during the early seventeenth century, and it profoundly changed Western ways of thinking. René Descartes, who set much of the agenda for this new and enormously influential stage of intellectual history, aimed to break decisively with what he saw as unreliable and unproductive traditions. He sought a new and empowering path to genuine knowledge and well-being; in the process he transformed the way we think about the universe, ourselves, nature, God, knowledge, and philosophy itself.

Descartes' philosophy embodies the central, modern idea that each person can discover which beliefs are true, and what actions are right, without imposition of outside authority. But his individualism is especially radical. He pursues truth in the solitude of his own thinking, using extreme doubt as a vital tool. He explains his methodology:

> I do not know whether I should tell you of the first meditations that I had . . . for they are perhaps too metaphysical and uncommon for everyone's taste. And yet, to make it possible to judge whether the foundations I have chosen are firm enough, I am in a way obliged to speak of them. For a long time I had observed . . . that in practical life it is sometimes necessary to act upon opinions which one knows to be quite uncertain just as if they were indubitable. But since I now wished to devote myself solely to the search for truth, I thought it necessary to do the very opposite and reject as if absolutely false everything in which I could imagine the least doubt, in order to see if I was left believing anything that was entirely indubitable. Thus . . . I resolved to pretend that all the things that ever entered my mind were no more true than the illusions of my dreams. But immediately I noticed that while I was trying thus to think everything false, it was necessary that I, who was thinking this, was something. And observing that this truth '*I am thinking, therefore I exist*' was so firm and sure that all the most extravagant suppositions of the skeptics were incapable of shaking it, I decided that I could accept it without scruple as the first principle of the philosophy I was seeking.
>
> (Cottingham, Stoothoff, and Murdoch, (1984–91),
> hereafter abbreviated CSM I 126–7)

Why did Descartes adopt this radical procedure? And how did it spur the two centuries of transformation that came to be known as modern philosophy? In this chapter I will motivate Descartes' project and isolate key features of modern philosophy in contrast with earlier traditions. I will then use a stage-by-stage discussion of the exquisitely developed *Meditations*, enriched by several of Descartes' other writings to assist your understanding and evaluation, not only to trace his method and system, but to highlight the landmarks that evoke the defining reactions of later moderns, and very many philosophers still. I will alert you when I treat some key phases of Descartes' philosophy more precisely or deeply. And I'll end with a rich set of questions to prompt further reflection, and a carefully selected, annotated bibliography to guide further research. This first chapter and the final chapter on Kant are quite the longest of the book, because both are intended as more painstaking models for approaching important thinkers with sympathy and layered levels of depth. Given the overriding educational function of the book, I cannot replicate fully this pattern in the other five chapters, though it pains me not to. Also this chapter must carefully prepare us for the rest of our exciting journey.

1.1   Background to Descartes' *Meditations*

Descartes gives a simple, autobiographical reason for why he was compelled to action. In his first published work, *Discourse on Method*, he recounts his deep disenchantment with school-books and the book of the world, which led him to study the book of his own soul. After years of voracious study at the new but well regarded Jesuit College of La Flèche, Descartes was frustrated with two thousand years of inquiry. Scholars disagreed on virtually every important issue, yet lacked a procedure for resolving their disagreements. There was even a long-standing dispute over how to conduct inquiry itself. This dispute was most heated in the battle between faith and reason.[1]

After the Roman Empire collapsed in AD 476, the Catholic Church oversaw all formal education in Europe for nearly a thousand years. A dominant question during this millennium concerned the proper relation between natural reason and revelation, a relation that underlies, and potentially threatens, the very nature and existence of philosophy. Some insisted that God sent revelations into the world as a substitute for all other knowledge. So philosophy, the champion of reason, is unnecessary and, since sometimes at odds with revelation, harmful. Others tried to combine religious truth with philosophy, treating philosophical wisdom as rational understanding of faith. On this view, revelation is the essential data of philosophy; unbelievers have nothing important to understand. This

---

1   An elegant presentation of the medieval debate on this issue is Gilson, E. 1938. My presentation parallels part of Gilson's.

approach took different forms, depending on how rational understanding was conceived. So, for example, St Augustine, who inaugurated this tradition in the early fifth century, offered a Platonic understanding of Christian revelation, since for him philosophy was largely the body of ideas from Plato, as revised by the Roman philosopher Plotinus (Aristotle's works were largely unknown in Europe at the time). St Augustine's faith-before-reason outlook was restated in different form seven centuries later by St Anselm, for whom logic was the model for proper understanding, and who therefore aimed to translate Christian beliefs into a series of logical demonstrations. And later, when mathematics and experimental science became the models of understanding, articles of faith were examined through math and science.

A different sort of combination of faith and reason urged seeking to know God in every possible way, and maintained that different types of minds take different approaches to the same truth. So, for example, followers of Averroës held that simple believers respond to imagination and emotion more than reason; theologians respond to reason, yet settle for probable answers because they fit with what they already believe; and philosophers insist on rational demonstration, and should be open to any probative source, including the so-called "pagan philosophy" of Greek thought. But some Averroëan doctrine, such as the denial of creation in time and personal immortality, contradicts Christian faith. This caused some convinced by Averroës to lose faith. But others retained both faith and philosophy by strictly separating them, treating faith and reason as two insulated ways of relating to the world.

The thirteenth-century philosopher St Thomas Aquinas introduced a fourth framework for inquiry, in which faith and reason can happily coexist. Faith cannot be endangered by reason because it is a different kind of commitment to a different kind of object. Philosophical assent is based on evidence, while no amount of evidence is sufficient to cause faith, which requires intervention of the will. But we cannot insulate faith from reason by allowing that a rationally necessary conclusion need not be true. True revelation can give everyone the insight they need for eternal salvation, including insight about God, humanity, and human destiny. Some aspects of this insight, like God's existence and the existence and immortality of the human soul, can be known by reason operating on its own. Other truths, like those of the Trinity, Incarnation or Redemption, are articles of faith, unverifiable by human reason. Yet even here, philosophical reasoning can be used to remove objections to articles of faith. If a philosophical conclusion conflicts with faith, there is something confused about the philosophy.

Many would not embrace Aquinas' conciliatory outlook. In the fourteenth century, important figures such as William of Ockham pressed the view that reason can prove nothing about God; increasingly, revelation was being divorced from reason. And by the fifteenth and sixteenth centuries – the doorsteps to modern philosophy – there was growing skepticism that philosophy has any relevance to religion. Theologians disagreed among themselves, and there was no way to tell whom to believe. In France, the essayist Michel Montaigne ridiculed philosophical attempts to know anything, and vividly reminded all serious inquirers about one of the deepest and most insistent challenges of the ancient skeptics: the problem of the criterion.[2] By what method or procedure do we choose the best or truest among several conflicting beliefs? And once we choose one of the available criteria, how can we tell if our criterion for choosing is itself valid?

It is tempting to say that a valid procedure or criterion is one that gives true results. But how do we judge which are the true results? If we appeal to our criterion to tell us, our argument is circular, and proves nothing. If we appeal to a second criterion, people who disagree with us will demand that we justify the new criterion. If we then continue to invoke more criteria, the process would repeat itself to infinity, unless unlikely, universal agreement on some later criterion emerges. But unless we appeal to other criteria, our only alternative seems to be foot-stomping, dogmatic reassertion of our belief against all who disagree, mere declaration of principle or statement of faith, no attempted justification. Ultimately, it seems that our views about important and contentious matters always rest on choices or assumptions that can never be fully justified. Montaigne warned that people tend to concoct arguments to support things they already want, and that this rationalization often hardens into intense, arrogant conviction.

Just as there were conditions frustrating the prospects of a sound, antiauthoritarian, individualistic philosophy, other events eased Descartes' efforts. During the fifteenth and early sixteenth centuries the Church had become increasingly secularized as it had become deeply involved in promoting the creative arts, and in studying non-religious, classical ideas to reconcile or integrate them with Church doctrines. On the one hand, a more secular Church made room for innovations such as Machiavelli's first purely secular treatise on politics. But even backlash had salutary effects, as when four years later Martin Luther accused Roman Catholicism of being too liberal in doctrine and too secular in operation. In seeking to purify Christianity and to return to its biblical foundations, reformers like Luther stressed that an individual can discover unbiased, objective truth, independent of vested authorities. Independence soon worked against Luther's intention, when the Bible itself began to be critically examined as a source of objective truth, especially by astronomers and other scientists. Predictably, the tension between faith and reason worsened.

The Catholic Church tried to counteract Protestant gains, but this only energized the individualist spirit of the times. For example, the Church established a superb educational program, headed by the Jesuits, to produce young Catholics who could outsmart heretics and promote the orthodox

---

2   The ancient skeptics' statement of the problem of the criterion occurs in Sextus Empiricus, *Outlines of Pyrrhonism*. Montaigne employs the problem in *Apology for Raymond Sebond*.

cause. In France alone, over 200 schools taught Thomism – the philosophy of Thomas Aquinas – as refined by the Spanish Jesuit Francisco Suarez. But the Jesuit curriculum also included full exposure to classical Greek and Renaissance materials, and this further opened the minds of students, including Galileo and Descartes.

The conflict between Protestants and Catholics highlighted why the problem of the criterion seems inescapable. Protestants insisted that the Catholic criteria for truth – which included the Bible, along with the authoritative declarations of the Church – were flawed: Protestants noted that popes and councils disagreed; they complained that popes had sanctioned activities contrary to Scripture, and so on. Yet from the Catholic point of view, the Protestant criterion of individual conscience was flawed: individuals obviously disagree, and Catholics believed that an authoritative interpreter was needed. Meanwhile, the new scientists relied on observational and mathematical evidence, and they dismissed any view – Catholic or Protestant – which said that God had created the earth as the center of the universe.

How can we tell where the truth lies? And if we cannot tell where it lies – if skepticism is victorious – then how can we rely on philosophy, religion, or science? The need to assimilate the new sciences, and the need to answer the skeptics, led Descartes to focus on the question of *how* we can know things. We must first solve this question before we can address questions of *what* we know. So Descartes set an agenda for the modern period by tackling central questions asked by philosophers throughout history, such as: what is the world like? What am I like? What is God's nature, and does he exist? What are the relations between God (if he exists), me (and humans generally) and the world? How should I live in light of answers to the previous questions? But he insisted that before one can responsibly broach any of these questions, one must decide by what method, if any, proper inquiry can be conducted. This ground-floor preoccupation with method is especially characteristic of modern philosophy.

So Descartes confronted a situation that motivated rejection of traditional paths to knowledge for a turn to his proposed alternative of rigorous self-examination. But he has much deeper, theoretical reasons also. A further look at his intellectual journey will uncover those reasons. And a road map will help. Descartes provides us much of this road map in the form of a metaphor:

> . . . the whole of philosophy is like a tree. The roots are metaphysics, the trunk is physics, and the branches emerging from the trunk are all the other sciences, which may be reduced to three principal ones, namely medicine, mechanics, and morals. By 'morals' I understand the highest and most perfect moral system, which presupposes a complete knowledge of the other sciences and is the ultimate level of wisdom. Now just as it is not the roots or the trunk of a tree from which one

gathers the fruit, but only the ends of the branches, so the principal benefit of philosophy depends on those parts of it which can only be learnt last of all.

(CSM I 186)

All the most empowering sciences depend on the science of physics. But physics, in turn, depends on metaphysics, or what Descartes calls *first philosophy*. If we add to this metaphor that one can plant and nurture to maturity the tree of lasting knowledge only if we use the correct method, and that when using this demanding method, one should follow certain provisional practical rules for living in the meantime, in order to get by, we have in miniature Descartes' philosophical project. Let us unpack some of the extraordinary detail of this project and make it more nearly full-size.

Nothing in Descartes' family upbringing explains his intellectual interests.[3] He was born in 1596 into an old, honorable and moderately wealthy French provincial family. His father was a regional politician; his mother died of a lung disease when he was only fourteen months old. Descartes himself inherited serious respiratory problems that plagued him at least until his early twenties; in fact, these problems led doctors to predict his early death. Descartes said that he eventually overcame these difficulties by habitually seeing things from the most favorable angle: he sought to make his happiness depend upon himself alone, not on things beyond his control.

Other evidence suggests Descartes was in fragile health all his life. At ten years old, he was sent to live and study at the Jesuit College of La Flèche. There he was excused from morning exercise and given a private room because of his frail health. Working in bed all morning became a lifelong habit. At La Flèche, he received his first exposure to science and math; traditional physics bored him, but math delighted him with its clarity and certainty.

Descartes left school at eighteen, and nothing of intellectual importance seems to have occurred for the next four years. But at age twenty-two he was befriended in Holland by an impressive thirty-year-old Dutchman named Isaac Beeckman, who got Descartes very excited about pure and applied mathematics. At one point, Descartes boasted that in less than a week he had found solutions to four math problems that had long remained unsolved. He told Beeckman of his intention to give the world a completely *new procedure* for solving any arithmetic or geometric problem:

. . . an entirely new science . . . will allow of a general solution to all problems that can be proposed in any and every kind of quantity, continuous or discontinuous, each in accordance with its nature . . . so

---

3   My account of Descartes' life is an amalgam of several sources studied over time, but is most directly contoured by Gaukroger, S. 1995, supplemented by Keeling, S.V. 1968, Kenny, A. 1968, and Rée, J. 1975.

that almost nothing will remain to be discovered in geometry."[4] He described his contributions as being "as superior to the ordinary geometry as Cicero's rhetoric is to the child's ABC.

Descartes was so stimulated by his interaction with Beeckman that he became increasingly engrossed in reflection. Some evidence says that he became obsessed, perhaps verging on mental breakdown. By the age of twenty-three, Descartes mulled plans for a completely new and powerful science. Then, on 10 November 1619, Descartes had a succession of three vivid dreams, which he interpreted as a vision expressing his mission in life.

Adrien Baillet, Descartes' first important biographer, wrote in 1691 that after Descartes had stripped himself of all prejudices, he clearly saw his goal. But he did not yet see the means of achieving it: "Nothing was left but the love of Truth, the pursuit of which was to be his sole occupation for the rest of his life . . . However, the means of making this happy conquest caused him as much trouble as that goal itself."[5] The search agitated Descartes' mind violently. Baillet wrote that Descartes found himself in a continual struggle, from which he could find no diversion:

> [He found relief neither] in walking nor in human society. This so exhausted him that his brain took fire, and he fell into a sort of enthusiasm, which so affected his mind, already over-tired, that it left him in the condition to receive the impressions of dreams and visions . . . He tells us that on 10 November 1619, having gone to bed *completely filled with enthusiasm*, and wholly preoccupied with the thought *of having found that very day the foundation of the wonderful science*, he had three consecutive dreams in the same night, which he imagined could have come only from on high.
>
> (Cole 1992: 32–3)

Descartes interpreted the first two dreams as a reproach for his past life; the third seemed to encourage his philosophical aspirations. Descartes' new approach would be to use a single method to unify all of the seemingly disparate sciences, and mathematics as well.

Descartes' central thesis was this. A mathematical understanding of the physical world, based on pure reason, is more objective than any picture of the world based on the senses. The only essential qualities of matter are measurable properties like size and shape, and all natural phenomena can be explained in terms of these geometric properties and motion. Descartes became the first to define motion by using the principles of conservation, a

---

4   Translated from Adam, C. and Tannery, P., eds (11 vols published 1964–74) *Oeuvres de Descartes*, 2nd edn, Paris: From vol X, 157. A different translation of this 26 March 1619 letter to Beeckman occurs in Gaukroger 1995: 92–3.

5   From Adrien Baillet's *Vie de Monsieur Des Cartes* (1691), cited in Cole, J.R. 1992: 32.

concept that would become more familiar through the physics of Isaac Newton in the later seventeenth century.

Descartes' method allowed him to take seemingly unsolvable problems and translate them into a precise mathematical language, in which they could then be solved. Most famously, he showed that relations between numbers can be represented by geometric constructions, and vice versa. This means that the same general results can be proved about mathematical relations between lines, between figures, and between numbers. Descartes showed that in effect, all measurable and orderable things can be treated in a similar way.

Descartes sought to identify the systematic and quantifiable features of things, or what he called their *simple natures*. This Cartesian view promotes a particular sense of what constitutes a good explanation, and it has profoundly influenced both our science and our ordinary thinking. Descartes required that good explanations be *reductive* and *compositional* – which means they explain many things in terms of a few basic features that make up a broader and more complex reality. By contrast, Aristotle had explained observable things in highly abstract and non-quantitative terms; he assumed that the natural world has a fixed, hierarchical structure, and that each kind of thing behaves in a characteristic way due to its specific nature, or *form*.

Descartes' new manner of explanation also differs from common sense because it does not focus on things that appear to our senses. How an object appears depends partially on the perceiver: appearances therefore depend on the context in which the object is perceived, the relations between perceiver and object, and so on. Appearances are relative to variable conditions. And we cannot even say which of several appearances is most accurate, for again we lack a criterion for choosing between them. An object's real properties are said to be objective qualities like size and shape, not subjective qualities like color or taste. Descartes argued that a sense-based or empirical conception of the world is open to doubt, but that a mathematical conception of the world is beyond doubt.

Finally, Descartes' metaphysics – his fundamental account of things – explains why his mathematical approach applies to reality so well. Cartesian metaphysics affirms that the human mind can successfully achieve this more *objective* conception.

Before he wrote the *Meditations*, Descartes made extremely important contributions in physics, meteorology, optics, and physiology: his studies included both theoretical work and hands-on activities like lens-grinding and anatomical dissections. He published the first unified celestial and terrestrial physics; his physiological studies aimed to cover everything from embryology to psychology, medicine and morals (theory of how to live the good human life). He pursued a panorama of other activities as well, from studying glaciers to computing the heights of mountains. Cartesian theory paved the way for a vast amount of experimental work, whose ongoing success has verified the modern science of matter. Yet some of Descartes' specific conclusions in physics were soon left in the dust by the work of Sir Isaac Newton.

Descartes was not the first to believe that physics is actually just a branch of mathematics. In *Il Saggiatore*, his elder contemporary, Galileo, also insisted that the book of the universe is written in the language of mathematics:

> Philosophy is written in this grand book – I mean the universe – which stands continually open to our gaze, but it cannot be understood unless one first learns to comprehend the language and interpret the characters in which it is written. It is written in the language of mathematics, and its characters are triangles, circles and other geometrical figures, without which it is humanly impossible to understand a single word of it; without these one is wandering about in a dark labyrinth.
>
> (Cited in Machamer, P. 1998: 64–5)

The brilliant astronomer Johannes Kepler also emphasized the role of quantity – that is, mathematics. He said that just as ears are made for sound, and eyes for color, the mind is meant to consider quantity; it wanders in darkness when it leaves quantitative thought behind. But it was Descartes who fully developed this mathematical, objective view of the universe and explained its revolutionary consequences. Descartes felt especially compelled to a give a philosophical defense of his physics because it aroused so much antagonism.

Descartes was charged with atheism because his views allow, for example, the possibility that the world has no beginning in time. In Descartes' day, almost no one professed atheism (as we understand the term today); virtually everyone professed to believe in God. But there were passionate disputes over what type of God exists, and how God is related to humanity and to nature. In trying to establish how to answer such questions, the problem of the criterion repeatedly arose, and it stymied any resolution to the issues at hand.

There were many threats to Descartes' scientific outlook. His work was chilled by the unexpected news that Galileo had been condemned and confined to house arrest by the Inquisition in Rome. Now Descartes' philosophical project became even more pressing, and in writing to a friend he referred to Galileo's book:

> I was told that it had indeed been published but that all the copies had immediately been burnt at Rome, and that Galileo had been convicted and fined. I was so astonished at this that I almost decided to burn all my papers or at least to let no one see them. For I could not imagine that he – an Italian and, I understand, in the good graces of the Pope – could have been made a criminal for any other reason than that he tried, as he no doubt did, to establish that the earth moves. I know that some Cardinals had already censured this view, but I thought I had heard it said that all the same it was being taught publicly even in Rome. I must admit that if the view is false, so too are the entire foundations of my philosophy, for it can be demonstrated from them quite clearly.
>
> (CSM III 40–1)

Descartes now faced a challenge: how could he persuade the Church authorities that his new philosophical principles were consistent with religion – and that they even support religion? If he could do this, then he could show that his physics follows from his philosophical principles. And if those philosophical principles could be understood to be absolutely certain from anyone's unprejudiced perspective, then his physics could safely see the light of day.

1.2   Descartes' innovations in how philosophy is written

In one of the truly great and beautiful philosophical writings of all time – the work entitled *Meditations on First Philosophy* – Descartes defends the foundation for his unified system of knowledge. Meditations are mental exercises designed to find truth within, and Descartes seemed to have been the first to use them in a work not chiefly aimed at morality or religion.

Descartes' style was deeply personal; he wrote in the first person, and invited his readers to think along with him from their own points of view. This approach reflects the spirit of modern thought, which is distinctively individualistic and anti-authoritarian. Descartes also achieved this extraordinary blend of the personal and impersonal in his anonymously published *Discourse on Method.* In this work Descartes proposed his scientific and philosophical revolution for the first time, and he solicited manpower and money for the innumerable experiments needed to uncover the laws of nature.

The *Discourse on Method* is what we might call an anonymous autobiography: it reveals Descartes the man, but in a way that treats his particular identity as irrelevant. Descartes thought of his own journey as representing all human inquiry: we all follow the path on our own, but we arrive at the same destination. The *Discourse* outlined four rules of theoretical method, and sketched a provisional guide to practical living to be followed while engaged in theoretical inquiry. The rules are quite general – so general that Leibniz later complained that they amounted to no more than the vacuous advice to take what you need, and do what you must, and you'll get what you want – but in the earlier fragment, *Rules for the Direction of the Mind*, and in the determinate execution of the *Meditations*, we can better appreciate their power.

Just as religious meditations seek to escape the darkness of sin and achieve spiritual illumination, Descartes' *Meditations* urge an escape from the confusion of sense perception so we can arrive at the certainty found in reason. Following the right path allows a philosophical novice to become a master of timeless truths. Indeed, Descartes stressed in the opening words of the *Discourse* that a correct method is essential:

> Good sense is the best distributed thing in the world: for everyone thinks himself so well endowed with it that even those that are the

hardest to please in everything else do not usually desire more of it than they possess. In this it is unlikely that everyone is mistaken. It indicates rather that the power of judging well and of distinguishing the true from the false – which is what we properly call 'good sense' or 'reason' – is naturally equal in all men, and consequently that the diversity of our opinions does not arise because some of us are more reasonable than others but solely because we direct our thoughts along different paths and do not attend to the same things. For it is not enough to have a good mind; the main thing is to apply it well. The greatest souls are capable of the greatest vices as well as the greatest virtues; and those who proceed but very slowly can make much greater progress, if they always follow the right path, than those who hurry and stray from it.

(CSM I 111)

Meditations are well suited to Descartes' aims because they naturally follow the method needed for a successful inquiry, which struggles to set aside all preconceptions and to start anew. This method, which he calls *analysis*, must follow the order in which truths are discovered:

> Analysis shows the true way by means of which the thing in question was discovered methodically and as it were *a priori*, so that if the reader is willing to follow it and give sufficient attention to all points, he will make the thing his own and understand it just as perfectly as if he had discovered it for himself. But this method contains nothing to compel belief in an argumentative or inattentive reader; for if he fails to attend even to the smallest point, he will not see the necessity of the conclusion.

(CSM II 110)

Descartes contrasted analysis with synthesis: whereas analysis accepts truths in the order that they're discovered, synthesis begins with axioms, postulates, and definitions and then logically deduces further consequences. Descartes argued that the synthetic procedure cannot work in first philosophy, since what he called *primary notions* – the axioms, postulates, and definitions – are often disputed. A person may not be ready to accept another person's starting points:

> In metaphysics . . . nothing . . . causes so much effort as making our perception of the primary notions clear and distinct . . . they conflict with many preconceived opinions derived from the senses which we have got into the habit of holding from our earliest years, and so only those who really concentrate and meditate and withdraw their minds from corporeal things, so far as is possible, will achieve perfect knowledge of them.

(CSM II 111)

Descartes cited the work of the English philosopher Thomas Hobbes to illustrate how synthesis can go wrong. Hobbes was a contemporary critic of Descartes; he claimed that the method of geometry, and concepts from the new science of motion, could be applied also to humans in society. Galileo had shown that all bodies are naturally in motion, rather than at rest; Hobbes now affirmed that everything is a variety of motion. Even thoughts are just motions in the brain. Hobbes said that sensation is the bridge that connects movements of the external world to human behavior; human actions are therefore merely reactions to stimuli received by the sense organs. Hobbes deduced that humans are naturally selfish beings, and that duties are nothing more than enforceable agreements made by rational and self-interested agents.

Descartes was unimpressed; he rejected Hobbes' starting point, arguing that the new science of motion could not be applied to the human mind. Descartes argued that thoughts cannot be motions in the brain; he said that philosophical disputes like this have to be resolved by establishing (and not assuming) how the mind works. Descartes saw the need for a method that would eliminate the controversial assumptions made by all parties to a dispute. Analysis, beginning with maximal doubt, is that method, simultaneously a method of discovery and justification.

As to the crucial role of meditation, I doubt whether we should make more of the use of the meditational genre than indicated a moment ago. If you look at a seventeenth-century dictionary, "meditation" is generically defined as earnest, attentive study of any topic, and Descartes does stress that attentive reflection is required of all who take his project seriously, and that frequent repetition is needed to implant in memory discoveries made. In its more specific meaning, meditations are devotional exercises prescribed by authorities; philosophers wrote treatises and disputations, not meditations. But Descartes' meditator will call dogma into doubt, and success by performing the proposed cognitive and volitional exercises is not presupposed. Nor is seclusion or first person narrative uniquely devotional. Finally, a homely but telling reason not to take the narrowest conception of meditation as controlling the work's content is that Descartes composed it before deciding on a title, and typically referred to it in process as "my metaphysics" and "first philosophy," not "my meditations."

Yet another of Descartes' innovations was to publish the *Meditations* along with objections from various philosophers and theologians. He also included his replies to those objections. This was another sign of the modern anti-authoritarian spirit: one should be both self-critical and responsive to criticisms from others. Yet this also was Descartes' attempt to incorporate a variety of theological objections to his work, in the hope that his careful replies would persuade the Church to embrace his philosophy. (All but the Seventh Set of Objections questioned his God-proofs. All questioned his proofs that mind and body are really distinct. Hobbes and Gassendi, who authored the Third and Fifth Sets of Objections, respectively, especially pressed Descartes' confidence that matter can't think.) Descartes also helped to broaden philosophical debate by conducting it through written correspondence. His friend and literary agent Marin Mersenne acted as mailman, and Mersenne was a friendly critic of Descartes' work as well; he had a hand in the Second and Sixth Sets of Objections. Even before his first publication, Descartes wrote Mersenne:

> I am very grateful to you for the objections which you have sent me, and I beg you to continue to tell me all those you hear. Make them as unfavorable to me as you can: that will be the greatest pleasure you can give me. I am not in the habit of crying when people are treating my wounds, and those who are kind enough to instruct and inform me will always find me very docile.
>
> (CSM III 52–3)

Descartes had to debate by mail because he lived in relative seclusion in Holland. This communication method not only became a popular and important source of intellectual growth: it also changed the kinds of people involved in philosophical debate. Until then, virtually all intellectuals had been university professors and clergymen; intellectuals now came to include physicians, diplomats, tradesmen, and so on. Learning became increasingly democratized, both in terms of who offered instruction and who was deemed fit to receive it. In the early modern period, most philosophical writing was generally intended for all intelligent people, not merely for scholars.

In large measure, this liberating change resulted from two other pioneering decisions made by Descartes. First, he wrote the *Discourse on Method* and related essays in French, his native language. This was a calculated departure from Latin, the language of Europe's educated elite. Other writers were soon writing in their native languages with great relish and national pride. And second, traditional Scholastic philosophy had been written in a regimented format, but now Descartes was conveying his ideas in richly different ways: his works were delivered as meditations, autobiographical sketches, short essays, conversational dialogues, and so on. Descartes' so-called "new philosophy" – including what we would now call science – offered innovations both in form and in substance.

1.3 Lead-in to the First Meditation

The full title of Descartes' masterwork is *Meditations on First Philosophy in which are demonstrated the existence of God and the distinction between the human soul and the body.* This work is commonly known simply as the *Meditations*, and it opens with a letter dedicating the work to the theological faculty at the University of Paris. In Descartes' religiously troubled times, a Catholic writer naturally sought an endorsement from this faculty. The dedication repeatedly stresses how religiously proper it is to offer rational proofs for God's existence and the soul's immortality. Indeed, rational proofs were necessary to persuade atheists who were dismissing the traditional exhortations based on faith. Descartes claims that his proofs are the best constructible by a human mind. You can judge for yourself whether this is just blusterous self-promotion, or whether it is of the nature of his revolutionary method that this be so.

By offering rational proofs, Descartes was already taking a stand on the relation between faith and reason. He stated his position even more clearly in a letter to Father Dinet, the head of the Jesuits in France:

> As far as theology is concerned, since one truth can never be in conflict with another, it would be impious to fear that any truths discovered in philosophy could be in conflict with the truths of faith. Indeed, I insist that there is nothing relating to religion which cannot be equally well or even better explained by means of my principles than can be done by means of those which are commonly accepted.

> (CSM II 392)

One of Descartes' major goals was to displace Aristotle's method for natural science and philosophy, and to persuade the Church that his replacement was more congenial to the Christian faith.

The theologians at Paris did not collectively or officially endorse Descartes; one of them, Father Gibeuf, did approve the work, and none of the other theologians were actively hostile to Descartes' efforts at the time. But unhappily for Descartes, many theologians outside Paris were most displeased, and some (like Professor Voetius at Utrecht in Holland) worked energetically to slander him. Another critic, the devout Catholic mathematician Blaise Pascal, said in his *Pensées* 77, "I cannot forgive Descartes. In all his philosophy, he would have been quite willing to dispense with God but he could not help granting him a flick of the forefinger to start the world in motion. Beyond this, he has no need for God."

In 1650, at age fifty-four, Descartes died in Sweden, where he had accepted a court appointment as the Queen's tutor. Thirteen years after his death, the Roman Catholic Church placed all of his writings on the *Index of Prohibited Books*. Four years after that, when Descartes' body was returned to France, a court order prohibited a funeral oration at Descartes' reburial services. In 1685, King Louis XIV renewed a ban on teaching Descartes' philosophy in the universities. And opposition to Descartes continued in French universities into the next century. Followers of Descartes, called Cartesians, were excluded from the Academy of Science.

Ironically, there is every indication that Descartes was a sincere Christian believer who gave God an absolutely indispensable role in his philosophy. So was he an enemy or a friend to the church? Perhaps we can resolve this puzzle if we carefully trace the development of his *Meditations*. Descartes clearly aimed to demonstrate the existence of God, and to demonstrate the distinction between the human soul and the body. But first he had to accomplish several other tasks. Most especially, he had to sufficiently understand the various natures of God, the human soul, and the body, so he could determine clearheadedly their relations.

The *Meditations* therefore used the analytic method to increasingly refine – or, in Descartes' terminology, to "make more clear and distinct" – the ideas of God, soul and body. Descartes also wanted to establish the legitimacy of one way of thinking about these things. He believed it's not enough merely to show that a chosen way of thinking is superior to every alternative; he wanted to show that our best way of thinking is certainly true. If it is certainly true, then it cannot be doubted. Hence, the First Meditation is entitled, *What can be called into doubt*.

1.4   The First Meditation

Some years ago I was struck by the large number of falsehoods that I had accepted as true in my childhood, and by the highly doubtful nature of the whole edifice that I had subsequently based on them. I realized that it was necessary once in the course of my life to demolish everything completely and start again right from the foundations if I wanted to establish anything at all in the sciences that was stable and likely to last. But the task looked an enormous one, and I began to wait until I should reach a mature enough age to ensure that no subsequent time of life would be more suitable for tackling such inquiries. This led me to put the project off for so long that I would now be to blame if by pondering over it any further I wasted the time still left for carrying it out. So today I have expressly rid my mind of all worries and arranged for myself a clear stretch of free time. I am here quite alone, and at last I will devote myself sincerely and without reservation to the general demolition of my opinions.

(CSM II 12)

Descartes began with familiar facts, like the fact that we acquire many of our beliefs when we are immature children. These beliefs are based on naïve sense perception, unexamined instinct, and the say-so of teachers, who sometimes give unreliable or conflicting lessons. Our minds are thus contaminated, and this has ongoing ill effects. Our minds must be purified, and then restocked according to a rational, reliable plan. One who seeks truths must therefore call into doubt whatever can be doubted. This cleans the slate, and lets us start anew. Of course this search for truth is most meaningfully done under optimal conditions. For example, you should wait for maturity. Failure by an immature inquirer shows nothing about our general human capacity to know. Furthermore, in deciding what to believe, you should set aside practical concerns; you should not weigh the costs and benefits of how to use your time. Practical matters are context-dependent, and Descartes acknowledges that we must often act even when we are uncertain. For example, if we were to eat only when we were absolutely certain that a food is not poison, then we would die from starvation. Our everyday notion of knowledge is influenced by the constraints of social practice, and the demands of action and community. We are implicitly aware of these constraints, so that we are ordinarily satisfied with less than full knowledge.[6] But if we aim for indisputable truth, we must constantly and fully criticize not only what we believe to be false, but also our uncertain beliefs, and even the things we strongly believe to be true. Lastly, Descartes indicated that the quest for truth should be conducted individually, that is, alone. The goal of enduring science motivates the solitary and uninhibited challenge to every standing opinion. Previous sciences have failed to endure. No matter how lustrous they have seemed, in time they have been replaced with new alternatives. This prompts the "pessimistic induction" that although scientists may now feel utterly confident they speak the truth on some issue, their views too are very probably false, and sooner or later scientists themselves will acknowledge that.

Descartes was seeking a rock-solid basis for a universal science. This new science treated the world like a huge, causally determined, physical machine, but Descartes believed it was crucial to have a place for human individuality, freedom, and spirituality. That's partly why he worked to demonstrate that the human soul is entirely different from anything physical. (Though I do not mean to suggest he orchestrated this result. In fact, he was an enthusiastic proponent of physiological explanations of an enormous range of human activity, but, as we'll see, concluded that a few things were in principle unamenable to such explanation.) Descartes' challenge was to show how this impersonal material world could be successfully integrated with a personal, meaningful existence. He tried to use doubt as the basis for a consensus – but is consensus possible? A much closer look at the nature and role of doubt will help us decide.

One of Descartes' earliest critics was a Jesuit priest named Pierre Bourdin, who rejected doubt as a basis for discovering truth. Descartes responded to Bourdin's criticism:

> Here I shall employ an everyday example to explain to my critic the rationale for my procedure . . . Suppose he had a basket full of apples and, being worried that some of the apples were rotten, wanted to take out the rotten ones to prevent the rot spreading. How would he proceed? Would he not begin by tipping the whole lot out of the basket? And would not the next step be to cast his eye over each apple in turn, and pick up and put back in the basket only those he saw to be sound, leaving the others? In just the same way, those who have never philosophized correctly have various opinions in their minds which they have begun to store up since childhood, and which they therefore have reason

6   An excellent discussion of this point is found in Stroud 1984: 39–82.

to believe may in many cases be false. They then attempt to separate the false beliefs from the others, so as to prevent their contaminating the rest and making the whole lot uncertain. Now the best way they can accomplish this is to reject all their beliefs together in one go, as if they were all uncertain and false. They can then go over each belief in turn and re-adopt only those which they recognize to be true and indubitable. Thus I was right to begin by rejecting all my beliefs . . .

(CSM II 324)

Descartes began his meditations as a philosophical novice would, so he started with commonsense beliefs. (So it would probably be better to call the early inquirer "the meditator," since Descartes does not uniformly speak in his own maturely-considered voice. To what extent he speaks in his own voice, and whether his imagined interlocutors are Aristotelian Scholastic philosophers as well as people of common sense, are interesting interpretational controversies.) Common sense tells us that all knowledge is based on sense experience – either personal experience or the hearsay testimony of others. So to challenge all other previous beliefs, the meditator first challenged the sense perception on which they are based.

Descartes used a model which compares knowledge to a multi-storied building: the upper floors rest on the floors below, and all floors rest on the building's foundation. A rotten foundation undermines the integrity of the entire structure – and so it is with knowledge. Descartes used the model of a building in two ways. First, he said that without a foundation, there can be no building at all; unless we have a valid source of knowledge (such as sense perception), there can be no knowledge at all. Second, he noted that a body of knowledge, like a building, is a hierarchical system in which some items necessarily depend on others. Descartes asked whether there is any valid source of knowledge at all – and he used his method of doubt to test proposed answers.

The First Meditation sets a pattern in which Descartes gradually develops his knowledge by repeated self-criticism. He first offers his best idea and examines its weaknesses; he struggles to remedy the weaknesses, and then works to incorporate his newly refined idea. He proposes a source of knowledge – the senses – and then doubts it; he revises the proposal to avoid the doubts, then finds problems with the improved proposal. He then repeats the process until every source of knowledge he can think of has been doubted.

In doubting the first principle, the meditator observes that the senses deceive when objects are far away or very small, but seem reliable when objects are nearby and there are ideal conditions for observing. For example, it's insane to suppose that my senses deceive me when they tell me I'm now writing something about the philosopher Descartes.

Here we seem to have a new, more defensible principle of knowledge that says "trust the senses when they operate under ideal external conditions." Descartes now asks whether this principle is valid:

A brilliant piece of reasoning! As if I were not a man who sleeps at night, and regularly has all the same experiences while asleep as madmen do when awake – indeed sometimes even more improbable ones. How often, asleep at night, am I convinced of such familiar events – that I am here in my dressing gown, sitting by the fire – when in fact I am lying undressed in bed! . . . As I think about this more carefully, I see plainly that there are never any sure signs by means of which being awake can be distinguished from being asleep. The result is that I begin to feel dazed, and this feeling only reinforces the notion that I may be asleep.

(CSM II 13)

As the ancient Taoist philosopher, Chuang Tzu, lyrically put it:

The Chinese philosopher awakened with a start, for he had been dreaming that he was a butterfly. And for the rest of his days, he did not know whether he was a Chinese philosopher dreaming that he was a butterfly, or a butterfly who was now dreaming that he was a Chinese philosopher.[7]

By showing that dream images cannot reliably distinguish between illusion and reality, Descartes has demonstrated that we cannot rely on sense images alone to know what is going on in the world. This, I think, is his really *deep* insight, not that we can never tell whether we're awake. Even if I knew I was now awake, my wakeful sense images alone could never give me knowledge. This is a plain matter of consistency, or what is sometimes called *epistemic universalizabilty*. My sense images in dreams, even if they happen to coincide with what's really going on in the world, do not, we all agree, provide knowledge of that world. So, the phenomenologically same sense data, occurring when awake, can't suffice from our point of view either. I'm going beyond the sensory presentations when I judge that I know in the waking case, but not in the dreaming case.

The other principle some see Descartes invoking here is *deductive closure*, such that if I know that p, and actively know p entails q, then I know that q – if knowledge can't be transmitted through known logical entailments, it can never be transmitted, and we are stuck in the skeptical mud. Its application is that if the meditator knows that she's sitting by the fire, and knows that if she's sitting by the fire she's not asleep in bed dreaming, then she knows that she's not asleep in bed dreaming; but she can't rule out that she's

---

7   The fuller version of this remark occurs in Chuang Tzu 1968: 49: Once Chuang Chou dreamt he was a butterfly, a butterfly flitting and fluttering around, happy with himself and doing as he pleased. He didn't know he was Chuang Chou. Suddenly he woke up and there he was, solid and unmistakable Chuang Chou. But he didn't know if he was Chuang Chou who had dreamt he was a butterfly, or a butterfly dreaming he was Chuang Chou. Between Chuang Chou and a butterfly, there *must* be some distinction! This is called the Transformation of Things.

now asleep in bed and dreaming the fireside experience; therefore, by *modus tollens* (if *p* entails *q*, and *q* is false, then *p* is false), she doesn't know she's sitting by the fire. And if she doesn't know by sense experience something as palpable as that she's sitting by the fire, she can't know anything about the world by sense experience.

Of course, some beliefs seem to resist even the threat of dreams; for example, the truth of mathematical beliefs does not seem to depend on circumstances: whether I am awake or dreaming, two plus three is five! So Descartes still hasn't challenged all his previous beliefs.

An even more potent doubtmaker is needed to demolish all unreliable beliefs, and Descartes supplied such a doubtmaker in the form of a dilemma. Either we are created by an all-powerful God or we have humbler origins. An all-powerful God could do anything, including deceiving us systematically. But to the extent that our origins are humbler, we are less perfect beings, and so more susceptible to getting things wrong. So in either case, we can't rule out pervasive error.

Here too there are interesting interpretive disputes, especially about whether the evil demon threat that the meditator introduces represents the contradictory of the perfect God, so that they exclude each other, but one or the other must obtain; or whether the demon represents the logical contrary of the perfect God — an all-powerful bad guy — so that they exclude each other (their contrary wills cannot both prevail, and the loser's limitations will be exposed), but they do not exhaust all possibilities, so perhaps neither obtains. The important point is to find the strongest doubt possible, and then use it as an acid test. If a belief can resist the strongest doubt, we admit it into our system of knowledge; if it cannot resist this maximal doubt, then we do not count it as knowledge. Descartes thought that a deceiving God would be the strongest possible source of doubt — but he realized how difficult it would be for his readers to accept this religiously offensive hypothesis. So he ended the First Meditation by replacing a deceiving God with the pretense that an evil demon was exerting all efforts to deceive him. This was basically a vivid depiction of the possibility that he was constituted in such a way that even his best efforts went astray.

The American philosopher Charles Peirce criticized Descartes' use of maximally stringent doubt. He thought it was an empty verbal utterance to talk of a contemplative doubt that makes no practical difference. Peirce commented:

> Some philosophers have imagined that to start an inquiry it was only necessary to utter a question whether orally or by setting it down upon paper, and have even recommended us to begin our studies with questioning everything! But the mere putting of a proposition into the interrogative form does not stimulate the mind to any struggle after belief. There must be a real and living doubt, and without this all discussion is idle.

A person may, it is true, in the course of his studies, find reason to doubt what he began by believing; but in that case he doubts because he has a positive reason for it, and not on account of the Cartesian maxim. Let us not pretend to doubt in philosophy what we do not doubt in our hearts.

(Peirce 1955: 229)

Descartes himself stressed that it would be impractical – perhaps even insane – to doubt every method or practice or habit of everyday life. But at the same time, he explained that systematic doubt is necessary when your goal is timelessly true belief. And he insisted that a dominant and constructive purpose for using doubt is to show – often against all tradition and expectation – that certain things, such as God and the soul, are in fact easier to know than seemingly familiar things, like physical bodies. In the Synopsis of the *Meditations*, he said:

The great benefit of these arguments is not, in my view, that they prove what they establish – namely that there really is a world, and that human beings have bodies and so on – since no sane person has ever seriously doubted these things. The point is that in considering these arguments we come to realize that they are not as solid or as transparent as the arguments which lead us to knowledge of our own minds and of God, so that the latter are the most certain and evident of all possible objects of knowledge for the human intellect. Indeed, this is the one thing that I set myself to prove in these Meditations.

(CSM II 11)

Which doubts are real seems to vary with perspective, and perspectives can change. The crux of the issue between Peirce and Descartes seems to be whether we should aspire to a wholly secure, infallible outlook. If we do, then a procedure based on maximal doubt seems necessary. Yet Descartes understood how the force of habit makes it psychologically difficult for us even to ask certain questions. So he didn't merely announce his resolve to doubt everything; instead, he tried to capture the reader's imagination with ever stronger skeptical possibilities. He emphasized the need to rehearse these doubts many times; he hoped this would help us liberate ourselves from long-entrenched beliefs that resist our initial questioning.

The First Meditation is best appreciated by highlighting the special features of the way Descartes uses doubt, which is necessary to, but not exhaustive of, his method. Here I summarize seven proposed (not unconnected) features of doubt that seem especially crucial.

1   The doubt is *methodological*, a tool required for the task of finding something findable. It's not designed to calm or eradicate some unsatisfiable urge (as with some forms of ancient skepticism). But we cannot assume,

just because it is methodological, that it does not eventually affect belief and action, but only challenges theoretical knowledge-claims (legitimately made only when exaggeratedly stringent conditions are satisfied). Descartes stresses that metaphysical inquiry sets aside everyday, practical concerns and matters of faith, and seeks only to discover what is true and false, and how the human mind can on its own distinguish the two. But this "pure inquiry" purports to have significant implications for living as well as is humanly possible. Still, as methodological, the doubts are used as epistemic filter to test the certainty of subsequent conclusions; hypothetical doubts are epistemically possible suppositions (not ruled out by anything known for certain) to be disconfirmed, overcomable by a superior perspective.

2   So, doubts are used *preemptively*. The more radical the doubt, the more secure is whatever survives it, and Descartes presents his attempts at doubt to be in principle maximal. Here the task is to walk the line between restricting the scope or attitude of doubt in self-serving, and hence question-begging ways (thus not successfully resolving the problem of the criterion) and eliminating every possible basis for addressing the doubt so that it cannot be non-circularly refuted or rebutted (so again not resolving the problem of the criterion).

3   So also, metaphysical doubt is *preliminary* (albeit essential) to the real business of scientific investigation and attainment of its fruits.

4   It is also portrayed as *foundational* in three senses: done only once in a lifetime (compare influential methods that require lifelong pursuit); demonstrates the possibility of knowledge and articulates the framework used to develop it; and provides first principles which enable the derivation of other truths, but not vice versa (though it should be acknowledged that, historically, Descartes completed most of his scientific and mathematical work before he turned to "first philosophy," prompting suspicions about how foundational it is, accusations of insincerity, political interpretations of Descartes' philosophical goals, etc.).

5   Doubt itself is *developmental* (from real but strictly limited to hyperbolical but universal in intent), and conditions the developmental (dialectical) character of the *Meditations*.

6   Specifically, it is *clarifying*, enabling explicit recognition of implicitly-held principles, both exposing hidden prejudices and assisting activation and recognition of truth-guaranteeing dispositions, clarifying the essential nature of things, and in the proper order (first self, then God, and then nature).

7   It also seems *therapeutic* (taking psychology into account), weaning of preconceptions, enabling actual withdrawal from materialist and empiricist suppositions, addressed especially to the unconverted prejudiced, both the naïve and the wrongheaded scholastic. Other features of Descartes' procedure, for example his use of paradigm, representative cases to test an outlook, seem to flow from these salient features of Cartesian doubt.

It is also useful to appreciate that Descartes uses skeptical considerations at different junctures to combat three distinguishable anti-rationalist postures:

- failure to use reason, as with prejudiced judgment;
- misuse of reason, as with precipitous judgment; and
- mistrust of reason, as with entrenched (dogmatic) skeptical judgment.

One of the alleged beauties of the Cartesian method is its discovery of truths which are preconditions for engaging in doubt, hence indubitable truths.

But a century after Descartes had proposed his method, the great British philosopher David Hume declared that he was not impressed:

> There is a species of skepticism, *antecedent* to all study and philosophy, which is much inculcated by Descartes and others as a sovereign preservative against error and precipitate judgment. It recommends a universal doubt, not only of all our former opinions and principles, but also of our very faculties, of whose veracity, say they, we must assure ourselves by a chain of reasoning deduced from some original principle which cannot possibly be fallacious or deceitful. But neither is there any such original principle which has a prerogative above others that are self-evident and convincing. Or if there were, could we advance a step beyond it but by the use of those very faculties of which we are supposed to be already diffident? The Cartesian doubt, therefore, were it ever possible to be attained by any human creature (as it plainly is not), would be entirely incurable, and no reasoning could ever bring us to a state of assurance and conviction upon any subject.
>
> (*An Enquiry Concerning Human Understanding* XII.1)

Is Hume correct to say that beginning with doubt leads us to end in doubt? Descartes thought not. Let's see why. (And we'll give Hume a chance to speak for himself in Chapter Six.)

1.5   The Second Meditation

Descartes' Second Meditation is entitled, *The nature of the human mind, and how it is better known than the body.* Just as the Greek mathematician Archimedes discovered the principle of the lever and boasted that it could lift the earth, Descartes now hoped to find one thing that is certain in order to support the entire structure of human knowledge:

> . . . I have convinced myself that there is absolutely nothing in the world . . . Does it now follow that I too do not exist? No: if I convinced myself of something [or thought anything at all], then I certainly existed. But there is a deceiver of supreme power and cunning who is deliberately and constantly deceiving me. In that case I too undoubtedly

exist, if he is deceiving me; and let him deceive me as much as he can, he will never bring it about that I am nothing so long as I think that I am something. So after considering everything very thoroughly, I must finally conclude that this proposition, I am, I exist, is necessarily true whenever it is put forward by me or conceived in my mind.

(CSM II 16–17)

This is one of the most famous reflections in all of philosophy. Its most famous formulation is *Cogito, ergo sum* – a Latin phrase that means "I think, therefore I am." This more famous formulation appeared four years before the *Meditations* in Descartes' *Discourse on Method;* the same formulation also appeared three years after the *Meditations* in his work entitled *The Principles of Philosophy.* The formulation does not occur in the *Meditations.*

For centuries, philosophers have argued about how to interpret the first truth of Descartes' philosophy. When someone is asked how he knows something, ordinarily he gives a reason: he appeals to some piece of evidence. If someone answers, "I just know it," this is viewed as unsatisfactory – as simply a dogmatic claim that has not been justified.

Descartes says that he knows with certainty that he is thinking and, therefore, that he exists. The facts of one's own consciousness and existence are the very first truths that anyone recognizes when doing rigorous philosophy, so they cannot be based on anything else. Judgments about consciousness and existence must therefore be self-validating. In the very act of my doubting, my existence is revealed: even if I am deceived, I must exist in order to be deceived; even if I am dreaming, I must exist in order to dream. In fact, I can be certain of my existence only so long as I'm thinking. I can't possibly conceive my non-existence here and now, for to conceive is to exist. However, if I ceased to think, I couldn't assert my existence; I couldn't know that I exist, though I possibly might exist even then. Finally, I know that I'm conscious because my consciousness is directly presented to me; it's not represented to me by an idea. Descartes referred to such self-evident truths as *simple intuitions* – and he said that such particular truths lead us to more general truths:

When someone says "I am thinking, therefore I am, or I exist," he does not deduce existence from thought by means of a syllogism, but recognizes it as something self-evident by a simple intuition of the mind. This is clear from the fact that if he were deducing it by means of a syllogism, he would have to have had previous knowledge of the major premise "Everything which thinks is, or exists"; yet in fact he learns it from experiencing in his own case that it is impossible that he should think without existing. It is in the nature of our mind to construct general propositions on the basis of our knowledge of particular ones.

(CSM II 100)

The *Cogito* is the first truth we reach by philosophizing in an orderly manner. More technically, we might say it is the first truth we encounter when we follow the analytic method under the most rigorous conditions of doubt. Descartes explains:

> In rejecting . . . everything which we can in any way doubt, it is easy for us to suppose that there is no God and no heaven, and that there are no bodies, and even that we ourselves have no . . . body at all. But we cannot for all that suppose that we, who are having such thoughts, are nothing. For it is a contradiction to suppose that what thinks does not, at the very time when it is thinking, exist. Accordingly, this piece of knowledge – *I am thinking, therefore I exist* – is the first and most certain of all to occur to anyone who philosophizes in an orderly way.
>
> (CSM I 194–5)

The *Cogito* is unsurpassably convenient; it is a certainty available to the inquirer at any stage of inquiry. And it serves as a perfect example (or model) of certainty to be used when we assess other candidates for true knowledge. It is unique yet exemplary, privileged yet a model for the rest of inquiry. Nothing can replace it as the first truth one arrives at when one philosophizes in an orderly manner, and it is the vital key to the discovery of other truths. (But note that "is crucial for the *discovery* of all other truths" does not entail "is the *sufficient* axiomatic basis *for the deduction* of all other truths.") But these other, derived truths of metaphysics, once recognized, are just as certain as the *Cogito* itself.

Let us penetrate more deeply this famous philosophical move. There are three main, influential species of interpretation of the *Cogito*:

1   The *Cogito* is a truth-professing *performative*, specifically, an enactment which is self-affirming or self-verifying, a semantically-contentful activity whose very occurrence inescapably provides immediate and conclusive evidence that what it says is true.
2   The *Cogito* is a *simple intuition*. Simple intuitions are a special subset of clear and distinct perceptions, namely those that can be grasped fully all at once, and not successively. These can be divided into three further subsets, the members of which are conceptual, propositional, and existential. If they are conceptual entities, they are not explicitly, in the order of recognition, conceptually dependent on anything else. These are Descartes' *simple notions* expressing *simple natures*. If they are propositional entities, they express necessary relations obtaining at a moment. These include immediate implications between particular items, which Descartes calls *first principles*. The generalizations immediately recognized on the basis of such particular implications, innate principles knowable by *the natural light*, are known implicitly first (i.e. are logically prior), but are brought to explicit awareness via knowledge of the

particular, so are posterior in the (epistemic) order of discovery. Descartes calls them *axioms* or *common notions*. If the entities are existential, they are the immediate objects of consciousness, thoughts. *Thoughts*, mental acts, are to be distinguished from *ideas*, the immediate contents of consciousness, or representations. Ideas belong to the first subset of intuitions, and necessary connections between them belong to the particular subspecies of the second subset. Whereas there are necessary connections between ideas, there can for Descartes be no necessary connections between thoughts, given the discrete (atomic) nature of time he countenances, at least methodologically.

3   The *Cogito* is an *inference*. But it is clear that this cannot mean it is a syllogistic inference. Syllogisms usefully re-present in a logical way knowledge already acquired. But syllogisms require axioms or major premises, and Descartes insists repeatedly that such major premises in philosophy are precisely what is centrally in dispute, so cannot be a starting point when following the analytic method of discovery. Sophisticated work has been done explicating Descartes' theory of inference. Here, suffice it to say, the kind of epistemically foundational inferences Descartes has in mind are propositional intuitions as explicated above.

The *Meditations* tests and finds candidates for foundation stones by their immunity to doubt, by their immunity to rational revision and/or false belief. *There ought to be no presumption that there's just one reason for supposing "I am" cannot be doubted.*[8] Descartes is discovering multiple conditions of foundational (underived) certainty. The *Cogito* is extraordinary in that it exemplifies simultaneously *all* the ways a foundational certainty can be discovered, indeed, discovered by any attentive inquirer, regardless of antecedent theoretical commitments. It is a performative or pragmatic necessity; its denial is inescapably self-refuting. Formulated as "If (whenever) I think, I exist," it is a propositional, simple intuition. Such a propositional intuition is an (immediate) inference. Focusing on the fact that I am *now* thinking (uttering or conceiving), it is an existential, simple intuition. All of its constituent ideas are conceptual, simple intuitions. Hence, the necessary connection between my thinking and my existing amplifies our knowledge, it is not merely formal or conceptual – there can be no conceptual containment between simple, unanalyzable notions, yet we can know that some such connections obtain – just the sort of position we would expect from a rationalist. The *Cogito* is the model for all foundational certainty. It is an indubitable intuition, inference, and performance. With other certainties within first philosophy (for example, "I seem to see a light," or "What's done is done and cannot be undone," or "Something cannot come from nothing"), we will have to account for their status in one way only.

---

8   This insight is nicely developed in Matthews, G. 1992: 11–28.

The *Cogito* has caused a major philosophical stir. Many scholars have applauded Descartes' innovative notion that the subjective self is the necessary starting point for all sound philosophy. But many others have criticized this innovation, suggesting that this emphasis on the subjective self necessarily denies or contradicts the existence of objective truth. Other critics note that if you aim to show that you indubitably exist, you're cheating if you start by saying that *you* are thinking, thus assuming what you set out to prove. Relatedly, some say we are just playing with the structure of language when we move from the verb "thinking" to a phrase that says "a subject doing the thinking." The eighteenth-century German satirist and philosopher, Georg Lichtenberg, seems to have been the first to level such a criticism at Descartes. He conceived philosophy as the frustrating effort to correct linguistic usage while inescapably using the very language being critiqued, and in this case urged that we should say, "There is thinking," just as we would say, "There is lightning," since as soon as we say "I think," it seems necessary to postulate an "ego." The nineteenth-century German philosopher, Friedrich Nietzsche, also made this sort of objection, and the twentieth-century British philosopher, Bertrand Russell, made a similar point:

> The word 'I' is really illegitimate; he ought to state his ultimate premise in the form 'there are thoughts.' The word 'I' is grammatically convenient, but does not describe a datum. When he goes on to say 'I am a thing which thinks,' he is already using uncritically the apparatus of categories handed down by scholasticism. He nowhere proves that thoughts need a thinker, nor is there reason to believe this except in a grammatical sense.
>
> (Russell 1945: 567)

A closely related objection claims that Descartes is jumping the gun when he says that the individual self, or what we might call the "ego," is necessary for doubt or thinking. This problem was posed by an anonymous seventeenth-century critic who called himself Hyperaspistes, the Greek word for champion: "You do not know whether it is you yourself who think, or whether the world-soul in you thinks, as the Platonists believe" (CSM III 192).

These are complex debates: suffice it to say that Descartes did not take the "I" to be a datum or an assumed fact. Immediately after he stated the *Cogito,* Descartes explained that the "I" stands for an unknown, whose nature must be explored. And it soon became clear that what is known for certain is not a concrete, persisting soul or self. After all, Descartes' existence is certain only so long as he is thinking – and most of his thoughts do not last very long.

Latching on to this fact, the English philosopher Thomas Hobbes voiced a more basic objection. He attacked the very possibility that you can be aware of your own thinking as it occurs:

I do not infer that I am thinking by means of another thought for although someone may think that he was thinking (for this thought is simply an act of remembering), it is quite impossible for him to think that he is thinking, or to know that he is knowing. For then an infinite chain of questions would arise: "How do you know that you know that you know . . . ?"

(CSM II 122–3)

This challenge seems to assume that if you can be aware of any of your thoughts, you must be aware of every thought. So if you pay attention to your current thought, you also must pay attention to the act of attention, and so on to infinity. Clearly, if an infinite number of mental acts must occur every time you think, then thinking is impossible.

It is doubtful that Descartes would have accepted Hobbes' assumption. But Hobbes' argument requires another assumption as well: if you can be aware of a current thought, such awareness must be a distinct "thought" in and of itself – but Descartes denied this assumption: "It is irrelevant for the philosopher to say that one thought cannot be the subject of another thought. For who apart from him, ever supposed that it could be?" (CSM II 124).

While some philosophers have considered the *Cogito* to be dubious, still others have thought it trivial. Pierre Gassendi, a contemporary of Descartes, was among those whose objections Descartes published along with his *Meditations.* Gassendi was a well regarded leader in the fight to revive and adapt Greek atomism, based on the ancient doctrines of Democritus and Epicurus. Gassendi also was an empiricist, affirming that the source of knowledge lies in sense perception; he therefore disagreed with Descartes' emphasis on the mind alone. Gassendi and Descartes agreed that sense perception merely gives us access to appearances, so Gassendi concluded that we cannot really know about matter. But Descartes was disturbed by this conclusion; while Gassendi adopted a pragmatic outlook based on probabilities, Descartes said that reason has the power to find the true nature of things. Gassendi thought there was nothing special about the *Cogito:*

But I do not see that you needed all this apparatus, when on other grounds you were certain, and it was true, that you existed. You could have made the same inference from any one of your other actions, since it is known by the natural light that whatever acts exists.

(CSM II 180)

Descartes replied:

When you say that "I could have made the same inference from any one of my other actions" you are far from the truth, since I am not wholly certain of any of my actions, with the sole exception of thought (in using the word "certain" I am referring to metaphysical certainty, which is the sole issue at this point). I may not, for example, make the inference "I am walking, therefore I exist," except insofar as the awareness of walking is a thought. The inference is certain only if applied to this awareness, and not to the movement of the body which sometimes – in the case of dreams – is not occurring at all, despite the fact that I seem to myself to be walking. Hence, from the fact that I think I am walking I can very well infer the existence of a mind which has this thought, but not the existence of a body that walks. And the same applies in other cases.

(CSM II 244)

Some critics concede that Descartes successfully gets to the "I" and to the existence of thought – but then they claim that no progress can be made beyond this point. They conclude that Descartes is stuck in what they call an *egocentric predicament* or a *solipsism*, trapped within the circle of his own ideas from which he cannot defeat skepticism after all. Other critics more charitably allow that a few more truths can be derived from individual consciousness. But they insist that Descartes could never have built a mature and reliable structure of knowledge – a high-rise building, if you will – based merely on a world of private ideas.

Descartes thought otherwise, and he began the construction in his Third Meditation. To appreciate his effort, however, it is necessary to dwell a bit on the nature of Descartes' private world.

Descartes knew that he existed, but he did not know what his true nature was. So he set out to test different familiar conceptions of "the self." For example, he tested the common understanding among some ancient Greeks, Egyptians, and early Christians, who believed that the self is some ethereal substance, or a kind of rarefied matter. He subjected these conceptions of the self to the strictest doubt, and he discovered that every sense-based and physical conception of the self ultimately failed. The only thing about himself that Descartes could not doubt was his thinking. So he concluded that, at this stage of inquiry, all he knew for sure was that he was a thinking thing.

Descartes presented a similar line of thought in the *Discourse on Method,* and some critics objected in a way that Descartes later paraphrased in the Preface to the *Meditations:*

From the fact that the human mind, when directed towards itself, does not perceive itself to be anything other than a thinking thing, it does not follow that its nature or essence consists only in its being a thinking thing, where the word "only" excludes everything else that could be said to belong to the nature of the soul.

(CSM II 7)

These critics charged Descartes with a fallacy called an "appeal to ignorance," which we can best understand by seeing it in action. The Greek playwright Sophocles created the famous character Oedipus, who unknowingly kills his own natural father. We might imagine that Oedipus protests his innocence by reasoning as follows: I know I did not kill my father. How do I know? Well, I perceive that I killed a man in the crossroads, but I do not perceive that I killed my father. Therefore, that man in the crossroads could not have been my father.

Here we imagine Oedipus appealing to his own ignorance, and it is a bad argument indeed. But critics charge that Descartes' argument about the mind seems to share the same form. Descartes explained why his argument is not an appeal to ignorance because he follows an analytic method by which clarity and insight gradually develop as he follows the order of explicitly recognized truths. So, in the Second Meditation, Descartes did not exclude the possibility that both a body and a mind are required for him to exist; he simply insisted that he could be certain that "he" existed, even if he did not have a body. In other words, self-certainty does not depend upon knowledge of the physical world, including knowledge of one's own body.

This conclusion has real historical bite, because it reverses the traditional order of knowledge. The traditional scholastic view had said that all knowledge comes from the senses, and that we therefore know matter more easily and more immediately than we know spirit. Descartes claims to prove his own existence, and to understand his nature, without assuming any physical existence at all. Defying tradition, he says we can know the self first, and we can know it more easily than we know the body. At the same time, he radically transforms the traditional notion of soul, which becomes the same as the mind or the thinking thing.

Descartes was excited by this deeper understanding of his nature. The idea that the self might be a disembodied mind was not just the product of skeptical suppositions: consider that some people have feelings in a bodily part that no longer exists; for example, they might feel itching in missing fingers. Since the fingers no longer exist, they obviously cannot be scratched. Descartes explained that feelings like this are caused by messages sent to the brain from the severed nerves in the stump; given past patterns, the brain wrongly but understandably interprets the messages as coming from the missing fingers. The generalized form of this phenomenon would be to experience sensations as though from a body, when there is in fact no body! This is how a disembodied mind could have worldly experiences. Yet Descartes found it difficult to escape old ways of thinking:

> . . . it still appears – and I cannot stop thinking this – that the corporeal things of which images are formed in my thought, and which the senses investigate, are known with much more distinctness than this puzzling 'I' which cannot be pictured in the imagination. And yet it is surely surprising that I should have a more distinct grasp of things which I realize are doubtful, unknown and foreign to me, than I have of that which is true and known – my own self. But I see what it is: my

mind enjoys wandering off and will not yet submit to being restrained within the bounds of truth. Very well, then; just this once let us give it a completely free rein, so that after awhile, when it is time to tighten the reins, it may more readily submit to being curbed.

(CSM II 20)

In a famous passage that follows – the so-called "wax passage" – Descartes mounted an important attack on knowledge-empiricism, the view that all knowledge is based on sense experience. Descartes tried to show that an empiricist who reflects on his own position will come to realize that it's false. Consider a simple example: how do you know a concrete physical object like a piece of wax? The empiricist would agree that there can be radical changes in our sense perception of a physical body like wax: cold wax is hard, heated wax is liquid – but it is still wax. The essence or real nature of an object obviously must continue throughout such changes, or the object will lose its identity. This essence must therefore be associated with unchanging features. However, the senses perceive only the outward appearances of a physical object. Descartes continued:

> . . . if I look out of the window and see men crossing the square . . . I normally say that I see the men themselves, just as I say that I see the wax. Yet do I see any more than hats and coats which could conceal automatons? I *judge* that they are men. And so something which I thought I was seeing with my eyes is in fact grasped solely by the faculty of judgment which is in my mind.

(CSM II 21)

Descartes says that the object itself – the object's essence – can be known only by a judgment of the intellect. Indeed, the very concept of *sameness through change* – a concept that applies to objects like the wax – cannot be derived from our ever-fluctuating experience; somehow it is supplied by the mind. Further, someone knows the existence of his or her own mind better than the existence of any physical object. Indeed, the basis we have for believing anything physical is based in our consciousness. States of consciousness are conclusive evidence that we exist, but they are not conclusive evidence for anything physical. Here is a structured presentation of the wax passage, where P means stated premise, MP, missing premise, and C, inferred conclusion.

P1) Sense perception of a physical body (like wax) changes even though (we agree) the same body continues to exist.

MP1) The essence (real nature) of an object is its unchanging features. (common conception)

MP2) Distinct perception of an object is perception of its essence.

C1) Distinct perception of a physical body is not by the senses.

P2)   Distinctly perceived, the body which continues to exist is some-
       thing extended, flexible, and indefinitely changeable.

P3)   The indefinitely changeable is not imaginable, that is, picturable in
       determinate images; for example, we can't even imagine (but we can
       conceive) the difference between a thousand- and thousand-and-one-
       sided figure.

C2)   Distinct perception of a physical body is not by the imagination.

MP3)   Perception is either sense perception, imagination, or intellection
       (these are the only representational faculties that supply mental
       contents for judgment).

C3)   Distinct perception of a physical body can be by the intellect alone.

MP4)   Objects themselves are objects as they are essentially.

MP5)   Only minds have (are) intellects.

C4)   Physical bodies themselves, as opposed to their external appear-
       ances, can only be known by a mind.

P4)   Whatever (now inconclusive) evidence I have for the existence of
       anything external to me is conclusive evidence for my own exis-
       tence, but not vice versa.

C5)   I know my own existence better than the existence of any physical
       body (like wax).

P5)   Each perception of an external body (like wax) is a state of my mind
       that I can become aware of, but not vice versa.

MP6)   (?) If one knows more features of X than Y, one knows the nature of
       X better than Y (?)

C6)   I know the nature of my mind better than (more distinctly than)
       the nature of any physical body.

I sprinkle MP6) with question marks since it does not seem acceptable, in
truth or to Descartes. After all, it is part of the complaint about sense
perception that accruing ever more observations of the changing wax by
itself tells us no more about its essence. Yet some assumption must be
supplied to link P5) and C6), or to get to C6) on some other basis, since C6)
is professed to be the main discovery of the Second Meditation, as its title
indicates.

In sum, you know you exist: you know you are a mind – a thinking
thing. The mind alone can uncover the true nature of things, and the mind
is easier to know than any physical thing. Descartes says that this realization
is a giant step toward weaning ourselves from a foolish prejudice in favor of
the senses.

Some have understood Descartes to be saying that sense perception is
irrelevant to life, a view that's hard to accept. But Descartes is not saying
this. As he will tell us in the Sixth Meditation, everyday experience is a
(divinely-instituted) useful guide to fulfilling our practical needs. He is
saying that there is a pre-experiential framework, or what philosophers call
an *a priori* framework, for interpreting reality, that his method proves that

the pre-experiential framework of reason is more certain and reliable than any sensory perception, and that it's needed to make proper use of sense perceptions when doing rigorous science. Without *a priori* guidance, observational science can go astray, using wrongheaded concepts and principles; but with correct *a priori* guidance, our sensory experience can unlock the secrets of the universe, and make us its master.

1.6   The Third Meditation

In the Third Meditation, Descartes sought to go beyond his own consciousness and to establish genuine knowledge of a wider world. He examined his thoughts from different angles to see what other knowledge might be based on them. He noticed that some thoughts are like mental images that represent things in a certain way; he called these thoughts *ideas* – a new way of using the term that has now become commonplace.

The critical question is: do any of these *ideas* allow Descartes to form a reliably truthful judgment about something other than himself and his thoughts? Descartes noted that there *appear* to be three types of ideas. First, there are the innate ideas, which are derived by reflecting on one's own nature. Second, there are fictitious ideas, which are invented. Third, there are what Descartes called *adventitious* ideas, which are caused by the observable physical objects in nature.

Fictitious ideas don't tell you how the world really is – and Descartes worried that all of his ideas about the outer world were fictitious. And what about the many adventitious ideas that seem to derive from the physical world; are they accurate and reliable representations? On reflection, Descartes discovered two main reasons for thinking that some ideas are genuinely adventitious:

> Nature has apparently taught me to think this. But in addition I know by experience that these ideas do not depend on my will, and hence that they do not depend simply on me. Frequently I notice them even when I do not want to: now, for example, I feel the heat whether I want to or not, and this is why I think that this sensation or idea of heat comes to me from something other than myself, namely the heat of the fire by which I am sitting. And the most obvious judgment for me to make is that the thing in question transmits to me its own likeness rather than something else.
>
> (CSM II 26)

But these reasons are inadequate. Descartes realized that he could not have full confidence in his natural impulses, since they had led him astray in the past. And dreams prove that unwilled ideas are not necessarily caused by external objects. And even if one knows that an idea is caused by an external object, it's a big leap to conclude that the idea represents that object accurately.

Descartes approached his ideas from still another angle. He noted that insofar as we view ideas as states of mind, they all seem to be the same sort of thing. They also seem to depend on him – the thinker – in the same way. But insofar as ideas are viewed as representing different things and so have different contents, they obviously differ from each other.

Descartes repeatedly concluded that each of his ideas could be explained without going beyond himself and his own capacities. Perhaps he was, after all, alone in the world. Finally, however, Descartes came upon one unique idea that his mind could not possibly have produced on its own. This is the idea of God.

Descartes arrived at the idea of God based on a logical sequence that begins with his fundamental observation: "I doubt." The sequence goes like this: to doubt is to lack perfect knowledge, so I have an idea of imperfection. This means I also have the idea of perfection, so I therefore have the idea of God, a supremely perfect being. The idea of God, like any idea or thing, must have a cause, since something cannot come from nothing. But I cannot produce the idea of God by myself. In fact, nothing short of a being with infinite properties could explain the presence of that thought in my mind. So I can explain my ability to think of God only by concluding that God does exist.

Some critics deny that Descartes (or anyone else) can have a real idea of an infinite God. Pierre Gassendi protested:

> . . . the human intellect is not capable of conceiving of infinity, and hence it neither has nor can contemplate any idea of an infinite thing. Hence if someone calls something "infinite" he attributes to a thing which he does not grasp a label which he does not understand . . . What an insignificant thing God would be if he were nothing more, and had no other attributes, than what is contained in our puny idea!
>
> (CSM II 200)

Descartes responded by making a distinction:

> . . . you fail to distinguish between . . . an understanding which is suited to the scale of our intellect (and each of us knows by his own experience quite well that he has this sort of understanding of the infinite) and . . . a fully adequate conception of things (and no one has this sort of conception . . . of the infinite).
>
> (CSM II 252)

Descartes had pressed a distinction like this in earlier correspondence to his friend Mersenne:

> . . . it is possible to know that God is infinite and all-powerful although our soul, being finite, cannot comprehend or conceive Him. In the same

way we can touch a mountain with our hands but we cannot put our arms around it as we could put them around a tree or something else not too large for them. To comprehend something is to embrace it in one's thought; to know something it is sufficient to touch it with one's thought.

(CSM III 25)

Whereas Christian apologists insist that God is incomprehensible, Descartes' rationalist approach requires an understanding that is sufficient for proof. In general, Descartes sought a compromise between the notions that human truth is completely independent of divine truth, versus the idea that our knowledge of truth completely depends upon divine illumination. In seeking this compromise, Descartes used an important distinction that was nicely captured in a textbook he published three years after the *Meditations.* The textbook was called *Principles of Philosophy,* and in it he says:

> . . . in the case of anything in which, from some point of view, we are unable to discover a limit, we shall avoid asserting that it is infinite, and instead regard it as indefinite. There is, for example, no imaginable extension which is so great that we cannot understand the possibility of an even greater one; and so we shall describe the size of possible things as indefinite . . . [I]n the case of God alone, not only do we fail to recognize any limits in any respect, but our understanding positively tells us that there are none.

(CSM I 202)

As Descartes searched for knowledge, he realized that he had the potential to know more and more, without limit. He said this does not show that knowledge is infinite; it shows only that knowledge is indefinite or boundless. Humans may have the potential to know without limit, but this does not make them all-knowing. By contrast, the claim that God is all-knowing means that God already knows all truths, and has no potential to know more. Similarly, negating the idea of finitude does not produce the idea of perfection.

Here Descartes followed what he took to be Plato's insight that the ideas of perfection and infinity are within us before we conceive of the limitations in us or in the world. Perfection and infinity are among the treasure-trove of innate ideas – but often they are hidden by the intellectual debris of prejudice. Descartes believed that the main reason for not seeing these truths is our foolish reliance on sense-experience and acts of pictorial imagination that are based on sense experience. In the *Discourse on Method,* Descartes observed:

> . . . many are convinced that there is some difficulty in knowing God, and even in knowing what their soul is. The reason for this is that they

never raise their minds above things which can be perceived by the senses: they are so used to thinking of things only by imagining them . . . that whatever is unimaginable seems to them unintelligible. This is sufficiently obvious from the fact that even the scholastic philosophers take it as a maxim that there is nothing in the intellect which has not previously been in the senses; and yet it is certain that the ideas of God and of the soul have never been in the senses. It seems to me that trying to use one's imagination in order to understand these ideas is like trying to use one's eyes in order to hear sounds or smell odours . . .

(CSM I 129)

Descartes summed up his Third Meditation with these words:

The whole force of the argument lies in this: I recognize that it would be impossible for me to exist with the kind of nature I have – that is, having within me the idea of God – were it not the case that God really existed. By "God" I mean the very being the idea of whom is within me, that is, the possessor of all the perfections which I cannot grasp, but can somehow reach in my thought, who is subject to no defects whatsoever. It is clear enough from this that he cannot be a deceiver, since it is manifest by the natural light that all fraud and deception depend on some defect.

(CSM II 35)

Here is a fully-articulated presentation of the Third Meditation's argument.

1   Ideas are like images in that they represent things as having certain characteristics.
2   Some of the objects of my ideas are represented as having more formal reality than others (i.e. some ideas have more objective reality than others).
3   Whatever exists must have an efficient and total cause with at least as much formal reality as it has (an instantiation of the evident truth that something can't come from nothing).
4   Every idea must have a first and principal cause with at least as much formal reality as the idea represents its object as having. (What is the status of this statement? Does it follow from 1, 2, and 3?)
5   I have an idea of God as an actually infinite, eternal, immutable, independent, all-knowing, all-powerful substance by whom I (and anything else which may exist) have been created.
6   I myself do not have all the perfections which my idea of God represents God as having.
7   I am not the first and principal cause of my idea of God. (This follows from 4, 5, and 6.)

8   The first and principal cause of my idea of God is some being other than myself who possesses at least as much formal reality as my idea of God represents God as having. (This follows from 4 and 7.)

9   God exists. (This follows from 4, 5, and 8.)

In interpreting and evaluating this argument, keep the following in mind. First, ideas are not identical with images (all images are ideas, but not vice versa), but are *like* them, that is, are intentional, purport to represent something beyond themselves. Second, "first cause" does not mean "uncaused cause." For example, the first cause of the idea of the sun may be the sun itself, but the sun is not uncaused. Third, idea as mode of the mind is the formal reality of the idea (as thought, as used in the *Cogito*.) All ideas are equal in reality in this respect. Idea insofar as it represents something other than itself is the objective reality of the idea. Degree of objective reality is a function of the formal reality its object would have, were it to exist. There are three degrees (types) of objective reality or types of mental content: of modes, of finite substances, and of infinite substance. "X is more real (more perfect) than Y" means Y's existence depends on X, but not conversely. Fourth, "in me formally" means the properties which by representation exist in the idea are actually present in me. "In me eminently" means "I don't have the properties, but do have superior ones, sufficient for the explanation of the properties." Fifth, a negative idea is one which designates the absence of something real (for example, ignorance). A materially false idea is one which is taken to represent something it does not (for example, ideas of secondary or sensible qualities).

Finally, we need to distinguish three increasingly strong notions:

1   An idea has representational character means it is *as if* of things, as if exhibiting something to mind.

2   An idea is *of* a thing (*res*) i.e. it represents something real i.e. it gives access to (cognizance of) a possible existent. (Clear and distinct ideas guarantee such access; sense ideas do not.)

3   An idea represents something that in fact exists.

3 entails 2, which entails 1, but not vice versa.

Is there a second causal argument in the Third Meditation? Some say the following is such, involving assumptions 4, 5, and 11 which have no analogues in the preceding argument.

1   I exist as a thinking thing, and possess an idea of God as a supremely perfect being.

2   Whatever exists has a cause with at least as much formal reality as it has.

3   The cause of my existence is either myself, or God, or some other being or beings less perfect than God.

4 Whatever causes its own existence can acquire any perfection it conceives.

5 Whatever conceives a perfection it can acquire, does acquire that perfection.

6 I conceive of perfections, such as knowledge, which, insofar as I doubt, I do not have.

7 I am not the cause of my existence. (4, 5, 6)

8 If the cause of my existence is some being (or beings) other than God, it (or they) must also be a thinking thing(s), possessing the idea of all the perfections I attribute to God.

9 If a thinking thing possessing the idea of all the perfections I attribute to God is the cause of its own existence, it is God.

10 If it is not the cause of its own existence, then it must be caused by some other thinking thing which also has an idea of all the perfections I attribute to God.

11 The series of causes of thinking things having an idea of God cannot be infinite; it must have a first member.

12 The first member of the series of causes of thinking things having an idea of God must be the cause of itself. (11)

13 The first member of the series of causes is God. (9, 12)

This argument has three underlying assumptions:

- There must be a sustainer of my existence.
- The same amount of power is required to conserve as to initially create (since there is no necessary connection between what exists at one time and another).
- It is more difficult to produce a substance than a mode, and whatever can do the more difficult can do the less difficult.

Note that Descartes tells Johannes Caterus, a Catholic theologian from Holland who authored the first set of objections (CSM II 77), that there is only *one* argument for God's existence in the Third Meditation, and that the above merely explains the original more fully. Note also that 2 is *prima facie* compatible with 11 only if something is its own cause, but the notion of a positive cause of itself relies on the ontological argument of the Fifth Meditation, so relies on something not yet in evidence.

Descartes says that a deceiving God cannot exist, since a non-deceiving God must exist. Thus he eliminates the strongest doubt that had emerged from his First Meditation, and he can begin to build the upper stories of his palace of knowledge.

When he ended his Third Meditation, Descartes was exhilarated, but not all of his readers were so thrilled. Many charged that his philosophy threatened religious orthodoxy, especially because the Cartesian God does not correspond to the providential God of the Bible. Even 350 years later, in a book by the late Pope John Paul II entitled *Crossing the Threshold of Hope*, Descartes is named as the main (though perhaps unwitting) culprit in destroying Christian belief. Pope John Paul claimed that Descartes' rationalism generates skepticism, which traps the mind in subjectivism: everything thus becomes based on human consciousness, and God is placed outside the world. This clearly undermines the medieval view that God is involved in the world, not distant from it. The Pope wrote:

> Though the father of modern rationalism certainly cannot be blamed for the move away from Christianity, it is difficult not to acknowledge that he created the climate in which, in the modern era, such an estrangement became possible . . . In fact, about 150 years after Descartes, all that was fundamentally Christian in the tradition of European thought had already been pushed aside. This was the time of the Enlightenment in France, when pure rationalism held sway . . . The rationalism of the Enlightenment put to one side the true God – in particular, God the Redeemer. The consequence was that man was supposed to live by his reason alone, as if God did not exist. Not only was it necessary to leave God out of the objective knowledge of the world, since the existence of a Creator or of Providence was in no way helpful to science, it was also necessary to act as if God did not exist, as if God were not interested in the world.
>
> (John Paul II 1994: 52–3)

The Pope accurately describes part of Descartes' legacy. He also correctly suggests that Descartes was more interested in God the mathematician and engineer than God the Redeemer. But it's less clear whether Descartes' posture ultimately was harmful to the God of faith. Descartes apparently believed that his posture was not harmful (and perhaps even beneficial) to the Christian tradition.

1.7   The Fourth Meditation

Descartes' Fourth Meditation, entitled *Truth and Falsity*, argues that since we can knowledgeably affirm a perfect God – and thus a non-deceiving God – we then have a reliable criterion of truth. According to Descartes, whatever we clearly and distinctly understand to be true must be true. Descartes will explain how we can infallibly avoid error by sticking to clear and distinct ideas, but first he has to confront the puzzle of how error is even possible in a universe created by a perfect God.

This puzzle is similar to a basic problem in theology, the so-called problem of evil, which asks why a perfect God permits evil to exist in the world. (The problem of evil is discussed with some care in Chapter Six.) Indeed, Descartes' interest in explaining the existence of error is the intellectual counterpart to explaining the existence of evil. Descartes introduced the problem by focusing on what he had deduced to be three indubitable truths. These were: God always does what's best; God could have made humans infallible; but instead God made us fallible. From these truths it follows that it is better to be fallible than infallible. But this result seems false – so should we reconsider any of the allegedly indubitable starting points which lead to this result? Descartes thought not, and he offered an explanation for why we make errors:

> So what then is the source of my mistakes? It must be simply this: the scope of the will is wider than that of the intellect; but instead of restricting it within the same limits, I extend its use to matters which I do not understand. Since the will is indifferent in such cases, it easily turns aside from what is true and good, and this is the source of my error and sin.
>
> (CSM II 40–1)

Descartes is saying that all judgment involves both an act of understanding and an act of will. The understanding presents mental contents, which determine what the judgment is about; the will adopts some attitude toward this content, such as an attitude of affirmation, denial, or withholding judgment. Our human understanding, created by God, is said to be perfect of its creaturely kind – but it is not absolutely perfect. If it were, we would be God. Our understanding thus has limits, but our free will does not: it can say "yea" or "nay" to anything (and pursue or strive to avoid anything) that comes before it. Descartes explains that error occurs when our limitless will outstrips our limited understanding; this is essentially a misuse of our free will. He says error would be impossible only if we lacked free will, but free will is our greatest gift, a gift that we rightly would not relinquish in order to avoid the possibility of error.

Now that Descartes has explained why errors occur, he can explain how to avoid them: he says we do this by restraining our wills from affirming things except where we understand those things distinctly:

> . . . if, whenever I have to make a judgment, I restrain my will so that it extends to what the intellect clearly and distinctly reveals, and no further, then it is quite impossible for me to go wrong . . . I shall unquestionably reach the truth, if only I give sufficient attention to all the things which I perfectly understand, and separate these from all the other cases where my apprehension is more confused and obscure. And this is just what I shall take good care to do from now on.
>
> (CSM II 41)

Descartes' account achieves two goals simultaneously. It acknowledges human fallibility and sin, as required by religious orthodoxy. But it also affirms that when humans scrupulously apply the correct method, human reason is infallible, and can therefore produce a scientific system of timeless truths.

By requiring an act of will in every judgment, Descartes once again seems to depart from the scholastic tradition that he aims to replace. His emphasis on the will also has spawned a host of often-repeated objections. One of them insists that we plainly cannot choose to believe or disbelieve as we wish, because most beliefs are involuntary. Indeed, in this Fourth Meditation, Descartes himself says he was *compelled* to believe whatever he clearly and distinctly understood to be true. Here Descartes and his critics disagree about the nature of freedom. For Descartes, freedom is essentially self-deter-mination, and one's understanding is one's true self. But for Descartes' critics, being free means you have the ability to believe or act differently than you do, even when your belief or act is based on the best of reasons:

> . . . the will simply consists . . . in the fact that when the intellect puts something forward for affirmation or denial or for pursuit or avoidance, our inclinations are such that we do not feel we are determined by any external force. In order to be free, there is no need for me to be inclined both ways; on the contrary, the more I incline in one direction – either because I clearly understand that reasons of truth and goodness point that way, or because of a divinely produced disposition of my inmost thoughts – the freer is my choice . . . For if I always saw clearly what was true and good, I should never have to deliberate about the right judgment or choice; in that case, although I should be wholly free, it would be impossible for me ever to be in a state of indifference.
>
> (CSM II 40)

We cannot resolve this disagreement about what constitutes freedom, but we can appreciate the appeal of Descartes' view. First, much of our daily conduct involves no direct choices; Descartes considers such unreflective behavior to be free so long as we are not forced to engage in it. Even if we train ourselves to automatically respond a certain way under certain condi-tions, we will have indirectly chosen that reaction – and it is therefore free. This is the sort of situation in which Descartes sees himself.

At the beginning of the *Meditations,* Descartes directly chooses to undergo the necessary cognitive therapy so that he will be able to withhold judgment on anything that can be doubted. He meticulously and methodically doubts everything until he confronts clear and distinct ideas. At that point, his will can't help but follow his understanding and affirm these truths. This is what Descartes calls the "freedom of *spontaneity*" – the highest form of freedom.

Descartes' view belongs to an important tradition in which degree of freedom is measured by strength of activity: the more a thing flows from one's true nature, the more strongly active it is, and the freer it is. (This view seems especially central to the rationalist tradition; for example, we will see it defended by both Spinoza and Leibniz.) By contrast, Descartes' critics belong to a tradition that measures freedom by how much we are in control – and ultimate control is the ability to do anything (absolute indifference). One central achievement of the *Meditations* is self-realization – transformation of the will from its divinely radical but unreliable condition of indifference to a stable condition in which it fully and reliably expresses one's true nature. By the end of the Fourth Meditation, I am as inquirer what I aspired to be. Fullest freedom = clear and distinct understanding = recognizing innate ideas = realizing the essence of the mind = self-actualization. (It will be valuable to compare Spinoza's understanding of these equations in the next chapter.)

Since Descartes' theory of judgment and his policy for guaranteeing indubitable judgments (his *ethics of belief* for first philosophy) are important to appreciating his system, let me say a bit more about each. Then, before leaving the Fourth Meditation, I will discuss more fully the explosive, seemingly anti-rationalistic implications of Descartes' avowal that God created everything, including the timeless truths first philosophy seeks to discover, so that they depend wholly on his will, so that the ultimate explanation for everything is just that God willed it, period. This doctrine is not highlighted in the *Meditations*, but forcibly maintained by Descartes elsewhere. I will try to disarm this threat to Descartes' method.

Descartes examines judging (the purely mental act) to learn more about the faculty (capacity) of judgment (what's in us that makes judging possible) – we don't automatically notice our faculties, but do when we turn our attention to their exercise – so as to learn more about mind. Judgments are those actions of the soul (they terminate in the soul) which are the primary bearers of truth-value (propositions, sentences, etc. are true only in a derivative sense), and so are the appropriate focus of pure inquiry (first philosophy). As mentioned above, the feature of his theory of judgment that draws most criticism is his requirement that free will be involved. Will is the mental capacity by virtue of which mind inclines in some direction with respect to ideational contents (presented by the understanding – understanding and willing are passive and active aspects of the same substance). Freedom is self-determination, which entails absence of external determination, but does not require direct avoidability or direct (current, deliberative) choice. We humans are most free when our will acts most powerfully, not when we have the most control. What appears to my understanding disposes my belief just as it disposes desire, and I'll believe if that disposition is not opposed by other perceptions, or habits resulting from cognitive training. The main considerations that lead us to associate the will with our conative mental acts apply equally to our cognitive mental attitudes. And belief as well as desire is necessary for action. We experience beliefs, doubts, etc. as having different intensities and correlation with action just as with desires and aversions.

Free inquiry proceeds in the *Meditations* by starting with direct or optional choice (freedom of indifference) to undergo necessary cognitive therapy so that one can withhold whatever is at all dubious. One persists in doubting until one confronts clear and distinct ideas (the activation of innate dispositions, implicit ideas and principles made explicit). Reconstruction begins with the *Cogito*; being attentively and distinctly aware of my thinking (non-analytically) necessitates my certain affirmation that I exist.

What does it mean to say my will is limitless? (Will's scope is greater than understanding's, which is greater than imagination's, which is greater than sensation's.) One meaning carries over from the Third Meditation – I have the limitless aspiration toward something else (that enables me to make explicit the implicit idea of God as actually infinite substance). A second meaning is as absolutely decisive power to say yes or no (affirming or denying) with respect to whatever can come before my (limited but perfect of its kind) understanding. This safeguards God's lack of responsibility for error. And the compelled assent of clear and distinct perception is no counterexample, given the aforestated conception of fullest freedom. What else does Descartes mean? Limitless in extension, as the capacity to apply oneself to all possible objects? Would this be one way to understand what it means to say that the will outstrips the understanding, and if so, do we have that capacity? How else can we interpret the outstripping claim?

We can outline the considerations which lead to Descartes' policy for acquiring beliefs as follows: (1) I am compelled to believe what I clearly and distinctly understand. But (2) when I do not understand something clearly and distinctly, my belief is optional. In particular, if I recognize I do not have a sufficient understanding of something, or recognize that the pros and cons on some issue counterbalance, I can suspend belief. And in particular, (3) I can disbelieve something while consciously recognizing its probability; indeed, the consideration that it is merely probable suffices to allow me to suspend belief. Now (4) I cannot believe what I totally fail to understand. And (5) I rarely believe what I recognize at the time I do not adequately understand, but I do often think I sufficiently understand something when in fact I do not. (Among the factors which contribute to this are intellectual laziness, reluctance to admit ignorance, prejudice, preference for lofty and obscure ideas over clear ones, focus on words instead of things, wrongly seeming to recall knowing something, cognitive hubris, and even the very lust for knowledge, when unguided by proper method.) (6) Though insufficiency of understanding is not naturally manifest, it is always detectable and often eliminable by proper method. So I may naturally enough be induced to believe what is obscure to me, but can avoid being so induced. But (7) it is not easy to avoid this; for example, instinctual beliefs and childhood prejudices are extremely difficult to shake. Still, (8) since by processes in my control I can avoid error, my mistakes are ultimately my fault; I am responsible for my errors because I can avoid error and I am responsible for what I can avoid. Of course, (9) when seeking the truth, I do not choose to be deceived, as such. But (10) choices I do make can bring about my deception.

So what should I do, given that my goal as theoretical inquirer is to maximize knowledge and minimize the risk of error? Generally put, (11) I should be maximally epistemically responsible. Now I realize that (12) what I believe depends at least in part on what sorts of evidence I take to be good, and that what sorts of evidence I take to be good depends at least in part on what method of inquiry (rules of acceptance, etc.) I adopt, because (as history shows) there are alternative methods. I have some control over the cognitive training, which will influence my cognitive habits, which will influence my dispositions to believe. (13) It would be epistemically irresponsible not to train myself to suspend belief on anything I do not have good reason to believe. And if my goal is to discover permanent foundations for systematic science, it would be epistemically irresponsible not to train myself to suspend belief on anything I do not have irrevisably adequate reason to believe. (14) Since I have irrevisably adequate reason to believe only whatever I understand clearly and distinctly, and my goal is to discover permanent foundations for systematic science, I should only believe what I understand clearly and distinctly. (15) This requires thinking for myself, beginning with internal testimony, beginning with particular notions and connections and forming generalities from them, and so on, as delineated by my rules for the direction of the mind.

Finally, what about the tricky issue of God's unlimited power? In correspondence (beginning in 1630, to Mersenne) Descartes sometimes stresses that God created everything, or that everything depends on God's will, including the eternal or timeless truths of mathematics and morality. This commitment to God's absolutely unconditional omnipotence is called *theistic voluntarism*. The puzzle is, if theistic voluntarism is true, then how is irrevisable knowledge possible? More broadly, how can Descartes be the father of modern *rationalism* yet embrace as ultimate explanation the brute, unguided will of God? Many commentators conclude that his voluntarism is out of place and systematically debilitating. Here's a sketch of why I disagree. Since it is compressed, it may be more challenging to master, but the deep interest of the issues makes your effort worthwhile.

Descartes views his creation doctrine as an unavoidable theistic commitment which has no deflationary implications at all for the status of modal propositions (propositions about what is necessary, possible but not necessary, and impossible), or for any other component of his rationalism, but on the contrary is required for his rational, permanent science.[9] The creation doctrine does entail that "For any eternal truth P, God could have willed

9   Elements of this account, especially as formulated in its first three paragraphs, coincide closely with the position in Dan Kaufman's 1999 American Philosophical Association paper, "The Creation of the Eternal Truths: A Defense of Descartes," on which I commented. That paper evolved into Kaufman 2002: 24–41. My own defense of Descartes goes further than Kaufman's; its last paragraph was enriched by exchanges with my former student, Jeff Teil.

that not-P is true," but it does not entail that there are no necessary truths, or that there are only contingently necessary truths. Indeed, the creation doctrine entails that there are *no* true modal propositions about *anything* other than God prior to God's willing, no pre-existing possibilities or necessities independent of God which would frustrate or impel his immensely powerful will. At bottom the creation doctrine aims to highlight God's absolutely indifferent will (required for his omnipotence); it is not a position about the correct modal logic.

The creation doctrine tells us that God has the power to make or not make the eternal truths, and that there are no possible or necessary truths before God decides to make them true. God is the source of the intelligible content of things, not just the bestower of existence on essence. Everything other than God is created by God. If God confronted essences as brute facts, he would be limited as in the kind of paganism on which Jupiter or Saturn is subject to the Styx and the Fates. Prior to his willing – and knowing, willing, and creating are the same thing in God – there is nothing to understand except God's own essence.

The doctrine allows that God can make what are in fact necessary truths to be not true, for example, make it not true that $2+2 = 4$ but rather $= 7$. But it does not allow that God could make competing eternal truths; make some current, positive impossibility to be true – for example, make it true that $2+2 = 4$ and $= 7$. In particular, it does not allow that God could make self-contradictory propositions true. (I controversially contend that none of the passages invoked by those who read Descartes as a radical voluntarist says otherwise.) Nor does it preclude knowing with certainty what are in fact necessary truths. Indeed the doctrine is first announced to Mersenne as an especial focus of his metaphysics of God and self which leads to the discovery of the foundations of his physics.

God makes or not makes the eternal truths by making or not making essences. For example, were God not to make the essences of the various modes of extension, all the positive claims of geometry would be false. If essences were actually existing, created things, they would be contingent (and the eternal truths based on them would be contingent) since dependent on God's moment-to-moment conservation of them. But they don't actually exist (as created substances and their modes do), don't require a cause of their continuation, but are established eternally by God's immutable will. God could change them if his will could change, but he is essentially eternal and unchangeable (yet free). So once they are created, there is nothing further to be done.

What are these essences? Platonic universals (independent of any mind) are incompatible with the creation doctrine, and are explicitly repudiated (for example in *Principles of Philosophy* I 48, 58, 62). But a moderate realist or conceptualist construal of Descartes (so that essences are just structures of the human mind) better fits his innatism anyway. Descartes seems to be following a familiar medieval view in which essences are the possibilities of the existence of things, that every reality, including mere possibilities, depends on God, and that given that God has made things possible there is nothing further to be done to make the eternal truths true. Further, if you read Descartes as holding that one can only conceive what's possible, and that to conceive x is to have an idea of x with objective reality, then the requirement that objective reality have a formally real cause just instantiates the general truth that all created reality, actual or possible, ultimately depends on God's will.

Are there some uncreated eternal truths concerning God's own existence and nature? If the set of eternal truths is equivalent to the set of broadly necessary truths, then God does not create, and cannot decide to violate, his own nature, and whatever is entailed by his nature, in particular, his omnipotence, is an uncreated, *absolute (not ordained) necessity*. We might then argue that the axioms Descartes uses to prove God's existence, *unlike* the truths of mathematics, the laws of motion, and the truths of morality which depend on God, are absolutely necessary. For example, though particular causal laws depend on God's will, the mechanism of efficient causation does not; God could not make his will causally inefficacious. Similarly, it is absolutely necessary that what is done is done and cannot be undone; God cannot retrieve a supremely willed past state of the universe; it would be a violation of immutability and omnipotence if the past were changed. So one need not know what essences (and so eternal truths) he created before coming to know that a veracious God exists – a methodological plus, in the face of the threat of circularity. But once we come to know that a non-deceiving God exists so that everything I clearly and distinctly perceive is true as I perceive it (so that my intellect reveals what divine *nous* has made true), we can achieve a rational science (*scientia*). To have clear and distinct perception is to actualize innate ideas with true (i.e. possible) and immutable (because created by God's immutable will) essences. Note specifically the apparent connection between God's real simplicity of essence (will is equivalent to intellect) and Descartes' conception of quantitative, unified science; hence his need to reject a plurality of God-independent essences with their own dispositions.

Not only do truths about God seem exempt from the creation doctrine, but so do purely formal truths based wholly on the law of non-contradiction. (This last result would help further fend off radical voluntarist interpretations.) Given that God creates the eternal truths by creating essences, we can offer an explanation. The law of non-contradiction is contentless; it is not about any particular essence. For it, there is nothing for God to create; there is no action he needs to take to make it true. When Descartes says that everything we can think about is something, and so requires a cause, he seems to be talking only about things with positive content in our conception of them (not, as he says in the Third Meditation, negative ideas or materially false ideas). The law of non-contradiction does not actually exist (is not formally real) and doesn't have positive content, as all essences do. An obviously contentious (and anachronistic, and Kantian) way of putting my leanings here is to say that all the created eternal truths are *synthetic necessities* (a notion explicated in depth in Chapter Seven). This gains some systematic support if you agree that the simple natures which ground Cartesian science – since simple – must stand in non-analytic relations to each other (where analytic relations are those of conceptual inclusion or exclusion); that Cartesian deduction (unlike the syllogistic inference he finds unuseful in the discovery of knowledge) is ampliative and both truth- and certainty-, but not logical necessity-preserving; and that the actual way he develops his rationalism, for example in the next, Fifth Meditation, in terms of true and immutable natures to be discovered, not necessities resulting from definition, indicates such Kantianism.

Penultimately, note how Descartes seems to stress the priority of God's unlimited power (and so absolutely indifferent will) at crucial junctures of rational theology. In explicating his ontological argument for Caterus, he repeats the two versions overtly present in the Fifth Meditation, and then purports to re-present them most deeply as follows:

1   I have a clear and distinct idea of God.
2   So God's existence is possible.
3   God is essentially all-powerful and independent.
4   So God can exist by his own power.
5   What can exist by its own power, does exist (necessarily).
6   So God exists (necessarily).

And as I read his causal argument in the Third Meditation, though the meditator understands (*de dicto*) God's nature, she does not comprehend (*de re*) it, and it is partly definitive of God that he is incomprehensible, the incomprehensibility derives first and foremost from his absolute freedom of indifference, and the incomprehensibility is essential for ruling out my ability to have the idea of God without God's causal assistance.

Finally, I'm not even sure we should think of Descartes as a theistic voluntarist at all, if we mean by "voluntarist" philosophers like Ockham and Kierkegaard who treat will as superior to intellect or reason, since for Descartes God's will and intellect are identical. It is natural to be perplexed at the meaning of this unexpected but simple thesis. So let me close by outlining Descartes' overall picture of divine and human will and intellect to help clarify things.

It is clear that Descartes thinks human freedom of spontaneity is superior to human freedom of indifference. Should we say that for God there is only freedom of indifference, and it is obviously superior to any type of human freedom? I suggest it is useful to distinguish conceptually, but not really, indifference from spontaneity in God as well. Put theologically, it is the greatest human freedom to assent to what God has created as true or good (by acting fully in accordance with our natures), not to create the true or good, which we lack the power to do. Our freedom of indifference, as functionally important as it is (for example, it is what allows us to pursue firm foundations for stable science beginning with the method of doubt, and in general deliberate), shows our weakness, and exists only because our intellects lack sufficient comprehension. One main goal of meditation is to convert indifference to spontaneity. Since what is true or good must be decided by God's undetermined will, God's indifference must be primary. But we can think of divine spontaneity following from indifference in the sense that those things that God indifferently created with true and immutable natures are now truly immutable, because if God creates them to be immutable with omnipotent power, then nothing could overturn the truths based on them, including God (otherwise they were never created to be immutable). So God always obeys the same eternal and universal laws, but these laws proceed from God himself. That is, God freely legislates for himself. So divine freedom, the basis for the creation doctrine, is structurally more like Kantian autonomy than voluntaristic, arbitrary willing; a cornerstone of rationalism, not irrationalism. (Kant's account of freedom occurs in Chapter Seven.)

1.8   The Fifth Meditation

Descartes' Fifth Meditation is entitled, *The essence of material things, and the existence of God considered a second time*. In this meditation Descartes authoritatively confirms his new, mathematical conception that physical things are spatially extended, flexible, and capable of changing form. Descartes immediately observes that whatever portion of space is carved out, the resulting geometric figure has what he called a *true and immutable nature*. This fixed nature of a geometric figure allows you to prove that the figure has certain properties.

Once you consider, say, a triangle, many necessary truths can be deduced from its nature. Descartes argued that just as you can prove geometrical truths based on a clear and distinct idea of matter, you also can prove theological truths based on a clear and distinct idea of God. In particular, you can prove with mathematical rigor that God must exist. God has all perfections, and necessary existence is a perfection; so God necessarily exists.

Caterus dismissed this proof on the grounds that it is impossible to deduce anything about the real world from a mere definition:

> Even if it is granted that a supremely perfect being carries the implication of existence in virtue of its very title, it still does not follow that the existence in question is anything actual in the real world; all that follows is that the concept of existence is inseparably linked to the concept of a supreme being. So you cannot infer that the existence of God is anything actual unless you suppose that the supreme being actually exists; for then it will actually contain all perfections, including the perfection of real existence.
>
> (CSM II 72)

Descartes agreed with Caterus' criticism to the extent that you cannot define something into existence. But that is not what Descartes took himself to be doing:

> . . . because a word conveys something, that thing is not therefore shown to be true. My argument however was as follows: That which we clearly and distinctly understand to belong to the true and immutable nature, or essence, or form of something, can truly be asserted of that thing. But once we have made a sufficiently careful investigation of what God is, we clearly and distinctly understand that existence belongs to his true and immutable nature. Hence, we can now truly assert of God that he does exist.
>
> (CSM II 83)

In other words, Descartes says he is not inventing a way of thinking, and then conveniently trotting out the consequences of that invention. Rather, he believes himself to be discovering necessary facts about an object of thought, as we do with geometric figures. To clearly think about God is to know that God exists necessarily; it is also to know that God is essentially all-powerful, all-knowing, and anything else that follows from the clear and distinct idea of a supremely perfect being.

Following Kant's taxonomy, we call this the ontological argument for God's existence. The ontological argument is the cornerstone of rational theology. In our next great thinker, Spinoza, it is the cornerstone of meta-physics, and so of all rationalist philosophy, since, as we will see, for Spinoza, metaphysics is first philosophy, and from a sound metaphysics one derives a sound theory of human nature (human knowing and emotion), from which one in turn derives a sound ethics (prescription for living optimally). Note by contrast, for Descartes, we must begin with an account of the nature and possibility of knowing, derive a metaphysics from it, and base decisions about how to live on that (supplemented by a physics). To take one more upcoming example, for Hume, sound philosophy must begin with a theory of human nature, which can only be developed empirically. These differences about the proper order of inquiry are deeply revelatory of a philosopher's position.

The last great Modern, Kant, famously criticizes the ontological argu-ment. His various theses (that existence is not a (real, determining) property which contentfully specifies objects of thought, that necessary connections among concepts or judgments don't entail necessary properties of things, etc.) all seem correct to me. And these insights do undermine the ontolog-ical argument as it is typically formulated. I also agree with Kant that no cosmological argument is complete without invocation of the ontological argument, so that rational theology does boil down to the ontological argu-ment. But, as Descartes clarifies in his reply to objections from Caterus, the deep structure of the ontological argument may escape Kant's critique. Here's how I think we should understand the argument; you judge its status.

God is (in its core meaning) properly conceived as the greatest conceivable being. If the greatest conceivable being doesn't exist, it can't come into existence. If it came into existence, it would either be caused to exist, or just happened to exist, which in either case implies limitation. So if the greatest conceivable being does not exist, its existence is impossible (not causable or just happenable). So if God exists, his existence is necessary. The notion of contingent existence or contingent nonexistence can't apply to God. So, God's existence is either impossible or necessary. So, presuming the concept of God is not absurd and so God is possible, God necessarily exists.

Leibniz realized this. Hence, he focused on the need to supplement Descartes' ontological argument with an argument for the (presumptive) possibility of God. Descartes himself thought he had taken care of this. For him, the concept of God is the most clear and distinct of all my concepts, and whatever I conceive clearly and distinctly is known to be at least *possible*, even before we prove that everything I clearly and distinctly conceive is *true* (Third Meditation). (Note: In fact, given Descartes' usage in the Third Meditation, a true idea (in contrast to a true judgment) is an idea of something really possible, not necessarily an idea of something that actually exists.)

It's important to recognize that ontological arguers like Descartes don't maintain that (mere) existence is a perfection; sometimes it would be better that some contingent thing not exist. The alleged property (perfection) of God is necessary-existence, just as his other perfections include necessary-omnipotence, necessary-omniscience, etc., all properties required by the conception of him as greatest conceivable. If this reasoning is not invalid, God necessarily exists if he is possible, so the only subject for debate is whether God is possible. Some have argued that the concept of God is self-contradictory, that God necessarily does not exist. For example, some have argued that the notion of necessary-omnipotence is incoherent (this line probably begins with the medieval "paradox of the stone," that God must be limited in power since he can't make a stone so heavy that he can't lift it). Note that Descartes himself avoids the possibility of such objections, which rest on construing omnipotence as ability to do *anything logically possible* (so that God's will must conform to the coeternal laws of logic, which are independent of his will), *if* he truly is a theistic voluntarist, for whom omnipotence is the ability to do *absolutely anything*, period, and for whom God is the creator of everything, including the laws of mathematics *and logic*. As is clear from Kant's full discussion of rational theology, he realizes that greatest conceivable being, necessarily existing being, absolutely independent being, unconditioned conditioner of all possibility, etc. are all equivalent. So maybe his critique of the ontological argument undermines the current version too. At least we now have a serious, clearheaded version of the argument before us.

Readers often focus exclusively on this new argument for God, but it is crucial to recognize the larger upshot of the Fifth Meditation. It is Descartes' defense of robust rationalism. *Concept-rationalism* is the doctrine that there is at least one innate concept. *Knowledge-rationalism* is the doctrine that there is at least one proposition that can be known *a priori* and whose truth is determined by extra-conceptual fact. *Concept-empiricism* and *knowledge-empiricism* are the denials of the above. *Strong concept-rationalism* affirms that most if not all of the concepts required for *a priori* knowledge are innate. *Strong knowledge-rationalism* affirms that most if not all of the *a priori* truths are determined by extra-conceptual fact. Descartes in the Fifth Meditation is defending strong concept- and knowledge-rationalism. My description of how this works is a bit complicated, but it will help if you cull the gist of the story.[10]

As he begins the Fifth Meditation, Descartes knows that he exists, has various thoughts, that God exists, etc., but (i) it's not clear this is *a priori* knowledge, and (ii) if it is, these cases may be special and anomalous, so a general argument concerning the status of *a priori* knowledge is needed. He begins with a geometric example, a triangle. Various properties can be demonstrated of the triangle; various entailments hold. The talk of "not expecting it to have those properties" and "which are not within my power" (i.e. unforeseen and unalterable consequences) suggest non-inventedness of the idea, but is not offered as the criterion of uninventedness, and so of having a true and immutable nature. Such irresistibility is rather a consequence of clear and distinct perception of necessary connections (entailments), as we've seen from earlier meditations. (Similarly, at CSM II 83–4, analyzability into parts (so compositeness) is not offered as a criterion of inventedness – complex ideas can have true and immutable natures; it's rather that when one cannot by a clear and distinct mental operation, but only by abstraction, separate component ideas, and that's because the ideas are necessarily connected.)

So, the argument goes: various properties can be demonstrated of the triangle, so the triangle has a determinate nature which is immutable. The demonstration is always based on the full set of defining characteristics of the item in question, not just some partial conception of it, and the entailments discovered are not purely logical (or analytic) ones – for example, the inference from "x is a three-angled polygon" to "the sum of the interior angles of x = two right angles" is not deductively valid, even given definitions. So, for geometry Descartes countenances a notion of geometrical entailment and postulates a true and immutable nature for an idea when, and only when, its full set of defining features geometrically entails some other property without logically or analytically entailing it. Revealingly, compare the view of basic necessary connections recognizable independently of any logical form discussed in connection with the *Cogito*.

Geometry is illustrative of a general doctrine about natures – there are entailments analogous to geometrical entailment, neither logically nor

---

10 My account is based on Edelberg's 1990 meticulously developed rendition.

analytically correct, but with correctness dependent in a crucial way on essential facts about the subject matter. Call the generalization on geometrical entailment "subject-specific entailment." Then, suppose you have an idea of A, defined in terms of a set of properties X. The idea is *innate* if (i) the properties in X jointly and subject-specifically entail some property F, but (ii) no proper subset of X does so, and (iii) the mind under certain conditions, namely when the entailment is clearly and distinctly perceived, lacks the power to deny, is psychologically compelled to affirm, that the entailment holds.

So, the flow of argument is: there are certain non-analytic entailments with corresponding psychological compulsions. True and immutable natures are the semantical ground of the truth of these entailments. Innate ideas are the ground of the corresponding set of mental compulsions that are manifested under the ideal conditions of clear and distinct perception. Therefore, strong concept- and judgment-rationalism are true. (So for Descartes, the direction of explanation runs from the necessities contained in the nature of things to the perceptions of the intellect. As we revealingly will see in Chapter Six, for the anti-rationalist Hume, in contrast, necessity is mind-dependent, a determination of the mind to pass from X to Y, accompanied by the propensity to project that subjective determination onto the world.)

We need true and immutable natures to meet the demands of the correspondence theory of truth, as follows:

1   Whenever a proposition is true (non-analytically), there must be something real in virtue of which it is true.
2   If I can demonstrate that some geometric property F subject-specifically entails G, there must be something real in virtue of which it is true that being F entails being G.
3   This real thing cannot be any actually existing F (or any existence), since the entailment would hold even if these things did not exist.
4   The truth of the entailment must rest on real, immutable, eternal essences.

The move away from geometry occurs as follows: It is extension (the nature of space or matter) which determines that a mode of space defined as a three-angled polygon has all the other properties it does. So the subject-specific entailments concerning geometric figures are all determined by the principal attribute of extended substance. Similarly, entailments among the modes of mind are determined by the attribute of thought, and entailments among the various specific perfections of God – we should avoid "mode" here since mode (unlike attribute) implies variability in its bearer (CSM I 211–12) – are determined by the attribute of supreme perfection.

The attribute of thought grounds entailments among modes (properties), which determine the behavior of modes (subjects of the properties) of the mind (mental events individuated by modes, in question). The subjects of these mental properties are just certain clear and distinct intellectual perceptions. And the properties that subject-specifically entail one another in virtue of thought (attribute of thought) are *intentional* ones, like that of being *of* – a three-angled polygon. Innate knowledge results from an appropriate correlation between entailments among geometrical and theological properties, on the one hand, and entailments among intentional properties, on the other. And we avoid the absurd result that we are omniscient about whatever we clearly and distinctly perceive by denying that we know every intentional property of our clear and distinct perceptions, that is, deny that we know everything contained in our clear and distinct ideas, as with our God-idea (CSM II 32).

So it's not that at birth the mind possesses a representation of the triangle that can later be retrieved and examined. It's only that the mind has a certain kind of disposition: if the mind invents the idea of a thing having as its content a three-angled polygon, the mind will be forced to think about this idea in certain ways, in virtue of entailments among its intentional properties. To have an innate idea is to have a certain kind of mental compulsion, grounded in entailments among intentional properties. The reason that ideas that give rise to mental compulsions must be innate, and could not be acquired from experience, is that the compulsions are rooted only in certain entailments, and no experience could bring about these entailments. Innate ideas (in this sense) with true and immutable natures can be composed, put together by the mind – a fact about the ideas' genesis. To be a thinking thing is to be a thing having innate ideas (the full range of subject-specific entailments among your potential modes is fixed). That's why brutes *think* not, which does not entail that brutes feel no pain. This explains the claim to Regius (CSM I 303) that "innate ideas" is equivalent to "the faculty of thinking;" "mind thinks" is equivalent to "mind has innate ideas."

The last five paragraphs of the Fifth Meditation (along with the fourth paragraph of the Third Meditation) characterize the structure of Descartes' overarching procedure in a way that has persuaded many readers (beginning with Descartes' astute contemporary, Antoine Arnauld, who authored the Fourth Set of Objections) that it is hopelessly circular. The charge is that, since Descartes purports to reliably establish the existence of a benevolent God by appeal to clear and distinct perceptions, and then deduces the reliability of clear and distinct perceptions from knowledge of a benevolent God, he assumes the reliability of clear and distinct perceptions to justify the reliability of such perceptions; and this is a question-begging procedure, formally valid, but probatively useless. Further, if Descartes describes his procedure as both showing that meticulous use of our most trustworthy faculty not only can, but must receive divine guarantee, so that certain theological knowledge is a prerequisite for all certified belief, and as successfully proving the relevant theological knowledge, he is contradicting himself, professing to prove something by steps insufficient to provide proof. Given that Descartes does argue for this theological knowledge, this contradiction can be avoided only by denying that all certified belief requires divine guarantee. Yet the critics insist that Descartes apparently affirms, not denies, this dependency. So in the search for indubitable knowledge, Descartes seems to argue in a debilitating circle; and in the search for the correct philosophical account of indubitable knowledge, he seems to hold inconsistent views. To someone who trumpets the unique success of his revolutionary method, this would seem a grave challenge. But each time he addresses the threat, he is unfazed. I do not think this is bluff or confusion. Here is a sketch of why I think he faces no problems of circularity or inconsistency.[11]

Consider the following, two principles:

A   For all p, if I clearly and distinctly perceive that p, then I am certain that p.
B   I am certain that (for all p, if I clearly and distinctly perceive that p, then p).

Early in the Third Meditation, A is true of Descartes, but B is not. A is true of the atheist as well. But when a clear and distinct perception of a theorem is remembered, the rational theist (Descartes in the Fourth Meditation) but not the atheist will be certain, since then B is true of Descartes, but not the atheist. A is true from the start, and provides the needed premises to prove God, and thence B. I need not have access to B before I prove God. My clear and distinct perception that p (and A itself) is not a *ground* of knowledge, but a *source* of knowledge that p. A is a fact that enables knowledge to get started. We authenticate the fact later, but need not do so at the beginning. Descartes becomes certain of different sorts of things, in the following order:

Proposition(s)	*Epistemic status*
Level 1. I think, causal maxims, etc.	Propositions known because they are clearly and distinctly perceived; immediately justified since A is true
Level 2. God exists, God is no deceiver	Propositions known because they are clearly and distinctly perceived to follow from premises at level 1
Level 3. Whatever I clearly and distinctly perceive is certain	Principle known because it is clearly and distinctly perceived to follow from propositions at level 2
Level 4. I perceive clearly and distinctly that I think, etc.	New premises, one corresponding to each premise at level 1
Level 5. I am certain that I think, etc.	Propositions known because they are clearly and distinctly perceived to follow from propositions at levels 3 and 4

11 I offered a much fuller solution to the challenge of circularity in Tlumak 1978. Here I also use Van Cleve's 1979 largely equivalent, perspicuous formulation as well.

These show initial premises were not arbitrary. These higher-order propositions that say the initial premises are immediately justified and certain are themselves justified by appeal to reasons.

We can rearticulate the structure of Descartes' procedure this way. Let *epistemic principles* (rules of evidence) be principles specifying the conditions under which propositions are justified; they are of the general form: If . . . , then p is justified for person S. For any sort of foundationalist, there are two types of epistemic principle. *Generation principles* tell us that propositions of certain types are justified independently of their (broadly) logical relations to other propositions. These lay the foundations of knowledge. *Transmission principles* tell us that if some propositions are already justified, then any propositions that stand in such-and-such relations to them are also justified. These are used to erect the superstructure of knowledge.

A is Descartes' generation principle. If [p is justified for S, and p entails q, and (p entails q) is justified for S], then q is justified for S, is Descartes' transmission principle.

Epistemic propositions are singular propositions that attribute some epistemic characteristic to another (object) proposition. (For example, I am certain that I think.) Epistemic principles are justified for a foundationalist either by:

(i)   being immediately justified, or
(ii) being mediately justified after epistemic propositions, or
(iii) being mediately justified before epistemic propositions.

Descartes' procedure exemplifies pattern (iii), which is neither circular nor arbitrary (dogmatic). The problematic issue is whether there are valid inferences from level 1 to level 2, and from level 2 to level 3.

Descartes occasionally entertains pattern (ii), for example, at the beginning of the Third Meditation: I am certain that I am a thinking thing; the only possible source of this certainty is clear and distinct perception; therefore, clear and distinct perception is a universally reliable source of certainty, that is, whatever I clearly and distinctly perceive is certain. This seems to exemplify a procedure called *particularism*, which begins with particular affirmations as data, and tests methods and principles in terms of their capacity to accommodate those particulars. But I read the meditator as rejecting the suggested route as premature, so that while the clarity principle is first *discovered* early in the Third Meditation, it is not adequately *justified* until the Fourth Meditation, as he acknowledges in the Synopsis. Interestingly, Descartes doesn't ever seem seriously to entertain alternative (i).

Summing up, Descartes' non-circular procedure may be outlined as follows:

1   If I clearly and (very) distinctly perceive p at time t, then I am compelled to assent to p at t.
2   If I am compelled to assent to p at t, then p is indubitable for me at t.

3 If I clearly and distinctly perceive an axiom at *t*, then that axiom is indubitable (demon-resistant) for me at *t*. (1,2)

4 If I focus my attention on an axiom, I clearly and distinctly perceive it. (Doubt therapy disabuses reliance on the sensory and allows such focused consideration.)

5 If I focus my attention on an axiom, it is then indubitable for me. (3,4)

6 If I clearly and distinctly perceive a theorem at *t*, then that theorem is indubitable for me at *t*. (1,2)

7 I clearly and distinctly perceive a theorem at *t* if and only if I provide a continuous and uninterrupted clear and distinct proof for that theorem at *t*.

8 I can know *that* a theorem has been clearly and distinctly perceived without now clearly and distinctly perceiving it.

9 When I do not clearly and distinctly perceive a theorem, even if I remember having clearly and distinctly perceived it, that theorem is dubious if and only if it is an epistemic possibility for me that even the best evidence is not a reliable guide to truth.

10 *Scientia* requires the indubitability of past demonstrations – I cannot attend to every lemma as the system of knowledge grows (*scientia* is not isolated, axiomatic certainties).

11 *Scientia* requires removal of the (second-order) epistemic possibility that even the best evidence – that of clear and distinct perception – is misleading or inadequate. (9,10) (This possibility is epistemologically equivalent to the possibility of inferior ("demonic") origins.)

12 At *t*, I provide a continuous and uninterrupted, clear and distinct proof for the theorem that God, an infinitely perfect substance (eternal, immutable, omniscient, omnipotent, and creator of all things (if any) which are outside me), exists.

13 At *t*, that God exists at *t* is indubitable for me. (6,7,12)

14 If God exists at *t*, then God eternally and immutably exists. (12)

15 At *t*, that God eternally and immutably exists is indubitable, that is, fully irrevisable for me. (13,14). (There is an immediate conversion from "the truth of what I perceive *now* holds" to "the truth of what I perceive *always* holds.")

16 I go on to indubitably prove that given that God is not a deceiver, and is the cause of all positive reality, since all clear and distinct perceptions are positively real, they must be true.

17 If it is indubitable that all clear and distinct perceptions are true, then it is epistemically impossible that the best evidence (the evidence of clear and distinct perception) is not a reliable guide to truth.

18 It is epistemically impossible that the best evidence is inadequate or misleading. (16,17)

19 Once clearly and distinctly deduced, all theorems are indubitable so long as there is correct record of the deduction. (9,18)

20 By the method of clear and distinct perception, born of the method of doubt, perfect knowledge (*scientia*) may be achieved.

The line of argument I have just sketched is neither circular nor inconsistent. And it is dogmatic only if a radical epistemological solipsism of the moment is dogmatic. The threat to the strategy is the claim that the deduction from axioms to the clarity rule cannot be continuously attended to – it is too long – and so the theorem that God exists becomes dubious when its further implications are being elicited. I think Descartes' response would be that until you clearly and distinctly realize the implications of God's existence, the final epistemically possible doubtmaker is not ruled out, and that is why you have to meditate seriously and repeatedly before you succeed. Achieving indubitable knowledge of the truth requires strenuous application of the mind. "But all things excellent are as difficult as they are rare." This is how Spinoza, the subject of our next chapter, concludes his *Ethics*. He will reject the very problem of the criterion.

To help you grapple with this very important philosophical question yourself, note that all of the basic strategies for defending Descartes against the charge of circularity seem to be determined by three main variables. First is one's view of his psychology or theory of mental activity. Descartes frequently uses the notions of clear and distinct perception, natural light perception, intuition, and reason. Commentators who identify these see the project either as one of self-validation, using a faculty to exonerate its own reliability, pulling oneself up by one's bootstraps (if initially everything is dubitable), or as validation of an entirely different faculty, such as memory (if clear and distinct perception is never dubitable). Those who distinguish at least some of the four notions, for example, treating intuition as a species of clear and distinct perception, tend to agree that no single mental function can be vindicated by its own use, and relieve the appearance of circularity by arguing that the clear and distinct premises of the God-proof are not of the same sort as those whose reliability depend on God, but are better, autonomously certain (demon-resistant since certain on the supposition of the demon).

The second variable is one's interpretation of metaphysical certainty and its relation to truth. Nearly all interpretations are variations on one of three themes: that certainties are indefeasibly justified beliefs (irrevisability); that certainties are optimally justified beliefs (maximal warrant); or that certainties are beliefs which cannot be mistaken (unmistakability). I have argued elsewhere that viewed abstractly, these three notions are logically distinct, but when we are sensitive to Descartes' usage and other doctrines (such as that warrant is a qualitative, not quantitative notion, that pre-God-proof modality talk should be construed epistemically, not logically – for example, "necessarily" means "certainly," as in his summation of the *Cogito* – and so on), we can show that for him they are equivalent, and amount to what we would think of as irrevisability. A proposition p is irrevisable for a person S at a time t if and only if S is justified in believing p at t, and it is impossible that any additional considerations at any later t' would warrant S's retraction of p, that is, warrant S's withholding p or believing not-p at t'. Certainty thus understood is a purely evidential notion, which does not logically entail belief or truth.

The third variable is one's interpretation of "compelled assent" (*persuasio*) and its relation to metaphysical certainty and to moral certainty (justification sufficient for practical purposes). The one datum in connection with the third variable is Descartes' unwavering contention that he cannot refrain from believing (is compelled to believe) whatever he clearly and distinctly perceives, so long as he clearly and distinctly perceives it. Fixing the meaning and role of this pivotal contention is central to discovering the structure of Cartesian method.

Underlying all this is a powerful theory of innate ideas. There are four, main influential species of interpretations of innate ideas. They are typically seen as competing. Analogously to my earlier effort to show that all the main interpretations of the *Cogito* are true, I will conclude this section by arguing that all the interpretations of Cartesian innatism are true, indeed logically interdependent.[12] The four, ostensible competitors are these:

1   On the *reflective theory*, innate ideas are ideas discovered by reflection on ourselves, by reflection on our existence or our nature alone (in contrast with adventitious or factitious ideas).
2   On the *anamnesis theory*, recognition of innate truths should be understood as a kind of reminiscence or recovery of knowledge had all along.
3   On the dispositional (or better, *transcendental*) theory, innate ideas are activatable dispositions or structures of the mind; the product of successful activation through proper method is clear and distinct perception, the occurrent manifestation of an abiding disposition.
4   On the *there-but-covered or hidden by intellectual debris theory*, what's innate is there to be seen all along if only we shine light on it (*lumen naturale*).

As the whole structure of the *Meditations* exemplifies, Descartes' talk of innate ideas as capacities or dispositions (a faculty), as implanted (imprinted, impressed) in the mind, as implicit in thought and discovered by reflection on ourselves, as present but covered over, as retrieval or recollection of what has been there all along, expresses logically interdependent, not fluctuating nor, *a fortiori*, competing accounts. The key to seeing this is recognition that systematically, at bottom, there are three senses of "idea" for Descartes: taken materially, they are operations or acts; taken objectively, they are (immediately represented) objects; and taken dispositionally, they are capacities to form certain ideas (in the material sense) or perceive them (in the objective sense). All (three sorts of) ideas that have objective reality (represent something) can be taken materially and objectively. Every idea taken objectively has a correlative idea taken dispositionally; every idea taken objectively need not have a correlative idea in the material sense. So, for example, "innate

---

12   I've embraced the thrust of this account for a long time, but I rely on Boyle's 2000 superior formulation of our agreement.

idea of God" could mean "God as he exists objectively in the intellect" (the "true" nature of God which we may aim to articulate), or "the capacity to perceive that idea, to summon up the nature of God," or the actual ideas in the material sense that are clear and distinct, or obscure and confused (clear and distinct *perception* – adverbial uses signify mental operations).

Next, for Descartes we are *conscius* of all that happens (all acts, not faculties) in our minds when it happens, but *conscientia* is an implicit awareness, which always precedes reflective knowledge. Cartesian consciousness is not consciousness as we tend to use that notion nowadays, but more like potential consciousness (an implicit awareness accompanies every thought). Similarly, Descartes allows that there are two senses in which we can know what thought is: implicit knowledge (*cognitio interna*), because we're *conscii* of thinking, or explicit realization, through a further mental act, of what thought is (*scientia reflexa*). And once I have explicitly perceived some thought I can further reflect on it to discover its properties, including what it contains, and in this latter case only still higher levels of reflective knowledge are possible; in the former case, there is only one mental act involved – implicit knowledge is had simply by virtue of having the thought, and it is an awareness not separate from the thought itself. One can explicitly notice that one is thinking without explicitly noticing what thought is.

So in the *Cogito* the meditator comes to know explicitly that she thinks, but not yet know what thought is. By attending to the process of thinking, she begins to come to know explicitly what thought is too. More generally, there are some ideas we can perceive because we have an implicit awareness of them, because they're relied on in the very process of thinking. To have such an implicit awareness is to have the capacity to perceive them explicitly, a capacity exercised when, through an act of will, we attend to our thoughts. And again, once they are explicit, they can be examined to generate explicit awareness of other innate ideas, but such examination requires meditative skills. Putting it retrospectively, in light of doctrine allegedly established by the end of Meditation Five, God created the intellect (i.e. us) to think, and in the very process of thinking, we implicitly rely on various natures and truths which exist, objectively, in the intellect, and we therefore have the correlative capacities to perceive those things, which are exercised when we attend to our thoughts and ideas in order to discern that which we implicitly know.

The will can direct intellect's attention so that it focuses on certain objects. Keeping the intellect focused on non-sensory things, contrary to habituation and the attention-grabbing liveliness of sense ideas, requires more than a single act of will, but sustained effort (promoted by meditative training). And while, insofar as will can affirm or deny a proposition (or pursue or shun some end), our will is perfect (like God's), unlike God's, it (our acts of attention, judgments, etc.) vacillates. Structurally, the *Meditations* is an exercise in developing constancy of will (only guaranteeable when one restricts oneself to the clear and distinct). What is needed is the ability to concentrate, to use the will to focus the intellect on innate ideas for a sustained period of time, indeed, before coming to know God, to even hold deductions together in the mind as intuitions, to fix those ideas in the mind so as to avoid sensory relapse, etc. To put it more melodramatically (but I intend accurately), the *Meditations* enact self-realization, becoming who the "I" truly is, a rational being (an intellect, or pure understanding), which means using the lower grade of human freedom – freedom of indifference, which entails choice and avoidability (could have done otherwise) – to achieve the higher grade of human freedom – freedom of spontaneity, which entails neither choice nor avoidability, but rather is manifested in compelled assent, acting in accordance with one's true nature in a wholly unfettered way. This process involves various transitions. Articulating these transitions optimally invokes all of the innatist metaphors. Descartes' remarks suggest that the dispositional (better, transcendental), reminiscence, reflective, and there-but-submerged accounts all dovetail, given the aforementioned resources. And the inevitably first instance of indubitable knowledge by clear and distinct perception for one who rigorously follows the analytic method of discovery, that which provides the basis for the discovery of all the rest, is the *Cogito*, which as intuition, inference, and performative, uniquely and fully plays its role in Descartes' foundationalist system.

1.9 The Sixth Meditation

Descartes' Sixth Meditation is entitled, *The existence of material things, and the real distinction between mind and body*. Here, Descartes completes the process of making philosophical ideas clear and distinct; in fact, Descartes was confident that he had vanquished defective methods of inquiry. For example, he believed he had vanquished the notion that truth is found through sense experience, and that a natural process is explained by identifying its purpose. Descartes also was confident that he had eliminated all rational resistance to theism. And he believed he had validated the reliability of human efforts to achieve knowledge through reason. Now he proceeded to ring the death knell for remaining misconceptions about human nature and how humans are related to the physical world.

Descartes said it is a fundamental misconception to think of a human being as being identical with his or her body. Rather, a human being is a compound of a body (which is spatially extended) and a mind (which has no extension in space). The mind is the thinking "I" or "self" first discovered in the *Cogito;* it can exist independently of any body, including the brain. The brain weighs about three pounds, while the mind is weightless. Since the mind is a completely different kind of thing from the body, one crucial condition for personal survival of bodily death is met. In a living human being, however, the mind and body causally interact through the nervous system. The body affects the mind, for example, when a wound causes pain; the mind affects the body when it chooses to initiate a bodily movement.

Descartes provided as much detail as he could about these causal processes in essays like *Treatise on Man*, *Dioptrics*, and *The Passions of the Soul*. In the *Meditations*, he approached the connection between mind and body more broadly:

> Nature . . . teaches me, by . . . sensations of pain, hunger, thirst and so on, that I am not merely present in my body as a sailor is present in a ship, but that I am very closely joined . . . with it, so that I and the body form a unit. If this were not so, I, who am nothing but a thinking thing, would not feel pain when the body was hurt, but would perceive the damage purely by the intellect, just as a sailor perceives by sight if anything in his ship is broken. Similarly, when the body needed food or drink, I should have an explicit understanding of the fact, instead of having confused sensations of hunger and thirst. For these sensations . . . are nothing but confused modes of thinking which arise from the union and, as it were, intermingling of the mind with the body.
>
> (CSM II 56)

One of Descartes' legacies is that this so-called dualism of mind and body has become a familiar way of understanding human beings. Indeed, the British philosopher Gilbert Ryle began his famous attack on Descartes with these words:

> There is a doctrine about the nature and place of minds which is so prevalent among theorists and even among laymen that it deserves to be described as the official theory. Most philosophers, psychologists and religious teachers subscribe, with minor reservations, to its main articles and, although they admit certain theoretical difficulties in it, they tend to assume that these can be overcome without serious modifications being made to the architecture of the theory.
>
> (Ryle 1949: 11)

After outlining Descartes' official theory, Ryle continued: "I shall often speak of it, with deliberate abusiveness, as 'the dogma of the Ghost in the Machine.' I hope to prove that it is entirely false, and false not in detail but in principle" (15–16). Ryle wrote these words in the middle of the twentieth century; since then, philosophers and other thinkers have increasingly moved away from any form of mind–body dualism. They generally have moved toward different forms of materialism, including some uncompromising versions that regard consciousness itself as an outdated superstition (to be rejected along with things such as ghosts). Even in Descartes' own time, many people rejected his view – mainly because it seemed impossible to explain exactly how the mind and body interact. For example, about a year after the *Meditations* was published, Descartes began a correspondence with the exiled Princess Elizabeth of Bohemia, who conveyed her puzzlement: "How can the soul of man, being only a thinking substance, determine his bodily spirits to perform voluntary actions?"[13]

Every major philosopher in the modern age has grappled with this problem. How can something which does not occupy space cause things to change their spatial location, and vice versa? The very possibility of such influence also seems to destroy central components of Descartes' philosophy: if the mind influences the physical world through our bodies, then how can the physical world be a self-contained machine (whose total energy is conserved) explainable by mechanistic science? And if a merely physical force on one's body causes changes in the mind, then our mental life does not seem so free after all.

Descartes acknowledged that the interaction between mind and body is quite mysterious. In fact, he insisted that this interaction cannot be understood scientifically. He replied to Elizabeth:

> The soul is conceived only by the pure intellect; body (i.e. extension, shapes and motions) can likewise be known by the intellect alone, but much better by the intellect aided by the imagination; and finally what belongs to the union of the soul and the body is known only obscurely by the intellect alone or even by the intellect aided by the imagination, but is known very clearly by the senses. That is why people who never philosophize and use only their senses have no doubt that the soul moves the body and that the body acts on the soul. They regard both of them as a single thing, that is to say, they conceive their union; because to conceive the union between two things is to conceive them as one single thing.
>
> (CSM III 227)

Several years later, Descartes wrote to Arnauld, whom he held in high regard:

> That the mind . . . can set the body in motion – this is something which is shown to us not by any reasoning or comparison with other matters, but by the surest and plainest everyday experience. It is one of those self-evident things which we only make more obscure when we try to explain them in terms of others.
>
> (CSM III 358)

Here Descartes seems to concede that the mystery of mind–body interaction makes it impossible to have a science of human being. So why didn't he explain all human behavior mechanistically? Indeed, he believed that most

---

13 Descartes' responses to Elizabeth, beginning in 1643, are deeply revealing.

human behavior can be explained by mechanistic accounts. The question is, why did he feel obliged to embrace separate minds at all?

Descartes' writings offer different answers. Let me isolate a few crucial points that will enhance your understanding and appreciation of the real Descartes. First, since substances are things that can exist independently, substance dualism is a quite strong form of dualism which entails that mind and body are *really distinct*. A and B are really distinct just in case it is possible for A to exist without B, and B to exist without A. Two things can be different, or *numerically distinct*, without being really distinct. Two things are numerically distinct if one has a property the other lacks. So, for example, my entire body and my head are numerically distinct. But my entire body and my head are not really distinct, since the existence of my entire body depends on the existence of my head. In general, things with parts are numerically but not really distinct from their parts.

Second, it may be that some kinds of phenomena we nowadays call "mental" require the existence of an irreducibly non-physical mind, but other kinds of phenomena do not. Types of mental states include (at least partly) cognitive states, such as perception, memory, belief; motivational states, such as desire and emotion (not to deny they involve a conceptual component), and more obviously mixed cognitive/conative states involving will, such as attention (selective focus) and intention; and sensations, including feelings such as pain. Awareness or consciousness seems able to accompany any mental state. And conscious beings seem always to have a point of view or perspective; consciousness is *ontologically subjective* – it exists only as experienced by the agent. Descartes doesn't knee-jerk postulate mind. He thinks much can and should be explained physicalistically. This includes his much-misunderstood position on animals. Animals lack minds or souls. They can be explained wholly mechanistically. But that doesn't entail, and it is false, that they lack sentience, so can't experience pain, or that they lack what we'd call short-term memory. Bodies without minds, automata, can feel pain and have some memory. But, for example, a non-mind couldn't consciously reflect on the sensation of pain, nor suffer more because it worries about the pain's persistence nor about what the pain signifies, and so on. So while animals lack minds, they are not indistinguishable from toasters, just as a dog is distinguishable from a worm, even though all are purely physical entities. Remember that for Descartes mind is essentially understanding or intellect, that all (including sensory and imaginative) acts of mind presuppose acts of understanding or intellect. He makes this plain in the Sixth Meditation before launching into his proofs of mind–body dualism.

Now, the key question: on what definitive grounds can we know that mind is essentially and so substantially different from body? In the *Meditations*, the official proof of this result occurs in the Sixth Meditation (and *not* before – the proof requires having clear and distinct ideas of both mind and body, and the criterion that whatever one clearly and distinctly understands is true, and these results are not jointly available until a ways into the Sixth Meditation, as the Synopsis advertises), but Descartes is thought to have offered other proofs elsewhere. Many of these arguments rely on a principle called the *indiscernibility of identicals*, or *Leibniz's Law*, which tells us that if x is identical to y, then x and y share all their properties in common, and vice versa. So, if I know that there's a property that x and y do not share, I know that x is at least numerically distinct from y. So, what do I know to be essentially distinctive of mind, and not true of body?

Consider one cluster of answers, all flawed for the same reason.

- Mind is distinctively intentional. If x stands in a mental relation to y, then that very relation can obtain even if y does not exist. I can believe in ghosts and yearn for your love even if there are no ghosts and you love me not. But if x stands in a physical relation to y, then that very relation can obtain only if both x and y exist. I can't kick a football unless both I and the football exist.
- Mind distinctively exhibits privileged access; I can refer to my mental states demonstratively (directly, as if by pointing) and no one else can. Note distinctions among the strengths of claims I might make, as between "I have unique access," "I have access epistemically superior to the access of others," and "I have epistemically ideal access."
- Mind distinctively exhibits incorrigibility, interpreted weakly as saying that my evidence for my beliefs about my mental states cannot be over-ridden by other evidence (a conception assimilatable to stronger forms of privileged access), or interpreted strongly as saying that my beliefs about my mental states literally cannot be mistaken.
- Mind is distinctively self-conscious. Note distinctions among construals: that I know when all my mental states occur (self-intimation); I can know when any mental state occurs (by attention); I know the *content* of all my mental states; and I can know the content of all my mental states.

It is debatable which of these claims Descartes really held. For example, I think he affirmed the intentionality of the mental, but not strong incorrigibility or strong self-consciousness, but we can bypass such detail. None of the claims prove mind–body dualism. Consider intentionality. It strikes me as a profoundly interesting fact that objects of psychological attitudes need not exist. But that the accusative object need not exist does not entail that the acting subject need not exist (it obviously must), nor that the subject has some particular ontological status, namely being non-spatial. The thing performing what we regard as mental activities may be physical, for example, the brain. And we may have strong but not decisive reasons to conclude that it is something like the brain. After all, forms of thinking seem systematically to depend on neural activity, evolutionary biology provides a story on which higher thinking emerges from our more sophisticated brains, and so on. The crucial point, again, is that peculiar features of *what* we think about don't establish the nature of *the thing doing the thinking*. I invite you to replay this objection with the other theses about mind. (I myself judge things to get a bit muddier with respect to self-consciousness.)

I do not think Descartes argued from any of these features to substance-dualism, mainly because they are inferences that go too directly from agent-centered epistemology or philosophy of mind to timeless metaphysics, from some perspectival fact to a non-perspectival reality. Instead, he seemed to put most stock in the view that minds are distinguished from matter by their creative use of language and reason (at bottom an argument from free will guided by reason). This argument, best stated in *Discourse* V, doesn't suffer the previous defect, and is, I think, the other main argument (besides the two in the Sixth Meditation) he took seriously. Descartes argued as if he were engaged in a present-day debate about whether a robot or a computer could be conscious:

> . . . if . . . machines bore a resemblance to our bodies and imitated our actions as closely as possible for all practical purposes, we should still have two very certain means of recognizing that they were not real men. The first is that they could never use words, or put together other signs, as we do in order to declare our thoughts to others. For we certainly can conceive of a machine so constructed that it utters words, and even utters words which correspond to bodily actions causing a change in its organs (e.g. if you touch it in one spot it asks what you want of it, if you touch it in another it cries out that you are hurting it, and so on). But it is not conceivable that such a machine should produce different arrangements of words so as to give an appropriately meaningful answer to whatever is said in its presence, as the dullest of men can do.
>
> (CSM I 139–40)

Descartes elaborated on this notion that the mind is what makes humans so versatile: "Secondly, . . . it is for all practical purposes impossible for a machine to have enough different organs to make it act in all the contingencies of life in the way in which our reason makes us act (CSM I 140)."

Thinkers still vigorously debate the notion that language is *the* feature that distinguishes the rational mind from any merely physical entity, no matter how complex it may be. For example, linguist Noam Chomsky stresses how, with only a finite vocabulary and a set of grammatical rules, people can understand and produce an indefinitely large set of grammatical sentences, including brand new ones. Descartes' point is that while a complex machine can do enormously many things, and do some things better and faster than any of us, it cannot exhibit the complete open-ended adaptability of rational, language-using humans.

We've seen that Descartes analyzed judgment in terms of free will, and he believed that whatever exhibits this divine ability must be made in the image of God. At bottom what he is now arguing is that beings with free will must be different from physical things, which are governed by the mechanical laws of science; things that have free will must be immaterial.

A controversial but striking twentieth-century parallel to Descartes' reasoning invokes Kurt Gödel's proof of the incompleteness of higher-order logics. An axiomatic presentation of subject-matter X is complete if all the truths about X are derivable from the specified axioms, are theorems of the system. The long-standing Euclidean assumption was that each area of genuine human knowledge could be axiomatized in this way. Gödel showed that there can be no complete and consistent axiom system for the elementary arithmetic of natural numbers, showing once for all that mathematical truth cannot be identified with derivability from any particular set of axioms, toppling the Euclidean assumption. In more complex areas of inquiry, the human mind can always discover truths that in principle can't be cranked out by any finite, generative structure; the mind (the analogy goes) has capacities that no mechanism can match, and on the operative scientific conception of the times, the physical is the mechanistic, a machine governed by causal laws. Language-use and mathematical insight are examples of such capacities.

Finally, the only other arguments for the real distinction between mind and body that I read Descartes as endorsing are the two actually given in the Sixth Meditation. The first, which is the culmination of so much of the *Meditations'* earlier analysis that we ought to refrain from tracing its underpinnings, now summarizes that one can clearly and distinctly perceive that the mind is a thinking but unextended thing, and clearly and distinctly perceive that the body is an extended but unthinking thing, and since everything clearly and distinctly perceived is known to be true, one can know that the mind is really distinct from the body.

The second argues that since (extended) body is essentially divisible and mind is essentially indivisible, mind is distinct from body. This is often criticized as clumsily question-begging, on the grounds that we aim to *prove* that mind is unextended and so indivisible, hence we cannot *assume* that it has no spatial parts. But I'm pretty sure that this criticism misconstrues what Descartes means here by the indivisibility of mind. (If the familiar reading were right, this wouldn't even be a new argument, since the first argument already claimed to know that the mind is a thinking thing with no spatial parts.) Rather, he aims to capture a profound but elusive fact about the essential unity of consciousness, a unity that has no counterpart in our conception of physical things. Since Kant penetrates deeply into this fact (see Chapter Seven), I omit further discussion of it here.

Descartes now returned to all the doubts expressed in the First Meditation in order to answer them. He was especially concerned to resolve the doubts about the physical world and how we know it; with this doubt resolved, the foundations for his new science would be secure. Descartes' arguments on this topic set the agenda for much of the work by the philosophers who were to follow. The main interpretive dispute is whether

Descartes confidently deduced the existence of the external world from the faculty of sense-perception and the fact that God is no deceiver – it's agreed that he thought the faculty of imagination may be best explained by postulating an external world, but that this postulate is only probable, not certain – or whether, as the Synopsis's closing remarks suggest, he aimed to highlight the fact that as cogent as any argument for the physical world might be, it cannot achieve the level of (metaphysical) certainty that characterizes our self-knowledge and knowledge of God.

1.10   A summary of key Cartesian commitments

To conclude this chapter, here is a list of especially important commitments of Descartes' philosophy that centrally frame subsequent philosophical inquiry, followed by a rich list of paper topics (which largely prompt reflection on themes I've addressed, but sometimes introduce new material). It will be useful for you to consider not only how Descartes' critics react to these commitments, but how and why you are inclined to do so as well.

- *Knowledge rationalism*: we can know important, universal truths about ourselves, God, and the natural world by (and only by) the proper use of reason, independently of sense experience.
- *Concept rationalism*: we have substantive concepts (innate ideas with true and immutable natures) which cannot be derived from sense experience.
- *Metaphysical realism* about the physical world: the physical world exists, and has at least some of its properties, independently of the beliefs, attitudes, etc. of perceivers.
- *Representational realism* about the physical world: when we have cognitive access to the physical world, it is always indirectly via our mental representations (ideas).
- *Substance-kind pluralism*: there is more than one kind of substance. For Descartes there are three kinds of substance: finite thinking substances (finite minds), finite extended substance (the spatial world), and infinite thinking substance (God, supremely perfect (actually infinite) being).
- *Individual-substance pluralism*: there are more than one individual instances of (at least) one kind of substance. For Descartes, there are many individual finite minds (souls, selves, "I"s). It is controversial whether Descartes also thinks there are many individual finite bodies, or whether there is only one extended substance, the whole physical world, and the particular concrete bodies we familiarly distinguish are partitioned off on pragmatic and other grounds. God is *sui generis*; there can be only one instance of supremely perfect, absolutely infinite, necessarily existing being.
- *Ahistoricism*: there are timeless, eternal truths (though in Descartes' case the method for validating them begins with temporally-indexed, momentary truths), independent of time, place, culture, etc.

- *Essentialism*: things have non-trivial properties necessarily; they have to have those properties in order to continue to exist. Descartes holds that created minds have an essence that determines what kind of thing they are (species-essences), but not an essence that picks each one of them out uniquely (individuates them), not a *haecceity*. It follows that individuation of minds requires appeal to contingent (non-essential) properties (modes).

- *Explanatory reductionism*: Good explanations of phenomena in the natural world are *compositional* and *reductive*, that is, they explain the wide diversity of phenomena in terms of a few, basic, ubiquitous properties of things (what Descartes calls *simple natures*). All the fluctuating, sense-observable features of things (their *secondary qualities*) are explainable in terms of their geometrical features and motion (their *primary qualities*). So a single method unifies seemingly disparate sciences and mathematics. Indeed, physics is a branch of mathematics. And indeed, all measurable and orderable things can be treated in a similar way (think of his discovery of analytic geometry, and recall the tree of knowledge metaphor). All explanations properly invoke *mechanistic* laws, which appeal only to *efficient causation*, never to *final causation* (purposes, teleology). The explanatory situation with respect to minds is different.

- *Epistemological foundationalism*: the structure of a system of genuine knowledge is such that there is some basic, underived knowledge (self-evident, immediately evident, etc.) that must be used to derive (by the legitimate forms of inference) all the rest of our knowledge. Foundationalisms vary depending on their accounts of basic knowledge and the rules for transmitting knowledge. Descartes' account of basic knowledge is given by his theory of *intuition*, and in the sphere of *first philosophy* (in contrast to the pursuit of specific empirical sciences) he restricts transmission to *recognized, valid deduction*. Descartes is an epistemological foundationalist in a second, distinct sense as well, as is manifested in his announced need to overcome skeptical doubt. In this second sense, a foundationalist requires that one refrain from pursuing the development of knowledge until the possibility of success is established. Such foundationalism is defined by embracing the challenge of the problem of the criterion. This also allows us to note that Descartes is a *methodist*, not a *particularist*. He refuses to begin philosophizing with any list of unchallengeable, particular data, but seeks a meticulous implementation of a presuppositionless starting point and neutral method, and is prepared to accept whatever results from this procedure. He thinks this requires what we might call *individual autonomism*, on which foundational inquiry must be conducted by the solitary individual, by exclusive appeal to his or her own rational reflection, without appeal to any outside authority. This is related to what is called *epistemic internalism*, the view that assessments of epistemic claims (claims to be justified, to be rational, knowledgeable, etc.) must be made in terms of the available perspective of the agent, not merely in terms of objective facts (such as causal connections) of which the agent is unaware (the opposing view is called *externalism*). This is also related to his insistence that first philosophy use what he called the *analytic method*, not the synthetic method. Analysis (in Descartes' technical sense) follows the order of discovery, of indubitably recognized uncertainties and certainties, not what may turn out to be the abstract, logical or ontological (in terms of what really exists, known or not) dependencies among things or kinds of things (which is how things are presented synthetically). Since people disagree, we must begin with analysis. Analysis (beginning with systematic doubt) enables gradual attainment of sufficiently clear and distinct ideas of mind, body, God, knowledge, etc., so that we can recognize authoritatively their relations. It also produces consensus. Once we've discovered what we truly know, we can re-present it logically in a synthetic way. A synthetic presentation is basically a geometric one, in which we set out our axioms, postulates, and definitions, and then deduce our theorems.

- *Atomism*: in some ways paralleling foundationalism, *conceptual atomism* insists that all our concepts are constructions out of a set of simple, unanalyzable concepts, which we therefore should strive to isolate. Descartes (as with reductionism above) is also an *explanatory atomist*, and also a *metaphysical atomist* when it comes to the natural world in the sense that he thinks macro-objects are all really constituted by corpuscles (though he rules out that such corpuscles should be true, indivisible atoms, since he's committed to saying that whatever is physical is extended, and whatever is extended is divisible, so that a physical atom would be a divisible indivisible (a contradiction)).

To tie up a few loose ends, Descartes holds that in order to unlock the secrets of the universe and allow us to be its master, observational science requires a framework of pre-experiential, rational concepts and principles, uniquely discoverable by his revolutionary method. The method validates the new science's treatment of the world as a huge, causally determined, physical machine while making a place for human individuality, freedom, and spirituality. The impersonal, material world, and our personal, meaningful existences, can coexist. However, their full integration (highlighted in our existence as human beings (not merely souls, minds or selves), which are mind–body composites (such that there is intimate causal interaction between the mental and the physical)) is not subject to clear and distinct understanding, so that no strict, metaphysically certain science of the human being is possible. We can assert some things with certainty, such as that the scope of understanding exceeds that of imagination, and the imaginable extends farther than sense perception, and that will is unbounded, and has broadest scope of all.

1.11 Topical highlights from Descartes' correspondence

In this chapter I have used the *Meditations* as the organizing skeleton for the invocation of other texts published during Descartes' life. I've cited little private correspondence. If you seek to test interpretations further, here's a list of topical highlights of especial interest from Descartes' correspondence (CSM III):

13	universal language and true philosophy
19–20	relativity of beauty and pleasure
22–3	metaphysics, theology, and theistic voluntarism
24–6	perfection of world; knowing is different from grasping
40	neurophysiological explanation of imagination, memory, etc.
53	aims of *Discourse on Method*
55	limitation of *Discourse*
62	sensation and reason
85–6	limitation of *Discourse*
97–100	theory–practice; thought is in our power; *Cogito*; mind–body; animal thinking
106	proving versus explaining
120	science and revelation
124 ff.	Galileo's work
132	matter is space
139–40	simple notions; light of nature as criterion of truth; faculties and objects
141–2	infinite will is the respect in which we are created in God's image; common notions are undeniable
143	pineal gland as seat in brain of soul; cooperative search for truth
147	source of idea of infinite; clear and distinct perception; memory
148	precipitate judgment not necessitated by embodiment; pain in the strict sense requires mind
154–5	distinct conceivability and possibility; body divisible, without inclination
157	report of mailing of *Meditations*, its foundational character
158	Sorbonne endorsement
159	*Cogito* is in Augustine, but is used differently
160	only some thoughts in our power, no absolute power over material things
161	my philosophy coincides with faith; free will a primary notion
162	soul joins body at pineal gland
163	*Meditations* follow order of reasoning, from easier to harder
166	"don't know everything in x" doesn't entail "don't know what x is"
169	God is beyond comprehension, yet we can articulate more about Him than anything else
173	my philosophy will undermine Aristotelian principles
179	freedom, indifference

1.12   Questions about Descartes

1   What is the nature of the method of doubt? What is its scope? How does Descartes plan to execute it? Does he actually do what he plans to do? Is it a feasible thing to do? Why or why not?

2   If you interpret any of the skeptical arguments of the First Meditation in an unusual way (in terms of structure, role, etc.), present your view and justify it.

3   a)   What is Descartes' conception of the structure of a rational system of knowledge? How does his conception motivate his philosophical method?

    b) Is the production of certain psychological states essential to Descartes' success? Are the *Meditations* crucially meditations in a traditional religious sense?

4   What is going on in the *Cogito* passage? Present your view and justify it.

5   Discuss Descartes' conception of thinking. What is the significance of his conception to his overall project? Is his conception too broad (does it include too much)? If so, what important consequences follow? If not, what?

6   a) Is self-consciousness, in Descartes' sense, possible? Explain Cartesian self-consciousness, and why you think it's possible or not. Why is it important?

       b) What is Descartes' position on the thinker's privileged access to his or her conscious states? On the unmistakable (incorrigible) access to such states? And on the self-intimating character of such states? How do these positions interrelate? Are Descartes' positions defensible?

7   What do you think Descartes is saying in the wax passage of the Second Meditation? Assess what you take to be his view (or some important component of his view) there.

8   Critically discuss Descartes' theory of ideas – in general, or focusing on innate, adventitious, or fictitious ideas. What is the relation between ideas and what they are ideas of? What is the relation between ideas and thoughts?

9   Explain what you understand by clarity and distinctness in Descartes and then, in light of this, evaluate Descartes' claim that his idea of God is the most clear and distinct of all he has in his mind.

10 Is there philosophical value (coherence, etc.) in a degrees-of-reality (degrees-of-perfection) doctrine such as Descartes'?

11 Evaluate Descartes' defense in the Third Meditation of the claim that his idea of infinite substance is neither "negative" nor "materially false."

12 Evaluate what you take to be Descartes' best argument for God's existence. Or analyze a key premise in one of those arguments in detail.

13 a) What is the nature and role of the divine guarantee of knowledge for Descartes? What sorts of belief require the guarantee? Why? If some beliefs are exempt from the requirement, why? How is this issue the issue of Descartes' overall line of argument?

      b) Do you think that Descartes assumes what he sets out to prove? How so, or not, and what is at stake? What is the relation between self-knowledge, knowledge of God, and knowledge of matter in the *Meditations?*

14 If belief, disbelief and withholding are acts of will, not acts of understanding, for Descartes (the Fourth Meditation), why did he give skeptical arguments in the First Meditation for withholding judgments? Why didn't he just resolve to withhold and proceed from there?

15 a) How in the end does Descartes explain the fact that God makes us capable of error? Is the explanation coherent? If so, is it adequate?

    b) What is the relation between Descartes' account of error, his view of human freedom and divine omnipotence, and his method of clear and distinct perception? Explain each related component.

16 a) What is the character and role of Descartes' doctrine of things with "true and immutable natures" (Fifth Meditation)?

    b) Why does Descartes give the ontological argument for God's existence when he allegedly has proven God's existence already in the Third Meditation?

17 What is it to be a substance for Descartes? How does substance relate to essence? Are there different conceptions of substance operative in the *Meditations*? How do they emerge and interrelate?

18 What is the nature and importance of the distinctions between understanding (intellect) and imagination for Descartes? How does it relate to knowledge of physical objects? How does it tie in with his conception of mathematics? How does sense perception relate to the others?

19 What is the nature of Cartesian mind–body dualism? How is it established? How does Descartes' discussion of the self in the Second Meditation relate to things he says in the Sixth Meditation?

20 Exactly how are metaphysical foundations (first philosophy) supposed to help secure practically desirable fruits on the tree of inquiry?

21 Is there any important internal inconsistency in Descartes' philosophical system?

22 What exactly is "first philosophy"? If it is exhausted by what Descartes would think of as metaphysics, how does Descartes conceive metaphysics? After all, there are historically distinguishable (albeit sometimes interrelated) conceptions of metaphysics: ontology; the science that precedes all other sciences, since all other sciences receive their principles from it (in what sense of "precedence," "receive," and "principles"?); etc. Is it (in "our" sense) some combination of metaphysics and epistemology, and if so, how are the two related? Is it epistemology alone, hence the familiar claim that Descartes inaugurated the primacy of epistemology over metaphysics, which prevailed until displaced by the primacy of philosophy of language (and/or logic), perhaps now displaced in some circles with the primacy of philosophy of mind? The more general, historical question: What are Descartes' innovations? Why is he the father of modern philosophy? What are his relations to Augustine, to Aristotle (especially Aristotle's logic), to other pre-modern philosophers?

23 What is immediate intuition? What is its scope? What is knowledge based on inference? How does it relate to intuition? What is *persuasio*? What is its scope? How does it relate to *vera et certa scientia*?

24 What is the nature and scope of "materially false" ideas? Do they fail to "represent" altogether, represent a "non-thing" as a thing, or misrepresent reality in broader ways? Are materially false and clear and distinct ideas contradictories or only contraries? If only contraries, what is the *tertium quid*?

25   What precisely is it for the will to "go beyond the limits" or "restrict itself to the limits" of the understanding? By what right does Descartes invoke will at all in the analysis of judgment?

26   In private correspondence Descartes stresses that God created the eternal truths, not just what we think of as contingent things such as ourselves. Does this doctrine appear, or operate subterraneously, in any of Descartes' published writings? If so, where and how? If not, why not? Relatedly, is it in virtue of his omnipotence that God can deceive even in truly recalled clear and distinct matters, prevented only by his logically independent goodness?

27   What is consciousness? thought? attention? What are their interconnections?

28   Is Descartes a representationalist? Does he really embrace the fourth in my list of his key commitments (see p. 66)? What's at stake in deciding?

29   Explore any of the central, perennial objections to Descartes: that systematic doubt (were it possible) is intellectual suicide; that only thinking, not thinking substance, can be proved; that thinking in time could not occur without objects ordered in space and time; that ampliative inferences are impossible; that reason's self-validation must be viciously circular; that metaphysical dualisms (pluralisms) are impossible; that the transcendence of the ego degrades nature; etc.

1.13   Transition to the remainder of the book

In Descartes' day there were two main efforts to break with tradition and to establish a new route to productive knowledge. One alternative was Descartes' rationalism, which emphasizes the function of the human intellect alone; the other alternative was empiricism, which expects all knowledge to be derived from sense experience. Empiricism could be found in the tradition that Descartes wanted to discredit, but it also was defended by some of Descartes' contemporaries who rejected tradition as well. For example, two of Descartes' critics, Thomas Hobbes and Pierre Gassendi, were continually at odds with Descartes both because they thought that all knowledge must be based on sense experience, and because of their belief that everything in the world can be reduced to a physical reality.

A central plank of Descartes' platform was that an exclusively physical picture of reality, such as that held by Hobbes and Gassendi, is caused by a misguided, exclusively empirical method of inquiry. Yet many, especially in Britain, were unpersuaded by Descartes' critique of empiricism. They found inspiration instead in an older contemporary of Descartes, Francis Bacon. Bacon began a competing tradition that, following Hobbes and Gassendi, is taken up by Locke, Berkeley, and Hume. We will examine the interestingly different counter-cases of Locke, Berkeley, and Hume in Chapters Three, Five, and Six, respectively. We will examine rationalists like Descartes who nevertheless argue that rationalism leads to very different views of the world and our place in it in the persons of Spinoza and Leibniz in Chapters Two and Four, respectively. And we will conclude our journey in Chapter Seven with the revolutionary philosophy of Kant, who both positions himself with respect to all these predecessors, and is the watershed for most of subsequent philosophy up to the present.

1.14   Some Recommended Books

Curley, E.M. (1978) *Descartes Against the Skeptics*, Cambridge: Harvard University Press.

Recognizing both that Descartes actively contributed to the scientific revolution yet was seriously disturbed by skeptical authors, Curley discusses the main topics of the *Meditations* through building an account of Descartes' strategy for turning skeptics against themselves, arguing that it requires a break with his earlier methodology in *Rules for the Direction of the Mind*. If you are interested in readings of Descartes on which his positive insights fully emerge from his own skeptical method, Broughton, J. (2002) *Descartes's Method of Doubt*, Princeton: Princeton University Press, is especially useful.

Frankfurt, H. (1970) *Demons, Dreamers, and Madmen: The Defense of Reason in Descartes's Meditations*.

A lucid, engaging interpretation of Descartes' procedure for justifying human reason.

Gaukroger, S. (1995) *Descartes: An Intellectual Biography*, Oxford: Clarendon Press.

An historically sensitive account of Descartes' intellectual development, especially notable for its argument that Descartes developed his foundational philosophical project to immunize his already established scientific views from religious condemnation, not to abstractly meet the challenge of skepticism.

Gueroult, M. (1984–5) *Descartes' Philosophy Interpreted According to the Order of Reasons*, 2 vols, trans. R. Ariew, Minneapolis: University of Minnesota Press.

An outstanding, transformative treatment of Descartes (published first in 1952) governed by taking consistently seriously Descartes' conception of how successful philosophical meditation must proceed. Volume I covers First through Fifth Meditations; Volume II covers the Sixth Meditation.

Hatfield, G. (2003) *Descartes and the Meditations*, London: Routledge.

An excellent guide through the *Meditations*, highlighting its role in grounding a new science of nature through cognitive training which enables the mind to discern how things really are.

Kenny, A. (1968) *Descartes: A Study of His Philosophy*, New York: Random House.

A stimulating discussion of the epistemology, metaphysics, and philosophy of mind in the *Meditations*.

Miles, M. (1999) *Insight and Inference: Descartes' Founding Principle and Modern Philosophy*, Toronto and Buffalo: University of Toronto Press.

A deeply informed, largely supportive study of *cogito, ergo sum* with especial focus on the meaning of *cogitare*, the certainty of *sum*, and the nature of the inference designated by *ergo*, which naturally extends to analysis of many other topics of the *Meditations*, and which stresses the dominance of metaphysical concerns. The reinterpretation of Descartes' theories of intuition and deduction exposes the weakness of much criticism based on misunderstanding, clarifying what sort of rationalist Descartes is, why thought is not the same as consciousness, etc.

Moyal, G.J.D. (ed.) (1991) *René Descartes: Critical Assessments*, 4 vols, London and New York: Routledge.

A rich collection of fine essays on the different aspects of Descartes' philosophy.

Rorty, A.O. (ed.) (1986) *Essays on Descartes' Meditations*, Berkeley, Los Angeles and London: University of California Press.

An especially worthwhile, single-volume collection of essays, some of them provocatively controversial.

Williams, B. (1978) *Descartes: The Project of Pure Inquiry*, Middlesex and New York: Penguin Books; published simultaneously at Atlantic Highlands, NJ: Humanities Press.

A rational reconstruction of Descartes' thought, couched in contemporary terms but driven by Descartes' most interesting concerns, launched by the classic articulation of why maximally stringent, universal doubt is necessary to know the truth.

Wilson, M. (1978) *Descartes*, London, Henley and Boston: Routledge & Kegan Paul.

An often novel, always defended, interpretation of Descartes' philosophy, developed through analysis of the key issues in each meditation.

For a lucid and engaging history of western thought to help contextualize our modern period, I especially recommend Tarnas, R. (1991) *The Passion of the Western Mind: Understanding the Ideas that Have Shaped Our World View*, New York: Ballantine Books.

2 Spinoza

2.1 Overview of Spinoza's philosophy and life

Baruch Spinoza's (1632–1677) masterwork is *Ethics Demonstrated in Geometrical Order*. His title alerts us to the guiding ideas of our discussion. Spinoza aims to discover and lead the good human life, indeed the way to blessedness. Success requires, or is at least best achieved by, use of the deductive, axiomatic method of mathematics. How to live must be impartially deduced or explained as a necessary consequence of one's status as a finite aspect of Nature, conceived as a completely intelligible, unique, infinite and self-contained causal system. We must understand our position in Nature and the true causes of our imperfections to free ourselves from them. This understanding will be a movement from inadequate to adequate ideas, from an illogical, psychological association of ideas by the imagination to logical, coherent thought by the understanding. It is not incidental that Spinoza begins the *Ethics* with a purportedly undeniable metaphysics, from which he aims strictly to derive a correct model of human nature, including a theory of knowledge (which explains how to move from inadequate imaginative cognition, to rational scientific knowledge, to rational intuitive knowledge) and a theory of the emotions, which he thinks leads inexorably to an ethics or way of life (optimally, blessedness, an abiding, self-sufficient well-being). Contrast this with Descartes, for whom it was vital to begin with epistemology, thence to derive a metaphysics. This deep difference will explain a lot. And you will appreciate Spinoza's stunning system best if you keep firmly in mind the ethical aspirations that drive his efforts.

I will outline the argument of Part I of the *Ethics*. Its main conclusions are that nothing exists except the one *substance* – the self-contained, self-sustaining, and self-explanatory system which constitutes the world; that this system properly may be understood in different ways, as God or Nature, as mind or matter, as creator or created; that this system can be known clearly and adequately through what Spinoza calls its *attributes*, but only confusedly and partially through what he calls its *finite modes*; and that to understand it in its totality, under the aspect of eternity, is to recognize that everything exists by necessity, so that nothing could be other than it is.

Our central task is to understand how Spinoza argues that more consistent implementation of Descartes' own rationalist commitments leads to these conclusions, undermines Descartes' God–Nature (and, as we will trace in Part II, mind–body) dualism, by entailing a *monism* and thoroughgoing *naturalism* on which God = Nature = substance = cause of itself (self-explanatory being) = infinite being = necessarily existing being, and to explain how this monism entails *necessitarianism* (nothing is contingent, or could logically be other than it is), so that there is no *free will* (and so, by the way, no possibility of Cartesian doubt, which presupposes free will), yet there are *degrees* of *freedom* (i.e. activity), properly understood, which we can learn through proper method to maximize.

Ultimately, going beyond Part I, we need to appreciate Spinoza's overall account of how we humans can know, act on, and find happiness in the world. We need to understand why for Spinoza another rich set of equivalences is true, including virtue = happiness (so virtue is its own reward) = knowledge (living under the guidance of reason) = self-determination = freedom (power over, not slavishness to, our negative emotions (i.e. passions))(where = stands for strong, logical (necessary) equivalence). To appreciate how his system begins to evolve, note that Part I can be structured as follows: propositions 1–15 establish the essence of God and his necessary existence; 16–30 establish the nature of divine power or causality (= the infinite power of Nature) and so God's relation to the world, and so the basic structure of reality; and 31–36 use the preceding work to critique features of the Judeo-Christian religious tradition. The Appendix reframes some of the key results more intuitively.

Before outlining Part I's critique of religious tradition, it is useful to get a sense of how his philosophy intertwined with his life.[1] Spinoza was exiled from a group of exiles. He was born to a wealthy Portuguese Jewish family in 1632, the year Galileo published *Two Systems*, which, the next year, prompted Galileo's house arrest by the Inquisition; the year John Locke was born; four years after Descartes moved to the Netherlands from France. To escape religious persecution, his family had immigrated to Amsterdam, where tolerance was unusually high. There Jews were free to practice their religion and contribute to commerce, so long as they didn't try to convert or marry Protestants, though even there Spinoza lived among many *marranos*, transplants from Spain and Portugal who publicly lived a Christian life but privately preserved Jewish tradition. His mother died when he was six; his father questioned rituals and doctrines, but was not outspoken enough to antagonize either Dutch Calvinist or Jewish Synagogue authorities. While his father lived, Spinoza muted his own challenges to what he judged harmful superstitions and professed mysteries. But when his father died, Spinoza expressed himself publicly and regularly, heretically denying personal immortality, affirming that God is a physical as well as a spiritual thing, etc. His God was not God the legislator and judge, planner and protector. He was warned, but did not relent, and at 24 was excommunicated

---

1   I have read many good accounts of Spinoza's life, but the only one on which I rely specifically for some details here is Damasio 2003, especially chapter 6.

by the Synagogue. His banishment was unusually severe. His condemnation, or *cherem*, contains uncharacteristically harsh language, and altogether severed him from the community – precluded contact with any Jews, including family and friends – not just from the religion. At that moment he changed his first name from the Hebrew "Baruch," meaning "Blessed," to its Latin counterpart "Benedictus," meaning "Spoken well of" or "Praised." In 1660 he left Amsterdam. Thereafter he lived a frugal, virtually property-less, solitary life in various Dutch cities, soon acquiring a reputation as an astute interpreter of Descartes' metaphysics and natural philosophy – publishing a commentary on Descartes' *Principles of Philosophy* in 1663 – eventually at 38 settling in The Hague, where that year he anonymously published the *Theological-Political Treatise* and eventually completed the *Ethics*, which he held back from publication.

The adult Spinoza always led a materially minimalist existence. He refused a healthy family inheritance, later refused a stipend from his close friend Simon de Vries, and refused an academic appointment at Heidelberg (offered at Leibniz's recommendation). As indicated by his introductory remarks in the fragment, *Treatise on the Emendation of the Intellect* (TIE), he didn't find money or social status rewarding. And he consistently refused any arrangement that might threaten his intellectual freedom. So he earned his living grinding lenses, never occupied more than a bedroom and a study, and kept only one piece of inherited property, the canopied, four-poster bed with closable curtains used by his parents. Long, thin and frail, with wors-ening respiratory problems at least exacerbated by glass dust inhalation, he died at 44.

Spinoza's *Opera Posthuma* was published by his friends by the end of that year, with the *Ethics* its centerpiece. Dutch and French translations began to appear the next year, despite a ban issued by the Jews, the Calvinists, and the Vatican. His writings managed modestly wider distribution, but suppres-sion largely succeeded for nearly one hundred years following his death. And the rule was: you could only comment on his ideas negatively, or put your-self at risk. Still, his ideas gradually seeped into philosophical consciousness, especially through Bayle's *Dictionary*, whose entry on Spinoza – ostensibly dismissing his ideas – was the longest in the book, and later through Diderot and d'Alembert's *Encyclopedia*, which devotes five times more space to Spinoza than the touted Locke. Whatever their public posture, several thinkers were privately influenced by him.

After the Enlightenment, with secularism flowering, Spinoza's influence became more openly acknowledged, not only by philosophers, but by literary giants including Goethe, Coleridge, Wordsworth, Shelley, Tennyson, and Eliot, and founders of psychology such as Wundt and von Helmholtz. Eliot applauded him as a hero of scientific rationalism and materialism and vanquisher of superstition. Coleridge and Shelley admired his ability to convey an almost mystical sense of the ideal unity of Nature. The great nine-teenth-century philosopher, Hegel, said: "To be a philosopher you must first be a Spinozist." The greatest twentieth-century scientist, Einstein, made plain how deeply his views of the universe and of God were influenced by Spinoza. And still other watershed thinkers, such as Freud, were undeniably influenced, though not apt to say so.[2]

What extraordinary system of ideas could so unmitigatingly alienate some yet so profoundly guide others? How can the same thinker appear to some as a man obsessed with God (a "God-intoxicated" man), who interprets every natural phenomenon as a revelation from an immanent but impersonal God, but appear to others as a cold materialist and determinist who drains morality and religion of all significance? Let's examine Spinoza's fullest articulation of his worldview to see for ourselves. Let's try to understand his goal of discovering "a true good, one which was capable of communicating itself and could alone affect the mind to the exclusion of all else . . . something whose discovery and acquisition would afford me a continuous and supreme joy to all eternity" (TIE 1). Let's try to appreciate how he lived and died in accordance with his own description of the free person, who lives guided by reason, as one who "thinks of nothing less than of death, and whose wisdom is a meditation on life, not on death" (*Ethics* Part IV P67). And let's try to see how Spinoza's philosophy can in large measure be seen to arise from internal critique of Descartes' philosophy, from embracing a thoroughgoing rationalism but arguing that it leads systematically to strikingly anti-Cartesian conclusions.

2.2　*Ethics* Part I: On the nature of the universe

It is the metaphysics behind the rest of Spinoza's philosophy that elicited the greatest outrage from Spinoza's critics. I begin by rather starkly outlining Part I of the *Ethics*, which contains that metaphysics, so you can see its proof. Then I will retrieve its overarching message and sketch the account of human nature and human well-being that follows from it. The general idea is that how we should live depends on who we are, who we are depends on our place in the universe, and our place in the universe depends on the nature of the universe. Spinoza provides a comprehensive conception of the

---

2　And still others could not suppress their inspiration. Instance Nietzsche's 30 July 1881 letter to Franz Overbeck:

> I am utterly amazed, utterly enchanted. I have a *predecessor*, and what a predecessor! I hardly knew Spinoza: that I should have turned to him just *now* was inspired by "instinct." Not only is his overall tendency like mine – making knowledge the *most powerful* affect – but in five main points of his doctrine I recognize myself; this most unusual and loneliest thinker is closest to me precisely in these matters: he denies the freedom of the will, teleology, the moral world order, the unegoistic, and evil. Even though the divergences are admittedly tremendous, they are due more to the differences in time, culture, and science. *In summa*: my solitude [*Einsamkeit*], which, as on very high mountains, often made it hard for me to breathe and made my blood rush out, is at least a duolitude [*Zweisamkeit*].

universe that, he claims, must be accurate, since any alternative is demonstrably contradictory. Against Descartes, he argues that the conception of the world as a plurality of substances, each persisting through time in possession of certain essential attributes, and causally created by a transcendent God, is self-contradictory. There is just one substance (monism), cause or rational explanation of itself, conceived through itself (i.e. infinite), necessarily existing, which is God, which is Nature. In the outline, P stands for proposition, C for corollary, S for scholium, D for definition, A for axiom, and N for note. I will set the pattern for your own fruitful efforts by identifying the source of each inference through the early, crucial stages of Spinoza's argument. Then I present the core arguments of subsequent stages without identifying the source(s) of every step, to avoid distracting detail. But before we even consider a full outline, let's isolate the core argument for monism, which seems to go as follows:

1   Substance is independent. (consensus conception of substance)
2   Whatever has an external cause can't be independent.
3   Substance doesn't have an external cause. (1, 2)
4   Everything must have a cause. (principle of sufficient reason)
5   Substance is its own cause. (3, 4)
6   No finite thing is its own cause.
7   Substance is infinite. (5, 6)
8   Substance has all (infinite) attributes. (P11, equivalent to 7)
9   There can't be two substances with the same attribute. (P5)
10 At most one substance exists. (8, 9)
11 There can't be two substances of the same kind. (P5 re-expressed)
12 Substances of different kinds can't cause each other. (P6)
13 Substance can't be caused by anything except itself. (5, 12)

5 entails 14, Substance must exist. This means that at least one substance exists, which is P7, since what causes itself necessarily exists; its essence necessarily involves existence. And 14 together with 10 entail that exactly one substance exists. God is identical to Nature. Only Nature as a whole satisfies the conditions established above – is its own cause, exists in itself, doesn't causally depend on anything else, so that knowledge of it doesn't depend on knowledge of anything else, so that it is conceived through itself. Spinoza will argue that this result has supreme ethical significance. As we proceed, we must explore more fully the way in which for Spinoza rationalism leads to monism, which in turn leads to naturalism and necessitarianism, the recognition of which leads to abiding joy.

Here's a fuller outline of Part I. The central flow is from the impossibility of *interacting* substances, to the impossibility of *more than one* substance, interacting or not, to the need to identify substance with God conceived as identical with Nature, to the need to recognize that everything is as it is necessarily.

God is identical to the world, and cannot be an immaterial, transcendent cause of it. If there were an immaterial God distinct from the material world, then God would have nothing in common with the world, since then God and the world would have different essences, and, by P2, if attributes (representing essences) are different, the things having those attributes have nothing in common – that is, the conception of one does not imply the conception of the other. (It is important here critically to compare "*need* have nothing in common" and "*can* have nothing in common.") But if God had nothing in common with the world, then there could be no causal relation between God and the world, since by P3, if things have nothing in common, they cannot be the cause of one another. (This is a common criticism of metaphysical dualisms. The point is that you can't have your cake and eat it too; you can't say that two things are essentially, non-overlappingly different, utterly disjoint, yet in the same breath affirm that one can affect the other.) So transcendence of an immaterial God rules out God's causal efficacy – God cannot be reintroduced into the world. But not only can we say, if God affects the world, then the above version of metaphysical dualism is false, but we positively can affirm that God is identical with the world. To suppose that they are not identical requires supposing that they have different attributes or modifications – difference of substance implies difference of attributes or modifications, as stated in P4. In other words, P5, there cannot be two or more substances of the same nature or attribute. On the other hand, the converse is false: having distinct attributes doesn't imply being distinct substances, as he makes plain in P10S; each attribute is independently conceivable from others, yet many, indeed infinitely many may (and do) characterize the same substance. And again, difference cannot be introduced by appeal to causal relations, since one substance cannot be produced by another (P6, which is equivalent to P3). And since all that exists in the universe are substances and their modifications, substance cannot be produced by anything external to itself – another substance can't do it, surely modifications can't either, and there is nothing else; substance cannot be the effect of transeunt or external causation (6C). Since substance can't have an external cause, it must be its own cause (logical explanation), that is, cause of itself, which, by D1, means that its essence or nature implies that it exists (P7). Since substance essentially exists, it must be infinite, for if it were finite, it would be limited by something else of the same kind (D2), nature, or attribute, which we showed above (P5) to be impossible (P8). Again, if substance were finite, it could be acted upon. But if it were susceptible to effect by external cause, then it would not be understandable solely through itself. So substance, by definition cause of itself, must be infinite.

But this infinite substance, whose essence involves existence, must be numerically unique, since plurality doesn't follow from its nature, and for each individual existent there is a reason (cause) why it should exist; so since there is no reason for plurality, there is none (8N2). (Compare P11: if there is no reason to prevent X's existence, then X necessarily exists.). Further, this unique infinite substance must have infinitely many attributes, since the more reality (essence), the more attributes (P9). Hence, infinite reality requires infinite attributes. But infinity of attributes does not destroy the numerical unity of substance. And in particular, the divisibility of substance is impossible (P12, P13). The argument in P12 seems bad, wrongly assuming that the parts of a whole must have the same nature as the whole; but P13 is more convincing, claiming that the parts of divided substance would either have the same nature as the infinite whole of which they are parts, or not. If so, we'd have a multiplicity of substances of the same nature, shown to be impossible in P5. If not, then substance could perish, since its parts could perish, but this contradicts the truth that substance *necessarily* exists. Finally, again, there is just one substance (God). For God has infinitely many attributes. And so if we supposed the existence of another substance, it would have to be explained by some attribute of God, since God has them all. But then two substances would share an attribute, which once again, by P5, is impossible. No substance distinct from God is conceivable.[3]

And so everything conceivable depends on God and everything that exists depends on God – God is conceptually and ontologically basic.[4] After all, only substances and modes exist. We've shown that there is but one substance, God Himself. And modes are not independently conceivable or existing. And what is not independently conceivable is conceivable through something else, if it's conceivable at all. Since modes are conceivable, they must be conceived in terms of God. And since modes exist, they exist in God. One mode (infinite immediate, meaning that it follows directly

---

3   Notice how frequently proposition 5 is invoked; you should take special pains to evaluate its proof.

4   It will help you characterize and compare philosophers' concerns and positions to define a basic kind of entity as a kind of entity that is more basic than, or prior to, or independent of – or better, allowing for pluralisms, no less basic than, or not posterior to – any other kind of entity, and then interpret the philosophers' claims to basicness in terms of distinct, applicable senses of *priority*. For example, Xs are *conceptually* prior to Ys if and only if one could not understand what it is to be a Y without understanding what it is to be an X, but not conversely; Xs are *ontologically* prior to Ys if and only if Ys could not exist unless Xs did, but not conversely (where X and Y are categorial terms and "could" is construed metaphysically); Xs are *epistemically* prior to Ys if and only if one could not know anything about Ys unless one knew some things about Xs, but not conversely; Xs are *experientially* prior to Ys if and only if Ys are experienceable only if Xs are, but not conversely; Xs are *explanatorily* prior to Ys if and only if you cannot explain Ys without appeal to Xs, but not conversely; and so on for *logical* priority, *temporal* priority, *doxastic* priority (dependency among beliefs), *identificational* priority (dependency in picking out and referring to things), etc. Important differences between every philosopher discussed in this book can be highlighted using such taxonomy. To take a current application, I am saying that for Spinoza logical, ontological, conceptual, epistemic (in the strong sense of knowledge), and explanatory priority (and so basicness) coincide, whereas crucially for Descartes the logical and ontological orders differ from the epistemic order (the order of being as presented by synthetic method differs from the order of discovery generated by the analytic method), helping to explain why Spinoza comfortably begins with metaphysics, Descartes, relentlessly with epistemology. For a discussion of some important ways the taxonomy has been used, see Tlumak 1983.

from an attribute of substance) is extension, or more strictly, the totality of motion and rest. Attributively construed, the attribute of extension applies to God. A particular finite thing is a mode; it can have a certain integrity and degree of independence, but it cannot possibly be a substance.

God is a necessary cause acting without will and design; God is conscious of himself, but his consciousness of himself does not imply design and purpose. All logically possible things are necessarily actualized. (This is known as the principle of *plenitude*.) After all, everything possible falls under an infinite intellect. But it would be irrational if existence arbitrarily accrued to some finite essences but not to others. Whatever is in God's power necessarily exists, and since his power is (within the constraints of consistency) unlimited, every characteristic of the world is utterly inevitable. Since nothing could conceivably have been otherwise, nothing can be said to manifest purpose or preference. There is no genuine contingency; everything is part of a single, intelligible, causal system. To explain why things possess the properties they do, we must deduce such from the total scheme of Nature, which is really inseparable, but logically distinct, from them. There is a conceptual distinction only between God (*Natura naturans* = God conceived through himself = active or generative Nature = substance with infinite attributes) and the law-governed, aggregate totality of modes, the sum of the parts of the universe conceived through the attributes (*Natura naturata* = passive or generated Nature = divine causality as it is expressed in the system of modes). This relation between *Natura Naturans* and *Natura Naturata* is precisely Spinoza's non-Judeo-Christian way of explaining the relation between God and creation.

Spinoza takes up the problem of free will at later stages of the *Ethics* as well, but immediately we should acknowledge that he is not blind to the phenomenon that his necessitarianism proves illusory. We do imagine ourselves to act in ways that are not wholly determined by prior events and natural laws. But, he explains, the subjective experience of free will stems from ignorance of the objective causes of our action – ignorance of cause is taken to be absence of cause. Consider a rock that has been thrown across a room. We can agree that its subsequent trajectory is not free. But now imagine that in mid-flight the rock acquires self-consciousness of the sort we enjoy. We can thence imagine the rock exhilaratedly experiencing itself *as if* it were moving freely, forming the preference to land in the corner of the room to which it is heading, and so feeling sure it is free. But as objective observers of the situation we know that the rock's subjective experience is delusory. Well, Spinoza argues, objective knowledge shows us that we are all like that rock. Belief in free will, and in contingency in general, is just ignorance of the necessary.

Already Spinoza has rejected Descartes' substance dualism and commitment to free will. As I distill key considerations throughout the *Ethics*, recall that one pedagogically useful way to organize these considerations is as the consequences of steadfast rationalism, the unwavering application of the principle of sufficient reason, which states that there must be an explanation of the existence of any being, and of any positive fact whatever. Spinoza thought Descartes, the intended father of modern rationalism, was in fact a lapsed rationalist, who began rightly with his strictly deterministic, mathematical conception of the physical, but who retreated to the mysterious when it came to the mental and to God. Spinoza is telling us, here is what mind and God must be if studied in the same rigorous way as geometers study matter. For example, as he strikingly says in his Preface to the Third Part of the *Ethics*, where *affects* are actions and passions:

> I shall treat the nature and power of the affects, and the power of the mind over them, by the same method by which, in the preceding parts, I treated God and the mind, and I shall consider human actions and appetites just as if it were a question of lines, planes, and bodies.

Also, as my distillation unfolds, there are three especially influential controversies to weigh. First, what's the status of definitions and axioms in relation to subsequent propositions? If they are shielded from criticism as either immediately self-evident or stipulative, and claimed to provide asymmetrical support for later propositions, then has Spinoza unjustifiably chosen self-serving starting points? (Remember the problem of the criterion.) For example, I A4 says that the knowledge of an effect depends on, and involves, the knowledge of its cause. So if I am an effect of God's creation, then my self-knowledge would depend on knowledge of God. But this *seems* to beg the question against Descartes, who distinguishes the order of knowing, in which I come first, and the order of being, in which God comes first. (I'm not concluding that it *does* beg the question. It depends on how knowledge is being conceived. If a momentarily recognized certainty is knowledge, Spinoza is definitely at odds with Descartes; if knowledge of X entails complete understanding of X's nature, then the meditator would admittedly lack self-knowledge at the *Cogito* in the Second Meditation.) And I A4 is the sole official basis of II P7, that the order and connection of ideas is the same as the order and connection of things, a proposition monumentally important to the development of his argument and seemingly flagrantly anti-Cartesian. The general question is, do axioms and definitions provide linear support for propositions as theorems, or are all the statements of the system mutually supporting, even so that a proper understanding of the first definitions and axioms depend on seeing their implications? Is Spinoza a foundationalist, like Descartes, or an innovative holist and coherentist? For example, in Part I, are substance, cause, attribute, freedom, and necessity logically interconnected notions used to define God or Nature?

The second controversy concerns the relationship between imagination (and emotion) and reason, and the purity of Spinoza's rationalism. No doubt his philosophizing purports to replace inadequate ideas of the imagination, which include local, temporal perspectives (*sub specie duratationis*) based on sense perception, ordinary language, and passion, with adequate ideas of the intellect or reason. The question is whether we can overcome the phenomena of the imagination altogether and achieve God's point of view, the view from eternity (*sub specie aeternitatis*), or whether there is in principle no human prospect of eliminating imagination, but only the goal of rationally understanding, so positively transforming it. I take it the question is not whether a human qua human, a finite mode, can be purely rational. That issue seems definitively decided in the negative. For example, early in Part IV Spinoza explicitly insists that we are inescapably parts of Nature, and so are necessarily always subject to passions (P4 and corollary). The question is whether we can overcome the human (and any finite) perspective and become immortal, or more, by achieving the divine perspective, become God (so no longer be human), who, remember, is not, for Spinoza, a separate, transcendent person. Still, I'm committed to reading him as rejecting these possibilities as well. This debate comes to a head in how people read the culminating Part V of the *Ethics*.

The third, long-debated question is how to interpret *attribute*, "what the intellect perceives of a substance, as constituting its essence" (D4). Remember from the outline above that Spinoza's metaphysics includes three ontological categories: substance, attribute, and mode. I will rehearse again all the key relations between these three elements in his inventory as I would formulate them before explaining our third controversy: since things are conceived through their causes, and substance is conceived through itself, substance is the sole cause of its own existence, and since a thing is properly conceived if conceived by its essence, substance's essence entails its existence, which means that it exists necessarily. Also, the more perfect or real a thing is, the more attributes it will have. So the most perfect being, God, must have infinitely many attributes, each of which is infinite within its own realm. Each divine attribute is a basic way of being for God, each constituting the essence of God insofar as God is considered as existing in that particular way. And every mode of a substance is a particular modification of an attribute of that substance, entirely caused by the substance. God expresses himself in limitless ways through these infinitely many modes. So all causation is the self-determination and self-expression of a substance.

Some modes are themselves infinite, meaning that they are permanent and ubiquitous features of an attribute, following from the attribute without need to appeal to the existence of any other modes. For example, conservation of energy (motion and rest) so characterizes the attribute of extension. Other modes are finite; they can be deduced from the attribute of which they are modes only in conjunction with appeal to other finite modes. Each such determinate mode is caused by another, and so on ad infinitum, but ultimately they are still caused by the substance, since the whole infinite series depends on substance. (This thought is the kernel of some so-called cosmological arguments for the existence of God, which is discussed by some of our later philosophers, most critically by Hume; see section 6.12.) Causation through its modes is one way in which a substance can express or exert its power, and since substance is infinite, every way it can manifest itself, it does manifest itself. Modal determinacy entails modal difference, and a fundamental way of differentiating things is by temporal-indexing. On this account, what Descartes counted as finite substances are not substances at all, but the local and temporary expressions of the divine Nature, limited expressions of God's attributes.

So what is an attribute? The wording of its definition may suggest that it is a *subjective* means of access to the nature of substance, and not true of substance itself, and talk of substance as simple, so not having *really* distinct attributes, may further encourage a subjectivist reading. The alternative is to construe attributes *objectively*. Spinoza says several things to encourage such a reading, including most obviously that God is a substance consisting of an infinity of attributes (D6), and occasionally even more baldly – what seems in tension with (D6) – that an attribute is not really, but only logically, distinct from substance. But what would such objective attributes be? We should not in principle expect an Aristotelian-style definition in terms of genus and differentia, since attributes are known only through themselves. The simplest answer would be that they are essential properties as in Descartes. Well, it seems that they can't be *precisely* what Descartes meant, since for him each kind of substance – whether it be body, finite mind, or God – must and can have *exactly one* principal attribute (extension, thought, and supreme perfection, respectively), but for Spinoza, substance must and can have infinitely many attributes. And more generally, if an attribute is *identifiable* with an essence, why does Spinoza constantly say that each attribute *expresses* the (or an) essence of God?

We may be boxing ourselves in by uncritically thinking of substance as a singular *thing* which has various properties, whereas much that Spinoza says powerfully suggests that we'd do better to think of it as a (necessary and universal) *order* or *realm* of things, such that the things depend for their existence and intelligibility on the whole scheme, without in any normal sense being properties of the scheme. Then attributes could be different forms in which this order is *expressed*, different ways of enabling the specifics of the universe, the modes, to present themselves to us, or, to use his own apt metaphor, different *faces of existence*. But wondering just how subjective or objective the expression relation is reintroduces some of the interpretive uncertainty with which we began. For example, should we take as a model of expression the different angles from which I can see my computer, which seems to introduce some element of subjective perspective, or the relation in Cartesian analytic geometry (which Spinoza knew well) between a geometric figure and its logically equivalent algebraic equation, which seems to be a wholly objective, timeless relation? (Notice that even logical equivalence of the attributes happily does not entail their identity, just as the logical equivalence of two linguistic expressions does not entail their synonymy.)

For the most part I think we can proceed without detailed resolution, so long as we agree on two things about which the text at least seems to me unambiguous. First, notice that Spinoza always says that the *intellect* attributes a certain nature to substance. But what the untainted intellect perceives to be the essence of something *is* its essence. That helps bridge the apparent gap between subjective and objective readings. Second, he never waffles in insisting that, for example, Nature (or God, or substance) *is* extension for the physicist, or that one explains human physical behavior by biology, not psychology. The explanations of things conceived under any attribute are incommensurable with any explanation of those same things under any other attribute. What this amounts to practically is that physicalistic and mentalistic explanations can never be combined within a single, coherent account. And this purports to have devastating, anti-dualistic implications, as when Spinoza argues that you can't coherently explain the creation of the extended world by invoking God's free will.

A brief recap as we transition to Part II. Part I taught us that there can be only one substance, which is cause of itself, and which must be identified with the universe conceived as a whole. Spinoza calls this unique, all-inclusive, intelligible totality *God or Nature*. Unless "substance" and "cause" are conceived this way, contradiction occurs. Substance originates change in accordance with the laws of its own nature. To explain the changes of state (modifications) substance undergoes is to exhibit them as the logical consequence of its essential nature. There could not fully be such explanation if there were more than one interacting substances. Then substance would have accidental or contingent features, which would violate the principle of sufficient reason, the cornerstone of rationalism.

2.3 *Ethics* Part II: On the nature and origin of the mind

The Preface to Part II signals the aim of the rest of the book: to elicit those implications of God's essence that allow us to know the human mind so we can know its highest good and the means to achieve it. So it is the application of general (monistic, naturalistic, necessitarian) metaphysics to the specific category of mind. The first fifteen propositions of Part II explicate the nature of mind and its relation to body. On this basis, 16–47 establish the nature of intellect and the extent of human knowledge, and 48–49 clarify the nature of will, its relation to intellect, and its (wrongly) alleged undetermined freedom.

A mind is a particular modification of God or Nature, a finite mode fully integrated into nature, subject to universal, scientific laws; a mind's powers are just its own, limited portion of the infinite power of Nature; it is or has no faculty or power beyond its activities, and its unity and individuality are just the unity and individuality of these activities, so that the understanding is identical with its ideas, and the will is identical with its volitions; therefore, since ideas are identical with volitions, will is identical with understanding (intellect), in humans as well as in God.

The mind is the complex idea of the body. To each component of the mind there corresponds a bodily process. But correspondence does not imply non-identity, and as I (somewhat controversially) understand him, Spinoza is affirming a kind of mind-body identity theory that privileges neither mind over body nor vice versa. When you describe behavior in mental terms you are describing bodily changes, but you are using concepts that are not assimilable to the concepts of physics or physiology, yet concepts sufficient in their own right to be used in adequate, causal explanations. Humans are unified beings with correlative but irreducibly distinct mental and physical aspects. There aren't two parallel series of finite modes, but one series describable in two important ways; indeed, these two descriptions or conceptualizations *cannot* be applied to two ontologically distinct things. But doesn't the tight fit between mental and physical captured centrally by the claim that the mind is the idea of the body contradict the obvious fact that we don't spend our whole lives thinking only about our bodies? No. Of course in the ordinary sense we think about external objects distinct from our bodies. But we do so only through perception of our unique bodies insofar as they are causally affected by those other bodies.

Finite minds are composed of adequate and inadequate ideas. Insofar as a mind consists of inadequate (confused) ideas, it is passive. This means that it predominantly reflects the things in its more immediate environment that are acting on it, which means it is being largely reactive, not proactive or self-determining, and myopic, not global in outlook. Adequate ideas are adequate (clear and distinct) causes (explanations, understandings) of their effects. When we understand why things appear as they do, we're active, free, rational, as opposed to having beliefs foisted on us by circumstances, passively reacting to our environment.

We already know that in contrast with Descartes, for Spinoza, an individual human mind is not a created substance (a self-contradictory notion) but only a particular modification of God or Nature's infinite power of thought; it is constituted by the set of ideas whose objects are the states of an individual human body, constantly affected by other, external bodies, which also are reflected in the ideas. Put more plainly, mind is just a way of conceiving the successive states of the body, and that succession is influenced by all other natural bodies. Of course ordinary thought and language suggest otherwise, but they reflect habits of the imagination, not scientific thinking, confused ideas, not logically coherent ideas of the intellect. Vague experiences and everyday, knee-jerk perceptual judgments are paradigm cases of confused ideas. When I make a perceptual judgment about an external object I am literally confused because my idea is caused both by the state of my body and the state of the object perceived, without distinction, so that it represents neither the true nature of my body nor the external body.

Also in contrast with Descartes (recall the Third and Fourth Meditations), ideas for Spinoza are never like lifeless pictures, and need not wait to be made into a truth-value-bearing judgment by adoption of a psychological attitude either of affirming, denying, or withholding. Ideas involve statements or assertions, so may be true or false, follow from one another, etc., and a (really) true idea is an adequate idea, having a place in the system of ideas which constitutes God's thinking. Spinoza is a *gradualist* about truth (and freedom, and everything else). Since an idea in its inherent nature, as a modification of the attribute of thought, must necessarily agree with its object, there is nothing positive in ideas by virtue of which they are called false (P33). Falsity is a lack of knowledge "which inadequate, or mutilated and confused, ideas involve" (P35).

Ideas are *more or less* true or false. So, for central example, ideas of the pure intellect are truer than what we'd normally describe as accurate perceptual judgments, which are truer in turn than what we'd normally describe as erroneous perceptual judgments, which are truer in turn than hallucinations. So, to reject an ordinary perceptual judgment as false is to say that it is *false in relation to a more coherent system of ideas*, namely clear and distinct ideas of the intellect, which more adequately represents the order of *things* (the *ideata* of the ideas). But an ordinary perceptual judgment is truer than an hallucination, because the hallucination occurs in an even less coherent system of ideas. But even the hallucination reflects *some* modification of a finite mode in Nature, so error is never absolute. Inadequate ideas are always *incomplete* in that they fail to represent the true order of causes in Nature. Error is always the privation of knowledge. Returning to our earlier example, perceptual experiences represent the interaction between human bodies and other things, but do not represent adequately the causes of those interactions. As we move from commonsense to scientific thinking, our ideas increasingly reveal more of the causes of the modifications of our body. The complete representation of the true order of causes in Nature requires one complete deductive system, a unified science that is the infinite idea of God, which, given the identification of mind with idea, is the absolutely infinite intellect (substance, viewed under the attribute of thought).

One anti-Cartesian implication of saying that ideas are just ideas of bodies, occurring in an order determined within the order of Nature as a whole, is that minds are not utterly spontaneous agents. Only if one's body became identical with Nature conceived as extended (conceived under the attribute of extension) could one's mind permanently possess absolutely complete knowledge. So, interestingly, the route to intellectual progress (emendation of the intellect) is expansion of one's physical powers, as we will see in the next section.

What is not useful for intellectual progress is systematic doubt. Spinoza thinks Descartes' method of doubt is pointless and impossible. It is pointless to generate doubt in order to overcome it when doubt can be avoided in the first place by following proper order, since doubt is incomplete understanding of the relations of ideas (and so things), and incomplete understanding only occurs when one acquires ideas in the wrong order, not from causes to effects. So, and this is where use of geometric method helps, knowledge will be ensured if you consistently begin with adequate ideas of causes and derive ideas of effects. That's why Spinoza begins with the richest possible adequate idea of all, the idea of God or substance; why Part I is metaphysics, "Of God." He then elicits all of its logical consequences, from the immediately proximate to the more distal, carrying the attentive reader's mind along.

Descartes' method of doubt is also pointless because it is prompted by the search for an independently identifiable criterion of truth, a mark external to truth that guarantees truth. But clarity and distinctness (= adequacy) is not properly distinct from truth itself. Since ideas are identical with their objects, the internal adequacy of an idea is just the correspondence between idea and object considered in two different ways. Also, since the principle of plenitude, that everything possible is actual, has already been established in Part I, we know that clear and distinct ideas are true, their ideata are actual, since, as Descartes would agree, clarity and distinctness guarantees possibility. And again, in characteristic gradualist fashion, Spinoza treats *falsity* not as a positive feature of ideas, but as a relative incompleteness. Since understanding is through causes, ideas of things that do not include knowledge of their causes are incomplete, and in that sense to some degree false.

Finally, Cartesian doubt is impossible because its initiation requires free will, which requires undetermined or uncaused effort, which is an illusion ruled out by Part I's necessitarianism.

So optimal method seeks to prove the existence and understand the nature of God head-on, and then elicit their implications. But we are blocked from understanding God by (especially anthropomorphic) images, including passions, and our ignorance of the laws of Nature. Images can't be logically related to each other, so can't provide real understanding or explanation. So we need to trace the hierarchy of ideas, from most confused and inadequate ideas of the imagination to most clear and adequate ideas of the intellect. To do so is to discover the hierarchy of things, from the finite and perishing to the infinite and eternal order of Nature.

But progress is difficult. Inadequate ideas are connected by psychological associations, not (like adequate ideas) logical necessity, and thus are to that extent passivities of the mind (passions). Most have become entrenched through repetitions in the modifications of the body, and are accepted by testimony, habit, and memory, not by systematic and logical inquiry. We have similar ideas only if we have had similar experiences, have undergone similar modifications. But since human bodies share roughly the same structure, so react similarly to similar inputs, we tend to share uncritically the same inadequate, commonsense view of things.

Spinoza explicitly distinguishes between three kinds of cognition (II P40 S2). Imagination presents objects in images, which never provide a full understanding of their causes. So ideas of imagination are never adequate. Imagination includes unscientifically refined sense perception and hearsay, including authoritative testimony. The intellect is capable of two kinds of adequate ideas. Reason shows *that* something is true based on common notions, what all things of a given kind have in common and what is present in each part of the thing as well as the whole thing. The beauty of common notions is that they cannot be grasped partially, but are adequately grasped if grasped at all. Still, the intellect is capable of a third kind of cognition, intuitive knowledge (*scientia intuitiva*), which is superior to reason, because it guarantees insight into precisely *why* something *must be* true. This occurs when one knows things in the proper order, by conceiving essences of things through their causes, fully back to the self-caused cause, God.

So how can we overcome our unhealthy, constricted view of the world and progress to scientific knowledge? As just indicated, the key first step is the use of *common notions*, such as ideas of extension and motion, and what is deducible from such ubiquitous properties. Geometry, for example, is based wholly on common notions. Common notions are adequate ideas, clearly and distinctly perceived. An adequate idea reflects the real nature or defining properties of its object. Adequate ideas immediately convey necessity, so certainty (self-evidence). If we have one adequate idea, we're on our way to purifying our minds, since we ipso facto have a model of clarity, a way of distinguishing adequate from inadequate ideas.

There is no problem of the criterion. A criterion of truth is neither necessary nor possible. Truth is its own standard. Having a true idea is entertaining a self-evident or logically necessary proposition, and the falsity of such propositions is inconceivable, so their truth is indubitable. Were it dubitable, skepticism would be total and permanent.

For Descartes you might happen to know something, but have to develop an arduous case to show that you know it. For Spinoza, when we have genuine knowledge we necessarily realize that we do. Knowledge is reflexive; it is, as he says, the idea of an idea.[5] So, once we have a single adequate idea, we can distinguish it from all lesser perceptions, discover its distinguishing features, and so enable ourselves to discipline our minds so that we make a true idea the norm of all our thinking. What the true or adequate or clear and distinct idea does not suffice to provide is knowledge of the causes of things, which is what the deductions of the *Ethics* will achieve. The goal is a complete and unitary deductive system (at the limit, *scientia intuitiva*, where we see how details within the system follow from the nature of the whole), and the methodological task is to find the simple ideas on which the whole order of adequate ideas can be based, and to exhibit the ideas in their logical relations. As we saw in Part I, the adequate idea that

---

5   To put it in terms of contemporary debates, Spinoza is committed to the (KK)-thesis, that to know that p is to know that you know that p. I think everyone agrees with this attribution. I am claiming by contrast that Descartes rejects the (KK)-thesis with respect to individually, sequentially discovered truths. This is more controversial. See section 1.8 for Descartes' position.

Spinoza invokes is the idea of substance or God, as captured by the ontological argument. And this idea precludes initiation of Cartesian skepticism, since the idea of God makes it self-evident that God is not a deceiver.

"As the light makes both itself and the darkness plain, so truth is the standard both of itself and of the false" (P43S). The intrinsic property through which truth manifests itself is explanatory completeness. While adequate ideas, which suffice for the determination of all of their object's essential properties, are absolutely true, the converse does not hold (I'm retrieving Spinoza's gradualism above); inadequate ideas are not absolutely false, but are false in degrees. Degree of falsity is a function of degree of incompleteness of understanding, degree of passivity of the mind, degree of confusion of the idea, as when one takes partial truth about something as the complete truth, as when one thinks about an effect without a cause, as when one affirms a conclusion without having grounding premises. This most familiarly happens when the sequence of our ideas is ordered by how they are received in sense perception or imaginative association, that is, by how the body is affected. And this happens when the idea is not viewed as a determinate member of the total system of ideas, not logically ordered in terms of what really depends on what, that is, not connected back to God. So, for example, an image of the sun accurately portrays its appearance relative to one's body, but an adequate idea of the sun includes the explanation of why it so appears, and so its real distance.

Part II concludes with further attack on the traditional notion of free will. Spinoza applies the theory of mind he has just developed to conclude that the more we understand, the more we recognize that temporal freedom is unreal, since the more we know that the mind is determined to will a specific action by a cause, which is determined by another cause, and so on ad infinitum. These infinite chains of causal necessity are the expression or reflection in time of what atemporally is the eternal and immutable action of God.

Many readers are perplexed at how there can be ethical ideals and prescriptions to approximate them in a philosophy which treats free will as nothing but ignorance of the determining causes of action. How can the reader choose to follow Spinoza's path? Isn't she fated to do so or not? A well-elaborated answer requires materials from subsequent parts of the *Ethics*. But since those parts are often omitted in Modern Philosophy courses, I here sketch how Spinoza thinks freedom is properly conceived and possibly enjoyed. Some elements of the account will be elaborated in subsequent sections of this chapter. Overall, Spinoza's position is that: Descartes' freedom of indifference, which implies that at the time of action one could have done otherwise, is impossible; that complete freedom is a strong version of Descartes' freedom of spontaneity, on which one exists from the necessity of one's nature alone and is determined to act by itself alone; that indeed only God can be completely free; but that humans can be more or less free insofar as they are self-determining. The key then is to understand degrees of self-determination.

For Spinoza, human freedom is a relative matter, involving the proportion of clear ideas to inadequate ideas in the constitution of a mind. The process of becoming free is inherently incompletable. We have the power to bring it about that we understand ourselves and the things that affect us, and hence, be less victimized by, and less merely reactive to, them. But a mind in which all affects were clearly understood would be a mind that is not part of Nature. The mind can destroy the causes of its sadness and achieve joy, not through removing the causes, but only through understanding their causal force, transforming passions into active, rational emotions. We are free to the extent that we are free from passion. Freedom from passion (avoiding being determined to act by passion) is acquired by pursuing through reason a state of harmony with Nature. It is not by shunning the passions, but by accepting their necessity and attempting to understand their operations, that we become free and virtuous. In sum, human beings are free to the extent they pursue their own real advantage through their own *conatus* (effort to persevere) without being overcome or disturbed by passions.

So action is adequate causality, events understandable through our own nature. Passivity is partial causality. For a singular thing (finite mode), a determinate mode of the power of substance, to persist is for it to have effects on other things (to exert power, whether adequately or partially), within the totality of modes under an attribute. The good is what we strive for; there is no independently identifiable good, and no natural hierarchy of good and bad (of perfection) – what's good is relative to one's condition. Our appetites are part of the chain of causes, so have effects as well as causes. The sole basis for evaluation is power to affect ourselves to our advantage or disadvantage, which is to increase or diminish our own power, which is joy or sadness. But the power of external causes and the power by which we strive to persevere do represent different strivings but don't necessarily compete and produce rival outcomes. Things often enjoy shared interests. But when an external thing's power does overcome mine, my mind can wrest from that thing its status as determining cause by understanding it (contrary to the self-deceptive state of free will, as with the stone, whose state arises from ignorance of causes). The remedy for the passions is understanding the causes of what we undergo, thence appropriating to ourselves the status of determining cause (which is not first or spontaneous cause, which is nonsense for a singular thing).

You can begin to see the argument that theory of human nature, including theory of knowledge, is necessary for salvation, or blessedness, that state of complete and permanent well-being that Spinoza seeks. Epistemology shows us the difference between freedom and bondage or servitude. And epistemology itself must be grounded in metaphysics. Ethics without metaphysics is mere idiosyncratic autobiography. We must understand ourselves and our situation as parts of Nature; otherwise our claims about our purposes and our happiness will be mere projections of our myopic outlook as caused by our limited experience as finite modes in Nature. Ethics requires knowing ourselves *sub specie aeternitatis*, that is, as necessary consequences of our situation within *Natura naturata*. It requires understanding ourselves scientifically, through the universal laws of Nature.

In sum, since we are parts of Nature, the moralist must be a naturalist, and ideal freedom and happiness must be impartially explained as the necessary consequences of our status as finite modes in Nature. This begins with understanding the causes of our passions. Passions, as we'll see, are negative emotions. Spinoza will argue that the key to freeing ourselves from our passions is understanding them.[6] And to achieve a full philosophical understanding of oneself, through understanding the world and our place in it, is to achieve, and is the only way to achieve, our greatest happiness and peace of mind. This takes us to the next stage of the *Ethics*.

2.4 *Ethics* Part III: On the nature and origin of actions and passions

Part I was a metaphysics of the universe. Part II was a metaphysics of the human mind and body that is part of the universe, and the epistemology it implies. Parts III through V comprise the account of human life entailed by all of this. Part III provides a wholly naturalistic treatment of the nature of human emotions and our susceptibility to them. Part IV frankly portrays the burdens of our human condition and the ways of overcoming them to live well. Part V portrays the ideal life, a non-traditional vision of human blessedness. Since I regard Parts III–V as constituting a continuous argument, though this and the next two section headings divide Spinoza's text into their standard, sequential parts, I occasionally blend material from all three parts when it serves cogency.

As we turn to Part III, remember that there can be only one substance, God, or in other words the whole, self-sufficient system of Nature, and that finite individuals are sub-systems of varying degrees of complexity of the system as a whole, and can always be viewed from a wholly physicalistic point of view and, equally appropriately, from a wholly mentalistic point of view. But given the complete interdependence of all finite things, how can we say that any of them are separate, or *individuals* at all? Part III fleshes out what it means to say that even though only substance is fully ontologically and conceptually independent, finite individuals, what Spinoza earlier called *singular things* (I P28, II D7), can exist with their own natures and their own modes, modeling in a limited way the one true substance whose power they use and express. *Finite individuality in general* is explicated in terms of the fundamental, organizing concept of conatus

6   An example of Spinoza's foreshadowing of Freud.

(striving to persevere in existence), and *human individuality in particular* is explicated through an account of the emotions (affects), which itself is grounded in the theory of conatus.

A finite mode is viewed as an individual to the extent that it exhibits integrity, which is nothing other than successful conatus, or persistence as what it is for as long as it can. Gradualist talk is once again appropriate. For example, all other things being equal, something that lasts longer is more of an individual than something that is more fleeting; something whose character remains stable for however long it lasts is more of an individual than something whose character changes during that same lifespan; something with a greater repertoire of capacities is more of an individual than something that can do fewer things, etc. And degree of individuality turns out to be a function of organic complexity. A highly complex body like the human body can respond to a myriad of external and internal changes without disintegrating. Think of all the remarkable ways we achieve homeostasis in the face of physical and psychological stresses. People often go through extraordinary trauma and survive, and healthier people are likelier to survive than sicklier ones. On the other hand, take a much simpler physical body such as a diamond. As hard as a diamond is when mined, there are so many simple ways to destroy its identity as a diamond; if you strike it from any but a few angles, it will shatter utterly – no more diamond! Indeed, if you knew the weak spot in its structure and how to apply pressure to it, you could destroy it with your fingernail.

So let us stress that for Spinoza every finite mode strives to persist for as long as it lasts (III P6–7), endeavors to increase its vitality to – put negatively – ward off destruction and – put positively – preserve its integrity (what it is). This is its conatus, and for humans, who are conscious of this striving, this is the *desire* (conscious appetite) for self-preservation, which is our human essence (III P9S). To be human is to desire to persist in a network in which others are doing the same. Mind's basic desire is to affirm the existence of the body, to imagine things beneficial to it, to increase its vitality (III P12). So all finite things exert their power to maintain their existence. And since each mode of extension is identical with a mode of thought, conatus is mental as well as physical. But only some finite things are complex enough to satisfy two conditions: their self-preserving power undergoes noticeable increases and decreases, and they are able to form and retain images of external things toward which their striving can be directed. Those more complex singular things, like human beings, have *emotions*.

A human being's well-being is a function of what emotions she has. "Emotion" refers to both mind and body, but in the mental sense, emotions are ideas in the mind corresponding to events in the body in which the power of that body is affected either positively or negatively. He defines three basic emotions – joy, sadness, and desire – and then defines all other emotions in terms of combinations of one or more of these three plus some other cognitive state(s).[7] *Joy* boils down to the *transition to* greater vitality, from lesser to greater perfection, *sadness* or sorrow, to the transition to lesser vitality, from greater to lesser perfection (III P11). Joy and sadness are changes in an individual's relation to its environment. Spinoza's definitions of the various emotions are developed throughout the remainder of Part III, and are elegantly recapitulated in the *Definition of the Affects* section that concludes it. For example, love and hate are joy and sadness with an awareness of their external causes, longing is desire conjoined with a memory of the desired object and an awareness of its absence, and pride is joy born of the fact that one has an unjustly inflated self-image.

So desire itself is conatus (the striving for persistence) insofar as the mind is conscious of it, and all of our emotional life is defined in terms of our effort to persevere. Emotions have both a physiological and psychological aspect, and a thing's emotional condition depicts its body's level of vitality or capacity for action. Some emotions are draining or enervating. These are the negative emotions, or passions. Some emotions are fulfilling or uplifting. These are the active emotions. So Spinoza is not condemning emotions as such, but only the passive ones. As I read him, all ideas have an emotional coloration to them, so it is not a question of extinguishing emotion, but of having the empowering ones. Indeed, optimal thinking, impersonal global understanding, is promoted by emotional acceptance, without regret, frustration, etc., of the way things are.

Relating this back to the epistemology of II, Spinoza is now saying that all ideas, all acts of thinking, have a motivating force as well as cognitive content. Minds, which are just complex ideas, are passive insofar as they are inadequate ideas, only partial causes or explanations of their states, and this occurs to the extent that their desires are based on sense perception, imagination, conditioning, and other forms of psychological association (all forms of opinion), the ways they cognize virtually all external things causally affecting them (so with respect to which they're passive or reactive). Minds are active insofar as they are the adequate, that is, sufficient or complete cause or explanation of their states, and this occurs when their desires are grounded in rational knowledge, in the limit, when their states are conceived as infinite intellect would conceive them. Active emotions of desire and joy, that express one's own power, are always good, and include most importantly the desire for knowledge, the joy of understanding, and, optimally, the abiding, overriding joy of the intellectual love of God, which is human blessedness, or, as we might say, salvation here and now.

---

7   This is the correct way to translate Spinoza's Latin, *laetitia* and *tristitia*. Edwin Curley so translates it. Samuel Shirley, in a generally excellent, reliable translation, in this case wrongly substitutes "pleasure" and "pain" for "joy" and "sadness." But as Spinoza makes plain in *Definitions of the Affects* III and at P11, pleasure and pain are species of joy and sadness, species chiefly related to the body, so not comprehensive enough for the explication of all the emotions (affects). For our purposes, not much is at stake.

Overall, Spinoza aims to take the mystery out of emotions, arguing that they are natural phenomena explicable in terms of general, causal laws, just like everything else in Nature. And like other things in the causal nexus, a change in cause can bring about a change in effect. We can transform our passions, species of sadness, to active, rational emotions, species of joy. We can liberate ourselves from bondage, live affirmatively, not like slaves.

In sum, it is as enduring and finite modes that we enjoy the conatus that distinguishes us from the self-sufficient whole of things, but as such our cognition is always partial or confused. So long as we see things temporally and partially, we are pulled in contrary directions, between natural sensuous concerns and the rational aspiration for eternal totality. Freedom from this psychic division requires escape from the bondage of time by seeing things *sub specie aeternitatis*. God is completely free because he acts from the necessity of his own nature alone. We are free to the extent that we act from the necessity of our own self-preserving nature, which means guided by reason.

It follows from the preceding account of human nature that guidance about how to live must come from one's own reason, and not from any external authority. (Kant will most famously develop this insight as applied to a narrower sense of ethics in section 7.4.) The key to living well is understanding what is truly advantageous (useful) and, given human nature, ipso facto being motivated to act on that understanding. What is objectively good is not the same as what is subjectively good. Subjectively, what's good is what I like, and what's evil is what I don't like. But my subjective preferences are largely induced by short-sighted reactions to the world around me, not clear understanding of what will really enhance my capacities to flourish.

The upshot of the *Ethics* thus far is that, given a correct (based on reason, not imagination) model of human nature, we can ground a new morality, in which virtue = freedom = self-determination (not lack of determination) = acting in accordance with the laws of one's nature (= laws of a common human nature) = self-realization = acting under the guidance of reason = being the adequate cause of one's states (modifications) = having adequate ideas (= knowledge = understanding = clear and distinct conception) = having power over, not being slave to, passions (passive emotions) = having active emotions (which enhance conatus or striving) = one's true self-interest = happiness.

2.5   *Ethics* Part IV: On the burdens of human existence and the ways to overcome them

Part IV catalogues the impediments to self-realization and gives a forthright account of human weaknesses. As regards the obstacles to flourishing, Spinoza is not naïve about reason's efficacy, and begins by acknowledging the limits of reason in the face of passion, invoking insights from Part III. One representative line of thought goes as follows: there are laws governing passions. For example, there is the law of association, by which X becomes a cause of pleasure by association – via similarity, contiguity, or contrast – with Y that has been such a cause; and there is the law of imitation, by which X becomes a cause of pleasure if it is such a cause in others whose emotions we tend naturally to imitate. Now remember that virtue requires rational desire, which is desire as active emotion, which is desire that arises from a true knowledge of good and evil, which is effort to self-preserve guided by scientific knowledge. But it is difficult to replace passive with active emotions, to become freer. After all, given the metaphysics of Part I, we can't even be conceived without other things, so to some extent we are always passive. Further, there are always more powerful things that can destroy us. And still more, truth and goodness per se can't displace falsity and evil – there is a gap between knowing the good and doing the good.

But there are ways of coming to live more actively (rationally, virtuously), approaching the greatest good of knowledge of God (system), the very source of intelligibility, but they demand psychological transformations which require, for example, cooperation and concern for others' well-being. Insofar as people live in harmony with reason they live in harmony with each other and so are mutually useful; insofar as they are governed by passion (determined by external things, not self-determined) they are necessarily different, not in harmony.

When he classifies specific virtues and vices, emotions that promote or inhibit conatus, he isolates the special value of those that are intrinsically good and can never become excessive. For example, you can't have too much joy, because joy means you're getting stronger and so more resistant to harm. But there are also many emotions that are good in moderation only, and only in certain contexts, such as localized bodily pleasure and love. What must be avoided or controlled as much as possible are intrinsically bad emotions such as hate, contempt, envy, anger, and revenge. They tear us apart, psychologically and physically.

Spinoza's earlier prescription for concern for others may surprise if misunderstood as the Christian commandment to love one's neighbor. It is an implication of Spinoza's ethics that *all* forms of sadness are bad; they are decreases in your conatus and so are disadvantageous. This includes all species of hate, including retribution; we should never return evil for evil, though we should always return good with good. This prescription is not offered in the Christian spirit, but is motivated by the realization that whenever we hate we hurt ourselves. (It is often said of negative emotions such as anger and hate that they hurt us more than they do their target.) Indeed, pity, repentance, and humility (IV P50,53,54), all Christian virtues, are condemned by Spinoza, since all are species of sadness. So, for example, one should be benevolent or charitable as an expression of one's abundant capacities, but not out of pity.

More generally, we naturally might be tempted to conclude that, given the primacy of conatus, Spinoza's ethics always demands selfishness. But it does not. Since in fact cooperation and friendship are in many ways crucial to enhancing one's life, he urges social harmony, not competitive self-interest. Also, he thinks it's just a mistake to see all joint pursuits of goods as zero-sum games, with winners and inevitable losers. This mistake is most obvious when it comes to the highest good of understanding God. Not only does another's understanding of God not hinder your efforts to do so, but joint inquiry helps each searcher succeed. For remember that God is Nature, so all knowledge of God is scientific understanding of nature, and it seems uncontroversial that scientific progress benefits from division of labor, communication with co-workers, and other forms of cooperation.

2.6   *Ethics* Part V: On the power of reason to liberate us to live blessedly

Part V is an account of self-care through restraint or moderation of the passions by the understanding, the power of the mind. An affect that is a passion (a confused idea) ceases to be so when we form a clear and distinct (adequate) idea of it. P1–20 outlines the way to freedom, nicely summarized in P20S.

There are percepts (remedies) for achieving mastery of the passions. Enabling control is the fact that insofar as ideas are properly, intellectually ordered, their physical correlates (appetites) are similarly ordered. One needs to break established patterns of association among ideas. So, for example, to remedy excessive hate, sever the object of the emotion from this idea of the external cause, by uniting it to the thought of another cause; for example, think it is only a contributing cause, and is itself conditioned by an indefinite succession of prior causes, a mere link in the causal chain. Doing this is forming a clear and distinct idea of the emotion; the affect ceases to be a passion. We can form a clear and distinct idea, understand in terms of general laws, all bodily affections, and emotions are ideas of bodily affections, so we can form a clear and distinct idea of any emotion – emotions can be scientifically understood, in a detached, objective way. We thus gain control of our loves and hates, desires and appetites.

Our strongest emotions are toward things we think could have been otherwise, so recognition of necessity weakens emotional force. Though perhaps less intense, the greater endurance of a rationally grounded emotion (directed toward the common properties of things) enables it to prevail in the long run over stronger passions directed toward absent objects and obsessions with particular objects. So, the alternative to the illusory Cartesian notion of training the will, to condition the imagination to respond appropriately, is to memorize rules for correct living while in a detached state, and then apply them when eventually assaulted by dangerous emotions.

Centrally, condition yourself always to be moved to action by the emotion of joy. Concentrate on people's good points, not their faults. The ultimate positive thought is love of God. Its special power is based on two main things. First is its connection with intuitive knowledge, the third, highest form of knowledge – a form of clear and distinct perception, where to conceive something clearly and distinctly is to conceive it in relation to God (= substance = Nature = infinite being = self-explanatory being = necessarily existing being). Second is the fact that it can be suggested by, and conjoined with, all our physical states, and the more things a given emotion can be associated with, the more frequently it can be evoked, and the more constantly it can occupy the mind. Intuitive knowledge is more potent than deductive knowledge since it has more explanatory power. It goes beyond abstract generalities and shows how general principles relate to particular instances. And by comprehending things in relation to God, it grasps them in terms of their source of intelligibility. We come to see that God lacks emotion, so can't feel joy or sadness, pleasure or pain, so can't love or hate. So our love of God must be unrequited, can't be turned into hate nor tainted by envy or jealousy.

We are blessed insofar as we increasingly appreciate our small but meaningful role in the infinite universe, and the more we act, the more what we do follows logically from an understanding of the situation as it really is, the more we function effectively, the more we contribute to the universe, the more significant we are. And the more progressively efficacious and significant we become, the more joyous we become, and deservedly so.

In elaborating the nature of human blessedness in the last half of Part V (P21–42), Spinoza says things that have been interpreted as inconsistent with the view he has developed thus far, including talk of mind without body, a finite mode being eternal, and duration being the same as eternity. For example, he says that the human mind cannot be absolutely destroyed with the body, but something of it remains which is eternal (P23). This is not a relapse into theism, but the claim that adequate knowledge is eternal, and so allows part of the mind (which is just a complex idea) to be eternal. So insofar as our thought is knowledge of eternal, necessary truth, it is detached from the limitations of time, and we are part of the eternal framework, united with the eternal aspect of reality, God or Nature, qua thought. And insofar as we take this rational view of things, we will treat those things equally whether we think of them as past, present, or future. We will no longer be driven by short-term desire, but will be truly prudent. We will no longer taint or muffle the joy of life because we will lose the fear of death.

To elaborate, to have adequate ideas is to see things as they are necessarily, *sub specie aeternitatis*, and so, to have eternal ideas, ideas which have eternally been in the infinite intellect of God. But since our finite minds just are complex ideas, when we think adequately part of our mind becomes eternal (V P23). Put a more familiar way, that part of our mind which is our intellect, as opposed to our imagination, is eternal (V P40). This eternality is our immortality. It is not the personal immortality of theism, which involves the persistence of a distinct self with memory after death, but occurs during one's earthly life in the form of the joyous tranquility which true understanding brings. Such understanding transforms our limited, specific perspectives from which so much around us seems contingently threatening, to a global, impersonal, embracing vision of things (seeing things "from the perspective of the universe") in which everything has its place, and so in which we even immunize ourselves from the fear of death (V P38).

Spinoza concludes the *Ethics* by acknowledging the effort required to follow his path to salvation. "But all things excellent are as difficult as they are rare."

2.7   Questions about Spinoza

1   Discuss all or part of the following rendition of Spinoza's views: Belief in free will is the epitome of error. We have such belief because we are conscious of our strivings and actions while being ignorant of their causes. Such belief is incoherent, anti-explanationist, the focal point of moralism (regret, recrimination) and self-deception. Determinism teaches us to understand rather than praise or blame. Freedom is self-determination. Within the most comprehensive determinism, we can have the power and responsibility to shape our own characters and moral destinies, so as to live up to an ethic of love and understanding, facing life calmly even in the most adverse circumstances.

2   How does Spinoza reconcile the world's (God's) timeless unity with the manifest diversity and change in Nature and experience, without making God a refuge of ignorance (by talk of mystery, ineffability, etc.)? Is the world of finite individuals, of duration, of contingencies and the passions they engender a) an illusion of the imagination to be transcended, or b) the real world of experience, constituted by the imagination, and to be critically examined (exposed as inadequate) but not transcended by reason? Relatedly, are imagination, reason and intuition modes of cognition which form an ascending hierarchy, each superior mode replacing its inferior ancestor, or do (must) all three coexist in a unified perception of the world?

3   Unpack as fully and clearly as you can Spinoza's claim that the individual mind is the idea of a body inserted into the totality of determinate modes of extension. Consider including analyses of what it is to be a body, how the account purports to explain why we inherently lack self-knowledge, have confused grasp of the physical world, are not mere spectators but active consciousnesses, etc. Or focus exclusively on how Spinoza accounts for the phenomena of mind–body interaction in terms of his theory of mind as the idea of the body.

4   Explain the notion of conatus (endeavor, striving) as essence. How does it function? Discuss a few doctrines which depend on it.

5   Why is Cartesian doubt impossible, according to Spinoza?

6   Write on the nature of emotions, or some particular emotion and its role.

7   Why does Spinoza lay out the *Ethics* as a deductive system in the style of Euclid? Is it essential to his aims or more of an instructional heuristic?

Is such linear derivation required by his monistic holism or (at the other extreme) inconsistent with it (or neither)? Descartes says he proceeds geometrically, but obviously he does not proceed in Euclidean style (in his analytic method of discovery). Why the different understanding of what philosophical rigor requires?

8   Spinoza's philosophy seems uncompromisingly naturalistic. Is it, and if it is, how should we interpret Part V P21–42? Some readers see Spinoza's final phase of thought in the *Ethics* as discontinuous or at variance with previously developed doctrine. Others see it as carefully prefigured in earlier material. Explore (some of) the sources of apparent tension and bolster the case of the detractors, the admirers, or some moderate position in between.

9   Articulate Spinoza's view of the relation between knowledge and virtue. What role ought education play in his scheme?

10   Discuss how Spinoza distinguishes among modes, attributes, and substance, with focus on the nature of attributes and their relation to substance.

11   How does Spinoza really understand the third kind of knowledge (intuitive), the grasping of the inmost essence of individual things as they follow from the essence of God (in relation to the second kind of (deductive) knowledge, or taken by itself)? For example, is Spinoza aiming to achieve a rigorously scientific understanding of mind and knowledge, or aiming to effect a mystical transformation of mind (or both, or neither)?

12   (A cluster of related questions, not to be addressed collectively): Why does Spinoza reject Descartes' sort of (substance) dualist theory of human being? If attributes are fundamental and mutually non-overlapping ways that things can be and be conceived, is Spinoza's different sort of (conceptual) dualism an improvement on Descartes? How does Spinoza account for the appearance of interaction, the utterly systematic but not causal correlation between mental states and physical states? (To what extent) is his explanation defensible? What exactly *is* the finite mode we call our mind? Is it real, or an illusion, or of some intermediate status? And while Descartes thinks the mind has ideas, Spinoza thinks that the mind is an idea. Why, and with what plausibility and philosophical benefit? And more specifically, Spinoza seems to argue that ideas are inherently judgmental, involving affirmation and negation, not "dumb pictures on a tablet" to which separable acts of will react (as in Descartes, as Spinoza reads him). Is Spinoza's account of judgment, including doubt or suspension of judgment, better or worse than Descartes'? Do both philosophers have difficulties explaining false beliefs; what are their different difficulties and who is worse off?

13   Why does Spinoza reject Descartes' notion of free will? What is his own conception of freedom? Can a determinist like Spinoza have an ethical theory?

14 What does it mean, and is it right, to say that the passions depend solely on inadequate ideas?

15 Pure knowledge rationalism is the view that all knowledge is based on reason. Pure explanatory rationalism is the view that everything must have a sufficient reason such that nothing is contingent. Is Spinoza both a knowledge and explanatory rationalist? Are the forms of rationalism he embraces defensible? Does Spinoza collapse logical and causal necessity? If so, is he conceiving the former too weakly or the latter too strongly? And what does it mean to say that God is the immanent cause of all things?

16 Why are the differences between the three kinds of knowledge important to Spinoza (and why does he characterize each the way he does, for example, calling sense perceptions "conclusions without premises"), and what is the relation between his view of knowledge and his ethics?

17 What is Spinoza's theory of blessedness, the intellectual love of God.

18 Reflect on Spinoza in relation to Cartesian commitments listed in section 1.10: rationalism, realism, representationalism, pluralism, atomism (conceptual, explanatory, metaphysical), reductionism, essentialism, foundationalism, individual autonomism, ahistoricism, and methodism (versus particularism and skepticism).

2.8 Some recommended books

Allison, H.E. (1987) *Benedict de Spinoza: An Introduction*, rev. edn, New Haven and London: Yale University Press.

A clear, skillful overview of Spinoza's entire philosophy.

Curley, E. (1988) *Behind the Geometrical Method: A Reading of Spinoza's Ethics*, Princeton: Princeton University Press.

A naturalistic and materialistic reading of the *Ethics* that aims to explain how its main positions, often masked by the axiomatic style of presentation, arise out of Spinoza's critical reflection on Descartes and Hobbes.

Delahunty, R.J. (1985) *Spinoza*, London, Boston, Melbourne and Henley: Routledge & Kegan Paul.

An account of Spinoza's main arguments in epistemology, metaphysics, philosophy of mind, philosophical psychology, and ethics, against the backdrop of Cartesianism, introducing alternative interpretations along the way.

Donagan, A. (1988) *Spinoza*, Chicago: University of Chicago Press.

Especially notable for treating Spinoza more dualistically than is usual.

Hampshire, S. (1987) *Spinoza: An Introduction to His Philosophical Thought*, rev. edn, New York and Middlesex: Penguin Books.

Originally published in 1951, this is the classic presentation of Spinoza as grand, rationalistic, system-builder.

Lloyd, G. (1996) *Spinoza and the Ethics*, London and New York: Routledge.

A well-crafted interpretation of the *Ethics* especially valuable for its insistence that Spinoza aspires for reason to understand, not displace, imagination; for its accessible presentation of some alternative, scholarly literature; and for its nice focus on the culminating discussion of intellectual love of God.

Steinberg, D. (2000) *On Spinoza*, Belmont, CA: Wadsworth.

A well-done, short, basic introduction unified by attention to Spinoza's uncompromising monism, naturalism, and geometric presentation, and with Descartes as backdrop.

Wolfson, H.A. (1934) *The Philosophy of Spinoza*, 2 vols, Cambridge: Harvard University Press.

An important early study of Spinoza's thought, especially as reaction against scholastic philosophy, and less in relation to his immediate predecessors (unlike Curley).

3   Locke

3.1   An overview of Locke's outlook in the *Essay*

At the beginning of the seventeenth century Francis Bacon inspired the modern empiricist movement. He was a highly influential organizer and promoter, but did not develop the empiricist project in the sustained, more sophisticated way John Locke did. So Locke (1632–1704, born the same year as Spinoza), is often treated as first in the lineage of modern thinkers articulating and applying what later came to be called *empiricist* method. (In Locke's time "empiricist" primarily referred to quack doctors; since Locke was a trained physician, he would not have welcomed the designation! *He* called his approach the "historical, plain" one (*An Essay Concerning Human Understanding*, Book I, Chapter 1, Section 2, hereafter I.1.2).) Locke began his important publishing in his late fifties, soon after he returned to England from six years of politically prudent, self-imposed exile in the Netherlands. (Had he been caught when fleeing England with the political manuscripts then in hand, he might well have been executed.) Indeed, his three most important works, the *Essay*, *Two Treatises of Government*, and *A Letter Concerning Toleration*, appeared in quick succession upon his return. His work soon became required reading for all educated people. In his final years, he and Newton, whose *Principia* was published three years earlier than Locke's *Essay*, were regarded in England as the two intellectual giants of their time.

Politically Locke was explicitly revolutionary, rejecting the absolute, divine right of kings, defending the right to rebellion by the misgoverned, and most influentially still, defending the right to private property as the pivotal, natural right. But many even found Locke's non-explicitly political ideas in our quarry, the *Essay*, dangerous, though you would be hard-pressed to find a seemingly more judicious, modest thinker. Locke may seem straightforwardly common-sensical, but his approach has some quite surprising implications. Let's begin by laying out his ground-floor goals and procedural guidelines, and then we can enjoy some of his more influential applications.

Locke tells us his *Essay* was instigated by an unresolved discussion with friends about principles of morality and revealed religion. He wondered whether and by what means he could hope to achieve resolution. This spawned the more comprehensive examination of the extent and limits of our cognitive faculties (= our understanding), to discover what we can and cannot expect from our understanding, so we can devote ourselves to acquiring well-founded beliefs about matters we are competent to investigate, or, as he puts it more precisely, "to inquire into the origin, certainty, and extent of human knowledge, together with the grounds and degrees of belief, opinion, and assent." His second, related goal is to serve as an "underlaborer" to the new scientists, clearing rubbish that could frustrate their progress. His general conclusion is that there are some things beyond human resolution, but that doesn't support a general skepticism. As he nicely puts it, "Our business here is not to know all things, but those which concern our conduct."

One especially central and influential demand on how we use our understanding in seeking the truth and conducting our lives is that we form beliefs and make decisions based on our own examination of evidence, not by appeal to supposed authority. Locke shares this individualistic ideal with Descartes (we know he was much-taken with his private study of Descartes), but disagrees about what the available evidence is. Locke prominently thought deference to the word of others relinquishes intellectual responsibility. He was especially concerned about the effects of dogmatic claims to divinely instilled religious and moral knowledge on social and political life. He was philosophical spokesman for England's Royal Society, whose motto was *Nullius in verba* ("On no man's word"). He was a major inspiration for the Enlightenment attitude to theoretical inquiry, on which each of us has a special responsibility for our beliefs, as for our actions. Kant took Locke's demand for intellectual self-reliance as definitive of enlightenment. Hegel took Locke's demand as definitive of modernity.

Besides distancing himself from Scholasticism, Locke writes in the midst of controversy between two other venerable traditions: the Platonic-Augustinian tradition, innovatively developed by Descartes, and the ancient empiricist and materialist tradition (as in Democritus), developed by Gassendi and Hobbes. To understand Locke's overall conclusions, note that he holds a hybrid view, different from any of his predecessors. He agrees with his rationalist predecessors that knowledge requires certainty. Anything less is opinion, belief, or faith. And like Descartes, he takes the intuitive understanding of necessary truth as the paradigm of certainty. But he famously disagrees about the status of the ideas or concepts that comprise knowledge-claims. *All* concepts are derived from experience; the "pure intellect" is not a separate representational faculty. Knowledge consists in grasping relations between empirically grounded concepts. But often when we cannot grasp these relations, so cannot know, we still can achieve reasonable belief adequate to our needs. In both his idea-empiricism and his modesty about our cognitive capacities, Locke notably influenced anti-Cartesian, European thought, as culminates in Hume in Chapter Six.

But a related, surprising commitment that warrants highlighting up front is that while there cannot be a science of physical nature based on the essence of things – even the much-touted, mechanistic, corpuscular explanation of nature, the "new philosophy," is only our best available, probable hypothesis – there *can* be an utterly demonstrative science of ethics and politics! This for Locke rests on a deep difference between *objects* of inquiry. Physics concerns substances, which have various powers and appear in various ways, and, Locke will argue, while we can know those appearances by the senses, we cannot know the real essences of the substances which are their source. In contrast, ethical and political theory concern either modes of or relations between substances, and with such subject-matter, he will argue, there is in principle no real nature lying behind what is accessible to us. Locke will have to develop this optimistic value theory without lapsing into the kind of dogmatism he abidingly abhors.

In preparation for deeper analysis, keep the following overall sketch in mind. Locke's *Essay* examines the operations of the human mind to learn what we're capable of understanding. It is divided into four books. The first book lays out Locke's goals and transparent method and contrasts them with the rationalist's unnecessary and obscure innatist alternative. The second argues that sensation and reflection (introspection of the operations of our minds, not rational, *a priori* reflection as in Descartes and Spinoza) can supply all the materials of our understanding, all of our ideas. The third traces the ways language can both promote and inhibit the communication of ideas. The fourth explains how abstraction and reason produce knowledge from ideas, how knowledge differs from probable opinion, and how the appropriate scope of reason and experience differs from that of revelation and faith. It reaches the ecumenical conclusion that we can prove that God exists, and in principle prove moral truths as reliably as mathematical ones, but cannot adjudicate sectarian disputes.

I begin my deeper analysis of Locke by distinguishing seven doctrines or attitudes held by many empiricists. I leave open whether all are essential to being a coherent, unrepentant empiricist (likely a question to decide by stipulation, not argument). What's vital to recognize is that they do not all stand or fall together. Some of the most important philosophical innovations, for example Kant's, may be formulated in part by complicating the relations among them.

- *Idea-empiricism* (or as it is more narrowly labeled in contemporary discussions, *concept-empiricism*) is the view that the representational content of all thought, the content of all ideas, is derived from outer or inner sense experience.
- *Knowledge-* (or *justification-*) *empiricism* is the view that all knowledge (or justified belief) is based on sensory evidence.
- *Meaning-empiricism* is the view that the meaning of a linguistic expression is some particular type of experienceable entity (ranging, for example, from private, sense-derived ideas to public, bodily behaviors).
- *Meaningfulness-* (or *intelligibility-*) *empiricism* is the view that a linguistic expression is cognitively meaningful only if it has in principle experienceable conditions of application.

- *Scientific Law-empiricism* asserts that the laws of nature can only be known on the basis of sense experience.
- *Explanation-empiricism* allows things or facts that lack sufficient explanation. (It is the denial of the Principle of Sufficient Reason, central, for example, to Spinoza, as we stressed in the previous chapter, and to Leibniz, as we will see in the next chapter.)
- Finally, *Philosophical Method-empiricism* is the prescription to base descriptions of the world on observation, and not abandon or revise these descriptions to accommodate antecedent philosophical theory.

My sketch thus far firmly asserts that Locke is an idea-empiricist, but is a knowledge-empiricist only if experience includes grasping necessary connections between ideas; suggests (depending on what the scope of knowledge and range of facts are) that Locke is a scientific law- and explanation-empiricist; has no obvious implications concerning meaning- and intelligibility-empiricism in the absence of an account of Locke's theory of language; and perhaps leans toward philosophical method-empiricism, but remains too inarticulate about what constitutes philosophical theory to nail that down.

3.2   *Essay* Book I: Locke's anti-innatist strategy

With these distinctions in tow, what is the *Essay*'s strategy, as delineated in Book I? Book I is obviously some sort of attack on innate ideas and principles, and so rationalism, but readers disagree about what sort of attack it is. Some see Locke as responding to an overall innatist argument that

1   certain principles enjoy universal consent, and
2   this can only be explained by appeal to innate ideas and principles, so
3   there are innate ideas and principles

by arguing that 1 and hence 3 is false. Such a straightforward attempt to *refute* innatism strikes me as weak, and indeed his strategy would be logically invalid unless it was also true that there are innate ideas and principles *only if* certain principles are universally accepted. Though he does think that 1 is false, I read him as posing a strong *challenge* to innatism, and advertising a superior *alternative*.

Locke's strategy unfolds as follows. He asks what the innatist thesis amounts to. Innatists argue that we all can know various *practical principles*, truths of morality and religion, independently of experience. Most hold such principles to be authoritative only if innate. They argue that we all can know various *speculative* or theoretical *principles* independently of experience. Most hold such principles provided the framework for defensible scientific inquiry. And they argue that we all have *ideas* with content in no way derivable from experience. Most hold that such ideas are required for coherent thought and successful communication. Locke supposes that innate principles presuppose innate ideas, and focuses his challenge on the postulation of innate ideas.

His challenge is a trilemma. First, if the affirmation of innate ideas means that we *can* (= have the capacity to) think various things before actually acquiring ideas through experience, the thesis is vacuous or trivial, insisting no more than that what's actual is possible. Second, if it means that we all *do* (occurrently) have various ideas prior to experience, the thesis is patently false; "children, idiots," and others are clear-cut counterexamples – why he also lists "naturals," who I understand to be people allegedly skilled at finding underground water with a divining rod, I've never been quite sure. Locke takes it to be evident that many lack these supposedly universal, occurrent ideas because he takes it as obvious that when someone has an occurrent idea, they are aware of (sensible of) having it, and if you ask these people whether they have the idea, they'll say no. (More likely, in their mental immaturity, they won't know what you're asking.) And third, innate ideas are explanatorily unnecessary, since there's a non-mysterious ("historical, plain") alternative explanation for everything that warrants explaining. The rest of the *Essay* exhibits that alternative.

On this reading Locke is imposing a weighty, he thinks unsatisfiable, burden on rationalists, and proceeding to show how his commonsense alternative succeeds. He is demanding that they make non-mysterious, substantive sense of the universally pre-experiential. Since they cannot mean by *idea* what is immediately before the mind when we think, they must be invoking some kind of potentiality, but about what positive, real, explanatory potentiality are they talking? As for the success of his own method, he invites us to watch and see.

Locke's critique of innate, theoretical and practical ideas and principles posed a threat. Given how widely they were supposed necessary for authoritative morality, religion, and science, many construed the *Essay* as a challenge to our most vital human practices, and to the possibility of salvation, which Locke himself agreed is our overriding interest.

3.3   *Essay* Book II: Perception as the basis for all thinking

Books II–IV explain, defend, and apply Locke's method, especially to topics rationalists have staked out in their own favor, such as modal thinking (thinking about what can, cannot, and must be true) and sameness through observable change (recall Descartes' wax passage). The layout of the three books displays Locke's atomist approach – like Descartes, unlike Spinoza – for example, begin with ideas, and among ideas, simple, unanalyzable ones; move to language which depends on ideas; move to knowledge and belief which involve complexes of ideas. I will now discuss a few crucial components of his story.

I begin with perception, which for Locke is the most fundamental act of the understanding. His theory of perception is called *causal representative realism.* It maintains that (1) *Material objects* or *substances* with (2) *primary qualities*, *cause*, under suitable external conditions, the occurrence of (3) *sensations* in the (4) body of a (5) *human being* with (6) sense organs, which, under proper internal conditions, *induces* (= causes?) (7) *ideas of sensation* in the (8) *mind* of the human being. He adds that the mind can then reflect on its own (9) *operations*, acquiring additional (10) *ideas of reflection.* Mental operations, such as *comparing*, *enlarging*, *compounding*, and *abstracting*, exercised on this stock of *simple* ideas generate new ideas. All ideas are acquirable in this way. And all 11) meaningful words *stand for* ideas. You may think my computer has a manic italics function, but I purposely highlight all the notions that need explication.

Being a representationalist, Locke holds that what we know immediately or directly are our own ideas. So he begins by providing an extensive classification of ideas.

There are *simple* ideas

- of one sense (for example, hardness, whiteness),
- of several senses (figure, motion),
- of reflection (perception, willing),
- of all ways (existence, unity, pleasure), and
- of primary, secondary, and tertiary qualities,

and there are *complex* ideas

- of *modes*: of simple modes such as space, duration, number, thought, power, and mixed modes such as obligation, drunkenness,
- of *substances*: of single substances, which are either divine, corporeal, or spiritual, or of collective substances, any collection of things such as an army, and
- of *relations*.

Simple ideas cannot be broken down into further components; they are either unanalyzable or phenomenologically homogeneous. They are acquirable only by direct acquaintance with their objects, not by description in terms of other ideas; they are not inventible, only discoverable. Locke seems to be an idea-foundationalist: there must be simple ideas for there to be any ideas at all, and all complex ideas are derived from simple ones by a finite list of mental operations. As the classification indicates, some simple ideas are specific to one of the five senses, some are acquirable through more than one sense modality, some depend on introspection, and some are so widely applicable that they can be attained through any form of inner or outer perception.

The classification also alerts us to an especially important distinction, introduced before Locke by scientists like Galileo and Robert Boyle as part of their conception of modern scientific explanation, and analyzed in his own way by Descartes, between the primary and secondary (and tertiary) qualities of objects. Locke sought to give mature philosophical form to this distinction (II.8). Ideas "of" qualities are either of primary, secondary, or tertiary qualities. Primary qualities "are utterly inseparable from the body," secondary qualities are "powers to produce various sensations in us by "the object's" primary qualities," and tertiary qualities are an object's powers to produce change in primary qualities of other bodies. But several competing views of qualities seem to be offered by Locke. Perhaps he holds that secondary qualities are really in the objects, but unlike the primary ones, they're only dispositional powers; or that they're really in the objects, but only primary qualities have resembling ideas; or that they're really not in the objects at all, but are only ideas in the minds of observers (unlike primary qualities). The "lights out," "manna," "pounded almond," and famous "hands in water" arguments seem to support the last interpretation (which, as we will see, Berkeley adopted). But realizing that, for example, when the lights go out, you see neither red (Locke's example of a secondary quality) nor rectangularity (if macro-shape, not just micro-shape, is an example of a primary quality), some of these interpreters add the contention that primary qualities are maximal determinables, where the determinable–determinate distinction is a relative one. X is a determinable of Y if and only if everything that is an instance of Y is an instance of X, but not conversely; it's similar to the genus–species distinction. Unfortunately, on this view, there can be no tertiary qualities, since determinables can't be changed; the object is always of some shape or other, and also, of some color or other.

The correct view, I think, is much like the first offered, and sees Locke as clarifying the claims of corpuscular science. Secondary qualities aren't just ideas in minds of observers; they are dispositions of the object itself. That they vary relative to the conditions of perception does not entail that they depend for their existence on perception, that is, are ideas. But these dispositions are ultimately reducible to or based on the primary qualities of the object, that is, the bulk, figure, number, and motion of the insensibly small parts of the object (its corpuscular constituents). The secondary qualities an object has under specifiable conditions, how those secondary qualities affect us, is in principle explicable in terms of the object's corpuscular composition. This is an immense gain in explanatory power. Also, the properties of bulk, figure, motion, and configuration are mathematizable, and so, according to the new physical science, objective, whereas there are no mathematical laws directly governing the behavior of colors, odors, tastes, etc. But to explanatorily reduce X to Y is not to ontologically reduce X to Y, that is, not to show that X doesn't really exist. Finally, the ideas of secondary qualities have no resemblances in the objects which induce them, since the secondary qualities themselves are powers, and an empirical content cannot resemble a power, and the primary, corpuscular structure of the object (which is not even perceivable) doesn't resemble what's empirically manifest in perception.

Qualities are supposed to be qualities of substance(s) – fundamental entities. The three main traditional conceptions of material substance are:

- as concrete individual, for example, Aristotelian-informed parcel of matter,
- as kind of stuff, element out of which the world is constructed, and
- as substratum, that which "underlies" or "supports" qualities.

Traditional criteria (tests) for substance include:

- ultimate subject of predication,
- can exist alone, and
- retains its identity through change.

Locke's stance on substance emerges later.

Perception is the initial way we can acquire ideas, and without which the mind can have no other ideas. Two crucial issues concerning perception are precisely what Locke means when he says that "in bare naked *perception*, the mind is for the most part only passive" (II.9.1) and involuntarily perceives its object, and what the significance is of Locke's stance on the Molyneux problem (II.9.8). Regarding the first question, one may be especially perplexed because some of Locke's immediately subsequent remarks at least suggest that the mind must *do* something to perceive what it is given. So, for example, is so-called subliminal perception, where something at a time has impact on one's thought or action but one is not consciously aware of that thing at that time, perception for Locke? And if perception does require that the mind take some kind of notice, is that an active contribution by the mind that threatens to open the floodgates to innatism? Locke thinks not, and I take his response to the Molyneux problem to illustrate this.

The Irish scientist Molyneux asked whether a person blind from birth, who can distinguish a sphere from a cube by touch, would be able to distinguish them immediately by sight were his vision repaired. Locke proudly agrees with Molyneux that he would *not*, and that *inference* from the visual data would be required to finally make the distinction. This shows that for Locke the idea of felt-sphericity is functionally distinct from the idea of seen-sphericity, and is an indication of just how simple – where again *simple* means either unanalyzable into component parts or phenomenologically homogeneous – simple ideas or mental atoms are for him. More specifically, by affirming that sight alone provides sensations of color and light, the man's need of experience to discover that patterns of color and light indicate the shape of objects at various distances from the eyes illustrates his lack of innate ideas. As normal adults we habitually and without notice make judgments of shape and distance based on color and light, but cases like Molyneux's show that we can only explain our tactile sensations by appeal to the sense of touch.

Perception begins to stock our minds with these ideas. Through reflection we acquire other ideas. Various other mental operations expand what we can think. Initially Locke seems to countenance four other basic operations. There's *retention*, which takes two forms: *contemplation*, which keeps something in view for some time, and *memory*, which is recollection in our contemporary sense. There's *discerning* or *distinguishing*, the perceiving of two ideas to be the same or different, which is basic to reason and judgment. There's *comparison* of one idea with another in respect of extent, degree, time, place, or any other circumstance. And there's *composition*, whereby simple ideas from sensation or reflection are put together into complex ones. Later he discusses two mental operations whose relation to the original list is debatable. One is co-presence without unity, leading to ideas of relations. Perhaps this results from contemplation and comparison operating jointly, or sustained perception and comparison, and may involve discerning. The second, notorious operation is *abstraction*, which in its basic usage means separating ideas from all other ideas that accompany them in their real existence. Since abstraction is the means by which all general ideas are made, and general ideas are pivotal to philosophical and scientific thought, successors such as Berkeley and Hume had much to say about the status of Lockean abstraction. Both thought that, unlike the other stock of mental operations, abstraction as Locke conceived it introduced a kind of indirectness and indeterminateness of thought which spawned nonsense.

Locke aims to show that all our ideas have their origins in these empirically verifiable processes. His purports to be a descriptively accurate account. Obscure innatism is unnecessary. Developmental psychology suffices. Three especially interesting test cases of this optimism are ideas of power, substance, and identity, familiar rationalist favorites. Locke develops his account of power in II.21. He develops his account of substance in II.23. And he offers his formative account of identity in II.27. Let us explore them in turn.

3.4   Test Case One: Thinking about power

Active power is the ability to make change; *passive power* is the ability to receive change. Physical action is *motion*; mental action is *thought*. *Will* is the mind's power to consider or refrain from considering any of its ideas, or prefer a particular motion of one's body. Willing (= *volition*) is the exercise of the power. If and only if a human being does what she wills to do, she acts (mentally or physically) *voluntarily*. But voluntary agency does not ensure free agency. *Liberty* or *freedom* requires more. So far as one can act *or* not act (think or not think, move or not move) in accordance with one's volition (choosing, preferring), so far is one free or at liberty. When an agent is not at liberty, she is under *necessity*. Beings without thought, so without volition, are altogether necessary agents. Freedom of action requires freedom of thought (if what brings about the action is necessitated, the action is necessitated), but not vice versa (consider a paralyzed person). Locke's claim is that experiencing actions gives us the ideas of the various kinds of *power*. In the end, he traces the source of liberty to the mind's power to suspend satisfaction and consider competing desires, or good and evil results, long- as well as short-term. And the ideas of good and evil themselves have their origin in the simple ideas of pleasure and pain. Conformable to his empiricism, he adopts a hedonistic theory of motivation and value (II.20.1–3).

Locke says many challenging things within this framework. For example, he notes that since both will and freedom are powers, we ought not ask whether the will is free, for that involves attributing power to a power, which is nonsense. But it is his derivation of the idea of power from the experience of action, and its exemplification in his warning not to confuse the voluntary with the free, that most pointedly invites critical assessment of his project. So, for example, he seems right to insist that if a man, transported while asleep to a locked room containing an old friend, were upon awakening to choose to stay and chat, he would then be a voluntary agent (doing then what he wants to do), but not a free agent (since he could not leave if he then wanted to). But this highlights the *methodological* question of how the idea of freedom, and more acutely, how knowledge of freedom, can be explained empirically. He partly anticipates Hume when suggesting that the idea of power arises from experience of regular patterns of change, which spawns expectations of recurrence, and then the thought that in one thing there is the possibility of being changed, and in another the possibility of making that change. But even repeatedly observing my desire to do X followed by my doing X does not uncontroversially give us the idea of voluntariness as we intuitively understand it. And freedom requires in addition the experiential genesis of *could have done otherwise*. What's the experiential basis for that? And supposing the *idea* were derivable from recollections of past occasions when I did do otherwise when I was so inclined, etc., how could any of that allow me to *know*, now or on any of those past occasions, that when I did what I wanted, I could under *those* circumstances have done otherwise?

If Locke means to explain the full-blooded idea of freedom as self-determination or spontaneity as found in a rationalist like Descartes, these objections seem serious. But I suspect his claims are, as usual, more modest. I read him as embracing a practically innocuous, theoretical skepticism. Sketching this reading provides opportunity also to say something about Locke's conceptions of mind (spirit) and body (matter), and to transition to II.23 on substance, where conjoined with II.1, IV.3.6, and IV.10.9–19 the richest remarks on mind and body occur.

Locke accepts a mind–body dualism, but conceives neither mind nor body quite like Descartes does, and doubts the metaphysical implications that Descartes drew from dualism. Descartes argued that extension is the whole essence of body, necessary and sufficient for being a body. Locke holds that extension is insufficient, and defines body as an extended, *solid* (meaning impenetrable, not hard) substance, *capable of communicating motion by impulse*. Descartes argued that thinking is the whole essence of finite mind. Locke holds that actual thinking is neither necessary nor sufficient, and defines mind as a thing *capable of thinking and of moving the body by will*. Thinking is to mind not as extension is to body, but as motion is to body; a body is always extended, but not always in motion. Minds cannot move but can initiate movement in body. Bodies cannot initiate movement but can transfer movement which they already have.

But imbuing Locke's discussions is confession that neither the power of thought nor the power to initiate movement is *comprehensible* – for example, since minds are conceived as lacking solidity, we cannot understand how they move bodies – but that's poor reason to deny the *reality* of either; *experience* shows us that mind *does* affect body. This lack of comprehensibility opens up for Locke all sorts of anti-Cartesian possibilities. For example, for all we know, a material thing could be immortal and an immaterial thing could be mortal. God could make matter persist forever in an afterworld just as he created it from the beginning. Granted sheer everlasting persistence isn't immortality, which also requires having thoughts. But for all we know, matter might think. We *could* be material. But the important point is that even if we are material, and are governed like the rest of nature by the laws of the developing mechanical science, we are not committed to atheism, because the careful study of that nature, whatever its underlying essence, shows that an immaterial God exists. (Locke uses a kind of design argument, discussed in section 6.11.) Philosophy cannot establish immortality. Only revelation can.

So applying this cognitive modesty to power, Locke insists that we definitely cannot get a *clear* idea of active power by external sense perception, for example, by seeing colliding billiard balls causing each other to move, because in those cases movement is not *produced*, but only *transferred*. A *better* source of the idea of motion production is reflection on our minds' effects on our bodies (II.21.4). But neither the transfer of motion nor our ability to initiate motion is well-understood. (For Descartes, the first but not the second can be well-understood. As we will see in the next chapter, for Leibniz, no form of communication of motion can be well-understood. Indeed, for Leibniz, the communication of motion never occurs; it is nonsense, requiring properties of the relation between the two objects that are not properties of either object individually.)

3.5   Test Case Two: Thinking about substance

Let's begin by retrieving Locke's distinction between modes, relations, and substances (II.12), and by recognizing that like Descartes he considers modes dependent on substances but unequivocally treats *individual* substances as distinct things subsisting by themselves. But here we have to detect a subtle distinction to appreciate the coherence of Locke's position (and, I might add, to better fathom Berkeley's distress with Locke). It is the distinction between being a mode qua mode, and being a mode qua relation. Think about the account of qualities Locke offered in II.8. Although he consequentially distinguished primary from secondary qualities, physical structures from the powers to affect us that those structures exhibit, I argued that he identified neither kind of quality with an idea – we have ideas *of* primary and secondary qualities. But qualities for Locke, certainly at least secondary qualities, are modes. Qua modes, they are not ideas or subjective sensations. But secondary qualities such as colors, tastes, sounds, and odors *as we sense them* are modes qua relations; they are partly constituted by their relation to us, for example, our perceptual mechanisms and changing conditions of perception. Qua relation, they *are* ideas. Hence we relieve the tension between II.8's realistic account of qualities and Locke's treatment of modes as ideas in our current II.23. *Usually* hereafter Locke fails to press any distinction between modes and ideas of modes, and this is crucial for understanding why he thinks we can genuinely know the objects of mathematics and morality, but not the substances which constitute the natural world, studied by empirical science.

How does he conceive such substances? The ideas of substances are compound ideas that include both ideas of a number of qualities, and the confused and obscure idea of Substance or substratum. In experience we notice a set of sensible qualities "going constantly together" which we "presume to belong to one thing." We readily identify such substances by their qualities, or causal powers, but contra Descartes, do not know well the inner structure on which the qualities depend. Still, we insist on supposing the substratum, as needed to support the qualities; we do not conceive things as mere bundles of qualities. To *support* qualities is not to *have* them. Substratum does not have properties, but the properties *inhere* in it. Further, as I read Locke, only some of a substance's qualities are supposed to subsist in its substratum, namely only those supposed to result from the arrangement of the corpuscles of the matter constituting the substance. So substance (used now as a mass term designating stuff like "water," not a count noun (enabling counting) like "an ounce of water") is not a featureless substratum but the universal matter of the burgeoning corpuscular hypothesis of the new scientists.

So is Locke's concept-empiricism up to the task of explaining the idea of substance, an idea Descartes argued was essentially not derived from experience, but innate? If Locke agreed with Descartes that we have a clear and distinct idea of substance, then that would be an idea whose origins cannot be explained empirically, and Locke's method would be shown to be inadequate. But I take Locke to deny the existence of such an idea. The idea of substance with which we actually operate is less penetrating, and it even has a component, namely the idea of substratum, which challenges empiricism. But empiricism plausibly can meet that challenge through the new mechanical science. The way it meets the challenge, however, virtually precludes the possibility that we could have knowledge of natural substances, could discern necessary connections between them and the empirical properties we perceive. I will explain this limitation in section 3.8.

3.6 Test Case Three: Thinking about identity

Locke's treatment of the third selected test case, personal identity, remains justly formative for ongoing discussions today, so I devote more space to it. He builds up to his position by first providing general resources for exploring questions about identity, and then proposing identity-conditions for perhaps less perplexing sorts of things. Here's how his presentation unfolds.

First, some conceptual distinctions, using my own vocabulary: To *individuate* an entity is to single out that entity, differentiating it from others. To *classify* an entity is to place it in a class, describe it as being of a certain kind or sort. To *reidentify* an entity is to individuate an entity as numerically the same at different times.

Second, some principles, affirmed by Locke:

1　If X and Y are numerically (strictly) identical, they can be classified the same, but not vice versa; so if X = Y, then if X is F, Y is F, and vice versa, but things of the same sort need not be the very same thing.
2　Identity is a transitive relation; that is, if X = Y and Y = Z, then it follows logically that X = Z.
3　Two things of the same kind can't exist in the same place at the same time.
4　One thing can't exist at different places at the same time.
5　One thing can't have two (spatiotemporal) beginnings of existence (from 4).
6　Two things can't have one (spatiotemporal) beginning of existence (from 3).

Third, the application of the principles to important kinds of things in preparation for the account of personal identity: There are three sorts or kinds of *substances*: *God*, *finite* intelligences or *spirits*, and *bodies*. Since God is eternal, unchangeable, and everywhere, there's no confusing him with anything else – there can't be two Gods, by the above principles. (But how do we positively individuate God on Locke's principles? Can there be one God on the above? What about principle 4? We need a definition of "place.") The identity over time (reidentity) of a finite spirit is determined by some kind of continuity relation from the start of its existence (to be fleshed out with respect to personal identity, since persons turn out to be finite spirits). And so with parcels of matter or masses: they strictly persist if continuous and without quantitative change. If you allow two parcels of matter simultaneously in the same place, all bodies may be in the same place, and identity–diversity relations collapse. *Modes* and *relations* of substances (motions and thoughts) are momentary existents, not continuants like substances, and so each temporally distinguishable one, having a different beginning of existence, is numerically distinct. A *living body*, vegetable or animal, is not the same as a mass of matter, and their identity conditions are not the same. A living body is a coherent organization of parts, partaking of a common life. The identity of *man* is the same as (or just includes as a prerequisite?) the identity of a living animal body of a certain (human) form.

Fourth, the focal debate: Locke holds that different sorts of things have different criteria of identity. So to determine the criterion of personal identity, we must know what (sort of thing) a person is. There are two main interpretations of Locke's overall view on identity. On one, Locke holds that there is no unambiguous analysis of the concept of identity, that the question "Is X the same as Y?" is nonsense as it stands, since incomplete, requiring filling out through specification of the respect in which identity is alleged to hold, the sort (mass, vegetable, man, person) involved. So there's no meaning to "identity" *simpliciter*, but there are multiple notions of identity, each with a different definition. This has come to be called the *relative identity thesis*. On the second interpretation, Locke accepts a univocal, absolute *analysis* of identity, namely X = Y if every property of X is a property of Y, and vice versa, but demands different tests or *criteria* for determining identity for different sorts of things. In either case, you cannot in practice answer questions about identity without specifying what sorts of things you're wondering about. Reidentification is logically connected to counting, and note how baffled you would be if someone asked you, "How many things are in the room?" You wouldn't know how to proceed, because you wouldn't know how to individuate things without some guiding classification. For example, qua desk, the item before you may be one thing, but qua atoms, it may be billions of things.

Let's consider one historically recurrent example, which I adapt slightly. Consider a venerable, wooden Ship of Theseus, transporting cargo of aluminum planks. In transit, a rotten wooden plank in the hull allows leakage; conveniently enough, it's replaced by an aluminum one. Unfortunately, other original planks go bad, and in each case are replaced by new aluminum ones, but all the original material is kept on board. A ship now reaches port, of the same shape, with the same crew, but now constituted entirely by different material. Soon the wooden planks are reconnected in their original relations to each other, and the result is placed in the local maritime museum. Question: Which, if either, is the Ship of Theseus? The aluminum ship at port? The wooden ship in the museum? Neither? (Given Locke's principles, it seems that we can rule out that both are identical to the Ship of Theseus. Two things can't at the same time be identical with one thing.)

Note that different philosophies seem to imply different answers. If a substance is always an (Aristotelian) informed parcel of matter, then it's the wooden ship, and in any event is not the aluminum ship. If *strict* spatiotemporal continuity is always a requirement of reidentity and there are no scattered objects (objects have to have some internal unity), then perhaps it's the aluminum ship, and in any event is not the wooden ship, etc. At the beginning of the *Essay* Locke announces he is not concerned with metaphysics. So it is natural to suppose his own response is not driven by any antecedent metaphysical theory (that he is a philosophical-method empiricist). Indeed, he resists an unequivocal answer. If by "ship" one means something that serves a certain function, say allows the sailors to do a certain job, the answer is the aluminum ship. But given different interests, for example the interests of an historical preservationist, the answer would be different. There is no, single correct answer. If this reading is right, Locke gives signs of being a forefather of pragmatism as well as empiricism, something that would be applauded by current thinkers who argue that the only consistent empiricism is a form of pragmatism. These general signs seem supported in his payoff discussion of personal identity.

Locke says that what constitutes personal identity depends on what it is to be a person. And he proposes that a person is "a thinking intelligent being, that has reason and reflection, and can consider itself as itself, the same thinking thing, in different times and places; which it does only by that consciousness which is inseparable from thinking" (II.27.9). Given this conception, he rightly draws several conclusions, for example, that a person is not the same thing as a human being, since being human requires having a living body of a certain form, but being a person does not. As we might say nowadays, *human* is a biological category, *person* is not. So a rational parrot might be a person, but could not be a human.

The really crucial question is, what is the status of Locke's proposed conception of person? His answer is that *person* is a *forensic* term, a term suitable to courts of judicature or to public discussion and debate. He is proposing a way of conceiving people so that they are properly held responsible, are treated justly, etc. This has nothing to do with whether or not they have some intangible soul, or a well-formed or monstrous body, but has everything to do with their state of mind, what they can be made to own up to, etc. At bottom, Locke's philosophical interests are largely practical, here, on the issue of personal identity, as well as elsewhere, throughout his writings. For example, what drives his earlier-sketched approach to liberty is the desire to conceive a viable social order (too).

To treat an account as practical and not logical or metaphysical is not to insulate it from criticism. And Locke's deeply interesting criterion of personal identity does raise concerns. When he elaborates his meaning, it becomes pretty clear that "consciousness extending backwards," or memory, is the central condition of personal identity. So let's compactly formulate his perspective as follows: X at time1 is the same person as Y at time2 just in case X is a person at time1, Y is a person at time2, and Y at time2 can remember what X did, thought, etc. at time1. But what does this mean? There are at least two senses of "can:" "can without contradiction" and "can in fact." There are at least two senses of "remember:" "seem to recall" or "claim to remember" – which does not guarantee the event happened – and "truly remembers." So we have at least four permutations for interpreting Locke's criterion. But "can without contradiction seem to recall" is far too broad; every person at time2 could be the same as X at time1 on that account! And "can without contradiction truly remember" is obviously correct, but provides no usable test for determining to whom the description applies. And "can in fact seem (perhaps erroneously) to recall" could lower the boom on lots of innocents – even if from the first-personal point of view someone feels responsible, perhaps due to a pathological guilty conscience, that's not enough in a decent legal system to decide that he's really responsible.

So the best candidate seems to be "can in fact truly remember." But some may dismiss that as too liberal. If others saw me (my body) at the scene of the crime, they'd say I shouldn't be exempt from liability just because I can't remember being there. Perhaps. But as I read Locke, he disagrees. As dramatically instanced in the case of amnesia, we should *not* punish a true (and not feigned) amnesiac for deeds caused by his body. Minimally, we should distinguish "can in fact readily remember" and "can with the most effective prodding remember." The former demand is too strong, and would let too many of the guilty off the hook. But the latter reflects the best practices of a compassionate society; if I sincerely can't be brought to acknowledge myself as the source of some bad behavior, that behavior is not (forensically) *mine*. I may warrant treatment, but not punishment. I am not responsible; I am not able-to-respond.

I am not taking sides, just focusing the debate. Of course, some think there are undebatable refutations of Locke's criterion. The most famous is Thomas Reid's. Locke rightly insists on the transitivity of identity. But suppose an old general remembers taking a battle flag into his first campaign as a young officer, and that the young officer remembers corporal punishment as a lad by his father, but that the old general cannot (be made to) remember the punishment. Then the young boy is identical with the young officer, and the young officer is identical with the old general, but the young boy is not identical with the old general. This absurdly violates transitivity. Does Locke have an answer?

One last example, designed to impugn the intuitions behind Locke's outlook.[1] Suppose you have two especially dominant characteristics. You are profoundly averse to pain and you are a monumental cheapskate. You require major, lengthy surgery. Normal procedure (including general anesthesia) will cost you six months' pay. But your doctor gives you a cost-saving option. For a week's pay, right before she takes up her scalpel, you will be

---

1   I believe that the thrust of this counterexample was conveyed to me in person by Roderick Chisholm in 1972, but it's been so long that I'm not certain.

given an amnesia-inducing drug, which will expunge all memories to that point. Then, for the next five hours, the body (so-described so as not to beg any questions about identity) on the operating table will be cut to its quick, but no painkillers will be used. Then, after the body is sewn up, another drug is administered which blots memories of the previous five hours, but restores memories of pre-surgery life, so only the five hours are irrevocably lost. Then care proceeds standardly, with post-op painkillers. Question: Which alternative do you choose? Claim: On Locke's view, you without hesitation should save twenty-five weeks' pay and select the unusual option. But you would at least struggle with the decision, and probably cough up that money you cherish so much to avoid the sustained agony *you* would otherwise experience. Even though recollections and anticipations of suffering increase total suffering, one can suffer deplorably without them. Our intuitions go against Locke. Or so Locke's critic avers. What do you think? How, if at all, would your thinking differ if during the five hours excruciating pain sensations occurred at every moment, but earlier ones were forgotten as successors took their place?

3.7   *Essay* Book III: Expressing thought in language

Some read Book III, especially its first two chapters, as offering a theory of meaning. Their story goes something like this. There are four predominant theories of meaning.

- Referential theories state that a linguistic expression's meaning is either the non-linguistic, mind-independent thing it either does, or is intended to stand for or refer to, or some specifiable relation between the expression and its referent.
- Behavioral theories identify a sign's meaning with some theoretically observable feature(s) of the body or behavior of transmitting or receiving organism.
- Use theories explicate meaning either in terms of expressions' use or rules for governing use.
- Ideational theories state that an expression's meaning is the idea which accompanies its use. One version is the imagistic theory, on which the ideas are images.

They then argue that just like Descartes, Locke is offering an ideational theory, on which a word's meaning is always a direct object of consciousness, while the word's referent is often an indirect object of consciousness; and, since he is an empiricist, for whom thought is ultimately a function of sensation, quite unlike Descartes, he is probably committed to imagism. Also, whereas Descartes construed ideas as both mental occurrences and mental dispositions (as with innate ideas), Locke restricts ideas to occurrences.

They then often level lots of objections: Many people lack imagery yet understand adequately. Many expressions, such as abstract terms, don't have images associated with them. Much of an image's content is irrelevant to the meaning function. Images themselves don't have meaning, but must be interpreted, so this "solution" to the problem of meaning just pushes the problem one step back. Since images are private, one person couldn't convey them to another, or know that sufficient imagistic similarity occurs, rendering successful communication impossible. The theory is unscientific, since scientific theories must be verifiable or falsifiable, but the occurrence of private images is neither.

Others read Locke as offering a theory of communication, not a theory of meaning. Language is a system for communicating information about ourselves, our physical and social environments, etc., and also serves other purposes of communication, such as greeting, intimidating, questioning, etc. Our natural, human languages seem to have some especially interesting characteristics. They are stimulus-independent: in most circumstances, no description of a person's physical environment suffices to predict his next utterance, and people don't exhibit a small, fixed repertoire of signals in relation to responses (like birds), nor inflexible but graded responses (like bees). They involve abstraction: we can focus on one detail in abstraction from others, and talk about more or less general classes or kinds of things. They are largely arbitrary: linguistic symbols usually have no intrinsic or necessary connection with what they refer to or convey. They are medium-independent: the same linguistic messages typically can be conveyed through a wide variety of media. They are productive or creative: the matching of signal and meaning is not learned case by case, but rather we seem to learn elements and rules enabling the generation of indefinite novelty. By dint of such characteristics, language is immensely powerful: it can deal with the past, the future, the absent, an enormous range of topics, etc. How can language express thought, and such an extensive range of thought?

This, I agree, is Locke's primary concern, with special focus on the function of language in philosophical and scientific inquiry. Successful communication of thought does not require identity of thought content, does not require replication of ideas from speakers' to hearers' minds, or knowledge based on intersubjective comparison of ideas. To understand what you intend, I need not see things just as you do. It is enough that I can imagine what I would see were I in your perceptual situation. And my ability to conceive things is a function of my recognitional capacities, which is a function of my knowing how such things appear to me. Non-vacuous conception is a function of what's imaginable, and whatever can be perceived, can be imagined. So, Locke seems to be saying, thought ultimately consists in having ideas of imagination, and language's primary purpose is to communicate or express one's person's thought to another. Hence, Locke is an influential proponent of the thought-precedes-language tradition that dominated the modern period, and which became especially widely contested in the second half of the twentieth century. But I think it's important to note how measured his version of this doctrine is. Although basic uses of language are wholly expressions of ideas in minds, he seems not only to allow, but insist, that only competent language users can form various highly complex ideas. For example, having language extends our memories, and so allows the formation of ideas that require extended memory, such as the crucial idea of personhood discussed earlier.

Whether he is offering a theory of communication or a theory of meaning, Locke makes an especially influential contribution with his account of names of kinds of substances – general terms which apply to each and all of the members of a kind – such as "gold." This account pairs up nicely with his just-discussed treatment of identity in Book II, especially by way of his distinction between real and nominal essences. He already has argued that our ideas of kinds of substances are complex ideas consisting of a collection of observable powers and qualities together with the idea of substance in general, or substratum. Now he argues that substance-names signify the complex idea of the sort of substance with which the name is associated. He calls this complex idea the substance's *nominal essence*, and crucially argues that nominal essences are "the workmanship of the understanding," by which at bottom he means a function of human agreement and convention. Of course we construct our ideas of kinds of substances based on observed similarities and regularities, but there are richly many similarities and regularities to be found in nature, and which ones are selected for inclusion in the nominal essence depends on human needs and interests, and sometimes, historical accident.

Locke contrasts nominal with *real essence*, "the very being of anything, whereby it is what it is," its "real, internal constitution" on which its properties depend (III.3.15). The Aristotelians, who the new scientists aim to supplant, identify real essence with substantial form. The new scientists identify real essence of a body with its microphysical constitution: the sizes, shapes, motions, locations, and relative situations of the body's solid parts. Although Locke deems the latter conception vastly superior – indeed he denies that we can even make sense of substantial forms – he argues through counterexamples in III.6 that the natural kinds into which substances are classified have no adequate basis in the real nature of things on either conception. The lessons he draws about our sorting of things into kinds are: that we have no access to real essences, so in practice all we can appeal to are the manifest or sensible qualities and powers of things; disagreements about classification are resolved by decision, not factual discovery; and specifically, there is no difference in how words for kinds of artifact and words for kinds of natural object function – classificatory disputes are managed in precisely the same ways.

In sum, we have no adequate basis for saying that our classifications accurately depict the divisions, if any, carved out by nature itself.

This is an epistemic, not metaphysical conclusion. He is not denying that there are pre-classificatory, real divisions in nature, or real essences as conceived by the corpuscular hypothesis. The conclusion is that our classificatory practices, as exemplified in our use of kind names, provide no grounds for asserting that there are joints in nature, identifiable by species–essences, however conceived.

Interestingly, Locke does go further, and seems to argue that however we treat *species*, there is nothing that is essential to an *individual* (III.6.4), and here the connection to his discussion of identity is most transparent. He embraces the intuition that the individual John Locke can persist as the very same individual despite losing properties we take to be necessary for him to be a human being (organized life), or a person (reason and memory), or any other sort of thing. And he reminds us that we count any quality or power of a thing as essential only relative to a nominal essence. "Person," "human being," etc. signify merely nominal essences too. Since nominal essences are products of agreement and convention given needs and interests, the so-called essential properties of individuals, which they never have qua individuals, but always qua members of whatever species they fit into given our pragmatically grounded classificatory scheme, are products of agreement and convention as well.

Hence, we get the striking conclusion that even real essences are *essences* only by reference to nominal essences – the empiricism and pragmatism go all the way down! Again, real essence is defined as what makes something what it is. This in turn is construed as the causal basis in the object of the qualities and powers which ground the proper sorting of the object. But which qualities and powers those are is determined by the nominal essence of the species. Real essences count as essences only because the nominally determined qualities and powers are considered those which cause the object to have its nominally essential properties. As usual, Locke shuns affirmative metaphysics.

3.8   *Essay* Book IV: Knowledge and opinion

With the discussions of substances, modes, and essences in hand, Book IV fulfills Locke's stated purpose of determining the nature and extent of knowledge, and the nature and grounds of the forms of assent that fall short of knowledge. He defines knowledge as the perception of the connection and agreement, or disagreement and repugnancy of any of our ideas (IV.1.2). He allows three different ways of achieving knowledge: by intuition, by demonstration, and by sense perception of a particular thing. With regard to what really exists, like Descartes, he holds that we can have knowledge of our own existence by intuition, knowledge of God's existence by demonstration, and access to anything else with a much lower degree of certainty only by sense perception. At least verbally unlike Descartes, he counts sense perception of a particular thing as certain enough to count as knowledge. (I say "verbally" because he would agree with Descartes that it doesn't count as *scientia*.) On the other hand, he does allow the *possibility* of demonstrative knowledge of universal propositions asserting *connections between* qualities and powers of bodies, and thus, the possibility of the new corpuscular theorist attaining *scientia* by wholly naturalistic methods. Still, given the modesty of *our* cognitive capacities, the limits on *our* ability to discriminate things by the senses (even when extendable through technology), and *our* irremediable inability even to conceive *how* the mechanistic features of bodies induce sensory ideas in the mind, he expects so little real success in pursuit of natural *scientia* (and he has long since dismissed the project of *a priori scientia*), that he encourages instead wholehearted pursuit of achievable, useful, probabilistic science.

Notice, finally, that Descartes himself, in the Sixth Meditation and elsewhere, insisted that we could not distinctly conceive the action of body on mind (or vice versa), so could not formulate physico-psychological (or psycho-physical) laws, so could not have a *scientia* of human perception (or physically efficacious willing). We feel such connections, but cannot do better than assign them to the benevolent will of God. Locke makes a similar point (IV.3.28–9), but ultimately is even more pessimistic about understanding mind–body relations. Descartes argued that we know that mind essentially thinks and cannot be spatially extended, and body is essentially extended and cannot think. Since Locke holds that we cannot know the real essence of either mind or body, he allows the possibility that matter can think (IV.3.6). But, anti-metaphysician that he is, he dismisses Descartes' inference from conceptual disparity to real distinctness. It is as easy to suppose that omnipotent God could attach the power of thought to a system of matter as to suppose that he adjoins it to an immaterial substance. More aptly, we don't know what either alternative amounts to. (Recall the supporting discussion in section 3.4.) The huge difference between Descartes and Locke here is that such metaphysical ignorance would profoundly dismay Descartes – if it were as thoroughgoing as Locke proposes, his very belief in God would be shaken – whereas Locke is unfazed. One shouldn't complain about lack of superpowers when one has enough to attain what matters. As he announced at the *Essay*'s start, "The Candle, that is set up in us, shines bright enough for all our Purposes" (I.1.5).

In Locke's strict usage, *knowledge* and *judgment* (opinion, assent) are mutually exclusive. *Knowledge* is ultimately based on intuition. Appeal to intuition is Locke's way to account for self-evidence or obviousness without postulating innatism. A proposition is self-evident when the ideas in it are such that the mind can directly perceive a connection between them. Crucially, this for Locke is an intrinsic or internal fact about the proposition, not some extrinsic or external feature of the proposition in relation to the mind (such as God's implanting it at birth), which is how he interprets innatism. He thinks that there are many obvious propositions that are not even supposed by rationalists to be innate, such as that red is not blue. (Look back to the discussion of Descartes' Fifth Meditation to decide whether he portrays innatism fairly.)

The only other way to acquire knowledge in the strictest sense is by demonstration, where the perception of connection is not immediate, but involves a chain of intermediate ideas. But each step of the chain must be intuited.

In contrast, one *judges* something to be true when ideas that are not manifestly connected are nevertheless presumed to be connected on the basis of considerations external to those ideas (IV.15.3). There are degrees of assent (IV.16), for example, belief, conjecture, guess, doubt, wavering, distrust, disbelief, etc. Degree of assent ought to be regulated by probability of truth (a form of *evidentialism*). Probability of truth is based on personal experience and testimony of others, and, with respect to judgments about what's unobservable, cautious analogical reasoning with what we do observe. But while opinion is never certain, assurance, the highest degree of assent, governs our thoughts and regulates our actions as fully as knowledge does. We then think our opinions are past doubt. Assurance is psychologically but not logically equivalent to knowledge. Further, it is psychologically true that neither knowledge nor assent is in our power (IV.20.16). But we are indirectly responsible for what we know or assent to because we are responsible for the ways in which we inquire – where we look, how hard we look, and so on.

Locke's account of assent, especially his evidentialism, which he takes to be the only reliable sign that an inquirer is a lover of truth, underlies his commitment to toleration (IV.16.4). He argues that it is reasonable to accept the Bible as revealed, but scripture should be interpreted critically, recognizing that it was transcribed by human beings under contingent socio-historical circumstances, and rejecting what's incompatible with what's naturally evident as being corrupted true revelation. The main reason to accept Christ's teaching, which is primarily moral teaching, is that it is reasonable. And only reason ought to be the final arbiter for determining whether some personal religious experience is immediate, divine illumination or utterly ungrounded, perhaps idiosyncratic, imaginings, which Locke calls *enthusiasm* (IV.19). Like innatism, enthusiasm threatens to oppress.

We are now in a position to understand his optimism about moral science despite his pessimism about natural science. Given his robust conception of knowledge, if we mean by "skepticism" doubts about the possibility of knowledge, Locke is skeptical in many arenas. For example, if I'm not now perceiving other men, I don't know that there are other men in the world, since I only know that X exists when I see it. And I can't know that stones won't nourish me, since we can't penetrate into the real essence of substances, and we can't know about anything which has a real essence that is hidden from us. I can't know whether a mere material being can think, or how primary qualities produce ideas of secondary qualities, etc. And yet we *can* have demonstrative knowledge of morality and politics. Why?

The answer is that the materials of moral (and political) theorizing are ideas such as those of human actions and institutions; these are ideas of mixed *modes*; ideas of mixed modes arise through combination of unlike (non-homogeneous) simple ideas; such ideas can be formed properly without regard to what does or does not actually exist; the unity of mixed modes is essentially conceptual or mind-conferred (III.5.10), and so, reintroducing Locke's crucial distinction from Book III, we can know the real essence of such modes, know what they really are, precisely because with them there is no difference between nominal essence, the marks we use to identify our entity, and real essence, the underlying constitution which makes the thing what it is, and from which its empirical, identifying features flow. Recall by contrast that our idea of a substance is always of a non-ideational *thing* possessing certain qualities, and the set of qualities or nominal essence of the substance by which we identify it is *not* identical with its real essence, best construed as its corpuscular structure. With modes, real and nominal essences are always the same. With substances, real and nominal essences are always different (III.3.18).

So the only universal propositions about substances that are certain are *trifling*, never *instructive*. Substantive scientific knowledge, instructive apprehensions of necessary connections, is possible precisely because their objects are constructed by us. Mathematics and ethics deal hypothetically with abstractions or ideal entities; the subject matter of mathematics and ethics are constructed by us. Natural science deals with real entities; its subject matter is not constructed by us. Therefore, there can be a science of mathematics and ethics, but, for us, not one of nature. To adopt a phrase that gained some currency, "genuine knowledge is maker's knowledge." And where we reach limits to human knowledge, where there are no perceivable necessary connections between relevant ideas, there we can only have probable opinion, and inquiry must be conducted by way of observation and experiment. And the benefits we enjoy from probable opinion, given our purposes and needs, make complaints about lack of knowledge unjustified. (How does this differ from Descartes?)

Finally, although Locke thinks a science of morality is possible, he does not think it is easy to develop. For him, moral law is divine law; morality is a function of God's will (II.28.8), and it is self-evident that we should obey his will. We can construct the idea of God from experience (II.23.33) and reason to his existence (IV.10.1), since we could not have come about by accident from chance arrangement of corpuscles. But working out in detail the relations between the ideas of the various modes which comprise our ethical concerns is exceedingly complicated.

3.9   Questions about Locke

1   Is perception, which is the original source of all ideas for Locke, active or passive for him? Give evidence, both textual and philosophic, for your answer. Consider how your decision influences other things Locke says (including his critique of appeals to innate ideas).

2 What is a simple idea for Locke? What is the relation between his criterion for simplicity, the claim that simple ideas are acquirable only by direct acquaintance with their objects, not by description, and the claim that they are not inventible, only discoverable? Can there be simple ideas? If so, can they only be acquired in the ways Locke insists, and do they generate all the rest of our (complex) ideas in the ways Locke traces? Must there be simple ideas? If so, why? Are Lockean simple ideas images (as Berkeley, in Chapter Five, will suppose)?

3 Is Locke a consistent idea-empiricist? Does he violate the strictures of empiricism in explaining the origin of some ideas in Book II such as extension, time, number (including unity), eternity, infinite space, good/evil, or God? And what precisely is his position on the idea of substance in general? If he countenances the idea of an underlying substratum, "I know not what," is he overtly retaining a non-empirical idea, an example of the very sort of rubbish he seeks to remove for the growth of the new experimental sciences?

4 What is at stake in the Molyneux problem, and is Locke's response to it defensible or not? How so? Is the debate a wholly empirical one?

5 Should we accept the distinction between primary and secondary qualities? Is it just a distinction of explanatory priority, or does it also have ontological import?

6 Can ideas such as power (necessity, obligation, etc.) be derived from experience? Can the reality of things such as power and obligation be known through experience? If so, how? If not, why not?

7 Is Locke's theory of liberty defensible? If there is a real difference between voluntary action and free action, what is the relation of each to moral responsibility? How does Locke's account of freedom relate to Descartes' and/or Spinoza's?

8 What role should mental as opposed to physical facts about an individual play in determining moral responsibility for present deeds? For past deeds? Discuss in terms of Locke's account of personal identity. And how should we construe Locke's "account" (the same could be asked of his account of freedom)? Is he aiming to elaborate an analysis of the true nature of personal identity (or freedom) that directly competes with and is arguably superior to earlier efforts, including Descartes' and Spinoza's, or is he abandoning their philosophical goals?

9 Are the conditions of persistence through time different for different sorts of things? Are sorts distinguishable by real essential differences, or only by human interests and decisions? What is the significance of answering one way rather than the other? Discuss in terms of Locke in isolation, or in relation to Descartes and/or Spinoza.

10 What is the role of the account of language in Book III? Does it really exemplify Locke's claim at the end of Book II that "there is so close a connection between Ideas and Words . . . that it is impossible to speak clearly and distinctly of our knowledge . . . without considering, first,

the Nature, Use, and Significance of Language?" Is it really essential to the *Essay*'s argument? Or, since words properly and immediately signify nothing but ideas, are words just conventions needed to communicate publicly, so that were we exploring the book's issues as private meditators, we'd beneficially dispense with potentially misleading words?

11   In III. 3, "Of General Terms" – presumably important because for Locke most of our knowledge consists of *general* propositions – Locke provides an account of the process *abstraction* by which we form general ideas. Later empiricists like Berkeley and Hume argued that this account is highly consequentially wrong. Support or criticize the account. Or ask yourself whether the account is even independently all that important for Locke, or whether it is just a prelude to his crucial distinction between real and nominal essences, which in turn prepares for the discussion of the science of nature in IV, as part of the rubbish-removal of the real essences of the passé Scholastics, and positively as an account of classification according to which the sorting of things is the work of the understanding.

12   When Locke in Book IV comes to fulfill his main goal of developing an account of the nature, scope and limits of human knowledge and reason-able opinion, he seems to many surprisingly non-empiricist. For example, his definition of knowledge as the perception of the agreement (entailment?) or disagreement (incompatibility) of ideas; his restriction of the sources of knowledge to intuition and demonstration, and his offering God's existence as the only example of sensitive knowledge of the existence of particular external objects; his commitment to the demonstrative certainty of morality as well as mathematics, but not of any claims about physical objects; etc. may make him seem like a knowledge-rationalist. And when he explains the self-evidence of basic axioms by appeal to intuition, why isn't he agreeing with the innatists he rails against in Book I, and what was the point of the idea-empiri-cism of Book II? (Specifically, how is intuition Locke's alternative account of self-evidence that does not postulate innatism?) Is he just giving an empirical–psychological account of the origin of the material for thought, and so knowledge, but then a rationalistic theory of the *justification* of our claims?

13   What kind of skeptic is Locke? For example, he seems to hold that I only know that a body X exists when I see it, cannot know anything whose real essence we cannot penetrate, etc., yet thinks many things probable, even beyond reasonable doubt, and that we're in good shape when it comes to things that really matter to us. On other things the skepticism may go deeper: for example, whether a mere material being can think, or how primary qualities produce ideas of secondary qualities. And yet we can have demonstrative knowledge of something as chal-lenging as morality. And how can Locke justifiably say we know some

body X exists when we do see it? Doesn't he hold that we never immediately perceive bodies? Or not? For example, is his view perhaps that we do directly perceive bodies, but the way they appear to us depends in large part on facts of our sensory apparatus – that we do directly perceive the secondary qualities of physical objects, but not the corpuscular structuring on which these qualities depend? In general, is our knowledge best understood as answering theoretical demands or as answering the practical needs of everyday life?

14 Now that you have studied Locke, to which of the seven empiricist doctrines or attitudes introduced in section 3.1 do you think Locke conforms, and to which not?

3.10   Some recommended books

Aaron, R. (1971) *John Locke*, 3rd edn, Oxford: Clarendon Press.

Originally published in 1937, still regarded as a useful, general survey of Locke's philosophy.

Ashcraft, R. (ed.) (1991) *John Locke: Critical Assessments*, 4 vols, London: Routledge.

Extensive collection of good essays on Locke.

Ayers, M. (1991) *Locke: Epistemology and Ontology*, 2 vols, London and New York: Routledge.

Knowledgably clarifies the meaning and point of the main arguments of the *Essay* in the context of Locke's predecessors and contemporaries, and assesses its overall success, with some appeal to current theory.

Bennett, J. (1971) *Locke, Berkeley, Hume: Central Themes*, Oxford: Clarendon Press.

Engagingly relates the thinking of Locke, Berkeley, and Hume on the topics of meaning, causality, and objectivity, with attention to textual detail but not systematic rendition.

Chappell, V. (ed.) (1994) *The Cambridge Companion to Locke*, Cambridge: Cambridge University Press.

Informative chapters on Locke's theory of ideas, and philosophy of mind, body, language, knowledge, religion, morals, and politics.

Hall, R. and Woolhouse, R. (1983) *Eighty Years of Locke Scholarship*, Edinburgh: Edinburgh University Press.

Together with *The Locke Newsletter* and *Locke Studies*, which Hall edited from 1970–2000 and from 2000 on, respectively, an optimal source for those wishing to think in greater detail about Locke's work.

Jolley, N. (1999) *Locke: His Philosophical Thought*, Oxford: Oxford University Press.

Presents a unified picture of Locke's effort in the *Essay* to analyze the nature and limits of human knowledge.

Mackie, J.L. (1976) *Problems from Locke*, Oxford: Clarendon Press.

An interesting examination of selected issues from Locke's *Essay*: perception and primary and secondary qualities, substance and essence, abstract ideas and universals, identity (including personal identity) and diversity, and innate ideas.

Woolhouse, R.S. (1983) *Philosophers in Context: Locke*, Minneapolis: University of Minnesota Press.

Aims to highlight and explain some of the *Essay*'s main themes in the context in which they were developed, with some attention to their current philosophical relevance.

Yolton, J.W. (1970) *Locke and the Compass of Human Understanding*, Cambridge: Cambridge University Press.

Yolton has authored several books on Locke, but this one is most relevant to our purposes, notable in part for its argument that Locke is not an indirect realist. For good history of ideas, his (1956) *John Locke and the Way of Ideas*, Oxford: Clarendon Press, surveys many early responses to the *Essay*, explaining how controversial it was, construed as a challenge to ethical and religious orthodoxy, especially to universal natural law and conscience, and how his opponents attacked his theory of ideas as generating radical skepticism.

4 Leibniz

4.1 Background to Leibniz's philosophy

Many consider Gottfried Wilhelm Friedrich Leibniz (1646–1716) history's last universal genius, a walking encyclopedia of the already-known and inventor of the radically new who juggled so many ambitious projects that he designed a chair in which he could both sleep and work, so as not to waste a minute moving from one location to another when at home. He was an international diplomat who served German nobility and was employed at five European courts, a logician (the forefather of modern symbolic logic), a mathematician (inventor of the differential and integral calculus), a lawyer (constructing new legal codes after completing his law degree at age twenty), an historian and librarian (producing new cataloging methods), a scientist (prompting the transformation of physics through introduction of the need for irreducible forces), an inventor (coming close to developing the computer even though electronic circuitry did not yet exist; he did develop the binary mathematics of computers in which all numbers may be expressed as combinations of 1s and 0s), an engineer and practical planner (with ideas for health care, the economy, dam-construction, even a department store), and, of central concern for us, a profoundly influential philosopher and theologian who exchanged ideas with luminaries of his time, including the three pre-eminent thinkers who were inspired by but in different ways moved away from Descartes, namely Malebranche, Arnauld, and Spinoza. Whether or not he was the last person to master every field of available learning, he was undeniably a Renaissance man whose far-flung writings addressed to different sorts of audiences make his worldview difficult to sort out smoothly and comprehensively.

But we can begin this sorting by recognizing three core aspirations that drove Leibniz from the beginning of his intellectual life. First, he sought to unify people. Leibniz characteristically saw merit in ostensibly conflicting positions, often thought the conflict was based on ground-floor misunderstandings, and developed a system to enable integration. He sought to unify all European states, to unify inquirers who dismissed purposive explanations with those for whom they were vital, to unify insights from ancient and modern philosophies, to unify science and religion, and to unify religions, not only the Catholic and Protestant churches tightly, but even Christian doctrine and (Jewish) caballah more loosely. So, for example, you can better appreciate the structure of *Discourse on Metaphysics* (DM) by superimposing these reconciliationist aims. Whether or not Voltaire justifiably mocked Leibniz's optimism that this is the best possible world, we are right to see Leibniz struggling to work out fully his vision of a universal, cosmic harmony.

Second, and relatedly, he sought a universal, logically perfect, symbolic language (a *universal characteristic*) whose grammar would correspond to the logical structure of the world. Complex concepts in all areas would be reducible to more elementary ones, and eventually to simple (not further analyzable) ones; simples would be represented by mathematical symbols, which would form an alphabet of human thought; and then the correct rules for combining these symbols would be specified. On this scheme, truths of the world would be expressed by those sentences that conformed to this perfect or ideal logical language, and falsities would appear as ill-formed or ungrammatical combinations. Whenever people disagreed, they could congenially settle their disagreement by calculation using this adjudicatory tool.

Third, he sought to improve on the physics of his time, and succeeded in initiating the move away from the Cartesian science of matter. We can skip technical details here. The important point is that Leibniz's fundamental account of the world, his metaphysics, blossomed largely from these three enduring missions. Projects in physics, linguistics/logic, and theology all lead him to the same metaphysical conclusions. Science, philosophy, and traditional Christianity can be integrated by this single, comprehensive metaphysics. And from this metaphysics other sound philosophy purports to flow. For example, if the basic structure of the world is provably rationally intelligible, then our minds must have some innate structure that enables them to discover universal and necessary truths.

I've said that Leibniz seeks to reconcile the strengths and remedy the weaknesses of both Scholastic and mechanical philosophies, to integrate the supposedly incompatible purposive framework of religion with the mechanistic character of modern science. Even his earliest reflections show special motivation to solve three crucial components of this problem. First, what makes something, especially a human, a genuine, unique individual, and the same individual over time? This is the problem of *individuation*. Second, how can we preserve both God's foreknowledge and human free will? This is one of two great *labyrinths*, that of the human mind. Third, what is the status of continuous magnitude such as Cartesian matter (extension or spatial spread), which is infinitely divisible, so not composed of real individuals? This is the other great labyrinth, of *the composition of the continuum*.

Reconciliation risks incoherence. One could line up pairwise crucial Leibnizian theses and superficially encourage the verdict of incoherence. For example, he says that all created substances are connected, that there are no purely external relations (*extrinsic denominations*), that every substance expresses every other, and yet, that substances cannot causally interact, are windowless, and each substance is like a world apart. He says that a substance's nature includes *every* truth about it, and yet what happens to a substance is not always necessary, and people are sometimes free, and only God exists by his own nature. He says that God is necessarily metaphysically perfect but freely morally perfect, and yet this is the best possible world morally as well as metaphysically, and we can know that. He says that there are no souls without bodies, and yet body is just an appearance based on really existing souls. He says that substances are indivisible, and yet the infinitely divisible are based on them. He says that all of nature can be explained mechanically, by efficient causation, as the new scientists insist, and yet ultimately an appeal to purposes or final causes is necessary. He says that whatever is true is provable by analysis, and yet many analyses are infinite and so incompleteable, yet we can be certain of those truths anyway. He says that no two substances can be exactly alike, and yet there can and must be precisely similar mathematical objects such as triangles. He says that all substances perceive, and yet many are unconscious. As we proceed, I hope to indicate why Leibniz is a master tightrope walker, not someone who wants to have his cake and eat it.

Notice that these prima facie conflicts swirl around the concepts of universal understandability and substance. Like Spinoza, Leibniz approaches philosophical issues committed to the existence of complete explanations for all truths. This is his ground-floor *principle of sufficient reason*. He develops a theory of substance he judges powerful enough to solve uniquely all the problems of metaphysics. It is commonly called the *complete concept* theory of substance. He naturally seeks solution in a theory of *substance* because substance is the most fundamental metaphysical notion. It is supposed that truths about substance explain the other elements of one's metaphysics, but not vice versa. And true metaphysics gives a comprehensive, systematic, general account of reality in terms of which we can explain why in general the world appears to us the way it does, but not vice versa. So Leibniz embraces an *appearance–reality* distinction, and seeks as philosopher a true account of reality and the way that appearances are based on it. As against Spinoza, he uses his theory of individual substance to explain a universe in which there are not only a multiplicity of substances, but, necessarily, infinitely many substances. And he centrally insists that to determine what exactly an individual is, we must provide a metaphysically adequate account of the distinction between an individual and its properties, and specify the conditions under which an individual remains identical through change. These tasks largely drive Leibniz's highly original philosophizing.

So, in this chapter my aim is to help you understand, appreciate, and begin to evaluate Leibniz's overarching goals, guiding methods, and resulting central, systematically-developed positions and arguments, with focus on his mature metaphysics (beginning in 1686 with the *Discourse on Metaphysics* and related essays and correspondence, culminating in 1714 with his *Monadology*). Along the way we should glean some of the relations between his metaphysics and his philosophies of logic, mathematics, science, mind, knowledge, value and religion, and to sketch his connections to some crucial predecessors and contemporaries.

4.2   Overview of Leibniz's philosophy

I will soon provide maps for reading the *Discourse* and *Mondadology*, and then go more deeply into the core of his metaphysical views through discussion of the problem of freedom, but first I offer a synopsis of Leibniz's whole system, so as to prepare for selective detail. The system has three levels of explanation. There is the fundamental level of metaphysics, which specifies how things really are, as provable by reason. There is the account of the system of sense-observable appearances, *well-founded phenomena*, whose general nature is explicable in terms of level one, the way things really are. And there is the account of the basic ways in which we relate appearances systematically to one another, in terms of notions such as space, time, and motion, which are abstractions based on features in the second-level realm of appearances. Level one constitutes reality. Level two is not illusory, but has only a kind of derivative reality based on non-confused truth at level one. And the items at level three are not real but only *ideal*, mental constructions, useful glosses on how things are, based on relations among the ways they appear to us, but twice-removed from the way they really are.

Reality consists of an infinite number of individual substances, monads (units). One substance, God, is absolutely perfect, and exists necessarily. God has a perfectly rational understanding and a perfectly efficacious will. Nothing outside God constrains his will, but his will does conform to his own supreme understanding, which is essential to his nature. His understanding includes infinitely many possible creation-choices, possible worlds, complete histories of ways a world could be, each actualizable by his will. Since he is perfectly good, he chooses to create the best among the possible worlds. A world's value must be assessed globally, not with finite perspectival bias. Since everything is interconnected, with preconditions and consequences, it is naïve to degrade a world because some locally accessible part of it doesn't suit us optimally – we do not know what the system-wide repercussions of change would be. Also, things that are possible individually may not be possible jointly (*compossible*), so Spinoza's commitment to plenitude, that *all* possibilities are realized, is rationally indefensible, and complaints that God did not bring about *all* identifiable goods are equally logically confused.

Created monads have no parts that could exist independently of them, so lack Cartesian extension, so lack form and divisibility. So they cannot be constructed or destroyed, come into or go out of existence gradually, but can only begin through creation *ex nihilo* and end through instantaneous annihilation, if they end at all. So monads do not come to exist or perish at some stage in the unfolding of the world, but are all actualized exactly when the world is created, and since the world is not created in or at a pre-existing time (and why would an all-powerful God wait until a certain time to create what he eternally knows is best?), but on the contrary, time is an asymmetrical function of relations among natural phenomena, time could not exist unless created monads existed. Further, since they have no parts, if we think of change ultimately as rearrangement of parts, as the new, mechanical philosophers do, no monad's nature can be changed or affected by any other monad.

Although no monad has parts, each created monad goes through a continuous series of states, its *perceptions*. Each of a monad's perceptions *expresses* or *represents* all of its own preceding and succeeding states, and the states of all the other, infinitely many monads. This is the sense in which everything is interconnected. X expresses Y if and only if it is possible to derive, in a rule-governed or lawlike way, properties of Y from properties of X. So each perception of each monad completely expresses, more or less distinctly of course, all of reality. By knowing a single state of a single monad, God knows all the states of that and every other monad. Each created monad represents the same, whole world – *what* it perceives is infinite – but each suffers from some degree of confusion (indeed most perception is altogether unconscious), so none is omniscient like God. In sum, every monad *mirrors* or reflects every other monad, and so, the whole universe, from a certain point of view, but none causally affects any other as on the dominant conception of causation (*transeunt*, external, influx-of-modifications-from-one-thing-to-another) that Leibniz inherits and rejects; monads are "windowless" precisely because all their states continuously unfold according to their timeless, inner, God-recognized nature; the appearance of mutual influence among their states is the result of a pre-established harmony. This harmony too is entailed by God's choosing the best, and is manifested by a world which optimally combines richness in phenomena with maximal order through governance by the fewest, simplest laws.

Harmonious interconnection is exemplified in many ways, including in Newton's recognition that every body gravitationally affects every other body, no matter how small or far away. Since every monad is associated with a (its) body and all its bodily movements are divinely coordinated with its perceptions (thus solving Descartes' problem of mind–body interaction), each monad perceives all movements in the universe (again) more or less confusedly. Indeed, to perceive a body (level two) is really to perceive confusedly the components of a collection or aggregate of monads (level one); we perceive each real substance in the collection with some clarity – it is not as if we are having an hallucination – but we don't perceive each or perhaps any one sufficiently distinctly, so that overall they merge together to appear to us collectively homogeneously, not heterogeneously. Further, since soul and body are coordinated but do not really interact, strictly speaking all ideas are innate, none are adventitious. Ideas are predispositions of the soul to have certain kinds of perceptions. Those perceptual states we call "sensory" may co-occur with observable, bodily states, but they are never produced by those physical states. Rather, like every monadic state, they are members of the continuous series that flow in lawlike fashion in accordance with the individual concepts, present timelessly in God's understanding, which constitute those souls' identities. (If we read "is in an individual's concept" as meaning "is essential to that individual," or "is a feature necessary to uniquely identifying (individuating) a thing" as entailing "is a feature that could not be otherwise," it looks like Leibniz must reject as incoherent any distinction between the necessary and the contingent. I will resist such a reading in section 4.4.)

Everything in the world is a living being. A living being is a body together with a single dominant monad. A monad dominates a collection of monads if it expresses notably more perspicuously the monads in the collection, than any of those other monads express it. And the body of the living being need not be, indeed strictly is not, the same body over time, since all bodies gradually change, such that even birth and death are just bodily changes, not absolute origins or termini. Again, all monads perceive. Souls are monads with relatively distinct perceptions accompanied by memory. If the living being's dominant monad is a soul, the living being is an animal. Souls that can reason and reflect on themselves, so stand in relation to God and be held morally responsible, are spirits. It seems that only humans among animals are spirits, but even humans in fact behave unreflectively, like souls that are not spirits, most of time, and species of animals differ gradually in degree. Reflection on myself establishes the reality of one monad, and provides the model for understanding monads in general.

Not only are there infinitely many monads, grounding infinitely many phenomena, but each of the infinitely many living beings is composed of smaller living beings, ad infinitum. The world is infinite from stem to stern, vertically as well as horizontally, as then newly invented microscopic examination began empirically to suggest, but as is sufficiently proven by reason alone.

4.3 How the *Discourse on Metaphysics* and the *Monadology* are structured

To help see where the components of Leibniz's system are developed, I begin by explaining his motivations and structuring in the *Discourse*. Its original title was *Treatise on the Perfections of God*. Its section headings were sent by the Protestant Leibniz through an intermediary to the Catholic Arnauld for feedback to help replace the obscure and controversial with the relatively clear and agreeable. Leibniz revised it for nine years before publishing any of it. It is an ecumenical project, seeking to achieve unity on issues of God's relation to creation, the nature of miracles, the origin of evil and the cause of sin, the immortality of the soul, grace, ideas enabling us to come to grips with these issues, etc. In *this* work Leibniz *assumes* that God exists, is perfect, and created the world. Sections 1–7 unpack what this means. One especially important subtext is Leibniz's effort to steer a middle course between the unacceptable extremes of the necessitarianism (the world could not possibly be otherwise) of Spinoza and the voluntarism (everything is a function of God's free will) and conventionalism (truth is a function of practical decisions that work), and so, as Leibniz sees them, irrationalisms, of Descartes and Hobbes, respectively. Sections 8–22 concern the basic nature of finite individuality and the many consequential truths about individuals that follow from that nature, at both the metaphysical level and the level of observable appearances, including physics (reconciling mechanistic and teleological explanation). I will make plain what all these implications amount to, and explain more fully the great significance of some of them. Sections 23–29 sketch the epistemology of spirits, including innatism. And sections 30–37 concern God's relation to human conduct and the soul–body union, and its consequences for morality and religion, culminating in the ideal community of persons, the City of God.

The programmatic *Monadology* (M) usefully rehearses central components of Leibniz's mature system. Most starkly, it is structured as follows:

Sections	
1–9	What monads are.
10–22	What the fundamental activity (perception) of monads is.
23–30 (with some retrieval from 19–21)	Hierarchy of monads, to the highest sort, spirits (what they are).
31–37 (and 53–55)	The two types of truth and the (two or three – an interpretational controversy) basic principles of truth (introducing the problem of contingent truth).
38–52	What God is, and how he is the "ultimate reason of things," and his relation to the two types of truth.
53–60	What possible worlds are, and the rationale for God's choice among possible worlds.
61–77	How this rationale explains the natural world, including the interconnectedness of all things throughout nature.
78–84	How properly understanding the natural world (organically) explains how mind–body coordination is possible without any actual interaction.
85–90	The special status of spirits in the City of God, and how understanding our role in God's plan should make us content.

Here is a richer, but still abbreviated version of its story that makes its development perspicuous and highlights its key concepts. Undoubtedly there are other useful ways to parse its stages, but this is one I find especially revealing. What are *monads* (*individual substances*)? They are the basic units of existence, so have no parts, are unextended, and must exist for anything else in nature to exist (1–3). They are causally insulated, so cannot begin or end in time, cannot result from natural construction (composition from pre-existing parts) or end by destruction (decomposition into parts), but can only be created or annihilated instantaneously (4–7). Though *without quantifiable parts*, they do have *qualities*, no two have all the same qualities, and these qualities continually and continuously change over time. These changing states are called *perceptions*, all perceptions stem from an *inner law of development* and are governed by an inner striving to develop, called *appetition*. Every perception expresses a unified multiplicity (which we are familiar with in our own case of conscious perception), cannot be explained mechanically, but again, proceeds wholly from the monad's own internal nature, so that each monad is the source of its own actions, and which is such that its later states naturally emerge from its earlier states (8–22). While all monads perceive, some, called *souls*, are also *conscious*, a more heightened or distinct, organized form of perception that involves memory, which brings with it psychological associations and a capacity for imagination (19–27). The most sophisticated monads additionally have the capacity for *reasoning from general truths*, which enables them to apprehend the necessary truths of mathematics and metaphysics and achieve a kind of reflection through abstraction which allows for *self-consciousness*; these monads are called *spirits* (28–30).

All metaphysical inquiry is governed by the *principle of sufficient reason*, that for every truth, there is a sufficient reason why it is so rather than otherwise. The *principle of (non)-contradiction* provides the sufficient reason for *necessary truths*, *truths of reason*; the *principle of perfection* or *of the best* provides the sufficient reason for *contingent truths*, *truths of fact*. The sufficient reason for any truth can be found by a process of analysis: *finite analysis*, which terminates in primitive, self-evident propositions, for necessary truths; *infinite analysis* for truths of fact (31–37, 53–55). The ultimate reason for truths of fact is God, who must be unique, exist necessarily, be perfect and infinite, and be the creator of everything that is good in creatures. All possible creatures (creatable things), found as options in God's *intellect*, without influence by his *will*, are necessarily imperfect (only God can be perfect). Since God's intellect is the region of possibilities, if (against possibility) God did not exist, nothing else would be possible, let alone actually exist. So the necessary truths depend only on God's understanding (i.e. intellect); the contingent truths depend on his will also. So, God is the perfect being, all-powerful, all-knowing, and all-good (38–48).

A created monad's degree of *activity* is the same as its degree of *perfection*, which is the same as its degree of *distinct* versus confused *perceptions*, which is the same as the degree to which God sees in its nature a reason for choosing other things whose behavior will be adjusted to it. But again, one created monad cannot actually influence another; its agency is *ideal*, not real, and always requires God's nod. So the fundamental, real action is God's creation choice, and what we call activity and passivity are functions of which things in the coordinated scheme accommodate which. For us, this is a relative, perspectival matter (49–53).

As regards God's creation choice, remember that God's understanding is the domain of possibilities. God freely decides what to actualize guided by the degree of perfection that the concepts of these possibilities represent. God *freely chooses the best*, which entails thoroughgoing *interconnection* of all things, such that each monad represents a particular (unique) *point of view* on the same universe; for each monad, the object of perception is the same, but the degree of perceptual confusion differs. The best entails that realizable perfection is maximized by means of the optimal combination of variety and orderliness. But the most *realizable* perfection still includes some unavoidable imperfection; an absolutely perfect world is impossible (53–60). Harmony exists at every level in an organically structured nature, between monad and universe, between monads, between dominant monads and the complex, living organisms that they organize and so unify. There is even empirical confirmation for this *a priori* determinable state of affairs (61–77). Specifically, universal, *pre-established harmony* explains the coordination between soul and body, even though they don't actually interact, and between the *efficient* causation of bodies and the purposive (*final*) causation of souls (78–81).

Since *spirits* have reason, and can know and act in pursuit of the good, they can enter into a special relationship with God and with each other, forming a special community, the City of God, a moral world within and in harmony with the natural world, in which justice and love prevail, and in which our greatest happiness resides (82–90).

A predominant, organizing theme of both *Discourse* and *Monadology* is that God achieves the best by creating a universe which expresses his perfections most fully, that such a universe is a harmonious collection of individual substances which reflect the qualities of God, its creator, by being simple, immaterial, causally self-sufficient, active sources of unity, and that this universe contains a subset of substances, spirits such as human minds, which further resemble God in their cognitive self-sufficiency because they have innate ideas, which further makes them eligible for membership in a special kind of moral community.

4.4 Understanding Leibniz's metaphysics by way of his defense of contingency

My own reading of Leibniz can be appreciated best by understanding how I think he handles the problem of contingency. The problem of contingency in Leibniz's philosophy is among the most vexing I have ever studied. Here I aim to provide a pithy, useful rendition of alternative positions on the problem, and defend my own. On both systematic and detailed grounds I will urge some unorthodox views, especially about what complete concepts, monadic properties, and infinite analyses are, which I believe go a long way to exonerate Leibniz from the charge of Spinozistic necessitarianism, which he centrally seeks to avoid. (Remember that Spinoza argued that the principle of sufficient reason, which Leibniz accepts, entails that nothing could be other than it is, which Leibniz rejects.)

In preparation, keep in mind the basic connections between (*alethic* or truth-pertinent) modal concepts. What is necessary is possible, but not vice versa. What is impossible is not necessary, but not vice versa. Nothing can be both necessary and impossible, but something can be neither (and then it is *contingent*). Everything must be either possible or not-necessary, and something can be both. Also, there are different grades of modality. For example, what is logically possible (consistent with the laws of logic) may not be physically possible (consistent with the laws of physics), and what is physically possible may not be technologically possible. Logical possibility is the weakest, easiest-to-satisfy, kind of possibility. Conversely, what is logically necessary must be physically necessary; logical necessity is the strongest, hardest-to-achieve, kind of necessity. So, a contingent truth would be an actual, so possible, but not a necessary truth.

At first blush at least, Leibniz confronts two distinct threats to contingency: its incompatibility with the nature of individual substance in general, and its incompatibility with the nature of God in particular. For first, on the most widely endorsed interpretation of his metaphysics, Leibniz adopted the view that truth is concept-containment – "A is B" is true if and only if the concept of A contains the concept of B; that, either as a consequence, or as an independent axiom or definition, all and only individual substances have complete concepts, which contain, at least implicitly, all the properties (or all the concepts of the properties) truly ascribable to the unique individuals which instantiate each of them; and that, in consequence, all truths about individuals are analytic, hence necessary, hence not contingent. And second, even if God's individuality does not rule out his contingent agency, his perfection may. For that this (actual) world exists follows from the three premises that this world is best, that God chooses the best, and that what God chooses exists. Assuming that the object of choice is possible, the last premise is undoubtedly necessary for Leibniz. So if the first two premises are necessary truths as well, there can be no contingency, since what follows from only necessary truths is itself necessary, and what is necessary is not contingent.

Though I don't think it significantly affects my subsequent discussion, let me register my conviction that the complete concept theory of substance is not axiomatic. Rather, Leibniz reasons as follows (DM 8): Aristotle is right, and it is a matter of general agreement, that individual substances are always designated by the subject-term, and never the predicate-term, of a logically perspicuous subject–predicate proposition. But by itself this is a merely verbal, metaphysically inadequate criterion. A metaphysically adequate account of individual substance requires a metaphysically adequate account of true predication. True predication is to be explicated in terms of concept-containment. So the concepts of individual substances must be maximally complex or specific, not forming part of any concept more complex than themselves. Therefore, substances (the ultimate subjects of predication, by pre-theoretical consensus) and only substances have complete concepts. I might add, still more controversially, that I take Leibniz's "subject–predicate logic," as it figures in the foundations of his system, not to be a significant syntactical thesis at all, but instead to be again a doctrine of pre-systematic agreement, from which Leibniz thinks he alone properly elicits the implications. Namely, substances are what's ultimately real, in the sense that all else is explainable in terms of them, so that all truths can be reduced to truths about substances and their properties. But again, truth is concept-containment. So all truths can be reduced to containments of predicate-concepts in subject-, that is, substance-concepts; again, substances are the ultimate subjects of true predication.

Returning to our main problem, how can Leibniz resist the threats to contingency? It is natural to begin by canvassing the solutions to the general problem of substantial contingency, and then to face special, additional problems posed by God.

Perhaps the simplest and most direct solution has been to deny that Leibniz held the troublemaking concept-containment theory of truth, to argue that containment or inclusion is not a logical connection, that deduction is not logical inference, but just innocuously means that the subject has the predicate. This negative move is then supplemented by some positive account of the necessary–contingent distinction concerning individuals (for example, that between what would be true of an individual even if other things in its world had been different (that is, true in all possible worlds), and what is true of an individual, given the world it is in), but I want to treat these logically distinct supplements separately. One premise of the variants on this solution strikes me as unchallengeable: that Leibniz steadfastly treats "B is in A" and "the concept of B is contained in the concept of A" as equivalent. Unfortunately, this decides nothing, since while proponents of this view proceed to urge that "in" is to be taken as reducible to "true of" (taken generically to apply to propositions of any modal status), opponents insist that Leibniz took himself to be providing a profound explication of "true of" in terms of "concept-containment," but then went on to distinguish necessity and contingency in terms of two species of containment.

I won't rehearse the detailed historical arguments citing the standard truth theories of Aristotle, Boethius, Aquinas, Ockham, Arnauld and Nicole, Clauberg, Descartes and Hobbes, which sometimes use "in" and "concept-inclusion" talk, as models that Leibniz followed. These arguments are unconvincing: either these philosophers had extensional accounts, where predication is understood in terms of one set being a subset of another (while Leibniz's is intensional, where predication is understood in terms of one concept being included in another – for example, "all monkeys are animals" analyzed as "the set of monkeys is a subset of the set of animals" versus "the concept of monkey contains the concept of animal"); or they only held the entailment from concept-containment to truth, not the problematic converse; or (like Aristotle) they simply did not identify in-predication with true predication in general; or (usually) all of the above. And Leibniz *admits* that his account of truth appears to generate a special obstacle to contingency. A more productive way to approach this dispute is to determine whether analysis is a logical procedure or not, since there is massive evidence that "containment" means "follows from by analysis." I will say something about analysis later.

But now I want to effect a reconciliation of sorts, with surprising results. It begins by adducing a strong argument which none of the proponents of the simple solution, so far as I know, has offered. It rests on what I take to be the true premise that the complete concept of X is just a perfect representation of X, is just God's knowledge of X (qua possible). Or as Leibniz puts it in terms of truth, truth always has its basis in the nature of things, where the nature of things is how things really are, as opposed to arbitrary convention (and where "nature" does not mean "set of metaphysically necessary properties" either), and the basis of the nature of things is God. Leibniz often says things such as Caesar's complete concept "pertains to him only because God knows everything" (DM 13). So it is plausible to interpret Leibniz as worrying about the threat to contingency of divine omniscience; his task would be to show that foreknowledge guarantees truth, but not only necessary truth. And ordinarily, knowing truth is not a matter of necessitating truth, so why is divine foreknowledge necessitating predestination?

We have two results thus far. First, there aren't two distinct threats to contingency: its incompatibility with the nature of individual substance in general boils down to its incompatibility with the nature of God. Second, everyone agrees that for God to know that A is B, all that must hold is the truism that the predicate B is truly applicable to the subject A. This explains Leibniz's exasperated insistence that, at the intuitive level, he shares the common conception of true (*in esse*) predication with all level-headed philosophers.

But we have only to go a little further to see why Leibniz thought this common conception has, at a deeper level, a commitment which is more challenging to contingency. Properly understood, divine foreknowledge is exhaustive, determinate knowledge beforehand of the histories of (what turn out to be) immaterial (so that matter can't be the source of contingency) individuals, in terms of which all the appearances that need explaining can be explained. But God does not apprehend any of the appearances, since his knowledge is fully distinct or adequate (as well as, importantly, intuitive, to which I will return), not confused or indiscriminating at all. In other words, and this is no limitation, God doesn't know sensuously or empirically the spatiotemporal aggregate of appearances (phenomena) we call "the world." God knows substances, and knows them conceptually (≠ discursively). So the ultimate basis of true predication is conceptual. And so, it seems as if individuals have all their properties in the same manner that abstracta like circles have theirs – necessarily. But they don't. Why don't they?[1]

A popular solution is that all and only contingent truths are existential truths (truths affirming the existence of something), and existence is the sole exception to the concept-containment theory of truth. Where "A" names an individual substance, "A is B" is contingent since equivalent to the conjunction of the analytically necessary "Whoever is A is B" and the contingent "A exists." I disagree with every component of this view, and judge it to be self-defeating. There are at least seven objections to it.

First, Leibniz repeatedly says that contingent propositions are not exceptions to the containment theory of truth. Second, he seems to hold that possible existence (*exigentia essentiae*) is explicitly contained in the complete concepts of all possible substances, and that actual existence is contained implicitly (in a way requiring infinite analysis) in the concepts of created substances. The question how analytic propositions can fail to be necessary would not arise if Leibniz held that contingent truths about existents were not analytic, but synthetic. Third, there are non-existential contingent propositions; these include propositions asserting connections within possible worlds, and asserting the bestness of this possible world. Actualization is the ground for truth, not for contingency. Since I appreciate how controversial these claims are, I will defend them soon.

In addition to these direct, textual criticisms, the proposed solution has false consequences. Fourth, the view implies that all true predications of actual individuals are contingent, but classifications of individuals according to their genus or species are necessary. Fifth, the view implies that all propositions with non-denoting singular subjects (subject-terms that don't refer to anything that exists) are false; but Leibniz's intensionalist treatment of propositions rejects this implication, which rests on the confusion of non-actuals with impossibilities, since Leibniz did seem to hold that impossibles (non-entities or non-terms) have no properties (nothing true can be said about them). Sixth, if a possible worlds account of necessity is adopted, the view implies that false predications of actual individuals are always necessarily false, since the predicate is not included in the concept of the actual individual, and in all other possible worlds – given the one concept, one substance doctrine, and the consequent rejection of strict identity through possible worlds – the actual individual does not exist, hence ascriptions to it

---

1   For those interested in researching the ensuing debate more seriously, excellent, early formulations of competing positions can be found in W. Abraham, R.M. Adams, C.D. Broad, E.M. Curley, G. Fitch, R. Grimm, H. Ishiguro, C. Jarrett, H.W.B. Joseph, B. Mates, T. Meijering, F. Mondadori, N. Rescher, B. Russell (1900), and M. Wilson. Many important contributions on this topic and others can be found in *Studia Leibnitiana*, the pre-eminent journal of Leibniz scholarship. Given the depth of the issue and my aspiration to cover the field, much of the remainder of this section 4.4 is challenging, but I urge your efforts to grapple with it. You need not follow it all to appreciate some key points along the way.

are false (via the previous point); hence the predication is false in all possible worlds. Finally, the view does not solve the problem anyway (*a fortiori* if the problem is the nature of God) since if only existence is contingent, then there is nothing contingent about God (who has necessary existence), and a necessitated God seems to rule out a contingent creation.

Most of the other competing solutions strike me as textually more sensitive. There are certain uncontroversial data that have to be captured:

- Leibniz's emphasis that not all possibles are compossible (possibly coexisting),
- his emphasis that contingency requires that some things are merely possible (unactualized),
- his unwavering repudiation of what he took to be Cartesian voluntarism (that ultimately everything depends solely on God's will),
- his affirmation that what is metaphysically possible is independent of God's actual (free) decrees (will), but not his understanding,
- his at least consistently mature position that a proposition is logically necessary if and only if it is an "identical proposition," or is demonstratively reducible (in a finite number of steps) to an identical proposition by use of identical propositions and/or explicit definitional substitutions only, and
- his central distinction, apparently put equivalently in different ways, between what is *intrinsic* (or *analytic*) but not *absolutely necessary*, and what is intrinsic and absolutely necessary; between what is necessary *ex hypothesi* and what is absolutely necessary; between what is *morally* necessary and what is *metaphysically* necessary; between *certainty* and *geometric necessity*; and between *infinitely analytic* propositions and *finitely analytic* or *demonstrable* ones.

To a large extent, interpretational disagreements can be diagnosed as stresses on the different ways of drawing, elaborating, and applying this central distinction, compatible with the other data. In other words, which, for Leibniz, is the ground-floor way of objectively making out the distinction, the way which explains the legitimacy of the others, and where does the distinction correctly apply?

Let me synoptically exemplify this. Begin with a popular account: The character of and relations between an infinity of possible alternatives (including the fact of bestness) are necessary. The root of contingency is the decision of God's free will, the one thing not essential to God. Final causes, God's purposes, are contingent, and whatever is based on them is contingent.

Now someone might agree that what is contingent *coincides* with what depends on God's will, but deny that it is contingent *because* it depends on God's will. So one might object: to explain the contingent by something contingent is either circular, or, if God's will to will to will . . . is appealed to, viciously regressive, if intelligible at all, and so is bad explanation. An ultimate sufficient reason must be found in the necessary, God's essence or metaphysical perfection. "God chooses what is best" is not contingent for Leibniz, since God's moral perfection follows from his metaphysical perfection. God's freedom consists in his supreme rationality (it's not the freedom of indifference.) Still, it is contingent that this world exists, because it is contingent that this world is best. And this – in spite of the fact that for Leibniz the value of possibles is independent of God's will, and is the ground of his choice – *because* concept-inclusions (truths) requiring infinite analysis are contingent, and the bestness of something infinitely complex among infinitely many alternatives requires an infinite analysis.

If God could demonstrate, that is, finitely analyze, contingent truths, the finite–infinite analysis distinction would be merely epistemological. But God cannot demonstrate contingencies, since it is impossible to do so. Yet he can know them *a priori* (through their reasons), whereas we cannot; we can only know them experientially. Further, though it is necessary that God wills the best, he doesn't will the best necessarily (*de re*), since alternatives to the best are possible in themselves, since not all possibles are compossible. But these alternatives are not possible in relation to God's necessary will; they are morally necessary. This by itself makes God's choice an ineliminable link in the explanation of the world (alternatives are excluded through choice, which is based on comparative value), and avoids the blind necessity in Spinoza. So this viewpoint takes the notions of unactualized possibles and infinite analysis, applied in the right spots, to be the fundamental explanation of contingency, and takes contingency to reside in the *objects* of God's choice, not his act of choosing.

Other interpreters take the need for infinite analysis as fundamental, but apply it at a different spot. So it is urged that, consonant with the demands of the Principle of Sufficient Reason, God's moral perfection does follow from his metaphysical perfection (which is absolutely necessary), but the deduction would require an infinity of steps. So, "God is good" is contingent, and the products of his goodness are therefore contingent.

Others dismiss the relevance of analysis length, and seek a solution in differing kinds of analysis rules. They emphasize Leibniz's tendency to include in a complete concept, not all the (concepts of) properties ascribable to the individual which instantiates it, but only a set of simples, which provides the basis for the derivation of the rest. Of course, if the derivation-relation is demonstrability, no gain has been made – you might as well have said that the rest were in the complete concept. The response is that some deductions are logical, based on the law of contradiction or identity, some are based on the principle of the best – whose auxiliary principles include the laws of nature and the maxims of conduct – which is contingent. Deductions employing non-logical inference rules (essentially) support contingent results.

But why are these latter rules non-logical? Because they reflect God's will, and are not implied in his understanding. And so we return to an earlier solution as more basic. Further, does the concept-containment theory of truth allow for non-purely conceptual *connections* between subject-concept and predicate-concept? In fact, what Leibniz usually says is that the laws which govern the universe in which an individual figures are included in the complete concept of that individual, that these are God's free decrees, qua possible, and that by a separate decree, he decides to render actual one world-governing set of possible decrees (for example in "Necessary and Contingent Truths"). And so these laws seem to be among those simples constitutive of complete concepts, premises instead of rules of inference. And again, the modal status of these premises is not an ultimate fact about them, but based on something else, namely divine will. And again, why is it contingent? (At this juncture one may begin to imagine lurking an Augustinian solution: it is part of a complete concept that some of the specifiable acts of its bearer are contingent; it is part of God's essence that he freely chooses the best.)

Notice that at bottom, what these last solutions are denying is the identification of the complete concept of X with the essence or set of metaphysically necessary characteristics of X. As I suggested before with respect to "nature," so more generally, I think that Leibniz does not use what is translated as "nature," "definition," or "complete concept" of an individual as equivalent to what Arnauld (and the Aristotelian tradition) means by "essence." The contingent is that whose essence does not involve existence, not that whose concept doesn't involve existence. If it weren't in the concept, given the concept-containment theory of truth and the deep explication of the principle of sufficient reason, it would be untrue and unreasonable (or better, untrue, that is, unreasonable). "Unreasonable" or "untrue" does not mean "metaphysically impossible;" they would if all possibles were compossible, but there are unactualized possibles.

How we circumscribe essences and marshall unactualized possibles leads to the final stage of the state of the art. If we ascribe to Leibniz the belief that "B contingently Fs" only if that very individual B might not have F-ed, and further suppose he interprets modal claims in terms of possible worlds, then we suppose that for him individual contingency requires trans-world identity, that is, that an individual exist in multiple possible worlds. But every possible individual is associated with a unique complete concept, and conversely. In the face of this situation, it has been proposed that Leibniz distinguishes between complete individual concepts and general individual concepts, the latter being metaphysical essences, no more than one occurring in any world, and one occurring in multiple, but not all, possible worlds. Trans-world identification is based on the inclusion of a general individual concept in a complete individual concept, which requires alternative disjunctions of possible properties of possible individuals. God freely wills the specific set of disjuncts, which are not part of the thing's essence. The merely intrinsic–absolutely necessary distinction is made in terms of the property's inclusion in some only versus all the worlds in which the thing's general individual concept appears. So on this view Leibniz is a kind of traditional essentialist: an individual remains the same (over time, counterfactually, etc.) so long as it retains its essence, and its essence is a conceptually proper subset of its complete concept.

Others favoring a possible worlds account of contingency, but construing the complete concept theory as precluding strict trans-world identity, have developed several variants of what is called *counterpart theory* solutions: for example, there's contingency because God could have chosen to realize *different, but similar* complete concepts. P is contingent if and only if there's at least one counterpart of the concept of the subject that contains the concept of the predicate, and at least one that does not. Let's suppose we impose all the restrictions on the counterpart-relation needed to avoid obvious trouble: a complete concept can't have two counterparts in one world; a complete concept can't be the counterpart of two others in one world; the counterpart-relation isn't both symmetric and transitive; counterparts are (in some sense) maximally resembling or similar. Still, does counterpart theory offer the univocal, basic understanding of Leibniz's account of contingency (and, according to its proponents, counterfactual talk and *de re* modal discourse generally)?

I think that it does not, since we cannot postulate other, counterpart possible Gods (infinitely perfect beings), since each would necessarily exist and, being omnipotent yet having divergent wills, all would have to be efficacious, so that incompossible worlds would coexist. It seems to me that the only route of escape – that only our God is metaphysically perfect and so necessarily existing, the counterparts are not, and so are innocuous – is a dead end. For I assume that counterparts have to be similar enough to count as counterparts – the most closely resembling object to me in some particular possible world might still be so dissimilar to me that it fails to support counterfactual contemplation. But any way we formulate it, this minimal similarity condition fails to work with God; God's essence is his metaphysical perfection. And even if we introduce a weaker notion of "same kind" it seems that Leibniz's God is *sui generis*, not just individually unique, but unique in kind. (I somewhat timidly add that no version of possible worlds semantics can coherently apply to God, since God does not exist in (at, truly of) any possible world, since Leibniz's God is transcendent.)

But what are we to make of all of Leibniz's talk of "possible Adams" and "several Sextuses?" To explain this, and to explain why I think the infinite–finite analysis distinction is fundamental and objective for Leibniz, I shall briefly sketch my view of how Leibniz conceives complete concepts, monadic properties, and infinite analyses. I shall then very briefly defend the infinite analysis criterion of contingency against main objections.

The key is to keep in mind that complete concepts are not infinite collections of mutually consistent abstract (universal) concepts, potentially shared by a multiplicity of individuals. The properties of monads, their perceptions, are always individual attributes. Leibniz is a nominalist. Note that this is not to say that they are individual relational attributes. The question of the individuality of properties is distinct from the question of their intrinsic relationality. The complete concept theory and consequent "each substance is like a world apart" doctrine implies that individual attributes are non-relational. This is consistent with the fact that they are all perceptions, that perceptions are representations or expressions, and that representations are intentional (of something). "A represents O" does not entail that there exists something which A represents; a substance doesn't depend for its existence or for the character of its perceptions on something independent of and external to it (other than God). There are relations between all monads, and between each monad and the phenomenal world, but these relations, which are ideal abstractions, are reducible to what is real, which are the perceptions (which are real states as well as representations) of the monads. And these perceptions are not intrinsically relational, for to conceive substance A fully it is not necessary to make any reference to any individual other than A. Distinct knowledge of A's state gives knowledge of the co-occurring states of all other monads, but "can know others by attention to A alone" does not imply "must know others in order to know A," and it is the latter which is relevant to the internal–external relation question. A is internally related to B if one cannot understand (identify, know, etc.) either except in relation to the other; A is externally related to B if one can understand etc. each independently of the other.

So I'm highlighting the fact that complete concepts are different in kind from the kind of conceptual abstractions that properly apply only to phenomena. Abstractions allow for shared, repeatable features. Real attributes don't, but are the unique, non-repeatable foundations of the identities ideally constructed from close similarities among points of view. One consequence is that the identity of indiscernibles, the numerical sameness of what is qualitatively exactly the same, does not hold for abstractions. Similar ideal things are distinguishable *only* numerically when co-present. And note that in saying that the simple *properties* of monads are non-relational, I am not saying that there are no relational simple *concepts*. Leibniz holds that there are, such as "the same," "acting on," "prior," "successor," and "number." There are infinitely many simple properties; there are a relatively small number of simple notions.

Concept B is included in concept A if each primitive concept of B is a primitive concept of A. If a complete concept were an infinite set of incomplete, abstract concepts (universals), then there would be no logical bar to determining predicate inclusion in a finite number of steps, and if the predicate itself were finitely complex (as it would be generally), then the first definitional replacement might fortunately explicitly reveal the predicate. So it must be that the properties, that concepts in complete concepts are concepts of, are unique, individual attributes, whose individuation is just as infinitely complex a process as is the individuation of the substance they are property of. And this, because what properties are depends on what substance they characterize. This explains not only why each substance expresses all others from a unique point of view, but why each state (property) follows from its predecessors, and contains its successors – a property is defined by its unique, infinite set of predecessors and successors (those constituting the history of the individual having it). Only A can have B_1, that is, only the being with B_1 C_8, D_{42} . . . can have B_1.

So the picture of constructing complete concepts, and then worlds, by including, or including the negation of, each of an enumeration of a stock of predicates through all logically permissible permutations, though perhaps graphically helpful, is strictly misleading. Yet we still preserve the law of excluded middle (everything is either F or not-F) since, if A has B_1, then everything else, which lack B_1, have some F_n which is the basis for saying not-B_1. And notice that the systematic needs of Leibniz's philosophy are retained on this account: we still have possibilities *sub specie aeternitas*; we can still generate incompossibility relations; and the various "noticeable paradoxes" listed in DM 9, such as the identity of indiscernibles, the mirroring thesis, marks and traces, etc. are more clearly deducible from the complete concept theory.

The point positively put is that a complete concept is a rule or law for generating an infinite sequence of non-abstractions, activities called *perceptions*. Laws governing abstractions such as numbers (laws relating generalities), even an infinite ordered set of such abstractions, can be wielded to exhibit geometrically necessary connections in a finite number of steps, as with proof by mathematical induction. The elements of such series are homogeneous, and can be similarly treated through repeated application of the same rule of progression. Not so with laws governing unique series of actions; they're not general laws, but all individual laws.

How do I account for the fact that some predications of individuals are necessary? The answer is this: those and only those predications are necessary which are entailed by the kind of point of view the individual has (where point of view (*situs*) is the monadic basis of the ideal world of phenomenal content, including space and time). This just comes down to what genus- and species-classification it satisfies (bare entelechy, animal soul, spirit or mind; dog, human being), and what those in turn entail; for example, being a mind entails being capable of apperception, which entails being able to apprehend necessary truths.

And now I can explain how I understand "alternative Adams" and counterfactual talk in Leibniz. Counterfactual predication is only possible *sub specie generalitatis*, and *sub species generalitatis* means empirically based. We identify a real individual via an actual world uniquely identifying description of the phenomenal body it dominates, and then, keeping in mind that it's *that* individual we're talking about, we wonder what the observable series of things would be like if not-F, given that F. (For those up on philosophy of language, my view is that in such talk about actual individuals, Leibniz is more like Saul Kripke than counterpart theorists like David

Lewis.) This helps explain, what is otherwise a puzzling feature of Leibniz's epistemology, his repeated insistence that (setting God aside), for us all real definition, that is, all proof of possibles, ultimately requires appeal to experience. From the perspective of our identificational semantics, possible worlds do not come first, so that the actual world is then conceived as one of them. The actual world comes first, and epistemic possibilities are constructed on the basis of the lawlike dispositions of real individuals, discovered by us only through encounterable, repeatable features.

What then about modal discourse about mere possibles? Such discourse is not *about individuals* but about complete concepts, though accessible to our contemplation only as incomplete concepts, just as "round squares are impossible" is not about round squares, but about the concept *round square*.

Trouble now is, all this is sounding very epistemological as far as the distinction between necessity and contingency goes. What about God's picture of things, and its implications? I think we can see that although his viewpoint is different in kind, it is not a difference that undermines the objectivity of contingency.

The realm of possibles in God's understanding is not an infinite array of complete, determinate worlds, that is, spatiotemporal aggregates. Leibniz's talk about the competing conatuses or strivings to exist of an infinity of possibles is to be understood conceptually as competing reasons for alternative creation-choices. If God did not have a sufficient reason for choosing, he wouldn't. Supreme rationality is acting on perfection-maximizing principles alone.

It is metaphysically necessary, not just an epistemological vicissitude, that creatures are imperfect. The best possible world is not perfect; otherwise it would be identical with God, which Spinozism Leibniz notably shuns (and thence we would need no theodicy). But degree of perfection is amount of essence or reality, is degree of activity, is, and here is the key one, degree of clarity of perception (but remember that perception is a generic notion, not to be identified with one of its species, sense observation, which is inapplicable to God). So it is metaphysically necessary that humans don't perceive adequately, and that God does. And here's the punch line: to apprehend by sense observation is to apprehend phenomenal, repeatable features, is to apprehend *sub species generalitatis*; to apprehend adequately is to apprehend wholly distinct, non-repeatable features, is to apprehend *sub species individualitatis*. Yet the latter way of apprehending need not be demonstrative and so of the absolutely necessary. Why? This brings me to the final task of explaining the objectivity and sufficiency of the infinite analysis criterion of contingency.

Infinite analyses or proofs of truths begin with the truth to be proved, proceed without exception in the direction of decreasing conceptual complexity, and converge on identical propositions (approach them as a limit). Infinite analyses are modeled on mathematical convergent series. But Leibniz says that his analogy with surd ratios (and incommensurable quantities) in mathematics is partial only, since the infinitesimal calculus he had just discovered provides the means to demonstrate or exhibit in a finite number of steps the convergence of certain infinite series, and to compute the exact values of the limits of their partial sums, whereas the analysis of contingents does not. There is no finite procedure sufficient for the complete analysis of complete concepts. So infinite analyses are non-terminating, infinite sequences. Since divine omnipotence is for Leibniz the power to do all and only what is possible, God can't complete the analysis of contingent propositions, can't demonstrate them, can't exhibit their coincidence with identicals. But God is metaphysically perfect (he is the only true or veritable infinity for Leibniz — no collection or aggregate is a true (actual, completed) infinity since not a true whole or unity; each is at best inexhaustible), and so indemonstrability is a metaphysically objective fact, not a matter of subjective limitation or perspective. All truth is ultimately conceptual truth, a matter of relations of concepts. But not all conceptual truth is demonstrable truth, and demonstrability is necessary and sufficient for (metaphysical, not moral) necessity, not certainty. And the analysis of truths about substances, with complete concepts, is always infinite, in virtue of the account of complete concepts and individual attributes I offered earlier. Indeed, it is revealing, and supportive of my view, that nowhere in Leibniz do we find an example of even the *initial* stages of an infinite analysis of a complete concept.

We can reinforce Leibniz's ingenious position by considering a few objections and replies. Objection: there is no contingency in the realm of possibility; all propositions about unactualized possibles are necessary. But, since possibles have complete concepts, analyses of predications about them will be infinite. Hence, many necessary truths require infinite analysis. Hence, infinite analysis doesn't guarantee contingency.

Reply: of course if by "contingent" you mean "true but not necessary," the unactual can't be contingent. But here by "contingent" we must mean "neither necessary nor impossible." And it is crucial to Leibniz's view that some connections between substance and properties, qua possible, that is, between their concepts, are intrinsic but not necessary.

Objection: the allegedly operative notion of contingency conflicts with the axiom that whatever is possible is necessarily possible, which Leibniz surely embraces. So Leibniz can't think of contingency that way. Full reply: "it's possibly necessary" does not imply "it's necessary but not contingent." Possible truths are necessarily possible, and independent of God's will. That is, the connection between Adam's concept and his not sinning in some merely possible world is not the product of God's will, but is an alternative residing (prior to creation) in his understanding. But this does not entail that if w_2 were actualized, the connection between $Adam_2$ and his not sinning would be necessary, that is, necessarily true. If that entailment held, then straightaway creation could never result in contingency (of connection). Creation makes for truth, not for contingency. The view that a necessary connection of concepts becomes non-necessary when instantiated is incoherent. Demonstrability is supposed to be the criterion of necessary truth, not necessary possibility.

So I think that intra-systematically, infinite analysis plays just the fundamental, objective, sufficient role Leibniz intends it to play. This is not fully to explain why, intuitively, the infinitely analyzable is the contingent. That requires more work, and like many scholars better than I, there I will leave you to brainstorm.

Summarizing, my overall thesis is that, beginning with the ordinary question of truth, Leibniz by common consent moves to the question of substantial truth, which he takes by common consent to be the question of truth as it really is, that is, as God sees it (and not how it merely appears). But as God sees it, truth is a matter of infinitely complex, exhaustively individuating substance-concepts analytically containing infinitely complex concepts of individual attributes (or states). He appreciates that, thus deeply understood, truth seems to be necessary truth. The distinction between two kinds of analytic or intrinsic containment, finite and infinite, allows him an objective distinction between necessity and contingency. He thus secures the rationalist desideratum that the true is the provable (knowable through reasons) and vice versa, while preserving a metaphysically adequate distinction between necessity and contingency.

Finally, defending metaphysical contingency is crucial because it is for Leibniz one of three requirements for freedom. The other two are intelligence, which implies distinct knowledge of the object of deliberation, and spontaneity, which means self-determination. Many philosophers invoke spontaneity to distinguish between free and unfree acts of intelligent beings. Strikingly, Leibniz cannot do this, since for him every change in every substance of every kind (all appetition) is a consequence of its spontaneous action; given the pre-established harmony, spontaneity is nothing special.

I don't think this is an awkward consequence for him. If you read late works such as the *Theodicy*, you see him explicitly developing an account of will on which it operates similarly in all creatures, such that it cannot be absolutely indifferent, but appetite requires representation of some good, strength of desire is proportional to apparent goodness of its object, and desire for the greatest apparent good prevails. So the monad certainly or infallibly chooses the greatest apparent good, but, in his now familiar refrain, certainty does not entail necessity – the monad is determined to act by motives that "incline without necessitating."

The way he does seem to distinguish free intelligent spontaneity from unfree intelligent spontaneity is in terms of the presence or absence of strivings toward perfection, the applicability or non-applicability of teleological explanations for action from the point of view of the agent. For an action to be free its agent's desire for a future good must change the agent's (perceptual) state. But desires for apparent goods are only a small subset of appetitions. So we might formulate his position as follows: everything that happens to a monad depends on it, but not always on its will. A monad's lack of physical constraint doesn't ensure its freedom to will as it should, which is necessary for moral responsibility. Key here is that the kinds of desires a monad can have depend on its representational capacities, so that the third condition of freedom, intelligence, is decisive. Freedom to will requires that one's will be governed by intelligence, or a distinct knowledge of the good. And, now sounding like Spinoza, this can be frustrated by psychological constraints, by passions, which, at bottom, are confused perceptions. So, non-rational agents are spontaneous agents, but not free agents in the morally relevant sense.

This account seems to introduce a troubling asymmetry. Good actions can be praiseworthy, but bad actions cannot be blameworthy, since not free. More needs to be said about how one can be responsible for confusion as well as clarity of perception. I will not do so here, but will try to enrich our understanding of the relation between clarity of perception and degree of perfection in section 4.6.

4.5 Understanding the debate about what things for Leibniz are substances

Let us retrieve some earlier claims in order to frame an important debate about what for Leibniz counts as substance. Leibniz is mainly a metaphysician, concerned to specify what sorts of things basically exist, how they relate to each other, and how they explain the world as we know it. His is an appearance–reality metaphysics, with three levels. What exists at the basic level are substances. Their activities explain the observable, extended world of matter, or *phenomena*. Other entities, such as space, time and number, are mental constructs (constituting an *ideal* world) based on facts about phenomena. What is ideal is continuous; what is most real is discrete. His metaphysics aims largely to solve inherited problems, such as what exhibits genuine agency, what remains the same through change, what in the universe depends on what. He strives to develop a theory of substance that solves all these problems. Individual substances (what in the last twenty years of his life he called *monads*) act, persist through change, are independent of other things which depend on them. Leibniz's ground-floor conception of the basic things, substances, is what have properties, but are not properties of anything else, and what are determinate, countable individual, not just mass or stuff. He argues that substances are *simple* or without parts. If they had parts, they would depend on the existence and nature of those parts. But substances are ontologically independent. Since all material or extended things are divisible into parts, it follows that there are no material substances.

But sometimes Leibniz seems to include biological organisms among substances. This would conflict with the generalization just made. There is sophisticated debate about whether Leibniz stuck to this generalization over the years.[2] I think he did. But biological organisms *are* special among *phenomena*. Things have different degrees of unity, are non-arbitrarily countable in varying degrees. Some, like a heap of sand, have virtually all of their unity imposed by our minds. Others, like a particular stone, have somewhat more internal unity. Among physical things, living organisms have the most genuine unity. If anything physical deserves to be considered a true, individual substance, it is they. This way of thinking represents an important tendency of Leibniz's thought. Unlike Descartes and like Spinoza, he is a gradualist. Of course things differ – indeed for Leibniz each real thing in the universe is unique – but deep down each monad differs from any other only in degree, and each physical thing differs from any other only in degree. As we'll see, every degree of difference is represented in this best possible, God-created universe. So he is not only a gradualist; he is an infinite gradualist. There is even good reason to read him as anticipating the application of so-called "fractal geometries" to the phenomenal world, so that each part of each infinitely complex thing is in turn similarly infinitely complex. The best argument for going further, and insisting that Leibniz was committed to saying that physical substances must exist, rests on saying that God cannot create monads without physical substances, since only God as the perfect being can exist as pure active force without a body.

But that all created monads have bodies does not entail that any of those bodies are substances. A bit more needs to be said about how bodies relate to monads. Certain aggregates of monads *appear* to minds as extended bodies; there are certain systematic rules governing what monadic conditions appear as what kinds of material conditions. This is why bodies are called "phenomena." But the unity of bodies results from a unifying thought of some mind. The strongest way to interpret this is that matter has only a conventional, not true unity. But are monads nevertheless parts of material bodies, as one thinks of atoms as parts of bodies? This too is debatable, but I am committed to saying no. Since monads are unextended, they can't be literally constituents of extended things. As the once-popular song goes, "Nothing with nothing still makes nothing." And Leibniz regularly analogizes the relation between monads and bodies with relations that are notably not part–whole, such as that between points and lines – we say a line contains points, but we don't mean that a point is a part of a line; point is a limitative notion, as the inventor of the infinitesimal calculus knew. (As with analogies generally, this is just a partial comparison, especially since points and lines are ideal entities, monads and bodies real entities.)

In sum, here's our situation. Substances are the ultimate furniture of the universe. There are three main alternative ways of interpreting Leibniz on substance. On the first, only spirits, souls capable of self-consciousness and (so)

---

2   Among the many talented contributors to this debate, two who set out many of the most important considerations are Adams, R.M. 1994: Part III and Garber, D. 1985: 27–130.

apprehension of eternal truths, are substances. This view is suggested especially by DM 14 and 34. On the second, only corporeal substances are substances, such that each of infinitely many soul-like entities is the form of some composite substance, which is a complete entity, consisting of an aggregate of other composite substances (i.e. its organic body), all combined into a single individual with true, substantial unity by a soul-like entity (i.e. the substantial form of that composite substance), all the way down (for each part) *ad infinitum*. On the third, only created monads, lacking parts, composed of primary matter and substantial form (*entelechies*), are substances. So-called corporeal substance has a greater unity than extended entities that are mere aggregates, but all bodies are phenomenal, such that all truths about bodies supervene on facts concerning the properties of monads. Leibniz may have begun with the spiritual theory, treating one's own mind (as in the Cartesian *Cogito*) not only as a paradigm of substance, but as its touchstone. But I'm almost sure he very soon abandoned (in the *Correspondence with Arnauld* and thereafter) that theory as too narrow. Ongoing interpretative debates swirl around variants of the corporeal substance versus monadological readings. Some think Leibniz vacillated as between these two. I read him as not only finally settling on monadology, but settling on it soon after the *Discourse*. This requires accommodating materials (especially letters) from the next three decades that seem to affirm corporeal substance in the strictest, metaphysical sense, but I think such accommodation is possible.

So far I have highlighted Leibniz's theological and logical grounds for monadology. Let me leave this phase of discussion by outlining Leibniz's basic argument from the extended world to monads, the labyrinth of the continuum argument for monads:

1   Matter is extended.
2   All extension is composite, divisible into a plurality of parts.
3   So, matter is a plurality.
4   All plurality exists if and only if its constituents exist – the reality of an aggregation is derived from that of which it is composed.
5   Perceptions of matter correspond to a real world outside us; extended matter is a "well-founded phenomenon," the appearance of collections of real substances (soul-like monads, centers of activity, having a true unity, spatially indivisible). Matter is a plurality of such monads (as they appear to us).
6   The admission of aggregates (requiring simples of some sort) might perhaps be well accounted for by the existence of atoms (Epicurean), or mathematical points. But the idea of atoms is inadequate because
7   The notion of atom is self-contradictory – they are material, and what's material must be extended, and so essentially divisible; yet they purport to be indivisibles, basic and ultimate. Also, atoms are supposed to be indiscernible and no two distinct things are indiscernible. So there is not more than one atom. But we need a plurality of such atoms.

8   And mathematical points can't explain aggregation. A mathematical point cannot be a constituent (part) of anything. It's not real (not capable of existing by itself), but only ideal. A point is only the *limit* of a process of infinite subdivision.

9   So (having excluded the remaining alternatives) the constituents of the plurality which is matter are either individual substances or their states.

10   But the constituents cannot be merely the states of substances, since the constituents exist simultaneously, and the states successively.

11   So the constituents of the plurality are true, indivisible, active substances (monads). Therefore, what appears to us as matter must be a collection (or organization) of simple substances.

4.6   Understanding the debate about Leibniz's essentialism

Leibniz is some sort of essentialist. Broadly, essentialism is the view that individuals have some properties necessarily, and that an individual has modal properties independently of the way it is referred to, described, or thought of. We can clarify this definition by distinguishing between *de dicto* and *de re* modality. "*De dicto*" means "of (or concerning) a dictum." A dictum is something with representative content. "*De re*" means "of (or concerning) a thing." The *de re–de dicto* distinction can apply more widely, but it has especially been applied to psychological attitudes such as beliefs and hopes, and alethic (pertaining to truth) modalities such as possibility and necessity. Belief *de re* is belief concerning some thing, that it has a particular property. Compare "I believe that some reader of this book will become a distinguished philosopher" with "I believe of you, Jane Smith, that you will become a distinguished philosopher." Or compare "Necessarily, humans are rational animals" – the proposition that humans are rational is a necessary truth – with "You (Jane Smith), necessarily have the property of being a rational animal." Affirming the latter, *de re* necessity, is a commitment to metaphysical essentialism. Someone who affirms *de dicto* necessities *may* be an essentialist, but only countenancing *de re* necessities *commits* one to essentialism. For example, suppose someone thinks certain sentences express necessary truths because of optionally-adopted linguistic conventions. They could still deny the existence of any necessary facts independent of how we conceive or choose to talk about things.

How should we understand Leibnizian essentialism? There are three main alternatives.[3]

Superessentialism embraces all of the following four propositions:

3   I model my presentation on Cover and Hawthorne's (1999). Proponents of reading Leibniz as a superessentialist include Mondadori, 1973 and 1975, who coined the word. Proponents of reading him as a strong essentialist include Cover and Hawthorne. Proponents of reading him as a strong intrinsicalist include Adams 1994 and Sleigh 1990 (and me).

1 An individual substance could not have a complete concept different from the one it actually has.
2 Every property of an individual is essential to it.
3 Substances are worldbound individuals (the numerically same substance cannot exist in more than one possible world; there is no transworld identity).
4 Talk of ways some actual individual x could have been or done F (counterfactuals, as well as other *de re* modal claims) may be understood in terms of one of x's *counterparts* (a possible, nonactual y similar to but not identical with x) having a complete concept which contains (immediately or derivatively) F.

Strong essentialism highlights the distinction between intrinsic (non-relational) and extrinsic (relational) properties by affirming 1 but denying 2 and 3 above – with 4 potentially left open, though the current, most notable proponents of a strong essentialist reading (Cover and Hawthorne) accept 4 – by saying that intrinsic properties are, but non-intrinsic properties are not, essential to their bearers.

Strong intrinsicalism is weaker still, denying that intrinsic properties need be essential properties, denying 2 and 3, and having no need for 4, but still wanting to say that for every property F had by an individual x, if an individual lacked F, it wouldn't be x. According to a prominent defender of the strong instrinsicalist reading of Leibniz, Robert Sleigh, complete concepts immediately include all monadic properties of an individual, accidental or essential, and include relational properties in some derived sense.

One task is to elaborate these three readings so as to determine what's at stake in choosing among them. In doing so, we can articulate much that Leibniz has to say about identity and relations as well. When we grasp Leibniz's theories of (*de re* and *de dicto*) modality, identity, and relations (and their interconnections), we will have the skeleton on which to develop a more adequate account of his entire metaphysics, and with that in place, an account of his epistemology, philosophy of mind, theory of value, theodicy, and so on. I began making headway in that direction in section 4.3. There and elsewhere I am clearly committed to reading Leibniz as a strong instrinsicalist. In the next three sections I elicit further implications from this understanding of his metaphysics.

4.7 Understanding what it means for the world to be the best possible

Degree of clarity of perception is the explanatorily basic criterion of degree of *metaphysical perfection*, so Leibniz's account of bestness can more fundamentally be restated in terms of the perceptual states of monads. For example, the necessary condition that laws invoked in explanations in the best possible world be most natural, which is explicated in terms of making appeal to the natures of created things, and not miracles, amounts to the condition that the laws appeal to the distinct perceptions of monads, since for Leibniz there are no miracles in the sense of contraventions of the general order, but only in the sense of contraventions of the subordinate regulations accessible to our minds. That is, all explanations for Leibniz must appeal to the natures of created things (voluntarism is false; the principle of sufficient reason is true), but as Leibniz says at DM 16, for example, a distinct understanding of the general order is beyond all spirits; what we call "natural" depends on less general maxims which creatures can understand. And understanding is a form of distinct perception. So, non-miraculous explanations are ultimately appeals to distinct perceptions of monads (though proximately they may appeal to phenomenal regularities – but remember that the phenomenal is based on the monadic, and the real individual attributes of all monads are just their perceptual states).

For those monads, namely rational souls or spirits, who are capable of *moral perfection*, metaphysical and moral perfection are necessarily correlated. This is true because spirits by nature attempt to bring about what seems best, and since the more distinct their perceptions, the more their apparent goods will be really good, the more distinct their perceptions, the more they will act virtuously or justly, which is what Leibniz means by "moral perfection." The same is true for physical perfection. It is necessarily connected to metaphysical perfection in that pleasure is for Leibniz, reminiscent of Spinoza, just conscious perception of an increase in perfection (and when that pleasure endures without leading to subsequent greater misery, it is happiness), and so animal souls and spirits (that is, those monads capable of a degree of physical perfection), given the essential interconnection of all things in a world, can't help but enjoy greater physical perfection whenever there's an increase in metaphysical perfection, so long as they're aware of it. (As an aside I note that awareness here must be construed as something more minimal than thought, since thought for Leibniz requires apperception, and only spirits, not animal souls, are capable of apperception.) So overall, the explanatory hierarchy seems to be this: the value of a just action (moral perfection) is founded on the fact that it produces pleasure (physical perfection), which is in turn explained by its effect in increasing the metaphysical perfection of the agent and the world. Metaphysical perfection is basic.

I think that if we didn't fundamentally associate increase in metaphysical perfection with increase in clarity of perception, it would not follow that increase in metaphysical perfection leads to increase in moral and physical perfection. For if overall the monads weren't more aware of the universe's development, even if such development were occurring, they wouldn't experience pleasure, nor would they more reliably act justly. I hedge by saying "overall" because locally it might seem that greater metaphysical perfection does not imply greater physical perfection. For example, in the metaphysical sense, one who suffers pain is more perfect than one lacking sensation altogether. But in this case the metaphysically more perfect one is physically less perfect, or at least that's so if the incapacity to have any physical perfection is properly described as being less physically perfect, rather than as being neither physically perfect nor imperfect. (In at least one place Leibniz himself seems to opt for the second description. In the 1714 letter to Bourguet (Loemker 1969: 662) he says that when an intelligent being loses his capacity to understand, it is still (metaphysical) evil, even if the loss involves no pain and no sin.)

Perhaps the best way of summing things up is this: though sufficient metaphysical perfection implies happiness and justice, the converse is false, metaphysical evil does not imply pain or sin, since without sufficient meta-physical perfection pain or sin is impossible, though of course some metaphysical evil is a necessary condition for pain or sin (witness God). Finally, that fact that metaphysical evil is only necessary for the other kinds of imperfections allows us to question the claim that, since metaphysical evil is just limitation, sin and pain must be purely negative too. Here I suppose the distinction between limitation and privation may be usefully invoked. The metaphysical evil exhibited by a group of monads which are the foundations of a rock, for example, is just a limitation, but, for example, the moral evil that a spirit perpetrates is not mere lack, but a lack of something which by nature it should have. (This distinction makes theodicy much harder.) Of course, given the complete concept theory of individuals, etc., it is arguable whether for Leibniz himself this distinction between limitation and privation is exemplified, but I leave that topic alone.

Turning more directly to theodicy – Leibniz's defense of theism against the problem of evil – we should note that God is morally perfect, and his moral perfection follows from his metaphysical perfection. But this does not entail the world is morally (or metaphysically) perfect, a conclusion ruled out by the identity of indiscernibles, since if the world were perfect, it could not be distinct from God. And since moral imperfection is sin, and admit-tedly there is sin in this world, this world is not morally perfect. To cite just one of several passages, *Theodicy* 21 says outright that even the best of all possible worlds contains some moral (as well as metaphysical and physical) evil.

On Leibniz's mature view, God does not disregard non-rational individ-uals when their welfare conflicts with those of rational spirits. Not even early and middle texts, such as the *Dialogue between Polidore and Theophile* (ca. 1678), transparently say or imply that rational beings need not fear that God will compromise their welfare for the sake of other kinds of creatures, since rational beings or spirits are infinitely more important. There's infinite gradation between us and other creatures, but so is there infinite gradation between God and us. If the welfare of the infinitely less is of no account, why does our welfare matter to God either? In general, the *Dialogue* conveys the metaphysical gradualism (which always nevertheless admits of infinite differences) and attendant metaphysical value commensurability and mutual accommodation theses characteristic of Leibniz's mature thought. And in texts such as DM 35–7 where Leibniz does affirm a spirit-dominated value theory, he just goes overboard, saying that spirits express God rather than the world, whereas other substances express the world rather than God, which contradicts sections 9 and 16, which explicitly say that each person expresses the world, and that an effect always expresses it cause, so all created substances express God too.

And even if each spirit's happiness were of infinitely greater importance than any other kind of thing, it doesn't follow that there would be no unhappiness. Each spirit's happiness might be infinitely more important than any other *kind* of thing, but since there is more than one spirit, more than one instance of the same kind – spirit – some spirits might be unhappy because of other spirits' activity.

Leibniz insists there is a uniquely best possible world. That world is supposed to be the richest, or contain the most variety. What does the notion of variety, taken by itself, and construed numerically, amount to? It would seem that, since every possible world is a compossible set of possible things, there are many possible worlds which are equally, infinitely varied and rich, and that the genuinely richest world would have to be one not characterized by more predicates, but by more intensive manifestations of (already) infinitely many predicates. So it seems variety itself is an intensive as well as extensive magnitude. And more intensive manifestations are just more distinct (more active, more intelligible, etc.) ones, so that the notion of variety itself must be explicated in terms of the clarity with which the monads perceive.

Let's restate the core of what's just been argued, to enable us to go further. Leibniz embraces the following ten-element equation: more perfection = more distinct perception = more activity = more quantity of essence = more positive reality = more affirmative intelligibility = more phenomenal variety governed by simpler laws = more harmony = more universal laws = more beauty. Degree of clarity of perception is the fundamental criterion of degree of metaphysical perfection, and degree of metaphysical perfection is necessarily correlated with degree of moral and physical perfection, so since the best is the most perfect metaphysically, morally, and physically, the most clearly perceiving is the best.

Now God's perfection is explained principally in terms of his power, knowledge, and will. Creatures acquire limited versions of these, and are more perfect to the degree to which they are less limited in activity (intrinsic force), perfection, and appetite (will). Every will naturally strives to bring about what seems best, and the perfection of will is only limited by its capacity to accurately distinguish the good. (So perfection of will is explainable in terms of perfection of perceptions.) The value of a just action (moral perfection) is founded on the fact that it produces pleasure (physical perfection), which in turn is explained by its effect in increasing the metaphysical perfection of the agent and the world. Metaphysical perfection is basic.

The best world is the richest, containing the most variety. Richest must be characterized not merely by predicates, but by more intensive manifestations of (already) infinitely many predicates. And intensive manifestations are just the more distinct (active, intelligible, etc.) ones. So variety itself must be explicated in terms of clarity of monadic perception.

I conclude this section by outlining how Leibniz's account of metaphysical activity and passivity undergirds his account of physical forces. In his usage, "primitive" means "characterizes monads" and "derivative" means "characterizes aggregates based on primitives." Primitive active force is clear perceptions and appetition toward new clear perceptions. Primitive passive force is confused perception (or prime matter). Secondary matter is extended mass (matter of seventeenth-century physics), whose two most important passive forces are inertia and solidity (impenetrability). From primitive active force derives the active forces of physics, especially live force (*vis viva*, roughly, kinetic energy). All phenomena of material objects, except perceptions, can be accounted for in terms of magnitude, shape, and motion. But the laws of mechanics themselves (and the concepts they invoke) don't derive from mere mathematical extension, but require metaphysical underpinning, which is teleological – the theory of well-founded phenomena rests on the pre-established harmony, which rests on the principle of perfection, which perhaps rests on the principle of sufficient reason.

To assist those reading Leibniz's essays on physics, I restate the position with his own terminology. A monad is a combination of *proto pathia*, primitive force of resistance, which accounts for the material properties of the world, the resistance and inertia of material objects, and the sinfulness and confusion of every non-divine mind, and *proto poeia*, primitive active force, which accounts for the presence of *vis viva* in material objects and for the perfections, the striving-towards-betterment, of every mind. At bottom, primitive active force is clear perceptions and appetition toward new clear perceptions, and primitive passive force is confused perception (prime matter); as before, greater activity is greater clarity of perception is higher degree of perfection. From prime matter derives secondary matter and extended mass, whose two most important passive forces (basic derivative passive forces) are inertia and solidity (impenetrability, *antitypia*). Secondary matter is an "aggregate" of monads (individual substances). From primitive active force derives the active forces of physics, especially live force, mass times velocity squared, mv^2 (kinetic energy is $\frac{1}{2} mv^2$), and conatus or virtual velocity. So the cause of material motion has its foundation in monadic appetition. So, the fundamental concepts of physics (terrestrial and celestial mechanics) are sufficiently accounted for by the monad's perceptions (primitive forces, since what's real in the monads are their perceptions). And appeal to metaphysical reasons (monads) is necessary.

4.8   Understanding debates about relations among key Leibnizian theses

After introducing his conception of truth and complete concept theory of individual substance in DM 8, Leibniz in DM 9 begins to trace several "noticeable paradoxes" – surprising but importantly true results – that logically follow. These include the following claims. The question is how are they connected to each other?[4]

- Whole-expression: Each individual substance expresses the *whole* universe from it own (unique) point of view.
- Same-expression: Each individual substance expresses the *same* universe from its own (unique) point view.
- Connection: Each individual substance is connected with every other individual substance.
- Mirroring: Each complete concept mirrors all other complete concepts in the possible world in which it is contained (their constituent concepts of properties are inter-deducible).
- State-inclusion: The nature of each individual substance is such that each of its states is a consequence of its predecessor (and contains it successors).
- Universal harmony: There is a universal harmony among all individual substances.
- Compossibility: Individual substances can coexist only if their complete concepts are compossible (and vice versa, if possible individuals *have* complete concepts).
- And recall from DM 8, Complete concept: Each individual substance has (exemplifies) exactly one complete concept, which allows for the deduction of all the true predications concerning it (and conversely, if possible individuals *have* complete concepts),
- and Truth: "S is P" is true if the concept of S includes the concept of P.

As a suggested account of compossibility: complete concepts are (mutually) compossible if every true predication contained in the one is deducible from the other, and vice versa. As a suggested account of expression: a given substance expresses the whole universe just in case what is true of the whole universe is deducible from what is true of a given substance, via its complete concept. Connection is the analogue in actuality of compossibility in the realm of possibility. Harmony is the analogue in actuality of mirroring in the realm of possibility (as applied to complete concepts). Talk of the law of the series of states is the counterpart in actuality to talk of the given complete concept in the realm of possibility.

---

4   The first half of this section is based heavily on Mondadori 1977.

In DM 9, 14, 15, 26, and 33, the *Correspondence with Arnauld*, *First Truths*, *New System*, *Principles of Nature and Grace*, *Monadology*, *Letters to De Volder*, and *Correspondence with Clarke* each of the following claims seems supported by different passages:

1   Mirroring entails Expression
2   Complete concept and Compossibility entails Mirroring
3   Complete concept and Connection entails Mirroring
4   Complete concept entails Whole-expression
5   Complete concept and Compossibilty entails Same-expression
6   Same-expression entails Complete concept and Compossibility
7   Same-expression entails Connection, regarded as a special kind of expression
8   Same-expression entails Harmony
9   Harmony entails Same-expression
10 State-inclusion entails Harmony
11 State-expression entails State-inclusion

I further suggest that 12 Truth does not entail Compossibility, and 13 Truth does not entail Same-expression. But add Connection to Truth and you get Compossibility and Same-expression. The structure of the relations among these principles and notions is supposed to be a consequence of Truth.

The task is to figure out whether there is a linear dependency between the various, distinct theses, or whether there's a massive circle, and if so, whether it is vicious and overlooked, or non-vicious and deliberate.

There is one question about the interrelations among theses that deserves special note. How can we square Complete concept (every possible individual substance instantiates some complete individual concept), Incompossibility (not all possible individuals substances are compossible), and Internal relations (the individuation of a substance does not depend on its relation to other individuals but depends only on its internal features)? As regards the last thesis, Leibniz argues that what makes a certain substance the substance it is cannot depend on how it is related to other things; substances are things that enter into relations, which presupposes that they have their individuality somehow determinate before entering into these relations.

(Complete concept) and (Internal relations) entail that complete concepts are at their core definable without relational predicates. This core concept fixes the identity of the individual and individuates internally at the fundamental level, metaphysically (from a human epistemological perspective we can identify things in relation to other things).

The perplexity is this. (Internal relations) excludes relations, but we ostensibly need relations to explain (Incompossibility). Compossibility itself is the external relation of existing-in-the-same world. How do we explain the fact that some possible substances can be in each other's way so that even an omnipotent God cannot create all possible substances? Also, world-boundedness of substances seems tied logically to the claim that what a thing is depends on how it is related to other things, which again fits uneasily with (Internal relations). On the other hand, recall that traditionally, substances essentially don't depend for their existence on the existence of anything else. What to do?

If "incompossibility of substances" means "logical incompatibility of their complete concepts," then it seems that (i) we must countenance relational concepts as components of complete concepts to get incompossibility, and (ii) individual world-boundedness implies that instantiation of one individual's complete concept logically implies the instantiation of its whole world, both ostensible assaults on (Internal relations). But if substances are logically independent of each other, how can we deny there's a possible world in which both exist? Perhaps by imposing constraints on possible worlds not grounded in incompatibilities between complete concepts. For example, Russell (1900: 67) says all possible worlds must have general laws (i.e. exhibit a general order); this is a metaphysically necessary external constraint on compossibility. But this won't do, since such a constraint is automatically satisfied by all logically possible worlds (for example, see DM 6).

Again the task is to bridge the gap between inner states of monads and relational predicates true of them needed for incompossibility, consistently with the internality of individuation and world-boundedness of individuals. It appears that a solution requires constraints on compossibility derived from a deeper understanding of what it is to be a world for Leibniz. Given his special pride in introducing the pre-established harmony, my best guess is that Leibniz held that for any two substances, there exists a possible world in which they both belong if and only if their states are in sufficient harmony with each other, that is, given that their states are perceptions, they can be conceived as two perspectives on the same world. Perceptions express or represent only insofar as the pre-established harmony ensures that they correspond in suitable ways with monadic states of other substances. So, possible worlds must be minimally harmonious. And, to retrieve the earlier ten-element equation and now add an eleventh equivalent, more harmony means simpler laws of nature, etc., so that we now understand Leibniz's claim that *the maximally harmonious, best possible world is the maximally compossible one.*

4.9   Space and time as relations among phenomena

Space is ideal, not real. If it were real, it would be either a substance or an attribute (since only those are real), but it is neither. It would be an attribute only if the essence of matter (which "occupies" space) were extension, but (since extension itself is the appearance of a plurality of continuously coexisting substances, and force is needed to explicate the behavior of the material) it is not. It's not a substance because since absolutely uniform, its parts would be indiscernible, and then there would be no sufficient reason for one arrangement of parts over another, which is absurd. Also, since spatial points don't exist (they're just boundary notions), and a whole can't exist if its parts don't, space can't be real.

Space is relational, not absolute. There is no absolute position, but only mutual relation of things, from which position is abstracted. Space is an order of coexisting things, an order according to which situations (points of view) are disposed. When the relation of situation of a body A to bodies C, D, E, etc. changes, while the mutual relations of situation of C, D, E, etc. do not, we infer that the cause of change is in A, not C, D, E, etc. If after another body B has, to C, D, E, etc. a precisely similar relation of situation to that which A formerly had, we say B is in the same place as A was. But really there is nothing individually the same in the two cases, since in the first case the relations of situations were (reducible to) attributes of A, in the second, attributes of B, and the same individual attribute can't be in distinct subjects. So the identity implied in "same place" is a mental construction – they are only precisely similar relations of situation (by the complete concept theory, since situation = point of view, which depends on a thing's complete concept, and for each complete concept there is one and only one substance). Spatial relations do not hold between substances, but only between simultaneous objects of perception of each substance (which correlate by the pre-established harmony in non-chaotic spaces). Space is a plenum – the smallest distances are infinitesimal, and the series of distance relations is dense (between any two there is another). There is no absolute motion or rest. Rest, for example, is the occupancy of a certain place by a body simultaneous with two events which are not simultaneous with each other. Situation is an intrinsic property (or set of properties) of individual substances; place is an extrinsic property, a possible relation between a limitless number of subjects at different times, and space is the assemblage of all places, taken together.

This is Leibniz's theory of space. His opponent, Newton, conceives space as a three-dimensional receptacle in which objects can be located (with an intrinsic metric) and which could exist even if no objects existed.

The Newtonian view of space is well-captured by the following claims:

1   Space is logically prior to matter
2   The volume of a body is distinct from the space a body occupies
3   Space is indivisible and continuous
4   Space is actually infinite
5   The points of space are not perceptible
6   There is absolute motion, which requires absolute space
7   Regions of space have absolute magnitudes, which are comparable
8   Space is an attribute of God, which immediately and necessarily follows from his (itself necessary) existence

In parallel fashion, Newton's conception of time is conveyed by these claims:

1   Time is logically prior to (independent of) events
2   The duration of a body is distinct from the time a body occupies
3   Time is indivisible and continuous
4   Time has no beginning nor end
5   Moments of time are not perceptible
6   Absolute motion requires absolute time
7   Stretches of time have absolute magnitudes, which are comparable
8   Time is an attribute of God

On the Newtonian, absolute view it is meaningful to suppose the universe as a whole rotates about an axis or does not, and the universe if finite has a motion of translation or is translationally at rest (moves uniformly in a straight line or not). These are not meaningful suppositions on the relational theory. On the relational theory it is not meaningful to say the universe is finite or infinite, and if it is finite, to say it might have been bigger or smaller at some specific time than it was previously, or might become bigger or smaller than it is now, or say matter is continuous or with holes.

So, on Leibniz's relational view, space is content-relative, relative to the things in it. It is an order of coexistence. Therefore it is an order among compossibles. Therefore there are no spatial relations across (possible) worlds. But since space is content-relative, spatial structures can be radically different in different possible worlds. Apparently each possible world must have some spatial order since even a chaotic arrangement is orderable (compare DM 6). Our best possible world is optimally rationally ordered, optimally lawful, and so our space lacks holes (and our time exhibits "equable flow"), but space is not in principle continuous. (What rests on the pre-established harmony of points of view of monads is contingent.) Our space is founded on the system of mutually coordinated perceptions (states, individual accidents) of monads. It (but not space per se) is a plenum. Apparently, space requires time and vice versa for Leibniz. As order of coexistence, that is, order among mutually contemporaneous states of things, there could be no space in an atemporal context. As order of succession, that is, order among the various different mutually *coexisting* states of things, it must have some sort of "spatial" structure. (I'm now talking about public time, not private or intramonadic time. Intramonadic time is appetitional transition from perceptual state to perceptual state.)

Leibniz has various interconnected goals: to refute the absoluteness of space, to refute the existence of a void, to refute the thesis that space is God's sensorium, and to refute the thesis that space is some sort of property, which is Samuel Clarke's view.

Here is a nice, representative argument, from his Fourth Letter to Clarke, in support of his account of space. If you have the pleasure to read the

Leibniz–Clarke correspondence,[5] keep in mind that Leibniz sometimes grants for the sake of argument claims he thinks he has refuted in his metaphysical writings.

1   If space is a property, it is a property of God or of things other than God.
2   If space is a property of God, things move about inside God, God's essence has parts, empty space is a property of God, etc.
3   The consequents of 2 are absurd.
4   So, space is not a property of God.
5   So, if space is a property, it is a property of things other than God.
6   If space is a property of things, there must be things in which it inheres in order for it to exist.
7   For Newton, there is nothing in the space between things.
8   So, for Newton, there are properties which do not inhere in substances, which is absurd, and contrary to 6.
9   So, the only way to salvage the claim that space is a property is to say it is an ordering property among things.
10 So, the only way to salvage the Newtonian claim that space is a property is to treat space as I do – the only coherent rendering of Newton's property-view reduces Newton's position to my position.
11 If space is an absolute reality, substances will depend for their existence on it and not conversely, even God would be unable to change it, there would be an infinite number of eternal things besides God (the parts of space), etc.
12 The consequents of 11 are absurd.
13 So, space is not an absolute reality.
14 The fundamental Newtonian claims about space are absurd unless they are interpreted as equivalent to my view of space; clearheaded Newtonians are Leibnizians.
15 There are no alternatives to considering space as some sort of property (broadly understood) or as an absolute reality.
16 So, my view of space is correct.

4.10   Key elements of Leibniz's epistemology

Leibniz was not especially interested in epistemology, and was largely dismissive of some of its traditional problems, such as skepticism. Nevertheless, an interesting, skeletal theory of knowledge does emerge from his metaphysics. The best rendition of this theory occurs in McRae (1976), whose presentation I summarize.[6]

---

5   The Third through Fifth Letters are especially wonderful.
6   To preserve coherence, I present his account without comment. But I do find some of its elements problematic, as indicated in Tlumak 1982.

1 Perception is the natural expression of a multiplicity in the unity of a subject.

2 X expresses Y if and only if the elements of X and Y are ordered in a one-to-one correspondence. (Conventional expression succeeds only for those familiar with applicable rules of correspondence, and application of different rules might result in different interpretations of the expression. No such conditions govern natural expression.)

3 A monad's immediate awareness of *its* perceiving *this* or *that* is apperception.

4 Minimal awareness requires apperception.

5 Perception itself is not a form of awareness.

6 Perceptions express the world as intentional object.

7 All subjects or monads have bodies, which are themselves expressive, though not, since composite, perceptive.

8 A subject expresses the world (mediately) through its body; so perception is expression once removed.

9 Mediate expression of the world is still expression of the world since expression is a transitive relation: if X expresses Y and Y expresses Z, then X expresses Z.

10 Both inter- and intra-monadically, there can be different expressions of the same thing, and it is a consequence of this that any two different expressions will have the same relation to each other that each has to the thing which they both express.

11 Only some substances are capable of sensation.

12 Sensation is perception heightened or distinct enough to be noticed. (The distinctness of a perception is a function of the distinctness of the sense impressions (modifications of the nervous system) it expresses.)

13 A noticed perception is really the cumulative result of a mass of separately unnoticed (*petites*) perceptions, which stand in one-to-one correspondence with bodily impressions (which are mechanically related to the rest of the material world).

14 Since noticing or recognizing perceptions amounts to apperception, sensation is a form of awareness.

15 Ideas or concepts are capacities to think something as occasion requires. Clear ideas are recognitional capacities, and recognition of an instance of a kind is the most basic act of thought, minimal awareness. Distinct ideas are capacities to enumerate sufficient marks for recognizing the item in question.

16 There is no sensation without clear ideas, hence thought, hence apperception.

17 Conversely, since recognition requires distinctness of perception, the senses are necessary to thought.

18 Apperception gives rise to capacities definitive of minds or rational souls. These capacities include the power to recognize possibilities and necessities through use of mathematical concepts; the use of metaphys-

ical concepts, concepts constitutive of mind, manifested in consciousness of the soul as one, as acting, etc.; the ability to reason; and the capacity for knowledge of one's thought-acts and thought-contents.

19 Only minds are capable of sensation.

20 Memory is a species of apperception; immediate memory is self-consciousness, since the object of consciousness is essentially past.

21 Perception is an immanent activity of the monad, governed by final causes (a pre-established harmony, reflecting the ends of the supreme cause).

22 Experience (knowledge of sensible phenomena) requires joint use of concepts produced by the senses, and innate mathematical and meta-physical concepts, which determine what is thought on the occasion of having sensations. Sensory data are recognized as approximating certain incomplete and abstract concepts (of possible but unrealizable, mathematically determinable objects) which comprise a pre-empirical conceptual framework, and will be experienced as phenomenal body only insofar as they are conceived as one entity, capable of acting and being acted on, etc., that is, only when metaphysical concepts (of real, intelligible and not sensible objects) are employed. The functions of sense and understanding are contingently related, both are necessary for experience, and their coordination relies on teleology.

4.11 Questions about Leibniz

1 Consider the following sequence:

1 God exists.
2 God chooses the best.
3 This world is best.
4 God chooses this world. (1,2,3)
5 What God chooses, exists.
6 This world exists. (4,5)
7 If this world exists, then Caesar exists.
8 Caesar exists. (6,7)
9 If Caesar exists, he crosses the Rubicon.
10 Caesar crosses the Rubicon. (8,9)

If 1, 2, 3, 5, 7, and 9 are all necessarily true, then 10 is necessarily true. The necessity of 10 is unacceptable to Leibniz, who aims to explain how Caesar freely crossed the Rubicon even though that crossing was contained in his complete concept. He insists that there are contingencies and true counterfactuals, that there could only be one God and one actual world, and that God always acts with sufficient reason. But he also clearly thinks that 1, 5, and 7 are metaphysically necessary. So, what does he say about 2, 3, and/or 9 to escape necessitarianism, and does his strategy work?

2   Is the complete concept theory the only or best way to capture the world's explicability?

3   Are all scientific explanations, such as the Big Bang, necessarily incomplete? Is physical atomism an explanatory failure? Must physics be supplemented by metaphysical explanation? Is the appearance–reality distinction itself obligatory? useful? coherent?

4   What kind of essentialist is Leibniz? Are there necessary truths about the world as it is in itself, independently of our ways of conceiving or talking about it?

5   Occasionalism is the view that since causation involves necessary connection, created things are themselves causally inefficacious, and God is the sole true cause of change in the universe. How does Leibniz's pre-established harmony differ from occasionalism? More generally, how does Leibniz make out the distinction between activity and passivity?

6   Can there be physical, individual substances for Leibniz, and in truth?

7   Does Leibniz have the resources to rebut the challenge to theism posed by the argument from evil? What does he mean in saying this is the best possible world? Why even suppose there is one uniquely best world?

8   Put starkly, Leibniz's two main arguments for God's existence are the argument from contingency – since there are contingent (dependent, not self-explanatory) beings, there must be a necessary being – and the ontological argument – since God is possible and is properly conceived as supremely perfect being, God exists necessarily. Evaluate elaborated forms of either of these arguments.

9   Many metaphysicians agree that if a is identical to b, then a and b share all their properties in common (the indiscernibility of identicals). Many fewer accept its converse, the "noticeable paradox" that if a and b share all their properties in common, then $a = b$ (the identity of indiscernibles). What is Leibniz's case for the identity of indiscernibles, and why might so many resist it?

10   Explain and evaluate how some other noticeable paradox is supposed to follow from the very nature of individual substance.

11   Is there a firm distinction between truths of fact and truths of reason?

12   Has Leibniz established on *a priori* grounds the fundamental nature of space and time that Einstein discovered empirically?

13   Does Leibniz adequately explain consciousness as a species of universal perception? What important role does unconscious perception play in his philosophy?

14   What is apperception, and why is it so important?

15   I am struck by the ubiquitous parallels between Leibniz and Spinoza, yet their radically different results. If you are similarly struck, what do you think is the deep diagnosis of their differences?

4.12   Some recommended books

Adams, R.M. (1994) *Leibniz: Determinist, Theist, Idealist*, New York and Oxford: Oxford University Press.

It is widely agreed that Leibniz is a determinist and theist. It is controversial whether he was steadfastly idealist. Adams painstakingly elaborates the forms of these three positions that Leibniz embraced and is sympathetic with the case for theism and idealism, but not determinism. An impressive amalgam of historical interpretation and philosophical analysis and argument, stylistically lucid but difficult because of its extraordinary detail.

Brown, S. (1984) *Leibniz*, Minneapolis: University of Minnesota Press.

An easy-to-read, general introduction, strong on exposition, light on detailed argument, especially helpful in highlighting some changes in Leibniz's thinking from pre-*Discourse* to *Discourse* and after. Treats the mature Leibniz as a problem-solver, not foundationalist demonstrator.

Jolley, N. (ed.) (1995) *The Cambridge Companion to Leibniz*, Cambridge: Cambridge University Press.

Fine collection of essays on a wide variety of issues, with useful bibliography.

McRae, R. (1976) *Leibniz: Perception, Apperception & Thought*, Toronto, Buffalo and London: University of Toronto Press.

An elegantly succinct and systematic reconstruction of Leibniz's theory of knowledge, smoothly incorporating numerous and well-chosen excerpts, and ingeniously and challengingly interpreting some of them.

Mates, B. (1986) *The Philosophy of Leibniz: Metaphysics and Language*, New York and Oxford: Oxford University Press.

Full of clear, interesting arguments on most of the topics that engage contemporary readers of Leibniz, expertly and extensively marshals texts, and includes a short but unusually good biography and outline of Leibniz's system. Especially notable for its stress on Leibniz's nominalism, and its relation to his theory of individual concepts, contingency, rational explanation, world-bestness, and perception.

Rescher, N. (1967) *The Philosophy of Leibniz*, New York: Prentice-Hall.

Still one of the best straightforward introductions to Leibniz's philosophy. Reissued by Ashgate in 1994.

Russell, B. (1900) *A Critical Exposition of the Philosophy of Leibniz*, reprinted 1997, London: Routledge.

A milestone effort to derive the whole of Leibniz's metaphysics from five basic premises – three about the nature of propositions and truth, the other two asserting that the "I" is a substance and that perception gives knowledge of a world other than the "I" and its states – which, Russell argues, ultimately involve inconsistency, stemming from Leibniz's theory of relations. An exhilarating read.

Woolhouse, R.S. (ed.) (1994) *Gottfried Wilhelm Leibniz: Critical Assessments*, 4 vols, London: Routledge.

Unusually rich collection of essays on Leibniz.

For an engrossing reading of modern philosophy as centrally concerned with the problem of evil (and not in the first instance with the epistemological and metaphysical issues which I place front and center), which maturely considers Leibniz's role in its development, I recommend Neiman, S. (2002) *Evil in Modern Thought: An Alternative History of Philosophy*, Princeton: Princeton University Press.

5 Berkeley

5.1 Overview of approach to the *Principles*

We can appreciate the elegant structure of George Berkeley's (1685–1753) thinking by tracing the flow of his most important work, fully and revealingly entitled, *A Treatise Concerning the Principles of Human Knowledge. Wherein the Chief Causes of Error and Difficulties in the Sciences, with the grounds of Scepticism, Atheism, and Irreligion, are inquired into* (hereafter *Principles*), which he published at 25. The title reflects Berkeley's self-conception of the work, which I want to take seriously. As a priest, Berkeley naturally aims to develop a position that combats various forms of irreligion. But he does not conceive religion as an enemy to sound science, philosophy, or core common sense.

There seem to be three main, interacting elements in Berkeley's method. First, he is an empiricist. His ultimate evidence is always the basic data of sense experience: one cannot be deceived about the contents of states of sensory awareness as one has them, and one should attend exclusively to such contents in determining what our experiences are experiences of. His advertisement of "close and narrow survey" and "strict inquiry" concerning the principles of human knowledge refer to this unwavering restriction. The senses by themselves make no inferences and impose no theoretical constructions. Those are functions of reason.

Second, he respects undistorted common sense, and consequently, is presumptively anti-skeptical. Unlike Descartes, he is no radical revisionist of ordinary thought, established by use or custom. If possible, the received opinions of the "vulgar" are to be preserved, not dismissed or contorted. But respect for common sense is not unconditional; if a component of common sense or ordinary usage is incoherent, it must be excised.

Third, he supplies philosophical, "strict and speculative," systematic explanations of coherent common sense, based on the contents of sense experience. The brunt of the *Principles* is to defend, powerfully and independently, these metaphysical explanations, show how they mutilate minimally ordinary thought and talk, and sketch several of the further implications, especially for science and mathematics, of seeing the world rightly.

So Berkeley's method tells us that crucial philosophical truths are immediately available to anyone who examines the objects of their own thought and perception in an attentive and unbiased way. This explains why his arguments are given from the first-person perspective. The main obstacle to appreciating such truths and their implications is witting or unwitting commitment to the doctrine of abstract ideas. The bulk of the Introduction to the *Principles* criticizes the use of abstract ideas, alleged source both of most bad theory and pessimism about the possibility of good theory. Berkeley will not complain about deficient human capacities or obscure subject-matter. Philosophical perplexity is not inherent to our situation in the world. Rather, as he poignantly says, "we have first raised a dust, and then complain, we cannot see" (*Principles* 3).

If you do not deny the existence of a problem, and do not evade addressing it, but propose and defend a way of overcoming it, we can call you a "solutionist." Berkeley thinks there are some real philosophical problems, and proposes an elegant, intuitive solution to them. But we also see in Berkeley a pioneering "dissolutionist," who aims to show that much philosophy is undetected nonsense. (In the second half of the twentieth century, lots of philosophers were dissolutionists.) And again, we are induced to mouth nonsense, utter words with no content, confront ultimately unmanageable subtleties and difficulties, because of palpably indefensible abstract thinking — palpably, because if each of us just straightforwardly confronts the challenge of forming the professed, abstract ideas, we will inevitably and notably fail. This confident expectation explains the performative character of pivotal stages of Berkeley's argument. When he avows that he can't do something, we're not privy to idiosyncratic autobiography, to which the reader may respond, "So much the worse for you; I can." And when he says he'll give up his position if the reader can perform a certain thought-act, I don't believe he's worried that someone more adept than he is will admirably succeed. In the experimental spirit, his claims need testing by appeal to content of sense experience. But he has already done those tests and presents us the opportunity to confirm his decisive results.

The most fundamental, decisive result, the core truth of philosophy, is that the universe consists wholly of particular spirits perceiving particular perceptions. There are at least two incontestably ground-floor elements to this position. One is that everything that exists is particular, so wholly determinate. This is his *nominalism*. The second is that the fundamental particulars which comprise the universe are perceivers, spirits, minds, or souls — active beings who think, imagine, remember, etc. — and that any less fundamental particulars must exist in these minds, so are perceived. This is his *idealism*. There is no doubt that Berkeley is also a theist, but for now I leave it open whether God's existence is only inferable from more fundamental nominalistic and idealistic data, or whether it is the third cornerstone of his system.

Before we move on, notice a distinction that allows you and other readers of Berkeley to disagree with me already. It's the distinction between anti-materialism and idealism. Everyone agrees that Berkeley is an anti-materialist, someone who rejects a certain (materialist) theoretical account of the phenomena of everyday life and science. He unambiguously argues that the notion of matter or material substance is unintelligible; that even were it intelligible it could serve no useful explanatory role (and indeed would taint the explanatory role of God); and that even if it had a potential explanatory role, we still could never be in a position to know of its existence. Someone could be an anti-materialist without going further and being an idealist, who insists that the basic constituents of the universe are active minds alone, and that all other existing things depend for their existence on being perceived by one or more of these minds. For example, many colleagues who I respect interpret Berkeley to be a kind of phenomenalist, not an idealist, and if you study some passages, you'll appreciate the temptation. For an idealist, to exist is to be a mind (a perceiver) or to be actually perceived by a mind. Phenomenalists allow that objects exist even if not actually perceived, so long as they *would* be perceived under suitably specified circumstances. It's a tricky business to formulate precisely such a conditional analysis of objective existence. (We will admire a world-class effort when we discuss Kant in Chapter Seven.) Here I merely make plain my own reading of Berkeley as committed idealist, with fuller rationale forthcoming.

A fuller rationale is forthcoming, but a sketchy rationale is already available. Given the methodology outlined above, I take Berkeley to be arguing roughly as follows: following a strict, rigorous survey, I am only aware of two sorts of entities. I am aware of mind, namely my own. I am aware of ideas in mind, at least my own. It is evident that ideas can't exist unthought of. What third sort of entity could there be? Any candidate you proffer will have to be something we can have no conception of, so your suggestion is empty or unintelligible. At best you are merely obliquely gesturing toward something, not saying affirmatively what it is. If you think otherwise, chances are you are under the spell of the doctrine of abstract ideas. So entities are either minds or thought by minds. Given a connection between thought and perception, natural to a strict empiricist, which I will soon elaborate, on which the scope of thought is a function of the scope of imagination, which in turn is a function of the scope of sense perception, we get the characteristic Berkeleian idealist doctrine that *esse est percepere aut percipi*, to be is to be a perceiver or to be perceived.

5.2   Structure of the *Principles*

I will now outline the flow of the *Principles* so that you can better understand and evaluate it and the subsequently written *Three Dialogues*, and know where to focus if some theme especially interests you. I will do so in three stages. First I will offer a coarse-grained structuring of the work. Then I will sketch selective, particularly revealing detail. Then I will isolate for fuller discussion what I take to be the truly crucial moments of the work.

It is useful to analyze the *Principles* into four main stages. Stage One (the Introduction) aims to diagnose and begin to cure the dominant source of bad philosophy and science, the doctrine of abstract ideas. Stage Two (1–33; numbers are paragraph or section numbers; if preceded by I, they are in the introduction; if not, or if preceded by P, they are in the main text) makes the fundamental case for idealism and exposes the deficiencies of prominent, competing positions. Some exposés rely on some premise in the case for idealism; others are wholly internal critiques. Stage Three (34–84) methodically addresses objections to idealism organized according to point of view, such as the point of view of common sense and the point of view of science. Stage Four (85–134) cites advantageous implications of idealism.

Even this coarse-grained outline allows me to alert you to some central interpretive controversies. First, how precisely does the critique of abstract ideas function? That it begins the work and is so sustained suggests a vital argumentative role. That it rarely is invoked explicitly as subsequent argument unfolds (and is virtually unmentioned in the *Three Dialogues*, though it does surface at the very end of Dialogue Three) suggests a more heuristic, less cognitively vital role. I side with those who construe the anti-abstractionism as crucial, and, I add, as influential methodological innovation. Second, proportionately how much is Berkeley concerned to bolster allegiance to idealism by refutation of alternatives and objections, and elicitation of consequences? By the end of 6 the case for idealism seems complete. Consider that paragraph.

> Some truths are so near and obvious to the mind, that a man need only open his eyes to see them. Such I take this important one to be, to wit, that all the choir of heaven and furniture of the earth, in a word all those bodies which compose the mighty frame of the world, have not any subsistence without a mind, that their being is to be perceived or known; that consequently so long as they are not actually perceived by me, or do not exist in my mind or that of any other created spirit, they must either have no existence at all, or else subsist in the mind of some eternal spirit: it being perfectly unintelligible and involving all the absurdity of abstraction, to attribute to any single part of them an existence independent of a spirit. To be convinced of which, the reader need only reflect and try to separate in his own thoughts the being of a sensible thing from its being perceived.

Is there any missing step in the case for idealism, to be discovered or developed later? Or is the sequel rhetorically useful but strictly superfluous? After all, as 7 opens, Berkeley declares victory, and turns to refuting competing theories, either by dint of their internal difficulties, or by appeal to the intuitive proof just completed.

To help address this question, let's outline more determinately the book's flow through the relevant first three stages. The Introduction tells us that philosophy causes more problems than it solves (1). The problems are of our own, avoidable making (3). One major source of problems is commitment to abstract ideas (6), according to which the mind can conceive qualities separately (7), can create an abstract idea of extension as what is common to all particular extensions (8), and can create abstract general ideas of kinds of things (9). But it is impossible to conceive separately qualities that cannot exist separately (10). And it is impossible for an idea simultaneously to have all and none of the properties of the things to which it applies (13). Ideas can be general without being abstract (12). A particular thing or idea can be universal in its signification (15). A proof about one triangle holds for all triangles if the particular features of that triangle are not mentioned in the proof (16). The abstractionist mistake arises from the mistake that the only purpose of language is communication of ideas, and that every significant expression on every occasion of use stands for an idea (19). Language has other purposes, and general expressions are often used successfully without associated ideas in either speaker or hearer (20). To avoid merely verbal disputes and problems with abstract ideas, we should focus on ideas directly, bypassing potentially misdirecting words (21–3). This completes Stage One.

We saw that 1–6 of the main body of the *Principles* ostensibly gives a sufficient proof of idealism. But idealism is contested by the favored theory of the new science, representative realism, whose three main components are that ideas in the mind are ultimately caused by mind-independent, unperceiving material objects; that some properties of those objects, the *primary qualities*, resemble the ideas they produce; and that other properties of those objects, the *secondary qualities*, are a function of the objects' primary qualities and the variable conditions of the perceiver and her environment. So Berkeley turns to excluding representative realism, relying on three considerations: that sensible (secondary) qualities are sense perceptions or ideas of sense (in Chapter Three I argued that this is a misreading of Locke, however accurate to some representative realists); that an idea cannot exist in an unperceiving thing since then it would exist unperceived – a contradiction (7); and that things outside the mind which resemble ideas cannot exist, since an idea can be like nothing but an idea (the *likeness principle*) – we can only conceive of likenesses (resemblances) between our ideas (8). He adds that primary qualities (figure, size, motion) can't exist separately, even in thought, from secondary ones, so they too can't exist in an unperceiving thing (9–10). Indeed, all the reasons, such as perceptual relativity, that philosophers give for the mind-dependence of secondary qualities apply equally to primary qualities (14). The bottom line is that we have no clear understanding of matter. Rather, it's described negatively as inert, senseless (incapable of sensing) substance, which has primary qualities, but qualities are sense perceptions and it is contradictory to suppose sense perceptions can exist unperceived (9).

Even if independent objects with primary qualities were possible, we could not know about them. Such knowledge would have to be based on either the senses or reasoning. But the senses acquaint us only with sensations. And even the realists admit that material objects are not necessary for having various kinds of experiences, as dreams show (18). Nor are material objects made probable by their capacity to best explain our ideas, since even their proponents admit they can't understand how body acts on mind. So matter is neither knowable nor explanatorily useful, and its superfluous postulation diminishes God (19). But again, the utterly disqualifying bottom line is that its very notion is contradictory.

Sections 22–4 succinctly reformulate what Berkeley stresses is his decisive insight, allowing his entire philosophy to rest on it. This passage is often referred to as his *Master Argument*, and given (along with 1–6) its professed centrality, I will treat it separately later.

We each perceive a succession of ideas, and since ideas are manifestly inactive (so can't be causes), some active spirit must cause the succession (26). But since some ideas are not caused by me (sense ideas are independent of my will), there is some other spirit causing them (29); that spirit is God, whose wonderful rules of regular succession we call the laws of nature (30), which enable us to reach our goals (31). These sense ideas are real things – more vivid, orderly, and coherent than ideas of our imagination, more independent than ideas of our will, but ideas nevertheless (33). This completes Stage Two.

This philosophy squares with everyday thought and action, and only undermines substance as understood by materialist philosophers, a main source of atheism and pointless dispute (34–5). A recap of doctrine confirms this (36–7). It is true we experience things outside or at a distance from us, but that doesn't entail that those things exist outside the mind, as dreams of distant objects prove (42). And many other philosophies, but not ours, are saddled with the consequence that bodies are at every moment annihilated and created anew, or don't exist at all when you or I don't perceive them, since on our philosophy it is only necessary that some mind or other perceive them (45–8).

This philosophy also squares with physical science, properly understood. Physical laws explain by appeal to properties such as figure and motion, which are ideas, not by appeal to some mysterious, underlying material substance. Such laws state regularities among phenomena (= ideas) (50). Strictly speaking, just as the sun doesn't rise, ideas like fire aren't causes, but it is convenient to talk that way; "we ought to think with the learned, and speak with the vulgar" (51). After all, ordinary usage is regulated by custom, so tracks common opinion, which may not be the truest (52). And note that others have realized that no object of sense can have active power, and have attributed all causation directly to God, but nevertheless have pointlessly retained such objects as existing outside the mind (53). This system fully allows for the exquisite mechanisms in nature (60). It is the materialist who invokes superfluous intermediaries, and again, their objects' admittedly inert features such as bulk and figure can't *cause* anything (61).

There are empirically discoverable, universal, general laws governing phenomena (62). Rare exceptions to them are reminders of God's agency.

But the harmony and efficacy of nature's regular operations suffice to convince of his wisdom and goodness (63). Indeed, a connection of ideas does not imply a cause–effect relation, but only a relation between sign and thing-signified. Combinations of ideas into machines (artificial and regular combinations) are just like combinations of letters into words according to rules. Real things are signs, prognosticators, from God (65). So science should not pretend to explain by appeal to material causes, which alienates us from the supreme spirit "in whom we live, move, and have our being," but should try to understand divine signs (66). This is what we need from Stage Three.

A central insight to carry forward is that to withhold attribution of any positive quality to matter, so to say only that it is *un*observed, *inert*, *senseless* substance, is to lapse into total unintelligibility.

5.3   A fuller analysis of four key arguments

I now want to consider a bit more expansively four arguments. The first is the Introduction's critique of abstract ideas. As I mentioned, scholars dispute the importance of this critique. Some see it playing no ineliminable, mature role. Some see it as *diagnosis* explaining the source of various mistakes, but not as part of the *proof* that they are indeed mistakes. I see it as a fundamental component of the argument, recurrently operative, albeit often subterraneously.

Locke exemplifies the target of Berkeley's critique. Berkeley reads Locke as believing that words are conventionally established, publicly sensible marks of ideas, needed because ideas, which are only introspectively discrim-inable items of consciousness, are invisible to others. Words not associated with ideas are noises signifying nothing. And he takes Locke to believe that we can construct or frame abstract ideas; they are not raw materials of consciousness, like simple ideas of sensation and reflection, but products of a special mental operation. We can abstract (= mentally separate off) a respect in which many particulars resemble one another. Those respects of resem-blance are a matter of attention and, in part, choice. This abstract idea can be assigned a name, so that the name immediately signifies the idea in our mind just framed by abstraction. Just as "Tlumak" names me, so "red" names the abstract idea Redness. The word, called a "general word," can be used to characterize particulars – for example, "red" can be used to charac-terize particular red things – because the particular(s) "conforms" to, is accurately depicted by, the abstract idea, which serves as exemplar. It is true that our ability to use general words depends on the fact that objects and events do resemble each other more or less closely – anything absolutely unique in every respect would defy description; we couldn't say what *sort* of thing it is, what it is *like*. But, as Berkeley sees it, Locke isn't just claiming that we do teach or learn the meanings of words by indicating cases of use, etc.; Locke rather offers his account as the *explanation* of our ability to teach (learn) the use of general words; that is, the essential step in understanding a general word is to frame an abstract idea. And our ability to frame these abstract ideas is not limited to isolated qualities of particulars; we can also frame generic ideas of kinds of substances, such as "human" and "gold."

Berkeley rejects the possibility of abstract ideas, as described by Locke. Berkeley's critique may be sketched as follows. He says: I can abstract x from y if and only if it is possible that x exists unaccompanied by y (I10). "Abstracting" means "imagining separately," "framing an idea" means "imagining," and an idea is any sensible or imaginable thing. So, substituting the definitions, Berkeley is saying that I can have an image of some quality x in isolation from an image of some quality y if and only if it is possible that x exists independently of y, in reality. Rather than formulating the principle of legitimate abstraction in terms of individual capacities, for Locke could then claim that he could do what Berkeley unimaginatively couldn't, we do better to formulate it in a logical mode, namely that the idea (image) of x is abstractable from the idea of y if and only if it is possible that x exists unaccompanied by y. That is, what *can't* be separated in reality can't be separated in imagination.

Since, for Berkeley, the possibility of real existence of things is equivalent to the possibility of actual perception of things, and since the limits of possible perception define the limits of conception or imagination (5), the principle states that the idea of x is abstractable from the idea of y if and only if it is possible that x is perceived at time t and y is not perceived at t, accompanying x.

Berkeley uses this principle of legitimate abstraction to refute the abstract idea theorist who claims, like Locke, that (1) we can think apart that which is necessarily bound together in sense (I7) and (2) we can form general concepts of classes of sensory things (I9). An example of the first kind is that extension, color, and motion are alleged to be abstractable even though the latter two could not possibly be perceived (exist) without the former. Note how this violates Berkeley's principle. An example of the second sort is that it's allegedly possible to frame an abstract idea that is a compound of ideas, each constituent of which is instantiated by every instance of the compound. But Berkeley says that if being a man, for example, entails being of some color or other, some size or other, etc., then it's impossible to have an idea of man which is not of some definite (determinate) characteristic of each kind. It's impossible to imagine a purely generic man.

Note that at I13 Berkeley rules out the possibility of a third class of abstract ideas – ones allegedly including all the properties of all the instances of the idea (for example, a triangle at once equilateral, scalene and isosceles) – but feels no need to appeal to his principle of abstraction, since this class of cases is incoherent; the cases are outright self-contradictory.

Although Berkeley rejects Lockean abstract ideas, he doesn't reject general words. But for him, an idea's generality consists not in its own nature, but in the *use* that is made of it. The particular idea (like all ideas, it is particular) is being used as an example, representing or standing in for all instances of all the relevant kind, and is not wedded to the particular, representative instance. So, for Berkeley, to say that a word is general is not to say what sort of (abstract) entity it names, but is rather to say how it is used in discourse about ordinary things.

The key to Berkeley's critique of Locke is the inference from *impossibility in existence* to *impossibility in imagination*. This might rest on the principle that to be an image of F is to be an image that is F. That seems false. An image of a sleepy, smelly dog is not itself sleepy and smelly. This raises the related, more general question whether images must in all respects be determinate. If not, then the fact that there couldn't be an object of a definite character does not imply there couldn't be an image of that object. Ask yourself how this relates to Berkeley's explicit commitment that an idea can only be like another idea. Also, has Berkeley got Locke right? The ensuing discussion of the Master Argument will bear on these questions. Minimally, here Berkeley is pressing the point that considering X and Y separately is not considering X and Y as separate.

Let me add that the relations between different senses of conceivability, imaginability, experienceability, and possibility, and between inconceivability, unimaginability, unexperienceability, and impossibility, are among the deep-core issues of much philosophy, especially modern philosophy. For example, many philosophers use conceivability tests for possibility, but it proves difficult to explicate a sense of "conceivable" on which conceivability is both identifiable independently of possibility and guarantees possibility.

We have seen that Berkeley wanted to undermine skepticism and atheism by refuting materialism. His anti-materialist thesis is that there is (are) no material substance(s). Material substance is understood to be (following Locke) some entity or stuff in principle unperceivable and unperceiving, which supports *qualities that are not in any mind*. "X is matter" means "*x* is *inert, senseless* substance, in which extension, figure, and motion [primary qualities] do actually subsist" (P9). Berkeley insists that he denies the existence of material substance not merely because he has no idea of it, a negative fact, but because its notion (definition) is inconsistent, a positive fact. That *ideas* should exist in what doesn't *perceive*, or be *produced* by what does not *act*, is self-contradictory.

Also, we don't believe a particular thing exists without some reason, but there's no reason to believe in the existence of matter. We don't (by definition) perceive matter, as we do ideas. We are not acquainted with it, as we are with ourselves, by a reflex act (immediately and intuitively). Nor do we mediately apprehend it by similitude of one thing to another, as in the inductive ground for belief in other minds. Nor do we get it by deductively reasoning from that which we do know immediately, namely from ideas and the self. But perception, immediate acquaintance, induction, and deduction from given data exhaust all grounds for belief. The notion of matter would explain nothing anyway. It is a superfluous intermediary between God and us.

It's worth attending closely to Berkeley's different, detailed arguments concerning matter in *Principles* 9 (to show the notion of matter is contradictory); also in 3, and 10–21, with isolatable arguments at 14–15, etc. that matter does not exist. They make use of his most basic intuitions, for example, that qualities (primary and secondary both) are mind-dependent.

Whereas Berkeley holds that there is (are) no *material substance*(s), he *does* think there are physical objects, but argues for a non-materialistic analysis of them. One of his more famous arguments for this conclusion, from paragraph 4 and our second for added attention, may be represented as follows:

1   Physical objects can be perceived.
2   Anything that can be perceived is either an idea or collection of ideas.
3   Physical objects are ideas or collections of ideas. (1, 2)
4   Whatever is an idea or collection of ideas can't exist unperceived.
5   Physical objects can't exist unperceived. (3, 4)

The most familiar objection to this argument is that it either begs the question or equivocates in moving from 1 and 2 to 3. It avoids equivocation only if "perception" has the same meaning in 1 and 2. Some causal–representational realists *distinguish* between *direct perception* and *indirect perception*. They maintain that we directly perceive only our own ideas, but indirectly perceive physical objects. So if we read the first premise in a way acceptable to them, perception is indirect. But all parties to the discussion would agree that reading "perception" as indirect falsifies 2. "Perception" in 2 must be read as direct. But then consistent usage requires that we read perception as direct in 1, and that begs the question against the realists. The key issue is whether Berkeley can affirm 1 innocuously. He thinks he can, that he's not making some contentious theoretical move, and his discussion surrounding paragraph 4 is intended to support that. I take it that the core intuition behind all this is that the nature of a sensible thing is *the way it is for sense*. The way you see or otherwise sense each particular object, the way you sense *it*, could not exist other than as perceived. In other words, what is presented to you in sense could not exist unpresented. This intuition in section 3 foreshadows the next, Master Argument in section 23.

Connecting this up with the Introduction, note that Berkeley believed that the only thing which led to the supposition that physical objects are distinct from perceptions is belief in abstract ideas, which he thought he refuted. In truth, objects are nothing but collections of perceptions (sensations) given a common name. If it be argued that ideas or perceptions are copies or resemblances of material objects, consider whether anything could be like an idea except an idea, etc. – and we begin the set of moves we've already traced. All this gives rise to the dictum: to be is to be perceived or be a perceiver.

Our third focal passage is the magnificent Master Argument of paragraph 23. For some, interpreting Berkeley is in large measure tantamount to interpreting this three-step proof!

1   It is impossible to conceive something that is not conceived of.
2   If it's impossible to conceive of something, then it doesn't exist.
3   Nothing exists which isn't conceived of (= something unconceived of doesn't exist).

Berkeley says he's willing to rest his whole case on this (22). On its surface at least, it's a lovely argument. Or perhaps you think it's a verbal trick. (People have similar, strongly opposing reactions to the ontological argument for God's existence that played such an important role in Descartes and Spinoza.) I urge you to grapple seriously with this terse gem. I will offer this much of my own opinion. I think how you parse the first premise determines how you treat Berkeley's methodology. So, for example, inspired by his introductory attack on indeterminate, indirect, merely allusive so empty thought and language (like Locke's substance as some-underlying-something-I-know-not-what), one might treat the first premise as reporting the inescapable failure to perform a certain thought-act, namely, the act of conceiving something-not-conceived-of. Reminiscent of one way we construed Descartes' *Cogito*, it's performatively self-defeating to say you're now readily conceiving of something unconceived-of, since you're right now doing the falsifying act of conceiving. On this construal, Berkeley practices a put-up-or-shut-up strategy, utterly confident realists will embarrass themselves into silence. (Consider Hylas' repeated failures to meet Philonous' challenges in the *Three Dialogues* explained below.) If the realist replies, "hear me unproblematically label the object of my thinking: the label is 'something not conceived of by anyone,'" one can appreciate Berkeley's rejoinder that that label lacks all positive content. But there are other ways to interpret 1. I leave further probing to you.

So far Berkeley has attempted to prove that there are no Lockean abstract ideas, that material substance is impossible, that both primary and secondary qualities are ideas in minds of perceivers, and that physical objects are collections of qualities (ideas) and so can't exist unperceived. Now (25–6), as our fourth focal passage, he argues that there is a spiritual substance, God, which causes our ideas to change. The argument is in two stages:

1A   If x is an idea and x has F, then the haver of x perceives that x has F.
2A   Nobody perceives that any idea has power or activity.
3A   No idea has power or activity. (1, 2)
4A   An idea can be like (represent) nothing but an idea. (P8)
5A   No idea can even represent anything with power or activity. (3, 4)

1B   Ideas constantly change.
2B   There is no change without a cause.
3B   Something causes ideas to change. (1, 2)
4B   Qualities, ideas, combinations of ideas, and substances are all the possible causes.

5B Qualities are not (the) causes (since qualities either are or are represented by ideas – each rejected in virtue of 3A and 5A respectively).

6B Ideas are not causes. (3A)

7B Combinations of ideas are not causes (if ideas aren't, combinations aren't).

8B There is some substance(s) that causes ideas to change (the other possible explanations have been ruled out). (1–7)

9B There is no material substance (previously shown).

10B There is a spiritual substance that causes ideas to change. (8, 9, and the fact that there are no other candidate kinds of substances besides material and spiritual)

11B God exists. (10, and the fact that no finite substance will suffice)

What do you think about this argument? Whatever its cogency, its existence suggests an answer to a main question I raised at the start. His epistemology is empiricist. But are there two or three cornerstones to Berkeley's metaphysics? Two surely are nominalism and idealism. Is theism the third? It seems not. Although Berkeley is a devout theist, indeed became a bishop, whatever he may also believe on faith, it seems that he aims to derive theism from empiricism, nominalism and idealism. On the other hand, once God is in the picture, he plays an enormous role. To highlight one final interpretive controversy, some think God vitally provides the basis for fully understanding what real, sensible things *are* (not just how to distinguish them from imaginary things in terms of vividness, coherence, and involuntariness): they are signs in the language of God, the way he benevolently communicates directly with us. The materialists distance us from God with their useless, intermediate mechanism. Idealism makes manifest how gratifyingly close we are to God.

Indeed, though I do not find it fully elaborated in our two famous texts, elsewhere Berkeley seems to use an argument from nature as language to support belief in God's existence. Its thrust is that I'm rightly convinced by analogy with my own case that other persons exist by the fact that they speak to me, since I know that my creative capacities for language-use signify the existence of my own mind. (Recall Descartes' similar appeal in Part V of his *Discourse on Method*.) But (and this comes mainly from Berkeley's *New Theory of Vision*) vision itself is language, a set of arbitrary signs which nevertheless have meaning. But obviously we humans did not construct those signs which constitute the language of vision. So there is some greater mind that communicates with us about the order of nature and future events, the kind of crucial information vision provides. In sum, the same reason we have to believe in other human minds shows that divine mind, God, exists.

Finally, notice how Berkeley's God purports not to be the more abstract, distant God that true believers such as Pascal and Pope John Paul II complained Descartes had perniciously wrought. In a rich, determinate sense, Berkeley's God is omniscient since he literally has everything in his mind, is omnipotent since he literally, directly makes all real things, is benevolent since he made the series of sense ideas so orderly that it allows us to learn about everything we need and to choose actions that provide pleasure and minimize pain, etc. This is the personal God in which we live and breathe.

5.4   Structure of the *Three Dialogues*

Let's now take a look at the *Three Dialogues between Hylas and Philonous*. "Hylas" is from the Greek for matter. "Philonous" means "lover of mind." Philonous tenaciously promotes revolt from exotic metaphysical notions and return to the plain dictates of nature and common sense. His target is any worldview on which the natural world, while it may occasionally stand in some relation to minds, does so only contingently. This is the worldview of most of Berkeley's predecessors. It is, for example, Descartes' position: our minds have access to the particular features of the physical world, enabling us to navigate it for our well-being, but only because of some lawlike correlation between our sensory ideas and that world that a benevolent God freely chose to institute. For Philonous, world-not-in-relation-to-mind makes no sense. On the contrary, objects of perception are ideas, and ideas are ideas in minds.

As we proceed, note three important things. First, for Philonous, perceiving is having something before one's mind. Perceiving is not limited to the five senses (= sense perception), but includes states such as imagining and remembering as well. Here is an important example of how sensing entails perceiving, but not vice versa: sense perception essentially involves limited control (recall Descartes and Locke's acknowledgment of the involuntariness of sense perception). Since God is omnipotent, his control is not limited, and so he does not *sense* the world. But an omniscient God does *perceive* everything that happens in the world.

Second, Philonous doesn't take himself to be defending a deflated conception of natural things. As he says in the third dialogue, "I am not for changing things into ideas, but rather ideas into things." So he is not using "idea" in contrast with the physical, but does insist that physicality implies mind-dependence. And he takes this dependence to support the common-sense view that we're in direct perceptual contact with the real world, not in relation to it by dubious inference or some other form of mediation. So we might say that a sense perception (in contrast with an imaginary perception) is both dependent on and independent of its perceiver's mind. It's dependent since it's an idea, and independent since it's real. There's no contradiction since there are two types of dependence relations between an idea and a mind. Perception is dependence of a quality on a substance. This relation cannot hold between a mind and − what is essentially different from it − something material. And this relation is different from the ontological dependence of some existent, say my computer screen, on its creator, which is not me, even though I'm perceiving it. Analogously, although pains only exist when they're perceived, we don't make our pains exist (hypochondria aside). And so it is for all sensible qualities.

Third, the organizing question of the *Dialogues* seems to be who is the biggest skeptic, meaning who either denies or doubts the reality of sensible things, or professes ignorance of their nature. Philonous' systematic goal is to persuade Hylas that every form of materialism, every view that allows that reality contains some things which are neither minds nor mind-dependent, leads to extreme skepticism.

In The First Dialogue Philonous convinces Hylas that the immediate objects of perceptual experience (sensible things) are mind-dependent, so, since matter is by definition mind-independent, sensible things are not part of material reality, so not real at all for the materialist. He does so by clarifying the nature of sensible things, showing that individuals of every species of sensible thing are mind-dependent, and rebutting two sorts of reply. His arguments recurrently assume that we only perceive objects by perceiving their qualities, and that we perceive qualities without inference or interpretation. Argument-pattern one: X (for example, pain) is incontestably mind-dependent; Y (for example, intense heat) *is just like* X; therefore, Y is also mind-dependent. Argument-pattern two: perceptual experiences (across and within sense modalities) conflict; therefore, not all perceptual experiences can be *of* a determinate, material world; therefore, no perceptual experience is of a material world. The success of the arguments hinge mainly on what "is just like" and "is of" amount to. The rebuttals reject the act–object analysis of perception (such that only the act, not the object of perception is in the mind), and pose the unmeetable challenge to conceive of a sensible thing that no one has perceived, that is, brought before the mind. Reintroducing a distinction from Chapter One, Philonous' underlying commitment here is that perception and legitimate conception are *de re* and determinate, never oblique and indeterminate.

In The Second Dialogue he argues that any notion of matter distinct from sensible things is either incoherent or empty, so that the materialist must profess abject ignorance. The notions of matter impugned include matter as cause of our ideas, matter as occasion for the occurrence of our ideas, matter as instrument of God's will, and matter as entity in general. These purport to exhaust the alternative conceptions of matter. So he feels justified in saying that there is no alternative conception of real existence, besides that in terms of spirits, against which the existence of ideas might be compared unfavorably (as *mere* ideas). He also argues that since sense perceptions are not dependent on our will, they must depend on another mind, namely God's.

In The Third Dialogue Hylas concedes the skeptical implications of materialism, but argues that immaterialism is just as badly off, and to that extent aims to neutralize the force of Philonous' attacks. He offers five kinds of worry, based on theology, science, metaphysics, epistemology, and inherent credibility. Roughly, the theologically-oriented complaints are these:

- We have no clearer an idea of God or ourselves than of matter.
- Immaterialism entails that God is responsible for all evil.
- If ideas derive from the mind of God, then God feels pain, which is an imperfection.
- Since we all falsely believe in matter, God is a deceiver.
- Since God's ideas are eternal, they can't be created. And ideas in our minds can't be created before we are created. But the Bible says that God created the earth and animals before us.

I skip details of scientific unease, but not Philonous' important reply below. The metaphysical challenges are these:

- The reality of sensible things implies only that they are perceivable, not that they are actually perceived.
- Anti-materialism can't distinguish between real and imaginary and dreamt things.
- Two people can't share an idea, so can't see the same thing.
- If some ideas have extension but minds don't, those ideas can't exist in minds.

Epistemologically, how can we distinguish true from false perception, as with optical illusions such as the straight oar that looks crooked when half-immersed in water, if not in terms of correspondence with reality? And how do we account for genuine, resolvable disagreement about the nature of objects? And as regards credibility, as a professed defender of common sense, it's at least controversial, and seemingly repugnant and even dangerous, to say that all things are just ideas.

Three notable new doctrines emerge from Philonous' replies:

- Scientific theories don't describe an unobservable reality controlling what appears to us, but are only tools enabling discovery of patterns in these appearances, which are then usable to explain and predict experienceable occurrences. This has come to be called an *instrumentalist* view of science. (On the other hand, a scientist committed to matter is obliged to confront lots of daunting questions about its extent, homogeneity, gravity, divisibility, etc., and to give mechanistic explanations of what's mechanistically inexplicable, such as secondary qualities such as colors and sounds.)
- We can make the distinctions between veridical perception and illusion, and between perception and imagination (and dreams) within sense experience – perception is illusory when it would mislead about future

experience if taken as veridical; perception is distinguished by its vividness, coherence, and partial independence of will.

- We can understand publicity, how different perceivers perceive the *same* object; they do so by perceiving different parts of the object, different individual ideas that make up the collection of ideas that is the object.

Philonous also tries to seal the deal on the unintelligibility of materialism. In the first dialogue he had argued that efforts to specify the relation between material substance and its properties signified in claims that a body *has properties* inevitably appealed to one or more inexplicable notions such as substratum and inherence. Indeed, we saw that Locke himself shared such worries. By contrast, he claimed that we can well understand the relation between a spiritual substance and its ideas. When in the third dialogue Hylas doubts this superiority, Philonous responds that saying that ideas exist in the mind amounts to nothing more than the familiar claim that the mind perceives them. This response might suffice if minds were wholly individuatable by their ideas. But minds not only have ideas, they have various positive capacities, etc. as well. How is the second "have" to be explicated non-mysteriously? Locke threw a version of this gauntlet at the innatists. Can his spokesperson, Hylas, turn the tables and expose obscurities in Berkeley's account of minds? Berkeley admits, indeed insists, that he has no *idea* of mind. But he is confident that he has an intelligible *notion* of mind. Is this confidence warranted?

5.5   A mini-glossary to aid interpretation

With some of our philosophers, it is so obvious that technical terminology must be understood to portray them fairly that I've offered definitions in their ongoing treatment. I find Berkeley a wonderfully clear writer. But there is a fairly manageable list of terms whose use by Berkeley is important, but may in some cases mislead. So I offer my understanding of them in a mini-glossary here. Perhaps you can notice commonalities and differences with the other philosophers we have engaged with.

An *accident* is a non-essential quality. An *affection* is a quality caused in a thing by something external to that thing. An *archetype* is an original model or pattern of things. An *artifice* is a skill. A *chimera* is a creature of the imagination. A *compages* is a collection or mass. *The economy of Nature* is the way the natural system is managed. A thing's *essence* is its intrinsic (non-relational) nature. A *faculty* is a power. The *fancy* is the imagination. To *frame* is to make. A *habitude* is a respect or a relation. To be *indiserpible* is to be indestructible or indissoluble. If something's *inherent* it belongs to or exists in a thing. A *minimum sensible* is the smallest thing we can sense. A *mode* is a quality. An *occult quality* is a hidden quality from which manifest, sensible qualities flow. A thing's *quiddity* is its essence, what makes it what it is. *Subserviency* is purpose. To *subsist* is to exist. A *substance* is an object that exists independently. A *substratum* is a substance viewed as bearer of qualities. To be *vain* is to be empty. To be *vulgar* is to be common or ordinary, and to be *wonted* is to be usual or customary, without pejorative implication. Finally, to be *without the mind* is to be outside the mind.

5.6   Questions about Berkeley

I hope that questions I asked in the course of this chapter provide grist for your reflective mill. I add the following, overarching questions, then retrieve a few focal concerns for your consideration.

1   Diagnosing the foundations of Berkeley's system, a critic might charge that he conflates the act and object of perception (unlike Descartes and Locke) because (1) beginning with the *mind-relativity* of *what* is perceived, that is, the object, he concludes that such sensible objects are *in the mind*; (2) he adopts a form of verificationism by thinking that the only discussable *objects* are sensible objects, by which he means objects of direct perception, so one cannot perceive causes – for example, sound is a sensation, existing in the mind, and so cannot be in the air, which is a senseless substance existing outside the mind; the sound is loud, acute, etc., but motion in the air is not, so sound is not the same as motion; (3) he thinks that perception is passive, and only will is active; and (4) he thinks that ideas are determinate images, so that perceiving is receiving images, and active imagination is an act of will. One might even be prepared to agree that if you grant Berkeley these four propositions, you grant him his entire philosophy, but argue that all four are false. Do you think this is a devastating analysis, or wrongheaded on one or more points?

2   Scholars disagree about how much weight Berkeley assigns to different criteria of theory-choice as he argues for the superiority of his own idealistic position. Once non-negotiable adequacy conditions such as intelligibility and non-contradictoriness are satisfied, main criteria include a) the theory squares with common sense, b) it can explain truths of science, c) it conforms to received religious truth, and d) it can solve actively debated philosophical problems without generating new problems of its own. On a close reading of his text, how do you think Berkeley applies these criteria?

3   Boswell famously reports that his British contemporary, Samuel Johnson (not the American Samuel Johnson, whose 1752 *Elementa Philosophica* is regarded as the first American philosophical textbook, and who was a great admirer of and useful correspondent to Berkeley) famously claimed to make short shrift of Berkeley's idealism by kicking a stone while announcing, "I refute him . . . thus." Does Johnson's performance have any probative weight, or does it merely reveal a colossal misunderstanding of Berkeley's position, or does it enjoy some third status?

4 Does Berkeley's test against abstract ideas set the standards for intelligibility too high; is his conception of conception too demanding?

5 Is the primary–secondary quality distinction, an influential innovation by early modern philosophers to provide theoretical underpinnings for early modern, mechanistic ("new") science, unsustainable, as Berkeley insists?

6 Is there any empirical test for deciding between Locke's materialism and Berkeley's idealism? If not, does it follow that there is no substantive difference between their positions? Or are there defensible, non-empirical considerations which favor one over the other?

5.7   Some recommended books

Creery, W.E. (ed.) (1991) *George Berkeley: Critical Assessments*, 3 vols, London and New York: Routledge.

A rich collection of essays.

Dancy, J. (1987) *Berkeley: An Introduction*, Oxford: Blackwell.

An introduction to the main doctrines of the *Principles* and *Three Dialogues* that is largely accessible to those with no philosophical background.

Fogelin, R.J. (2001) *Berkeley and the Principles of Human Knowledge*, London: Routledge.

A clear account of how the *Principles* unfold from its basic arguments and their intuitive basis, through efforts to refute competing positions, answer objections, and show advantages to science, math, and philosophy.

Foster, J. and Robinson, H. (eds) (1985) *Essays on Berkeley: A Tercentennial Celebration*, Oxford: Clarendon Press.

A well organized collection of essays by knowledgeable scholars on central topics in Berkeley's philosophy.

Grayling, A.C. (1986) *Berkeley: The Central Arguments*, La Salle, Illinois: Open Court.

An interpretation of Berkeley's main arguments for his version of immaterialism that considers them more defensible than commonly allowed, but still dubiously dependent on some metaphysical commitments that are not supported successfully.

Pappas, G.S. (2000) *Berkeley's Thought*, Ithaca and London: Cornell University Press.

Helpfully focuses on the underrated importance of Berkeley's case against abstract ideas, his overrated commitment to common sense, and his conception of immediate perception and its objects.

Pitcher, G. (1977) *Berkeley*, London, Henley and Boston: Routledge & Kegan Paul.

A study of Berkeley's metaphysical views as based on his theory of perception – especially his account of visual perception of distance (depth perception), size, and situation, and the heterogeneity of the objects of sight and touch – and his opposition to Locke.

Stoneham, T. (2002) *Berkeley's World: an examination of the Three Dialogues*, Oxford: Oxford University Press.

An overview, followed by a detailed account of Berkley's metaphysics and epistemology, largely as they are articulated in the *Three Dialogues*, that treats them as problematic in detail, but overall as plausible as competitors to materialism.

Tipton, I. (1974) *Berkeley: The Philosophy of Immaterialism*, London: Methuen.

A focused study of the case for immaterialism in the *Principles* and *Three Dialogues*.

Urmson, J.O. (1982) *Berkeley*, Oxford: Oxford University Press.

A brief but useful, sympathetic account of Berkeley's work as criticism of characteristic scientific thought from Galileo to Newton, and of its metaphysical basis.

Winkler, K.P. (1989) *Berkeley: An Interpretation*, Oxford: Clarendon Press.

Impressively and sympathetically develops the background to Berkeley's immaterialism so that it seems natural, and then discusses some of its important consequences.

6 Hume

6.1 Main alternatives for interpreting Hume

The main trends in David Hume (1711–1776) interpretation have changed over time, though the abiding task always seems to be to determine the nature of and relations between his skepticism, empiricism, and naturalism. Prominent Scottish contemporaries took him to argue that reason is not an independent source of substantive knowledge (there is no Cartesian faculty of reason which gives us transparent insight into the essence of things), but also that beginning exclusively with subjective experience (ideas) inescapably leads to a radical skepticism about the existence of causal connections, external objects, enduring selves, real human freedom, and objective values. Their favored, commonsense alternative involved repudiating the Cartesian–Lockean "way of ideas" altogether. For much of the twentieth century most read Hume as the forefather of logical positivism, which restricts meaningful statements to what's empirically testable or to an expression of concept usage. Since most traditional philosophical claims are of neither type, they are nonsense, and since empirically testable hypotheses are the purview of science, the only proper, special role for philosophy is conceptual analysis. Later in the twentieth century the competing interpretation emerged that Hume was primarily a psychological naturalist, optimistically using experimental methods to develop a science of human nature on a par with Newton's science of matter in motion. This new science would provide the essential foundation for explaining and so understanding as simply and generally as possible everything important in human affairs – thought, action, passion, valuation, language, society, etc. – rigorously restricting itself to experience, and exposing the limits on success. On this view, like Descartes Hume builds a complete system of the sciences on a new foundation, a science of human nature which reveals instinct and imagination to be largely responsible for how we think and act. An increasingly popular interpretation nowadays is that Hume was *both* a skeptic *and* a constructive philosophical naturalist, and that these two components, vitally, work together, indeed mutually define each other. I adopt this last view, which itself takes a variety of forms.

Some initial distinctions will help clarify what kind of skeptic, empiricist, and naturalist Hume is. (Hume did not use the terms "empiricist" or "naturalist," but did use the term "skeptic.") *Theoretical or speculative skeptics* purport to expose a certain incapacity. *Normative or prescriptive skeptics* (further) recommend withholding judgment given the alleged incapacity. And *practicing or actional skeptics* in fact actively withhold judgment. *Epistemological skeptics* purport to expose an incapacity to know or justifiably believe. *Conceptual or intelligibility skeptics* purport to expose an incapacity to understand or make sense of. *Antecedent skeptics* raise doubts before inquiry is allowed to get underway. *Consequent skeptics* discover doubts in the course of inquiry. *Excessive or unmitigated skeptics* doubt everything. *Moderate or mitigated skeptics* doubt selectively or discriminatively.

There are many types of *false philosophy*. But the *true philosophy* is the *Academical* philosophy, which is a *mitigated consequent skepticism*. This is how Hume explicitly identifies his philosophy near the end of *An Enquiry Concerning Human Understanding* (Section XII, Part 3). Hume is certainly skeptical of the excessively speculative claims and non-experimental methods of the dogmatic rationalists such as Descartes, Spinoza, and Leibniz; how much more broadly skeptical he is remains to be explored. On the other hand, he unequivocally rejects what he takes to be the most extreme form of doubt, Cartesian systematic doubt (unmitigated antecedent skepticism), which would inescapably abort the possibility of all inquiry, so would be useless if implementable, but is not implementable since psychologically impossible. So one central task is to understand what mitigated skepticism amounts to and how it is achieved. This will require also understanding what sort of empiricist and naturalist Hume is.

Concerning empiricism, he certainly announces and regularly applies principles which restrict legitimate ideas, uses of language, and knowledge-claims to those based on experience, but we need to decide what he means by "experience" – is it just subjective sensation and reflection, or something broader? – what are the ways of "basing" an idea or belief on experience – is inference the only permissible basing-relation? – and what is the status of these empiricist restrictions – are they inviolable methodological constraints or testable and in-principle revisable empirical generalizations?

Concerning his naturalism, the overriding interpretative question is whether it is a purely descriptive thesis, or a normative thesis as well. Some read Hume as arguing that traditional norms of justification can't support the central elements of our ordinary worldview (our belief in an objective world, governed by causal laws, standing in relation to our persisting selves, which can freely act on that world, guided by objective values), so we should give up on traditional, *justificatory* philosophy, and turn instead to the new, achievable project of developing a general *explanation* of why in fact we hold this worldview. Others read Hume as undermining traditional norms, but then as not abandoning normative aspirations, but developing and applying a revolutionary, naturalistic account of norms. On this second alternative we can see that many, but not all, of our most important beliefs are justified, given a proper, naturalized conception of justification.

6.2   An outline of the first *Enquiry*

With this orientation in hand, let's explore Hume's line of thought first in *An Enquiry Concerning Human Understanding*, then in the earlier, more wide-ranging *Treatise of Human Nature*, and then in *Dialogues Concerning Natural Religion*. The changes from the *Treatise* to the *Enquiry* – for example, the latter downplays the detailed associationist psychology as inessential specu-lation, omits the skeptical implications of the associationist accounts of cognitive errors, avoids so severely hobbling reason that it makes room for faith, bypasses accounts of certain ideas, such as those of space and time – are revealing. Still, much of the *Enquiry* parallels the central argument Hume identifies in his Abstract to the *Treatise*, written after the *Treatise* was completed; that Abstract is as beautifully a crafted summary of the core of Hume's position as I know, so I recommend its close study. Finally, I will approach the *Dialogues* as an application of Hume's method, as that method is developed in the *Treatise* and the *Enquiry*, to the topic of religion.

One thing Hume does in section I of the *Enquiry* is to contrast the person who conceives herself as investigating matters by the use of reason alone – a strong rationalist – with the person who has a more expansive self-concep-tion which also takes seriously her social and active nature. The solitary reasoner like Descartes typically, perhaps inevitably, takes her philosophizing to be the sovereign judge or arbiter of human practices or customs, poten-tially validating some of them and discrediting others. She really is the queen of all the other sciences. Hume thinks philosophy, besides being sometimes harmlessly pleasurable, is a vital antidote to superstition and pretension. Nevertheless, we will see how he is cutting the philosopher down to size, making her more ordinarily human – "Be a philosopher; but, amidst all your philosophy, be still a [wo]man." His positions are often described as *deflationary*. Whether that means they succeed only at the expense of eviscerating what we need, or whether they defensibly reconceive things in more modest ways, remains to be examined.

In Section I of the *Enquiry*, Hume positions himself within the traditions of philosophical inquiry. We saw that philosophers like Spinoza essentially begin with metaphysics, and then deduce in turn a theory of human nature (philosophy of mind and epistemology) and an ethics. Hume stoutly resists beginning with traditional metaphysics, and insists on the need to begin good philosophizing with a theory of human nature. Since he treats a theory of human nature as a factual theory, he proceeds to explore the character of factual claims and bases for factual thinking, belief and knowledge. This is the central mission of Sections II–VI: on the origins of our ideas (II); on the empirically testable principles of psychological association (which reduce to resemblance, contiguity in time or place, and cause and effect) which glue ideas together analogously to how the principle of gravitation glues natural bodies together (III); on the definitive characteristics of factual claims about the world, which relate ideas to the world, as contrasted with claims which merely relate ideas to each other (IV); and on the nature of all thinking concerning not-immediately-present matters of fact – what such thinking cannot be based on (IV), what in fact it is based on (V), and how this basis can occur in degrees, and is not all-or-nothing (VI). With this analysis in hand, Hume proceeds to explain what his predecessors regarded as necessary connection in the real world (causality) actually amounts to (VII); what human freedom means, and how we can now readily see that freedom is not only compatible with, but requires, universal causality (VIII); and how at bottom we are in the same boat as other animals in nature (IX). He then applies his theory of human understanding, with its prospects and limits, to various religious beliefs, including belief in miracles and in a providential God (X and XI). Hume's attitude to more attenuated, more general forms of religiosity is less clear, and will be discussed when we explore his *Dialogues* later in this chapter, but certainly one of his central goals was to undermine what he calls "vulgar superstition," which largely includes competing, sectarian religions. Hume concludes his *Enquiry* with an overall account of how, methodologically and substantively, we can and cannot legitimately proceed, especially contrasting his own *mitigated* skepticism (which he identifies elsewhere with *careless* skepticism) with other, ultimately unacceptable forms of skepticism. As I mentioned above, these revealingly include Cartesian doubt, *excessive antecedent* skepticism, which proactively tries to doubt everything as a precondition for legitimate inquiry, and Pyrrhonian doubt, *undifferentiated consequent* skepticism, which reactively defuses any dogmatic belief it happens to encounter. Hume unequivocally rejects Cartesian doubt. His attitude toward Pyrrhonian doubt is more controversial. I will argue that he endorses its attempted practice as a vital part of his method, but discovers that it is unsustainable and fails by its own modest standards.

6.3   *Enquiry* Sections I–III: Basic principles and materials of the understanding

Let's look more closely at some pivotal stages of his project in the *Enquiry*, attending mainly to what are often found the more difficult but important issues. To do so effectively, some clarification of usage helps. Here are my proposals. Hume uses *reason* in a broad and a narrower sense. In the broad sense it means the faculty of inference, and includes both understanding and reason in the narrower sense. Reason in the narrower sense is the faculty of immediate intuition or demonstration, where intuition is immediate rational insight, and demonstration is a (rationally perceived) sequence of necessarily connected intuitions. *Understanding* is the faculty of factual reasoning, reasoning from experience, notably inductive or cause and effect inference. Just as the *Dialogues'* concern will be *natural* religion, religious belief based not on revelation but on evidence and reasoning, centrally factual reasoning (so that a more exhaustive analysis of religion requires a *Natural History of Religion* to understand and assess "social scientific religion," and an essay *Of Miracles* to assess testimony about revelation, etc.), so now the *Enquiry*, part of the larger systematic *Treatise of Human Nature*, aims to treat scientifically, by experimental method, the faculty of factual reasoning, clarifying its relation to reason, narrowly construed, and other components of human nature such as imagination, the senses, and the passions or the sentiments, including emotions, feelings, desires, and willings. The *imagination* is the faculty of creating and connecting and separating items that are not all present to the senses, and it generates new ideas from old ideas by means of principles of association. (Early in the *Treatise* he characterizes the imagination as the representational faculty by which we repeat our impressions in the form of ideas having less force and liveliness; and he treats *memory* of past events as a separate representational faculty.)

What we will find is this: Hume's examination of human understanding severely restricts the scope of reason (narrow) and extraordinarily expands the role of the imagination. And further exploration of human cognition and conation in the *Treatise* extraordinarily expands the role of the *passions*, and relates the passions to the imagination. Finally, Hume altogether rejects the existence of a Cartesian *intellect* as some higher, non-imagistic, representational faculty. These are key results in a larger theory of human nature, which vitally reminds us that that we are social and active as well as rational beings.

The inquiry concerning human understanding aims to vindicate empirical science against superstition and bloated rationalist metaphysics, and to provide a framework for the introduction of particular principles of scientific inference covering hidden causes, reasoning from analogy, probability, etc., but with principled reasons for concluding that ultimate causes will escape us – a unified case for inductive science, with skepticism paving the way for legitimate science and inquiry by exposing the impotence and even the incoherence of any supposed alternative (theistic metaphysics; rational insight into the nature of the material world . . .). It is also written in part as a defense of the thrust of the *Treatise* against the clergy's accusation that his philosophy is self-destructively skeptical and atheistic, and against the "easy and obvious," inspirational thinkers, most prominently Francis Hutcheson, who accused Hume's writings of "lacking warmth in the cause of virtue." Note how Hume concludes Section I by professing aspiration to combine the best of the easy and obvious, and the abstruse (more theoretical (i.e. speculative) and painstakingly detailed) manners of doing philosophy, and how he argues that the abstruse can serve the obvious, as when scientific knowledge of an animal's anatomy enriches an artist's capacity to portray that animal.

Section II specifies the materials available to the understanding. Our mental life consists of perceptions. There are two types of perception, impressions and ideas, distinguished by their greater and lesser degrees of *force* and *vivacity*, typically construed as phenomenological properties we can all readily detect ourselves, not causal properties describing how they affect further thought and action. There are two types of impressions and ideas, of sensation and of reflection, and each of these may be either simple or complex. Impressions of sensations are sensations; impressions of reflection include (possibly overlappingly) passions, emotions, desires, and willings. The first principle in the science of human nature is that all our simple ideas in their first appearance are derived from simple impressions, which are correspondent to them, and which they exactly represent. This is commonly called the *Copy Principle*. I suggest that for Hume X represents Y = X resembles Y = X copies Y = X is an image of Y.

The Copy Principle entails the denial of the existence of innate ideas, hence the rejection of a cornerstone of rationalism (as we saw prominently in Descartes and Leibniz). It also entails the denial of abstractionism, and so of ideas such as infinite divisibility and of substance as something other than a collection of particular qualities. Ideas are always determinate, never abstract, yet are sometimes functionally general (as in Berkeley). Ideas are ideas of memory, where much of the vivacity of the antecedent impression is retained, or of imagination, where most of the vivacity is lost. The Copy Principle is very often construed as an irrevisable methodological constraint on an idea's legitimacy. I read it (and all of Hume's principles) as a purportedly true since massively confirmed empirical generalization, and claim that Hume's treatment of the missing shade of blue (where he acknowledges an apparent counterexample to the principle but thinks that's not weighty enough to give the principle up), as well as many forthcoming systematic considerations, show this. That is, for me, Hume adopts experimentalist procedures without exception. But again, this is controversial.

The Separability Principle, that whatever can be (distinctly) imagined as separate (existing independently) is possibly separate, and vice versa, and more generally, that what's (distinctly) imaginable is possible, and conversely, is the second principle in the science of human nature. "Different," "distinguishable," and "separable in thought" seem to be used interchangeably. Hume also equates the imaginable with the non-contradictory. It was then common to use words like "absurd," "repugnant," and "contradictory" interchangeably, and Hume seems to analyze them all in terms of (distinct) inconceivability, which for him, as a good empiricist, is (in contrast with Descartes) tantamount to unimaginability. Imaginability is not a purely formal or syntactical property; Hume does not say that what is not *logically* self-contradictory is automatically imaginable. Something simultaneously red and green all over is unimaginable but not logically contradictory, not reducible to something of the form P and not-P. So a key is to understand more fully what imagination is. This is complicated by the fact that in the *Treatise* "imagination" (sometimes called the *fancy*) has different uses, ranging from a faculty that more or less freely conjoins and separates ideas, to producer of permanent, irresistible, and universal (not changeable, weak, and irregular) beliefs. Finally, *belief*, and its contrast with mere conception or entertaining of an idea, is a crucial, vexed notion. I'll say a few things about belief later, and see section 6.15 for a statement of Hume's allegedly different accounts of belief.

6.4   *Enquiry* Sections IV–VII: The basis of all factual thinking

Section IV begins with what the literature dubs *Hume's Fork*, which states that all the objects of human reason are either *relations of ideas* or *matters of fact*. True relations of ideas are intuitively or demonstrably certain; their denials are contradictory (in the expansive sense just noted); they are discoverable by the mere operation of thought, without dependence on what exists. As their exclusive and exhaustive alternative, matters of fact are neither intuitively nor demonstrably certain, but are more or less probable; their denials are always possible (distinctly imaginable); they are only discoverable through experience. Given Hume's project, he devotes the rest of the book to examining the bases of beliefs in matters of fact. What I think sometimes goes unnoticed is Hume's careful formulation that these two kinds exhaust the concern of *reason* (understood broadly), where to be an object of reason is to *have truth-value*, to be true or false. This is important because there are other materials of the mind, other perceptions, which play a powerful role in Hume's philosophy, but cannot be subsumed under the fork, because although they may have all sorts of other explanatory properties, they can be neither true nor false. Passions are examples of this.

Next begins one of the most famous arguments in philosophical history, and its full development takes us through Section VII. First I will baldly sketch its general flow. Then I will articulate it more fully. Here's the sketch. First question: what assures us of any not currently sensed or remembered matter of fact? Answer: all such reasonings are based on the relation of cause and effect. Natural follow-up question: how do we arrive at knowledge of cause and effect? Answer: never by (*a priori*) reason or reflection alone, wholly from (past) experience. Deeper, heretofore neglected follow-up question: what's the foundation of all conclusions from experience? Answer: (negative) not any process of reason or understanding, that is, not any demonstration (valid deduction from self-evident premises) or non-circular inductive (probabilistic) justification; (positive) custom or habit, which is based on imagination or instinct, a primary propensity which reason happily cannot abidingly frustrate or assist, since it is essential to all goal-oriented action, including survival, and all forms of inquiry into the world. Conclusions from experience are expectations based on similarities. An "object" of kind A is called the cause of one of kind B if, in our experience, objects of kind A have always been followed each by an object of kind B. There is no real, necessary connection between the objects themselves, but only a felt propensity, which custom produces, to pass from an object to the idea of its usual attendant. (On a more modest, agnostic reading, there *may* be an objective connection, but there is no good reason to believe that there is. And on a third, *skeptical realist* reading, we *can* know *that* objective connections *exist*, but may not be able to know anything about their nature or character.) The felt connection is mistaken for a connection between objects because of the mind's tendency to project ("spread") itself out onto the world, a tendency uncovered by the study of human nature.

Now for the more detailed account. It begins with an analysis or diagnosis of our thinking, gives a devastating critique of that thinking, and then provides an accurate, substitute story. Consider:

1   There is an A-event;
2   There will be a B-event;
3   If there is an A-event, then there will be a B-event;
4   Past A-events have always been followed by B-events;
5   The future will resemble the past;
6   The future has always resembled the past.

We seem to move from cause to effect, from 1 to 2, as follows: Since 6, 5. Since 4 and 5, 3. Since 1 and 3, 2. But first of all, causal relations are not knowable *a priori*, but knowable only by inference from past experience. 1, therefore 2, is invalid; the strong, rationalist conception of causation is false, since we can imagine 1 without 2, so possibly 1 but not 2. 3 and 1, therefore 2, is valid, but 3 is inferred from past experience, that is, from 4. And second of all, inferences from past experiences (inductive inferences) cannot be rationally justified. 4, therefore 3, is invalid; we can imagine the future differing from the past. 4 and 5, therefore 3, is valid, but 5 cannot be established. a) One can only establish a proposition by argument by demonstration or induction. b) 5 cannot be demonstrated, because its denial does not imply a contradiction. c) 5 cannot be established inductively (from 6), because all inductive inferences presuppose 5, thus rendering an inductive argument for 5 circular or question-begging. We cannot use induction to justify the use of induction.

So, inductive inference cannot be rationally justified by any deductive or inductive argument. As I read Hume, that doesn't mean that it is irrational. It is one of our natural instincts *necessary for thought and action*, and *so* is normative. Indeed, refined rules of probabilistic, matter of fact thinking can be developed and ought to be followed – we ought to proportion the strength of our belief to the evidence (*evidentialism*), etc. (Again, others read Hume more skeptically as abandoning normative justification altogether and sticking exclusively to de facto explanation.) The proper understanding of causal (necessary) connection and the rules for its assessment is of great import. It allows us to develop our foundational theory of human nature. Its first application, which will transform the philosophical landscape, shows us that freedom presupposes, not precludes, necessity, which brings us to Section VIII.

6.5   *Enquiry* Section VIII: Implications for freedom and morality

Ostensibly, the influential argument of Section VIII – the longest section of the *Enquiry*, on the only topic carried forward from Book II of the *Treatise* – proceeds as follows: longstanding unresolved disputes about subjects of common life and experience are very likely caused by verbal impasse (ambiguity). Such is true for the question of liberty (freedom) and necessity (causality). This is a reconciling project. Everyone has the same view here, and verbal clarification will reveal this: all affirm both liberty and necessity. The moral point of view presupposes the scientific one.

All agree that physical events are causally connected. The apparent dispute is whether things are different with mental actions. As shown earlier, our commitment to physical necessity rests on perceiving constant conjunctions of similar events, and the consequent determination of the mind by custom to infer the one from the appearance of the other. But we perceive precisely the same relations in the mental domain – between characters, motives, volitions, and actions. (Hume gives evidence for the uniformities given, and accommodates superficially disconfirming variations and exceptions. For example, varied human conduct presupposes underlying uniformity and regularity, since custom and education (environment) form stable character, based on cause–effect relations.) Hence we ought consistently to be committed to mental (i.e. moral) necessity, and at least tacitly we all are so committed, in philosophy, in the special sciences, and in common life.

People sometimes disavow universal causality though all their practice and reasoning presuppose it because they seem to perceive a necessary connection between external cause and effect but do not feel such connection between motive and action. But first, it has been shown already that such necessary connection is *never* perceived; it's a projected illusion. And second, often we don't feel that expectation of transition from motive to action when we act, but do feel it when we reflect on our (or anyone's) actions. Hume admits that when *performing* actions we familiarly adopt a different perspective than when *reflecting on* actions (agential phenomenology differs from spectatorial phenomenology), and can feel that we are subject to our will but that our will is subject to nothing. But he insists that such a sensation is false, that we are deluding ourselves. As self-consistency and consistency with plain fact requires, we can only mean by liberty a power of acting or not acting as we choose or will. Other definitions, such as action uncaused by motive, are vacuous or incoherent. Properly understood, liberty is opposed to constraint, not necessity; otherwise liberty would be equivalent to chance (the opposite of necessity), a merely negative notion that designates nothing real in nature. We can often do what we choose to do and what other choices would have prompted; in those cases there's no interference with the exercise of choice; we're spontaneous, and unexploited opportunities are real. But we can never choose in a way other than the way we do choose; unexercised power of choice (i.e. indifference) is not real.

Morality requires both liberty and necessity, construed objectively, as constant conjunction of like objects, or (at bottom equivalently) subjectively, as the movement of the mind from one object to another. Hume highlights that his properly deflated account of necessity squares with orthodox views of voluntary action, and poses no threat to morality or religion; it is innovative only with respect to the operation of matter, but here we're not concerned with physics or metaphysics. He adds that only durable features of conscious creatures are properly subject to praise and blame – not, for example, transient actions performed unintentionally or out of ignorance – and these evaluative practices presuppose necessity. We praise or blame someone for something *he* or *she does*, not for some fortunate or unfortunate *happening* at his or her locus; the action must issue or proceed from one's character for it to be one's action. Similarly, we morally assess only what flows from internal character and passions, not from external force.

Hume's concluding discussion of an objection is wonderfully revealing of his philosophical outlook. The objection is that if every event has a cause, and physical and mental causation are indistinguishable, then the ultimate author of both the physical world and my volitions and so actions is the Creator, so that either no human action is evil, since proceeding from a good cause, or the Creator, who cannot plead that He didn't know or didn't mean it, is evil, since responsible for evil. But, so the objection goes, both alternatives are absurd and impious, so the account that entails them is absurd and impious.

How does he reply? He firmly insists that to say that each local evil, whether physical or moral, belongs to an optimal whole, may momentarily please the speculative imagination, but such an attitude is unsustainable, and ridiculous from the occurrent victim's point of view, given human nature. Uncertain speculations cannot counterbalance natural and immediate sentiments. So the first disjunct, that no human action is evil, must be dismissed. As regards the second disjunct, that the Creator is evil, we're out of our depths, and any proposal includes obscurities and unresolvable difficulties, properly driving us back to the difficult-enough but in principle manageable issues of common life. That this would be his predictable reply will be borne out as we increasingly appreciate his philosophy.

In sum, physical and mental events are equally patterned so as to generate the idea of necessary connection, so acts of will, as well as physical motions, are rightly supposed to have a cause, but having a cause per se is misconstrued if construed as some freedom-robbing form of necessitation.

So, my three-phase reading of section VIII has it that it is beyond reasonable doubt that human actions follow consistent patterns and that we draw inferences about them; that liberty can only mean the power to act or not act as one wills, a degree of freedom obviously enjoyed by most of us most of the time, and that we need only remind ourselves of the results of Section VII to dismiss as unintelligible any rival conception of liberty which takes it to invoke some form of non-necessary relation; and that necessity properly analyzed does not subvert, but is essential to the support of, morality, and that anyhow, the moral sentiments which lead us to ascribe blame or merit are unaffected by any such metaphysical niceties.

This presents Hume as at least a *compatibilist* (reconciling what wrongly seems in conflict) and perhaps as a *soft determinist*. Before leaving this section, let me mention one serious alternative interpretation, using the following definitions. *Strict determinism* states that every event is fully determined by exceptionless causal laws. *Determinism* states that every event has a prior cause. There's the custom-based principle that like objects, in like circumstances, will produce like effects. The *free will assumption* affirms that most humans have the capacity to act freely and are therefore morally responsible for their free actions. *Compatibilism* states that the conjunction of determinism and the free will assumption is logically *consistent*. Some add that free will entails determinism. Some add that determinism and the free will assumption are both *true* (this is *soft determinism*). *Libertarians* hold that there is a freedom worth wanting that is *incompatible* with determinism, a free will that is a precondition for central components of our self-conception such as moral responsibility, autonomy (self-legislation), desert for achievement, creativity, dignity, susceptibility to reactive attitudes such as resentment, etc.

Everyone agrees that Hume is not a libertarian. But on an alternative reading Hume predictably refuses to take *any* stand on the metaphysical issue of free will, but only exemplifies his overall, innovative philosophical project of tracing the origins of our ideas to determine their precise cognitive content, using his theory of definition – here solely rigorously tracing the origins in impressions of our idea of necessity – showing us once again how to resist the temptation to do any metaphysics. Since compatibilism, and *a fortiori*, soft determinism, are metaphysical positions, it is wrong, according to this interpretation, to attribute those positions to him.[1]

Since I agree that tracing the origins and relations of ideas is fundamental to Hume's method, how should I respond? First, not pressing a traditional, metaphysical thesis doesn't entail not being a compatibilist. Compatibilism merely makes a consistency claim, which is a relation of ideas, not matter of fact claim. Well, should we say that for Hume one conjunct of the consistent pair, determinism, or the doctrine of necessity, is *true*? Determinism goes beyond experience, so Hume must not be asking the question whether determinism is true in a metaphysical way; he clearly denies that we know it *a priori*. But it does not follow that he is only asking, "What is the cognitive content of our idea of necessity?" and that there is nothing more we can meaningfully say about determinism. Minimally, Hume does operate as if determinism is true, treating it as a regulative (practical, methodological) principle, because (among other things) we are social and active as well as

---

1   Ted Morris defended a rich, interesting version of this alternative at the 2005 Pacific Division American Philosophical Association meeting.

rational beings. Is his commitment stronger than this? I think so. I side with those who include determinism among the *natural beliefs* for Hume: commitments which are universal and unavoidable, rationally indefensible (unsupportable by successful deductive or inductive argument), but necessary for inquiry (including science, "speculative parts of learning") and action, including survival itself.

On the other hand, as I argued in section 6.3, the theory of definition is neither irrevisably prescriptive – that would be illegitimate *a priorism* about matters of fact – nor natural belief, on multiple counts. It is a crucial, powerful, empirical hypothesis, demonstrably well-instanced in the course of inquiry: every matter of fact is either a logically contingent proposition supportable to some degree of probability by external or internal observational evidence (those are the ones that are "objects of reason") or natural beliefs. "Like causes have like effects" and the Copy Principle have the same status as the theory of definition. They admit of possible, rare counterexamples, but that's no good reason to abandon any of them. Recall that the missing shade of blue is allowed as a singular (thus far in the inquiry) disconfirming instance of the Copy Principle, but Hume understandably just shakes it off. Similarly, Hume doesn't try to explain away all the counterevidence to L; the claim of parallelism between the physical and mental only amounts to noting that the relations between motives and action are *no less regular* than causal relations in any other part of nature, allowing they may be irregular and uncertain. But Hume typically proceeds to invoke the exceptionless, more general, principle of determinism to ground guidance for defending L's, and the parallelism's, reliability, prompting us to search for *hidden* causes when an action is out of character, for example.

The modest yet crucial commitment to determinism does seem to govern every discussion in Hume's writings. As we'll see later in Hume's treatment of religion, even in the limiting, exotic case of world-causation (creation), an event of which we have no experience whatsoever, even the spokesperson for agnosticism agrees that the *being* of God is unquestionable, since, he reasons, nothing exists without a cause, and the only cause of this world – whatever the *nature* of that cause may be – we call God, and piously ascribe to him (now shifting from the cognitive to the attitudinal mode) every species of perfection we can anthropomorphically conjure. But when we get to specifics, as when we wonder whether God as first cause of criminality must be morally flawed, or whether what we take to be criminality really is not so, Hume, thoroughgoing empiricist about matters of fact that he is, properly responds, "Who knows what to say about God, except to insist that we're right about the criminality." Remote and uncertain speculations cannot counterbalance natural sentiments, or natural beliefs. So we rightly return to common life, which involves habits and customs, which involve constant conjunctions, which induce expectations (inferences), etc.

I never see Hume lapsing into *traditional* metaphysics. So when he insists that persons are only responsible if their actions result from intentions, he is not further interested in questions about the ultimate genesis, or even of distal, prior causes of those intentions. He tends to be forward-looking, and shows little interest in counterfactual conditionals about what someone would have done under different, non-actual conditions. So unlike many other compatibilists, for Hume we need not assure ourselves that a person could have acted differently before punishing him, but it is relevant to ask if punishment will change his future action. So his "reconciling project" is not as far-reaching as more ambitious, compatibilist ones. But it seems to me overstatement to deny that he is a compatibilist (indeed one who holds that freedom presupposes causality), and that if we do deny it many more apparently constructive philosophical exchanges will turn out to be talking at cross-purposes, or changing the subject.

So, if we take Hume's method to include his theory of definition, seen as neither *a priori* nor irrevisably prescriptive, but to go beyond that theory as a mitigated consequent skeptic must (for whom stable, endorsable results are those which emerge from the confluence of efforts to be skeptical, manifestations of our human nature, and the presentations of experience), we should conclude that Hume occupies an especially important place in the history of modern compatibilism that began with Hobbes, but that of course his own brand of and route to compatibilism differs in identifiable ways from several others in this lineage.

Section IX reinforces Hume's naturalism, and the gradualism that goes along with it. He embraces the consequence that animals learn about the world the same way humans do. Differences in capacities among species, like differences among individual humans, are just a matter of straightforwardly explicable degree.

6.6   *Enquiry* Section X: Implications for religion based on miracles

There is disagreement about what Hume aims to prove in his famous discussion of miracles in Section X. He is certainly not arguing that miracles are impossible. That conclusion would contradict his deep commitment that no matter of fact is impossible. The issue is the credibility of testimony that a miracle occurred, which rests both on the general criteria for determining reliability of testimony and the criteria for doing sound history. But many think Hume argues for the strong conclusion that under no circumstance should we judge it probable that a miracle occurred based on historical reports. I think his conclusion is weaker, though effectively as damaging to one form of revealed religion, namely that no human testimony can credibly support a belief in miracles *that would make it a legitimate foundation for any specific religion*. Here is what I agree Hume's line of thought to be, taken wholesale from Don Garrett's perfect rendition (Garrett 145–50).

1   Experience is our only guide in reasoning concerning matters of fact.
2   Some events are always and everywhere found to be constantly conjoined; others are found to have been more variable, and sometimes to disappoint expectations.
3   A wise person proportions belief to evidence.
4   When conclusions are founded on invariable experience, a wise person is maximally assured, and regards past experience as a full proof of the future existence of the event. (1, 2, 3)
5   When conclusions are not founded on invariable experience, a wise person is more cautious, weighing the opposing past experiences, considering which side has the most support, and inclining to that side, with doubt and hesitation. His resulting judgment is no more than probable. (1, 2, 3)
6   Whenever we reason concerning matters of fact we must balance the opposing past experiences and subtract the smaller number from the larger in order to know the exact force of the superior evidence. (1, 2, 3)
7   All inferences we can draw from one object to another are founded solely on our experience of their constant conjunction. There are no necessary connections between them.
8   The connection between human testimony and any event is not necessary. (7)
9   We should lack all confidence in human testimony had we not discovered by experience that memories are reasonably good, people are generally inclined to tell the truth and feel shame when caught in a lie, etc.
10   Our assurance in any argument based on testimony and hearsay is derived from our observation of the general veracity of human testimony and the usual conformity of facts with the reports of witnesses. (7, 8, 9)
11   Testimonial evidence varies with the experience, and is regarded as proof or probability depending on whether the conjunction between any particular kind of report and any kind of object is constant or variable. (4, 5, 10)
12   A miracle is a violation of a law of nature, implementing a supernatural purpose.
13   Laws of nature have been established by firm and unalterable experience.
14   So there is a uniform experience against every miraculous event. (12, 13)
15   There is a direct and full proof against the existence of any miracle, and the proof cannot be overridden, or the miracle made credible, by an opposing, superior proof. (4, 5, 14)
16   When witnesses testify that something not merely marvelous or extraordinary, but miraculous occurred, and their testimony taken in isolation amounts to proof, there are conflicting proofs, and the stronger must prevail, but still with diminished force, in proportion to that of its opposition. (6, 11, 15)
17   No testimony suffices to establish a miracle unless the testimony be of such a kind that its falsehood would be more miraculous than the fact it

purports to establish; and even then there is a mutual undermining of argument, with the superior only assuring to the extent that remains after subtracting the inferior. (15, 16)

18 There have never been circumstances in which human testimony of miracles is fully assuring – there has never been any miracle attested by sufficiently many people, of sufficiently unquestioned good sense and education, to rule out their delusion, or of sufficient, undoubtable integrity, to rule out deceit, or of sufficient repute that they have too much to lose were deceit exposed, when attesting to facts performed publicly enough in a prominent part of the world such that the false-hood of their testimony would be bound to be detected.

19 Passions incline most people to believe and report, with vehemence and assurance, all religious miracles.

20 It is a strong presumption against miracles that they allegedly occur mainly in ignorant and barbarous nations, or if now believed by more highly civilized people, transmitted to them with a sense of authority from ignorant ancestors.

21 Incompatible world religions cannot all be established on solid foundations.

22 Each miracle invoked to establish a particular religion serves to over-throw all the other, incompatible religions.

23 In undermining a rival religion, one's miracle likewise undermines the evidential efficacy of those other miracles on which those others religions were based.

24 All the prodigies of different religions ought be regarded as opposing facts, and the evidences of those prodigies, whether weak or strong, as opposing each other. (22, 23)

25 It seems that no testimony for any kind of miracle has ever amounted to a probability, let alone a proof, and that even supposing it amounted to a proof, it would be opposed by another proof derived from the very nature of the fact that it aims to establish. (4, 5, 15, 18, 19, 20, 24)

26 Experience alone gives authority both to human testimony and the laws of nature. (1, 10, 13)

27 When these two kinds of experience oppose each other, we must subtract the one from the other, and embrace the opinion with the assurance resulting from the remainder. (6, 26)

28 This subtraction when applied to all popular (sectarian) religions amounts to their entire annihilation. (4, 5, 13, 19, 20, 24, 27)

29 No human testimony can have the force to prove a miracle and make it a legitimate foundation for any popular system of religion. (4, 12, 28)

Still today much effort is expended coming to grips with this argument. One leading strategy is to reject as too restrictive Hume's definition of miracle (step 12), for example, contending that miracles are better under-stood as *exceptions* that are not necessarily contradictory to standing law, as when a wise judge sees the merit of pardoning someone just found guilty under normal procedure. Another popular complaint is that Hume improperly restricts the relevant evidence that a miracle was witnessed, for example, ignoring or downgrading the long-term, life-transforming impact one can observe in believers. What do you think?

Issues from both Sections XI and XII will be folded into later treatment of the *Dialogues* (section 6.10), and XII's discussion of skepticism and method folded into the next section's overview of the *Treatise*. For now, the important core of Section XI is this: since observed conjunctions provide the only evidence for inferences to the unobserved, we cannot infer more in an unobserved cause than we have observed to be needed for an observed effect. This challenges the religious view that sufficient motivation for moral conduct requires reasonable prospect of rewards or punishments in an after-life. Either we experience correlation between merit (demerit) and reward (punishment) or not. Indeed, in a posthumously published essay, "Of the Immortality of the Soul," Hume goes further. He criticizes metaphysical, physical, and moral arguments for immortality, and notes that the moral arguments, which take the afterlife to be necessary to achieve the divine justice manifestly not realized in our earthly lives, not only assume without evidence that God has attributes beyond or different from those he has exerted in this universe, but undermine our most fundamental moral conceptions. Given *our* ideas of goodness and justice, punishment must have some appropriate purpose and be proportionate to the offense. *Eternal* punishment by God for the *temporary* offenses of such *frail* creatures like us, who *he himself created*, makes no sense. It violates, not supports, our deepest moral sentiments and the policies reflection tells us promote the interests of human society.

6.7   *Treatise*: Overview and key elements of Book I, on the understanding

Let's now turn to the *Treatise*. Hume downgraded its maturity, and said that his *Enquiries* (the one just discussed, and *An Enquiry Concerning the Principles of Morals*, published three years later) are the best representation of his work. Since he cared about the opinions of others, his assessment of the *Treatise* is understandable. The mere thousand copies printed did not sell out during Hume's lifetime, over the next three dozen years! Most philosophers nowadays do not share his assessment, and indeed most judge the *Treatise* to be the greatest piece of philosophy ever written in the English language. (So don't despair if you're not appreciated immediately.) Its subtitle is *An Attempt to introduce the experimental method of Reasoning into Moral Subjects*, where "moral" covers human nature and human affairs. It studies our cognitive and conative capacities and limits, so as to provide a new foundation for the sciences, seeking to do properly what Locke aimed to do. It carefully observes human behavior, and recognizes that it cannot do experiments on people in the same way we can with unperceiving matter, since the experimental setup itself can change the person's natural operation. Whereas it attempts a detailed human science, the first *Enquiry* seeks a more modest "mental geography" with focus on the nature and illustrative application of causal inference to the topics of free will, rewards and punishments in an afterlife, and miracles, all with anti-religious implications, helping to undermine superstition. (His second *Enquiry* was a recasting of *Treatise* Book III's account of virtue.) The *Treatise* is exhilaratingly jam-packed with argument, so I admit up front that I will not remotely do it justice. But I will trace some of its highlights, especially those that reinforce pivotal ideas or don't retrace ideas culled from the *Enquiry*. Given their compression, these sections on the *Treatise* are generally more challenging than the rest of the chapter.

Hume was bit by the philosophical bug early. His father died when he was 2. He was raised by a devoted mother. He entered university at 12, left at 15. After three years of work in France, deliberately working in the town where Descartes went to school, he completed the first draft of the *Treatise* at age twenty-six, settled in London, and published Books I and II of the *Treatise* anonymously in January, 1739; Book III appeared in late 1740. The book develops a new science of human nature, contributing to interrelated issues in epistemology, metaphysics, philosophical psychology, and ethics. Book I explains how we form such important concepts as cause and effect, external object, and personal identity, and explains how or why we believe in the objects of these concepts. Book II explains the origin and role of the passions and the nature of human freedom. Book III explains the origins and nature of morality. The unwavering commitment to experience and observation runs through all of Hume's philosophy. The other side of the same coin is criticism of any philosophy that gives reason priority. Reason can't establish that every event has a cause, that enduring, external objects exist, that someone is virtuous or vicious, etc. Yet experience too can only take us so far; it can't reveal the ultimate features of human nature; we only experience impressions and ideas, and sense experience alone doesn't account for belief in external objects, causation, and personal identity. Such limitations on experience are consequential too.

Hume thought predecessors like Locke and Berkeley had, intentionally or not, already exposed the skeptical implications of traditional philosophy – that philosophy can't tell us the real nature and relations of things. He concluded that the important remaining task of philosophy is to show how we get on with our intellectual and moral lives, to explain how, though nothing is ever present to the mind but perceptions, we not only have ideas of their objects, but naturally believe they really exist outside the mind (and, I'd add again controversially, do so with a newly-conceived kind of legitimacy).

The apparatus of the understanding he works with includes two faculties of having impressions, sensation and reflection, and two faculties for having ideas (representational faculties), memory and imagination. Memory preserves the character and order, and the bulk of the force and vivacity of the original experience. Imagination, now understood in a broad sense, need not preserve order, but can separate and recombine ideas at will, and typically does not preserve most of the force and vivacity of the original experience. There is also a narrower use on which imagination forms our fainter (non-memory) ideas, but *not* by any (deductive or inductive (probabilistic)) reasoning. The really important results to highlight here are these: (1) that Hume treats reason, and its characteristic product, belief, as *ways* of having ideas, so species of imagination. The force and vivacity of beliefs are weaker than those of impressions or memory, but stronger than ideas that are merely entertained or hypothesized, etc. Hume notably denies that reason (intellect) is a separate representational faculty at all; it follows that it is not a privileged capacity for insight into the true nature of things, contrary to the over-reaching claims of his rationalist predecessors; (2) that Hume explains the character of much thought and action in terms of the imagination, not the senses or reason. So reason (as argument) has its place, but its place is severely diminished, and imagination does most of the explaining, and, where applicable, justifying.

This is all part of the conceptual geography of the *understanding*. The other central force in human nature is *passion*, to be discussed in section 6.8. It is under the analysis of passion that Hume explains voluntary action, which results from volition (will), an impression of reflection, usually caused by desire or aversion, which naturally may be caused by prior passions. The mental operations involved in volition and morals also depend mostly on non-rational operations; reasoning has some role, but again, a noticeably diminished one.

How sensations arise is not Hume's (a moral philosopher's) concern, but that of anatomists and natural philosophers; he matter-of-factly says their causes are unknown, and moves on, never proposing a theory of perception, never trying to prove that there's an external world causing them. Whatever the ultimate source of sensation, impressions and ideas interrelate in ways that induce ineliminable beliefs in causes and objects. He explains belief, not perception. Belief is a way of having ideas. Ideas are causally dependent on impressions; more specifically, all ideas are either copied from resembling impressions or composed of simple ideas that are copied from resembling impressions. This first principle (our Copy Principle) is discovered by sustained experimentation, evidenced by the temporal priority of impressions to their corresponding ideas, the existence of simple ideas corresponding to simple impressions, and the lack of certain ideas by those who never had the corresponding impressions. So the way to clarify an obscure idea is to trace it to its source impressions, and the way to challenge an idea as meaningless is to fail with sincere effort to find a source impression. All ideas are determinate, but some function generally through association (annexation) with a term that disposes the mind to "survey" similar ideas as needed in cognitive operations. That's all that a so-called abstract idea amounts to, and there can be abstract ideas of substances, modes of things, and relations between things.

As regards relations, even when items are arbitrarily united, we may for philosophical purposes compare them, at bottom, in seven ways (I.1.5): we can ask:

1   whether the items resemble each other, or better, in what ways and how closely they resemble each other, since there can be *no* comparison without *some* resemblance, so that resemblance is presupposed by the other six relations;
2   whether the items are identical, the most universal relation insofar as it is common to every object which has duration, where identity is construed strictly to imply unchangeability, and where the negation of identity is difference, either in number or in kind;
3   whether the items are related to each other spatially and temporally, for example, contiguous or not, before or after;
4   how they relate with respect to proportions of quantity;
5   how they relate with respect to degrees of any quality they may share;
6   whether they are contrary (exclude each other);
7   whether they stand in the relation of cause and effect.

Among all possible relations, three – resemblance, contiguity in space or time, and cause and effect – can also function naturally to explain much of our mental life. These three forms of natural association are "the cement of the universe," the only links that bind the parts of our mental universe together, the forces which limit the extraordinary freedom of the imagination to join or separate ideas. These elements work together to produce our ideas of causal connection, external existence, and personal identity, (and space and time), matters in which we believe and on which life and action entirely depend. Experiences of events that we take to be causally related reveal only three perceptible features, but a non-perceptible necessary connection needs to be taken into consideration. How do we explain this idea of necessary connection, since apparently there is no impression from which it is derived? Even though we demonstrably cannot see or prove that there are necessary causal connections, we think and act as if we had knowledge of such connections, can make and cannot help make all sorts of predictions. By contrast, a suddenly-created Adam in full maturity couldn't make the simplest prediction. The difference between us and Adam is experience of invariant succession of paired objects or events, which prompts an expectation (a feeling), determining the mind to transfer attention from a present impression to the idea of an absent but associated object. The idea of necessary connection is copied from these feelings, but then is projected onto the world. That there is an objective necessity to which this idea corresponds is an untestable hypothesis, nor would showing that such necessary connections had held in the past guarantee that they will hold in the future. Hence we should be agnostic about the existence of real causal connections. (The controversy as reported concerning the *Enquiry* replays itself here. Many read Hume as *denying* causal ties in the world, others, as affirming their existence but confessing ignorance of their nature, still others as skeptical on all counts.) The same with belief in future effects or absent causes, required for effective planning. As for belief itself, it is just a different manner of conceiving an object, not a separate idea. Were it a separate idea, we could willfully join it to another idea to believe by choice, but experience shows us we cannot. Also, were it an added, separate idea, the content of belief could not remain fixed as specified by the original idea, as it should be – contrary to fact, what we believe would always be transformed by the event of our believing it.

We must take for granted that there are external – reidentifiable and distinct from and external to the mind and its perceptions – objects. But we can ask why we believe they exist, that is, is the belief produced by the senses, reason, or imagination? The senses can't account for the idea of continuity. (Recall Descartes' wax passage.) And the belief exists without even consideration of argument, so reason cannot be its source. So imagination must be the source. The imagination tends to continue a course once begun. No sense impressions exhibit a perfect constancy, but some exhibit a good deal of constancy and coherence, which prompts the imagination, working involuntarily and unnoticed, to belief; small differences are overlooked and taken to be identical, while bigger differences follow familiar patterns.

Is there a general account of proper belief-formation in Hume? It is plausible to propose that central positions and arguments found in modern philosophers predictably emerge from their ground-floor methodological commitments, and that their attitudes toward and use of various forms of skepticism is a most revealing diagnostic of methodology. We can understand Hume's model of belief-formation along such lines, as follows. Our human nature, what he sometimes describes as a set of *primary* or *original* (which implies uniform and basic) *propensities* (instincts, principles), conjoined with eliciting or activating cognitions and/or emotions, yield beliefs. Primary or natural beliefs – in the external world, causal connections, and perhaps personal identity – are indispensable for daily life and science, and hence are universal, the same across all cultures. Secondary beliefs are inessential but widespread. They sometimes compete with natural propensities, that is, oppose human nature, and when they do, they promote instabilities, intellectually and/or morally. Reason is a weaker propensity to belief-formation; it is too weak to neutralize primary propensities, and can only achieve a kind of momentary amazement, but it is potentially sufficient to neutralize secondary propensities, and thence achieve suspension of judgment, which is the victory of skepticism. Skepticism is the pivotal tool in discovering the status of all our beliefs – ordinary, scientific, moral, conceptual – given the facts of human nature. We should use the tool as vigorously as our nature allows, thus always beginning with Pyrrhonian or excessive consequent skepticism, indiscriminate doubts generated within inquiry, and methodologically analyzing when it succeeds by inducing equipoise, when it is mitigated by some counterforce (ranging from natural belief, to circumstantial feeling, to residual, probable evidence), when the mitigation leads to good results (from intellectual humility to social fulfillment to pleasure), and when to bad, such as interruptions or enfeeblings of natural propensities, as when superstition weakens natural benevolence or sense of justice. Superstition or bad religion is thus dangerous. Hume's attitude toward bad philosophy, and its contrast with true philosophy, is less clear.

6.7.1   *A famous perplexity about how to read* Treatise Book I

Perhaps the central interpretive puzzle of the *Treatise* is reconciling Hume's use and endorsement of the skeptical arguments of Book I, Part IV. He confesses himself "ready to reject all belief and reasoning" there, yet he prepares to launch the constructive philosophical project to provide a "solid foundation" based on experience for a "compleat system of sciences," which vitally uses a set of (eight) general rules or norms specifying the best ways for determining what causes what, discovered through a causal examination of causal inference, through reflection on the success and failure of past inferences from observed to unobserved matters of fact, as developed in Book I, Part III. Can Hume's commitment to science and philosophy, and reason over superstition, survive his skepticism? I now elaborate how I think Hume handles this challenge, using excerpts to focus its elements.[2]

In Part III he argues that inductive inferences (from observed to unobserved) are determined by certain properties of the imagination, not by reason, but that this does not entail that they are unreasonable. The imagination also explains the formation of precipitously formed rules, prejudice, which commonly guide the vulgar, and which generate beliefs that can be criticized and corrected only by comparing them with the more "philosophical" standards of reasoning, used by the wise, who strive to proportion their beliefs to the evidence. And in Part IV, so too, the instinctive workings of the imagination, not the senses or reason, are responsible for both the vulgar (on which the perception is the external object) and philosophical (on which we groundlessly think the perception represents something external) versions of the belief in body, and for the belief in the existence of a unitary self identical through time and change (the "fiction" or illusion of "perfect" identity). And the imaginative operation involved in causal reasoning

---

2   I have presented Hume roughly this way for many years. Nevertheless, since Paul Stanistreet recently has organized these considerations so nicely, and more elaborately, I am guided by the concluding chapter of his *Hume's Scepticism and the Science of Human Nature* (2002). Given its compression, this section is more difficult.

contradicts the imaginative operation involved in belief in external body — causal reasoning "utterly annihilates" all the qualities of external objects (by showing that secondary qualities are mind-dependent, which in turn undermines belief in primary qualities — recall Berkeley here). To waffle by embracing both principles successively is to relinquish the claim to be a philosopher. To accept neither principle violates human nature and extinguishes the possibility of science. And our scientific aspirations to discover the deepest, even ultimate, tie which explains how effects are really caused, has been crushed by the discovery that the tie lies merely in ourselves, though here too we persist given the imagination's propensity to "spread itself on external objects," another pervasive illusion. The question of the Conclusion of Book I is, "How far ought we yield to these illusions?" It would be absurd to "assent to every trivial suggestion of the fancy." But if we reject them all, and consistently follow the understanding only, we have seen how pure, solitary understanding subverts itself. If reason and the senses contradict each other, if our only choice is "betwixt a false reason and none at all," then why doesn't skepticism rule out a naturalistic philosophy? How can he persist to "make bold to recommend philosophy?"

Note the role of Hume's conception of belief, as grounded in the vivacity of ideas, not reason. On the one hand, were belief grounded in reasoning, skepticism would in fact subvert all belief (about what's not sensorily or memorially present). But if, on the other hand, belief is just a matter of the vivacious and forceful manner in which an idea is conceived, why do or should we prefer vivacious ideas produced by inductive inference to those produced by any other process? The fact is that unstable melancholy and delirium give way to submission to the everyday (from whose vantage point the solitary, abstruse speculations seem "cold, strain'd, and ridiculous," but also that restored good humor resuscitates intellectual curiosity (love of truth) and ambition, a felt desire to return to philosophy (for Hume). And his blind submission to the senses and the understanding is the proper manifestation of true "sceptical disposition and principles." Appeal to sentiments, desires, humors, and ambitions signifies the new stance that reason can only function properly in relation to the other faculties of mind. Autonomous reason inevitably leads to contradiction and self-doubt. "Be a philosopher; but, amidst all your philosophy, be still a man." "Where reason is lively, and mixes with some propensity, it ought to be assented to. Where it does not, it never can have any title to operate on us." So, when we return to philosophy, it is guided by reason working in tandem with the "trivial" qualities of the imagination. The reasonings by which reason is subverted are neither lively nor mixed with any propensity. And we need not assent to every trivial production of the fancy, since lively causal reasoning often will not support them. So the newly-constituted reasons to believe are neither false reasons nor no reasons at all. They are skeptical reasons. Pure reason is impotent concerning matters of fact. Reason integrated with the other parts of our natures (our passions and habits of mind) can succeed. Though it at first appears that pure reason is "in possession of the throne, prescribing laws, and imposing maxims, with an absolute sway and authority," eventually it steps down to the "serious good-humour'd disposition" of the mind "all collected within itself."

Is this return to chastened philosophy peculiar to those who find philosophy pleasant, or who are curious (i.e. love truth), or who are ambitious? Hume suggests that it is in fact near-impossible to restrict one's thoughts to the everyday, and that we ought to choose philosophy as the way to speculate. It is "almost impossible for the mind of man to rest, like those of beasts, in that narrow circle of objects, which are the subject of daily conversation and action," and since superstition is "more bold in its systems and hypotheses than philosophy" (fabricating an entirely new world and gripping the mind intemperately with its vision, not just assigning new causes and principles to observed phenomena in a way that does not disturb everyday living), and since we ought to prefer what is "safest and most agreeable," philosophy is to be preferred. As I think Book III argues, true philosophy, culminating in an account of morality, is not only most agreeable in that it least disrupts natural conduct, but also in that it leads to a kind of reflective endorsement and reflective equilibrium, where the mind can "bear its own survey" from all points of view, a result that other methods of belief-fixation cannot achieve. And false philosophy may be ridiculous, but it's not dangerous in the way erroneous religion is.

But the superiority of philosophy can't be proven by argument; in a way, the proof of the pudding is in the eating, or the practice, under the nurturing conditions of high energy and good humor. Those who do true philosophy recognize its superiority. This true philosophy is a true skepticism, a "more *mitigated* skepticism . . . which may be both durable and useful, and which may, in part, be the result of . . . Pyrrhonism, or *excessive* skepticism, when its undistinguished doubts are, in some measure, corrected by common sense and reflection." In true philosophy reason is preferred to all superstition, but is tempered with the "gross earthy mixture" of our ordinary work and recreation. It is a state of mind stable and secure enough to provide a basis for the naturalistic investigations of Books II and III. And the cornerstones of this basis are the natural beliefs such as the customary transition from cause to effect and belief in the continued and distinct existence of bodies, which "are the foundation of all our thoughts and actions, so that immediately upon their removal human nature must immediately perish and to ruin." These stable beliefs, "if not true (for that, perhaps is too much to be hop'd for) might at least be satisfactory, to the human mind, and might stand the test of the most critical examination."

But it seems precisely that this second condition is not fulfilled; even natural beliefs are fictions from the point of view of autonomous reason. But we've exposed the colossal weaknesses of solitary reason, and its ultimate reliance on sentiment. So the true philosopher "will be diffident of his philosophical doubts, as well as his philosophical conviction," inquiring with due caution and "deference to the public." He will be neither dogmatic nor hostile to his opponents. Specifically, reason gave us indication of its own infirmities, so it ought to induce caution in reflecting on the very doubts it generates when it attempts to sever the connection with the other faculties of mind on which it naturally depends. To put it flatly, we best exhibit our true, skeptical philosophy when, having reasoned our way to the intellectual abyss, "utterly depriv'd of the use of every member and faculty," we revert to the natural beliefs and propensities of the vulgar. Suitably chastened, philosophy is to confine itself to correcting and methodizing "the reflections of common life." True philosophy respects reason, but recognizes its limits, and commits to work within them. Reason has some authority, but not absolute authority. It has authority only when harnessed by propensities not themselves based on reason. With this insight, the systematic study of human nature (Books II and III, and subsequent work, including the *Dialogues*) can proceed, with ongoing sensitivity to where we can and cannot "expect assurance and conviction." One who does philosophy in this "careless manner" – as diffident of his philosophical doubts as of his philosophical convictions – is "more truly skeptical [*zetetic*] than . . . one, who feeling in himself an inclination to it, is yet so overwhelm'd with doubts and scruples, as totally to reject it." The true skeptic might still hope to establish causal principles that withstand the judgment of posterity, but he will calmly suspend his studies when offered some "innocent satisfaction," re-engaging when he is so inclined. (Socrates may have been right to say that the unexamined life is not worth living, but Hume is adding that the overexamined life is unlivable.) Hume invites all so inclined to follow his speculations. If you do so, don't be surprised if you read or use extorted expressions of certainty, but in a way that does not imply any abiding dogmatism. If you are not so inclined, do something fun. Maybe you'll get the philosophical urge later.

Donald Livingston's (1998) account of the structure of *Treatise* I.4 further enriches debates about how to interpret Hume. According to Livingston (using quoted material from Hume), while Hume addresses various first-order questions, his persistent, central concern, which gives all his inquiries their special character, is to answer the second-order question, "What is the nature and worth of philosophy?" – a question both about and in philosophy, which is essentially self-inquiry aspiring to self-knowledge. His science of human nature emerges as a resolution, satisfactory to the human mind (if not "true") and able to withstand the most critical examination, to the crisis such radical questioning spawns. He calls his the "sceptical philosophy," the true philosophy (true to its own nature and yielding self-knowledge), contrasted with false philosophy (alienated from its nature and yielding self-deception) and vulgar opinion. I.4 aims to determine the nature of philosophy and to develop the normative distinction between true and false forms of philosophical reflection.

The dialectic of Book I exemplifies the nature and limits of philosophy. Philosophical reflection is widely guided by three principles. Philosophy seeks to understand things as they are ultimately (Ultimacy). Philosophy is a radically free and self-justifying inquiry, withdrawing at least in thought from mere customs and taking itself as sovereign spectator and arbiter of them (Autonomy). Philosophy *feels* entitled to rule when it reaches its proper level of reflection (Dominion). Book I discovers that these three do not cohere with other principles of our nature (*primary* propensities), so philosophy typically understood is inconsistent with human nature; since philosophy is supposed to yield self-understanding, such philosophy is inconsistent with *its* own nature (cannot survive its own survey). If philosophy is to continue, it must take account of this discovery and reform itself. To pass through the disturbing sequence of philosophical self-understanding is to be a true philosopher; not to, is to be a false philosopher (insufficiently self-aware), not true (faithful) to what a more coherent philosophical perspective reveals. (I think we should explicate "coherence" in terms of "reflective endorsement," to be explained through Annette Baier's masterful work, sketched next.) While Hume repudiates vulgar living, true philosophy approaches nearer to the sentiments of the vulgar than false philosophy, reconciling philosophy with common life.

Hume's key discovery is that Autonomy must be reformed, that philosophical reflection wholly emancipated from common life (customs) is empty, and if consistently pursued ends in total skepticism. "The understanding, when it acts alone, and according to its most general principles, entirely subverts itself, and leaves not the lowest degree of evidence in any proposition, either in philosophy or common life." Most philosophies surreptitiously import prejudices to give content, and then purport to offer a work of autonomous reason, untainted by prejudice (the "monstrous offspring" of prejudice and reflection). So these philosophies are empty if consistent, inconsistent and arbitrary if not empty. At this stage, we have "no choice left but betwixt a false reason and none at all." A fourth principle is required, limiting the previously unrestrained autonomy of reflection: the autonomy of custom, on which custom is presumed true unless shown to be otherwise, and where showing it to be otherwise presupposes the authority of custom as a whole. "Philosophical decisions are nothing but the reflections of common life, methodized and corrected" (*Enquiry* XII.3). The false philosopher imagines himself to be the sovereign spectator and lawgiver to whatever domain of custom he is reflecting on. The true philosopher realizes he is a critical participant in whatever domain of custom he's reflecting on and so is not entirely free of its authority. So, Hume retains the principle of Ultimacy, but beliefs are viewed with some diffidence given restrictions on the principle of Autonomy. The task of true philosophy is to form general rules that can be used to render the customs of common life as coherent as possible.

This position emerges in Section 7, "Conclusion of this Book," after philosophical thought suffers self-alienation in the preceding six sections. In Section 1, "Scepticism with regard to Reason," reason is shown to subvert itself. In Section 2, "Scepticism with regard to the Senses," philosophical theories of perception that seek emancipation from vulgar perceptual (direct) realism subvert themselves. In Section 3, "Of the Antient Philosophy," the ancient philosophical theory of substance is shown to alienate the thinker from the true understanding of substance he possesses. In Section 4, "Of the Modern Philosophy," causal reasoning, which is the essence of modern scientific philosophizing, is shown to subvert itself and to destroy the possibility of belief in an external world. In Section 5, "Of the Immateriality of the Soul," the theological interpretation of the soul as immaterial is shown to support atheism, not theism. And in Section 6, "Of Personal Identity," the philosophical theory of a substantial mind is subverted and replaced with the image of the mind as a "bundle" of perceptions. (This is the only section in which the first-order question is in the foreground, but then in the Appendix Hume confesses his errors and rejects his account, without replacing it with another, neatly formulable alternative.) The conception which begins to emerge in Section 7 enables first-order theorizing which does not produce the self-alienation, self-deception, or self-subversion so vividly portrayed in the preceding traditions.

The end of Book I is preparation for the investigation of the *Treatise* proper, namely human conduct (broadly understood) and its source in the passions. Book I is also important because our passions are partly determined by our understanding of ourselves and the world. Book III examines the world of culture, which is the public display of the passions determined by the understanding. It's crucial to investigate philosophy since a disorder in philosophical reflection, if taken seriously, yields a disorder in the understanding of ourselves and the world. This in turn generates perverse passions. On Livingston's reading, the "foundation" of the *Treatise* comes not at the beginning of Book I when impressions are introduced, but at the end of Book I when true and false philosophy are distinguished. The upshot is that impressions perceived by passionate agents in culture are shaped by general rules, customs, and conventions. Analytically we can talk of impressions untainted by judgment and custom, but our concrete experience of impressions is always shaped by them. Hume is concerned to examine the concrete experience of human conduct as determined by our passions and by the understanding which generates those passions.

Much, but not all, of Livingston's provocative reading sits well with my own understanding of the *Treatise*. But the scholar whose work most transformed my long-standing opinions about Hume is Annette Baier, whose penetrating account (1999) of the Conclusion of Book I as a microcosm of the *Treatise*'s enactment I summarize for your benefit, and to close out this section.

As Baier presents it (with quoted material from Hume), Hume seeks norms with the sort of grounding a reflective naturalist can accept, mental operations that can "bear their own survey," that is, be revealed as neither unstable nor self-contradictory when self-consciously analyzed by the very processes that produced them. The development of the norms is progressive, "gathering new force as it advances." He comes to appreciate how to go from habits to norms. The *Treatise* examines three kinds of associations: among ideas, among passions, and among persons. Book I examines conflicts within solitary "Cartesian" reason. Book II examines conflicts between our sympathetic concern for others and the tendency to treat others as a mere backdrop for ourselves. Book III examines conflicts between the points of view of different persons, as they approve and disapprove of their own characters and the characters of others. The conclusion of Book I announces and enacts the turn from one-sided reliance on intellect and its methods (casting off the anxieties and tyranny of obsessive, restricted theorizing) to an attempt to use in philosophy all the capacities of the human mind, to proceed in a careless (i.e. carefree), hopeful manner, being a philosopher, but still a man. It exhibits a sequence of changes in self-conception, driven by the urge to get an honest version of the thinker, each stage driven by the realization that there was either illusion or contradiction involved in the previous version of the introspective protagonist. The conversions are:

1   From bold, original, independent thinker to solitary, shunned monster;
2   From solitary thinker to typical, fallible thinker;
3   From typical thinker, subject to the human imagination's distinctive habits, to the typical victim of its self-destructive workings;
4   From victim of imagination to willing adherent of "the understanding," namely the imagination in its most regular and established workings;
5   From one who discriminates between imagination's established workings (intellect) and its trivial workings (the fancy), to agent and witness of the vanishing of evidence, the total destruction of reason through subversion from within;
6   From total skeptic to one willing to be ruled by a "trivial property of the fancy," namely intolerance of long and elaborate reasonings, such as the preceding;
7   From banisher of elaborate reasoning to science-rejector, and breaker of one's own rules, since the path from conversion 1 to conversion 6 has been even longer than that from 1 to 5;
8   From breaker of one's own rules to renouncer of all rules, advocate of forgetting difficulties;
9   From liberator from norms and their difficulties to failed liberator, unable to forget that it was by reasoning that one came to banish the norms of reasoning;
10 From manifestly self-contradicting thinker to despairing self-doubter, "in the most deplorable condition imaginable."

To expand on this process a bit, boldness and independence in 1 turn out to be illusory; the thinker needs others, if only to impress with his originality, since he cares about how others see him. And he may need others to get a criterion of truth. So he seeks common ground, and finds it in reliance on shared propensities of the imagination. But these shared habits of thought produce conflicting principles, for example, between the ideas of physical objects and of causal dependency, now described too as "illusions." It's a choice between illusions. He switches back and forth between orthodoxies. At the despair point there is utter solitude (ironic outcome of Cartesian assumptions of self-sufficiency in Book I, Part IV), and with reason subverted, there are no longer any "reasons" for the present position, or non-position. The predicament is described as an intense feeling and an overheating of the brain. The turn from intellect to feeling is occurring. Hume now describes the changes in him. Paralysis and despair are relaxed by "nature herself." The very distraction that was offered and refused earlier, thoughtless amusement, which enables a forgetting of the difficulties, *now* takes over and "cures me of this philosophical melancholy and delirium," now that total despair sets in and is recognized *as* a state of feeling and overheating of the brain, for only then is there an acceptance of natural sentiment not as mere distraction but as a *replacer* of (narrowly construed) reason. Reason must be worked through, taken to the end of its tether, before sentiment can take over the guiding role. From now on moves are dictated by feeling, are swings in mood, not twists in argument. Here Hume gives us a short sequence of moods as a preview of the dialectic of the passions to be developed in Books II and III. (1) Sociable, cheerful mood, to whom preceding speculations and intellectual agonizing appear cold, strained and ridiculous, in which skeptical doubts can't be sustained, in which one finds oneself indolently believing in the general maxims of the world and having impatience with philosophical reasonings – blind submission to ordinary people and beliefs, renunciation of philosophy. No willingness to "torture my brain with subtilities and sophistries." Painfulness is what disqualifies them. Spleen is directed just at philosophers. (2) But neither spleen nor indolence in (1) can sustain itself. He tires of the company of the uncritical, needs relief from that uneasiness, experiences the return of philosophical curiosity, but now with "my mind all collected within itself" *indulges* in "a reverie in my chamber, or a solitary walk by a riverside." Then he is *uneasy* about judging without knowing upon what principles he proceeds. Then he realizes that aims of self-consciousness without uneasiness and of gaining a reputation are themselves sentiments. "Just" philosophy is now seen as the self-indulgence of self-conscious animals, and critical self-consciousness of mankind's procedures is stressed as preferable to all superstition, which needs to be counteracted. Hume's forthcoming program and method is announced clearly in the last pages of the section. His aim is to establish a system which is satisfactory to the human mind (squares with common practice and experience) and survives the most critical examination by posterity, a science of human nature, using cautious observation of human life as it occurs in company, in affairs, and in their pleasures. It's to be careless, free of tyrannizing obsessions, including an over-dedication to the new philosophy itself (follow me if you want), and expecting vacillation as to certainty "in *particular points*, according to the light, in which we survey them in any *particular instant*" – he expects correction – preparing us for Book II's examination of "those several passions and inclinations, which actuate and govern me," and Book III's principles of moral good and evil. Book I's failed, solitary intellect gives way to a more passionate and sociable successor. The self-destructively narrow conceptions of self and reason operative in Book I are superseded by encouragingly expanded conceptions in Book II (though some earlier conclusions, such as the denial of a simple self, are retained), which develop into the recognizable persons with morally evaluable characters of Book III.

6.8 *Treatise*: Key elements of Book II, on the passions

I shall now devote a few pages to Hume's Book II account of the passions. This is infrequently discussed in Modern Philosophy classes, and time constraints make that understandable, but given that passion plays such a dominant role in Hume's system, at least an outline is in order. For each passion, Hume seeks to know its nature, its origins (how it arises in us), and its manifestations (effects on our mental lives and conduct). To know its nature is not to analyze it; every passion is a unique, simple impression, so is unanalyzable. (Hume does say that hope and fear are "mixtures" of joy and grief; does that entail that some are not simple impressions?) But various passions have similarities and dissimilarities, so can be compared. A passion causes its manifestations, but remember that for Hume causation is a logically contingent relation. So a passion is recognizable independently of its usual results, and can occur without them. So we should not confuse symptoms or other typical accompaniments of a passion with the passion itself. Passions themselves are secondary impressions, arising either from original impressions (whose sources are unknown), or from ideas produced by antecedent impressions. So the causes of passions are all mental causes. But causes of passions can be different from their objects; it's the distinction "betwixt that idea which excites them, and that to which they direct their view when excited." The exciting idea can be of non-existent things. The object can also be merely intentional, and not exist in nature. With direct passions, the cause is identical with the object, but not with indirect passions, since they are not brought about only by the perception of some thing or quality, but require my awareness of the person to whom it is related – for example, myself with pride and humility; another with love and hate. Passions can cause one another, but they can also clash.

Passions are classifiable:

- according to how they arise,
- by their turbulence and felt intensity, and
- by their causal influence.

Direct passions are caused immediately by pleasure or pain (the same as good or evil for Hume); indirect passions are caused by pleasure or pain, but only through the mediation of ideas; original (i.e. primary) passions (implanted instincts) produce pleasure and pain when acted on, but do not arise from pleasure and pain. Non-original passions are also called "secondary" passions. Passions are inexactly distinguishable as calm or violent, and as strong or weak. Calm passions can be strong, exerting a steady and controlling influence on deliberation and conduct – for example, the general appetite to good and aversion to evil is calm but can be strong – and it is then often wrongly supposed that we act from reason when we act from them – that is, we mistake the calm, steady, and controlling influence of these passions for the operations of reason. So, original passions are often violent (for example the desire to punish our enemies, or bodily appetites), often calm (for example benevolence and love of life). Secondary passions which are direct are often violent (for example joy and grief, hope and fear), often calm (for example general appetite to good and aversion to evil). Secondary passions which are indirect are often violent (for example pride and humility, love and hate), often calm (for example moral approval (approbation) and disapproval, sense of beauty and deformity). Typically whether any passion is strong or weak depends on its possessor's character, the particular configuration of someone's passions as a whole. Keep in mind this is part of Hume's causal account of thought, feeling, and action. Naturally, the efficacy of some particular force depends on the cluster of its surrounding forces. Reason alone cannot be a motive that influences our conduct; it only has the secondary role of correcting false beliefs and identifying effective means to given ends. As we will discover, it is not reason but moral sense that is the epistemological basis of moral distinctions, fundamentally the distinctions between the various types of virtues and vices.

Hume's central concern as a scientist of human nature is secondary passions. Recall that there are two types of impressions, of sensation (of color, touch, smell, pleasure and pain, etc.) and of reflection (the passions, understood in the broad sense; it may be that in narrower usage, passions are distinguished from, for example, desire). Indirect impressions of reflection derive from impressions of sensation, the ultimate starting point of all experience and thought, via ideas. For example, a pleasure causes the idea of a pleasure, which causes a reflexive impression of a desire or hope (or with pain, an aversion or fear); these in turn may be copied by memory or (weaker) imagination, causing further ideas. Since Hume is interested in moral, not natural philosophy, in the science of human nature, not physics or physiology, he focuses on impressions of reflection, and given their complexity and discoverably crucial role, indirect impressions of reflection.

Two last sets of key, preliminary distinctions. In deliberation every chain of reasons in means-to-end reasoning is finite and has as its stopping point an ultimate or final, but not invariable, end, which is an aim or goal of one or more passions. A reason in the chain is a true or false statement saying that (doing) something is an (effective) means to something desired. Given the distinction between the temporally prior cause of an action, the state-of-affairs-to-be-realized aim of that action, and the temporally posterior consequences of that action, I do not think that Hume's view is hedonistic; that is, I do not take him to hold that the only thing that is ultimately valuable is pleasure and the absence of pain, and I am sure it is not egoistic, insisting that we always ultimately only seek to promote our own best interests. Pleasures and pains may be causes of passions, results of fulfilling passions, and aims of passions. Not all passions are concerned with self-centered objectives. Benevolence, for example, is not. The aims of passions need not be egoistic or hedonistic, and egoism is a doctrine about aims, not causes (motives) or consequences (results) of actions.

Finally, with respect to every indirect passion, we must as mentioned earlier distinguish its object from its cause. The object of a passion is what that passion is directed towards, its definitive intentional object. Others disagree with me, but I am committed to treating Humean secondary passions as intentional mental states, but we can distinguish intentional states generally from a proper subset of such states, namely truth-relevant representational states. When we soon grapple with Hume's famous claims about reason's relation to passion remember that reason always has to do with truth and falsity, passion never does. But again, this doesn't entail that passion lacks intentionality or object-directedness. So, for example, the object of the pivotal emotion of Hume's account, pride, is always "the self." Pride is a form of self-approval. But the cause or exciter of pride varies enormously, and includes every valuable quality of our mind and body, natural talents as well as achievements, our relations, our possessions, artificial as well as natural objects and qualities, etc. By understanding the nature and role of conflicting, fundamental passions, such as pride and humility, and love and hatred, we make great strides in penetrating human nature, especially its social and actional aspects.

The really important general thing to appreciate is that Book II is an essential prelude to Book III, *Of Morality*, because, as we will see, for Hume morality is tied closely to the emotions (not pure reason), always and forever. But Hume's view is not monolithic – sympathy, experience, reason, instruction, and habit are all involved in the development of our moral sense.

As regards Hume's theory of motivation and action, he says much the same about liberty (freedom) in the *Treatise* as he does in the *Enquiry*. Note that in the *Treatise* (including II.2.3, II.3.1–3, and III.3.4) Hume devotes much attention to what is relevant to someone in a *magisterial capacity* when determining responsibility. Such a judge's concerns are: was the person's action intentional? Did the intention flow from enduring motives in the person? Can these motives be changed by reward and punishment? The judge focuses on intentions because they better indicate the durable mind and temper of the agent than transient, external performance does, not because they were "freely formed" (in some way that implies that they could have been otherwise). Someone who loves a victim reacts differently from a judge – for example, desires revenge regardless of intentions (an instance of ill-will toward any "deformed" behavior). Strikingly, Hume does not tie fitting passions to what's earned – one can be proud of good looks or an inherited, splendid house as well as achievement through effort. The pattern of his discussion reinforces the picture that Hume is a confident searcher for uniformities, tests generalizations by observing what *did* happen in varying actual conditions, and does not try to give sense to any strongly counterfactual sense of "could have done otherwise."

Also note that he conceives Will as an (indefinable) internal impression we feel and are conscious of when we knowingly give rise to any new motion of our body, or new perception of our mind. Talk of will as a (possibly unrealized) power is eschewed. Hume insists that reason alone can never motivate, and that reason can never oppose or override passion. But these claims and their grounds are, I think, often misunderstood.

Part 3 of Book II explains passion's role in action. Hume's famous, important claim, is that given what reason and passion are, talk of combat between passion and reason, as in traditional philosophy and common discourse, is strictly nonsense. Since passions presuppose beliefs and incorporate the influence of reason, they would be in combat with themselves if they resisted the influence of belief (this can happen in the *pathological* cases of self-deception and weakness of will). (As revelatory of Hume's philosophical strategy, compare his earlier, reconciling conclusion that given what liberty and necessity are, talk of incompatibility between the two is nonsense – since liberty presupposes causality, it follows that it is compatible with causality.) X would not be an impression of reflection if an idea did not introduce it. An idea must be present for X to be a passion rather than just a pleasure, and belief is crucial in identifying a passion as, say, pride, rather than something else – for example, the belief that the fine thing *is one's own*. Our passions and their relative strengths are functions not just of original instincts and our sensitivity to pleasure and pain, but of what we know, what we attend to and with what vivacity, what others who matter to us think and how they convey their assessments, etc. While passions direct conduct, thought influences passion.

So one misreads *Treatise* II.3.3 as holding that passions lack intentionality. They cannot copy, but they do refer to, their objects. They are representations, but not representations that contribute to true or false judgments. The objects of reason (matters of fact or relations of ideas) have truth values. Passions lack truth values. So passion cannot contradict reason; the relata of contradiction are perceptions with truth value. What does lack even intentionality are "emotions" understood as mere bodily disturbances, but such are impressions of sensation (which are "original existences"), not impressions of reflection.

Still, though reason is relevant to practical deliberation, reason (timeless and beyond criticism) alone never suffices to cause action. Recognizing truth never by itself produces conduct, but must be conjoined with incentive-providing feeling. One species of feeling is sentiment. Sentiments are preferences. In particular, moral sentiment is a preference "for the happiness of mankind, and a resentment of their misery." Given that Hume is a gradualist, perhaps we should add that basic moral sentiment is a preference for the well-being of one's group, and disapproval of their misfortune. So when Hume says that preferring world destruction to scratching our finger is not unreasonable, that doesn't entail that it isn't criticizable in other ways, for example, as immoral or imprudent. It is wrong and foolish. To criticize the will of a person we need to consider not just the influence of belief but also the motives that led to the acquisition and retention of those beliefs and the motives those beliefs influenced. It is the world-destroyers' desires and preferences that make their will faulty. They act contrary to their long-term good, not to reason, which has had its say. And what they care about conforms less stably with our natural sentiments, so is destabilizing. Hume's philosophy always aims at living well by acting in accordance with nature. Stability is a component of well-being.

6.9   *Treatise:* Key elements of Book III, on morality

I conclude this all-too-compressed analysis of the *Treatise* with a few words about Hume on morality. Hume is disagreeing with traditional moralists about the source, form, content, and role of morality. The primary object of moral evaluation is character, the most stable indication of who we are. Sometimes Hume uses "character" to mean "character trait" (as recognized by others), sometimes "the whole cluster (economy) of traits." To discern character a special and especially "steady and general" point of view is required, so as to discern traits that affect human happiness, not, for example, just some concrete, unique individual as with romantic love. Moral evaluation must be shared, and articulated, and of generally recurring traits we have names for, and whose value we can discuss and make explicit, and whose value is there independent of our approval of it. (This last clause is controversial, but I consciously affirm it.) Virtues are approved passions, approved since agreeable or useful, even if circumstantially unexercisable. Virtues are powers of producing pride or love of various forms, especially esteem; vices are powers of producing humility (shame) or hatred. Book II explained many traits; Book III evaluates some of them. For Hume, we need psychological (scientific) explanations to evaluate knowledgeably. What's peculiar about moral sentiment is the generality of its concern, the abstractness of its objects from the human reality in which they are found, the social construction of the means of finding them, the generality or extensiveness of the sympathetic understanding of human reactions required (in the primary sense, *sympathy* is a mechanism of the mind which generates a special sort of emotional involvement with the experiences of others, in which we share their pleasure and uneasiness, that leads to the sentiment of approval or disapproval), the expected agreement from others who have met these earlier requirements, and so the calmness or steadiness of verdict from time to time as well as from person to person. The moral sentiment is a pleasure taken in other human pleasures or passions, a sentiment aiming at agreement with other persons' similarly reflective sentiments. Note that however the gradualist he typically is, morality is a *distinctively human* phenomenon for Hume, applicable to neither beasts nor superior beings. That human nature must first supply the motives (passions) before the moral sentiment can react to them, guarantees the reality of our moral subject matter, and the special reflexivity of moral pleasure. It is an impression of reflection that takes as its objects other impressions of reflection. This is a central reason why the skepticism about external objects never surfaces for morality, whose objects are accessible in a science of human nature properly restricted to perceptions (what is before the mind). In the Conclusion to Book III Hume sketches the turn of the moral sentiment on itself (paralleling earlier efforts at reflective examination, such as applying causal reasoning to itself), to see if it will "bear its own survey," and improve humanity's lot. He concludes that morality based on extensive sympathy with humankind will fare best, can approve of itself.

Note that consistent with his moderation elsewhere, including his recommendations for moderation in both belief and doubt, his standards for virtue are not excessively high – virtue must be the rule, not the domain of saints. Remember (for example, from our discussion of freedom and causality) that for Hume people can't through a voluntary act change their natures. But people can change their situations. The tendency of moral contemplation of character to regulate conduct is real, but weaker, more circumstantial and less dependable than most traditional theory suggests. It works indirectly, through approved natural motivations, through concern for the happiness of still malleable loved ones, and ability to control their situation, through sympathy, through desire for esteem, through pride in virtue itself, induced by use of wise artifices, that is, intelligently and purposely designed conventions.

6.10   *Dialogues:* Overview and stage-setting Part I

Hume had a lifelong interest in religion and its role in life. He offered histories, psychological explanations, and philosophical evaluations of religious beliefs. His manuscripts show how carefully he crafted his writings on religion. For example, he worked on and off for 27 years on *Dialogues Concerning Natural Religion* – widely regarded as the greatest piece of philosophy of religion in English – and carefully revised its final, provocative section as he faced death. These writings may seem to be a transparently and uncompromisingly negative assessment of religion in all its forms. Yet perhaps surprisingly, there remains vigorous and basic disagreement about Hume's final attitude toward religious belief. This disagreement is most especially prompted by several fascinating and on the face of it puzzling things the dialogists eventually say which seem inconsistent with positions they have otherwise consistently stressed throughout their discussion. You can get a lot out of the *Dialogues* on your own, and I won't offer running commentary. I do aim to provide you with a framework for making your own judgments about Hume's intentions and successes.

It is useful to classify religious beliefs by their origins.

1   *Revealed* religion, religious belief as it is most commonly found in the world, is based on alleged divine inspiration, either through a special kind of personal experience, or an historical claim to which others have testified, typically that a miracle was performed. We saw one challenge to revealed religion in Section X of the *Enquiry*, "Of Miracles."

2   Belief can also be caused by factors studied by social sciences such as psychology and sociology. These causes may vary with time and place, for example be a function of cultural diversity, or be common to all times and places, for example express psychologically universal fears and hopes. In either case the factors explain, but do not rationally justify, the belief. Hume gives a rich account of these sources of belief in *The Natural History of Religion*.

3   *Philosophical* religion is based on rational argument without appeal to revelation. Sometimes the argument rests on no specific, observable evidence. Let's then call it *a priori* religion. We already know that Hume rejects *a priori* justification for any substantive position. He overtly dismisses *a priori* religion in Part IX of the *Dialogues*. But if the argument is a natural scientific one, based on causal inference from observation, it is *natural* religion. This is the focus of the *Dialogues*, belief in God as the likely cause of observable evidence. One of Hume's infrequently noticed, penetrating achievements in the *Dialogues* is, I think, unearthing the hidden, unhealthy influences of *a priori* assumptions among those who sincerely strive to think about God scientifically.

4   We know these three origins for religious belief exist. It is an open question whether Hume thinks there also exists what we might call *original instinctual* or *presuppositional* religion, where religious belief is a fundamental expression of our common human nature in the same way that our beliefs in causal connections, an external world, and the persistence of ourselves are. This would be so if religious belief went beyond all justifying data but was based on an inborn instinct that is indispensable for normal life. Readers who conclude that religious commitments are natural instincts for Hume rest their case largely on Part XII of the *Dialogues*.

There are at least three interestingly different ways to view the flow and structure of the *Dialogues*. The structure you impose on the text will influence your reading of various passages.

1   It exhibits a linear development. Positions mature; minds may change. So if perspectives at the end conflict with earlier ones, we ought to look for Hume's final position at the end, and trace and evaluate its lineage.

2   It exhibits Philo's (and some suppose Hume's) unremitting Pyrrhonian (unmitigated consequent) skepticism, such that Philo aims to neutralize any positive, cognitively determinate assertion about God's nature, whenever it is made, and whoever makes it, so that no superior position emerges. There can be no worrisome inconsistency between Philo's earlier and later remarks, because he permissibly says whatever works (*ad hoc*) at the moment to defuse dogmatic pretensions.

3   It's just a good example of what honest dialogue does best, allowing thoughtful proponents of major positions to make their case interactively, without presumption of resolution.

The text begins with orienting remarks by Pamphilus. He is a philosophical novice and godson and tutee of Cleanthes, so you might dismiss his observation that dialogue is of special value when dealing with important but obvious issues, such as the existence of God, and obscure and undecided issues, such as the nature of that God, and his closing assessment that "Philo's principles are more probable than Demea's, but those of Cleanthes approach still nearer the truth." But you may choose to factor them in. For example, is the existence of God really supposed to be obvious? In Part I all the characters say it is. Here's an early instance where we must make another interpretive decision. To what extent should we read the dialogues literally, to what extent ironically? Many especially see Philo as a clever ironist. So when Philo matter-of-factly agrees that God exists, is he just insincere, does he believe in God in roughly the way Cleanthes does, does he believe in God roughly the way Demea does, or does he believe in God in a different, highly attenuated sense, and if so, how should we specify that sense? In this case, Philo tells us what he's agreeing to up front, namely that there's a cause(s) of the universe (to which we give the name, "God"). So all he's antecedently committing to is the principle of universal causation, nothing particularly theistic at all. The nature of that cause is left open, and when the discussion of its nature begins in earnest at the beginning of Part II, he categorically denies we can know how to answer the question, given that all knowledge is based on experience, and we can't have experience of world-creation. He adds that the honorific terms we apply to God function to express reverence and devotion in a house of worship, not subject-matter for debate in a university.

As the text ends, comparison is even ascribed to Hermippus, who "opposed the accurate philosophical turn of *Cleanthes* to the careless skepticism of *Philo*, or compared either of their dispositions with the rigid inflexible orthodoxy of *Demea*." Again, you may dismiss the judgment of a teenager, but if you don't, appreciate what his words might mean. For example, don't assume "accurate" means "correct," so that Cleanthes is being declared the winner. After all, Cleanthes himself near the end of Part III distinguishes *accurate and regular* argument – what I take to mean methodical, sequential argument aiming to fit some recognized valid inference-form – from arguments of irregular form which may nevertheless compel acceptance over their accurate counterparts. And the second sentence out of Pamphilus' mouth defines "accurate and regular argument" similarly. And don't read "careless" as "negligent," but as "carefree" (still one meaning of the term, the expected reading in Hume's time, as an eighteenth-century *Oxford English Dictionary* specifies), in the very sense in which Hume designates his own philosophy careless skepticism, i.e. mitigated consequent skepticisms, i.e. the Academical Philosophy (as in Section XII of the *Enquiry*). This reading is bolstered by the fact that Hermippus is comparing the participants' *dispositions*.

This notion of dispositional difference may be more important for understanding the *Dialogues* than readers typically recognize. For example, only once throughout the text does Hume speak in his own, unmasked voice. In a footnote in the middle of Part XII he says:

> It seems evident that the dispute between skeptics and dogmatists is entirely verbal, or, at least, regards only the degrees of doubt and assurance which we ought to indulge with regard to all reasoning: and such disputes are commonly, at the bottom, verbal and admit not of any precise determination. No philosophical dogmatist denies that there are difficulties both with regard to the senses and to all science, and that these difficulties are, in a regular, logical method, absolutely insolvable. No skeptic denies that we lie under an absolute necessity, notwithstanding these difficulties, of thinking, and believing, and reasoning, with regard to all kinds of subjects, and even of frequently assenting with confidence and security. The only difference, then, between these sects, if they merit that name, is that the skeptic, from habit, caprice, or inclination, insists most on the difficulties; the dogmatist, for like reasons, on the necessity.

Hume seems to be saying that all parties to the dispute acknowledge the same, cognitively significant evidence, but attitudinally react differently, as in the seeing the glass half empty versus seeing the glass half full contrast. (Given Hume's own promotion of the role of the passions in belief and action, he may in this regard be ancestor to William James' much-discussed later conclusion that when one inescapably has to make a very important decision and the intellect/evidence doesn't suffice to do so, one not only permissibly may, but really must, allow one's "passional" nature to prevail.)

It is useful to divide the *Dialogues* into five main phases. Phase One: Part I offers revealing stage-setting, including sometimes overlapping but sometimes competing conceptions of the nature and value of skepticism, and its relation to religious belief. Note especially that Cleanthes, the proponent of natural religion and professed *evidentialist* (believe only on the basis of evidence, and proportion confidence to the quality and quantity of evidence), is most dismissive of thoroughgoing skepticism, charging that it's either ridiculous, insincere, depressing posturing or a surefire recipe for death, since sincere beliefs always manifest themselves in conduct (so the genuine skeptic would just as soon leave by the upper-story window as by the door), and self-described skeptics end up acting just like the rest of us. Philo agrees that skeptical principles can't always hold sway, but even then will have beneficial aftereffects, and make the skeptic temperamentally different from the more optimistic or the indifferent. Then he sounds other, familiar Humean themes: we all as we live develop general principles of thought and action; philosophy is just a more precise and methodic way of doing so, hence better at achieving stable results. We can't even account for our everyday methods of reasoning (such as cause and effect) when they are applied to the issues of common life for which they're tailored, but use them by a kind of instinct or necessity; so surely we do not know how far to trust those methods on exotic issues such as God's nature. Reason in abstract isolation defeats itself; stable belief requires more natural, experiential considerations to counterbalance it. When natural grounds don't exist, suspension of judgment occurs, so skepticism triumphs.

6.11   *Dialogues* Parts II–VIII: Design argument for natural religion

Phase Two: Parts II–VIII examine the pivotal argument of natural religion, the argument for design, which, generally, argues from some general pattern of order in the universe or provision for the needs of creatures to a God responsible for these phenomena. Cleanthes presses variants of it, with a basic structure as follows:

1   We observe that intricate machines (or rational volumes, or articulate, coherent speech, or . . .) are the product of intelligent, purposive, human design.
2   We observe that the universe is significantly like an infinitely intricate machine (or stunningly impressive volume, or . . .).
3   Similar effects probably have similar causes.
4   So the universe probably is the product of an infinite, stunningly more impressive, intelligent, purposive designer. (1, 2, 3)
5   So God probably exists. (4 and our human conception of God)

Demea blanketly condemns such empirical, anthropomorphic argument as blasphemous. Philo is open in kind to analogy based on experience, but thinks Cleanthes' applications of the argument-form fail. Recurrent questions which shape the debate are:

1   What is the nature of the data to be explained; how should we conceive the universe? Cleanthes begins, "as an infinitely intricate machine," and then offers other models. Minimally, Philo suggests that each model is optional.

2   What is the nature of good explanation? An example from Part IV: does one advance understanding at all by explaining A in terms of another, particular thing B, if there's nothing to say to account for B? Cleanthes says "yes," Philo, "no." (Philo allows that you do make progress if you explain A in terms of a *general principle* G, even if you can't (yet) derive G from some more comprehensive principle.) In light of the answers to 1 and 2,

3   What is the best explanation of the data? Cleanthes says theism; Philo constructs several allegedly equally good (bad) alternatives.

The questions he asks about the origin of the observable arrangement of matter are:

* Is it spirit (voluntary agent) or matter or mind–body composite?
* Is it transcendent (external) or immanent (internal) to the universe?
* Is it infinite or finite?
* Is it perfect (including error-free) or imperfect?
* Is it one or many?

The answers are forms of the following alternatives:

* *traditional monotheism*: one perfect being distinct from the world who actively plans the world;
* *polytheism*: multiple gods (including henotheism: there are other deities, but mine is the best);
* *deism* (as that was understood in eighteenth-century Britain): a designer god who got things going but is no longer actively involved;
* *pantheism*: a god who is identical with, so not separate from, the universe (as in Spinoza, see Chapter Two);
* *limited theism*: a single excellent, but not perfect god;
* *atheism*: no god;
* *agnosticism*: can't know whether God or gods exist. A strict agnostic totally suspends judgment. A leaning agnostic thinks atheism is more probable than its alternatives, but not so probable that firm denial of gods is warranted. If atheists or agnostics propose an explanation for the order in the universe, it is most likely to be naturalistic one, such as Epicurean (Democritean) atomism (in terms of atoms moving in the void) or evolutionary theory.

Finally, I add *mysticism*, which plays a significant role in the conversation. It says something about our mode of access to God, namely that we can have an immediate, non-conceptual access to God, but that God is ineffable, his nature, inexpressible.

Philo's challenges to Cleanthes' case for theism seem to come in fortifying, supplemental waves:

- The analogy is not strong enough to make theism a good explanation (Parts II and III).
- Even if the analogy were stronger, available alternative hypotheses, at least equally strong, weaken confirmation of the theistic one (especially V–VIII).
- Even if the assumption of theism is well able to explain order in the world, its status as good explanation is challenged by the fact that the postulated explainer (the order of ideas, the divine mind) itself needs explanation just as much as order in the world; so we face explanatory regress, so might as well not venture the first explanatory move; and explanations with which we are familiar much more often go from matter to mind, not mind to matter – indeed, the only thing in experience that mind seems to influence directly is the person's own body (IV and VIII).
- Even if theism satisfied the conditions of good naturalistic explanation, its moral component is unsupported (some think, more strongly, disconfirmed, or even disproved) by the occurrence of unnecessary evil in the world (X–XI).
- Even if theism survived all the previous challenges, it would still be useless to argue from it to otherwise unknown features of the universe or our lives (including how we ought to act), since we are only entitled to ascribe powers to the cause sufficient to produce the observed effects, no more than that (XII).

Some underlying charges he makes along the way include that Cleanthes begs questions; ignores some evidence and tampers with other evidence; makes unverifiable assertions; assumes whatever unknowables are needed to make his case; and invokes, contrary to official methodology, various *a priori* assumptions. Important examples of the last charge are that order is *not* found where there is no designer; that material order is improbable, needing explanation in terms of mental order, which is self-explanatory; and that certain value commitments, about what is better than what, are true.

6.12   *Dialogues* Part IX: Cosmological, *a priori* proof of theism

Phase Three: one thing about which Cleanthes and Philo (and Hume) completely agree is that matters of fact cannot be demonstrated, or known *a priori* by reason alone. They react harshly to Demea's effort in IX. But whatever our final assessment, Demea's version of the cosmological/

ontological argument is really quite elegant. I make it fully explicit as follows:

1   Everything that exists has a cause or a reason.
2   Natural causes are temporally prior to their effects.
3   So nothing is a natural cause of itself. (2)
4   There's either a finite succession of natural events or an infinite succession.
5   If there's a finite succession, the first natural event would itself require a cause or a reason. (1)
6   This first natural event can't have a natural cause (by hypothesis – given 2 and the fact that it's temporally first) and can't be the cause of itself. (3)
7   So if nature is finite, it has a reason which is supernatural. (5, 6)
8   If there's an infinite succession, it, taken as a whole, requires a cause or reason, why there is any succession at all, why this one, and why not another.
9   There can't be a natural cause external to the succession (we are conceiving the succession as naturally all-inclusive, and anyhow, were there another natural cause, since 3, a regress would occur).
10 No natural event within the succession suffices to explain the whole.
11 The whole natural succession is not self-explanatory.
12 Invoking chance violates 1, and really doesn't mean anything determinate.
13 Invoking nothing is no good, since something, the universe, can't come from nothing.
14 So if nature is infinite, it has a reason which is not a natural cause. (8–13)
15 So nature has a supernatural cause. (7, 14)
16 The supernatural reason for nature necessarily exists, that is, can't be supposed not to exist without contradiction, since it carries the reason of its existence in itself (ending the regress) by having its existence entailed by its essence.
17 So Deity exists necessarily.

Kant famously and profoundly criticizes this argument. I think Cleanthes anticipates some of Kant's objections as he especially attacks steps 8 and 16. The resistance to 16 is straightforward enough; he explains why the words "necessary existence" have no coherent meaning. But I'll add two notes to his complaint about 8, which connect up with the recurrent question, What is the nature of the data to be explained? Cleanthes says that the unity of a series of things or set of parts is something we impose on them, not an additional reality that needs explanation. So if we can give a cause for each state of the universe, there is nothing more to explain. Let's mean by an *inorganic whole* a whole that can be exhaustively explained by explaining each of its parts and their relations to one another. A paradigm of an inorganic whole is a machine, the model of the universe with which Cleanthes began. It seems true that if you explain each component of a watch and their interconnections, there's no super-entity above and beyond that mechanical system that needs to be explained. Let's mean by an *organic whole* a whole that has properties that cannot be exhaustively explained by explaining each of its parts and their interrelations. Here the model is an organism, which many argue have *emergent* properties that are not explicable by internal analysis of the organism's parts (such as consciousness emerging from a complex brain). Demea, and many others who have defended the cosmological argument, conceive the universe to be an organic whole. Hence the otherwise seemingly frivolous banter throughout the *Dialogues* about whether we should view the universe as a vegetable, an animal, a machine, and so on. If the universe is rightly conceived as an organic whole, then it has a natural, not merely arbitrary unity, and step 8 has to be criticized on other grounds.

The second note purports to strengthen Demea's position. He might reply to Cleanthes that if *unity* is not objective, but merely a mental projection, with what right do you claim that *order* is objective, and needs to be explained? Perhaps we humans don't like chaos, so impose order on the otherwise blooming, buzzing confusion we confront. Further, suppose Demea grants real order in the universe. He might wonder why mere order requires a designer by distinguishing the increasingly rich notions of *order*, *complexity*, and *design*. Design may entail order, but order does not entail design. Cleanthes must argue *for* design, not *from* design; design is not something we "look and find," even if order is.

6.13   *Dialogues* Parts X–XI: Evil as challenge to theism

Phase Four: Philo gives the pivotal argument against traditional, religiously significant theism, the argument from evil. Here are a few helpful guides to thinking about it. The existence of so much apparently unwarranted evil in the world is probably the most serious challenge to belief in the existence of a God unlimited in power and goodness. If he is unlimited in power he should be able to remove unnecessary evil. If he is unlimited in goodness he should want to remove it. But he doesn't remove it – it's there. So he is either limited (and so not God as we have traditionally conceived him) or does not exist at all. An enormous amount of energy and ingenuity has been displayed by religious writers and philosophers trying to avoid, eliminate, or solve this problem of evil. Is the excess of evil real or can it be explained away? The task Philo takes to be most serious is to formulate a reasonable explanation for the apparent facts, not just a logically possible (merely conceivable) one. He begins with the strong logical form of the argument from evil, which claims that God and any evil are incompatible, but then shifts to the inductive or evidential form of the argument, which we may be tempted to outline as follows:

1   For something to be the Judeo-Christian God, it must be all-powerful, all-knowing, and all-good.

2   If it is reasonable to believe anything about the world based on human experience, then it's reasonable to believe that there is excessive evil.

3   If something couldn't prevent excessive evil, it wouldn't be all-powerful.

4   If something were unaware of the excessive evil, it wouldn't be all-knowing.

5   If something were unwilling to prevent the excessive evil, it wouldn't be all-good.

6   So it's reasonable to believe (if any empirically-based beliefs are reasonable) that nothing is all-powerful, all-knowing, and all-good. (2–5)

7   So it's reasonable to believe that God doesn't exist. (1, 6)

8   Given an appropriate standard of rationality, which requires that there be a preponderance of positive evidence for reasonable beliefs, if p is reasonable to believe (at a time), then the denial of p is not reasonable to believe (at that time).

9   So it is unreasonable to believe that the Judeo-Christian God exists. (7, 8)

I say "tempted to outline" this way because it's importantly debatable whether Philo or Hume himself would accept 6–9, which supports at least leaning agnosticism and perhaps even atheism, whereas much they say suggests strict agnosticism. Ask yourself how to proceed after 5 in order to conclude with strict agnosticism.

Of course the proposed explanation for the evil must be consistent with the overall theistic view — we can't meet a problem in one place by violating a requirement elsewhere in the belief-system. Efforts to justify God's ways in light of the phenomena of evil are called *theodicies*.

Philosophers typically begin tackling a problem by defining key terms (so we know clearly what we're talking about), and so one might expect a definition of "evil." In this case, I don't think Philo tries it or that it's worthwhile, because I think the problem pretty much remains the same on all plausible accounts of evil. For example, even if evil is the absence (privation) of good, the question is why there is so much apparently unwarranted absence of good, so much apparently needless privation. But while definition of the term "evil" is not important, outlining the coverage of the term, the range of things to which it applies, is important, so that we are clear what an adequate solution must address. Evils are standardly classified as *physical* (or *natural*) and *moral* (and there is *metaphysical* evil i.e. imperfection, but I will ignore what I take to be this innocuous form of evil here — if creation is not identical with the creator, then creation *cannot* be absolutely perfect). Physical evil includes terrible pain, suffering, and untimely death caused by natural disasters, diseases, etc., and defects and deformities which rob so many sentient beings of the full benefits of life — such evil seems to be involved in the very structure of the physical and biological world. Moral evil includes moral wrongdoing (like torturing, cheating, etc.) and character defects (like cruelty and deceit, etc.), and it may be either intrinsically (in itself) and/or extrinsically (instrumentally or in consequence) evil. Philo focuses on natural evil, but has a few things to say about moral evil.[3]

There have been four basic strategies for responding to the problem of evil.[4]

(i)   Try to evade confronting it at all.
(ii) Try to deny that it's really a problem by showing that it rests on some sort of conceptual or linguistic mistake.
(iii) Try to solve it within a traditional theistic framework.
(iv) Try to escape the problem without losing the crucial values of theism by carefully modifying theistic concepts (usually towards temporal and/or pantheistic concepts of God).

(i) and (ii) try to avoid the problem. (iii) and (iv) accept the problem as legitimate, requiring an answer.

We learn a lot about what we think and why by systematically exploring the problem of evil. Many solutions have been proposed. I will say a few things about five kinds of solution, with an aim of giving you some concrete idea of the conditions a good solution would have to fulfill, pitfalls that have to be avoided, and the wide range of interrelated issues that need to be addressed just to respond intelligently to this one problem. (That's characteristic of philosophical problems!) The solutions are these:

1   There must be evil because good requires evil.
2   Evil is justified as punishment for sin.
3   Evil is needed to freely develop character.
4   Goodness is defined by God's will, so it doesn't make sense to question God's goodness.
5   Evil is the result of misuse of freedom, but a world with free agency and evil is better than a world without free agency and no evil.

Proposal 1 unwittingly contradicts the position it aims to protect. It either means that (a) for any given thing, for good to exist in it, evil must also exist

---

3   Hume's reckoning of natural evil, especially animal suffering, seems justified. We often hear that humans are uniquely or at least especially murderous of their own kind. But this seems false. Many animals, for example some non-human primates, lions, and rats, non-idiosyncratically and under normal conditions kill others of their kind, including their young, as when there's male, group takeover. To achieve dominance, animals like chimps and wolves exhibit intergroup violence that easily surpasses our own. Sociobiologist E. O. Wilson argues that ants are the most warlike of animals, seeking the annihilation of neighboring colonies whenever possible. Hume's gradualism again seems vindicated. We are more alike than unlike the rest of nature.
4   This useful way of classifying theodicies is offered by Madden, E. and Hare, P. (1968) *Evil and the Concept of God*, Springfield, Illinois: Charles C. Thomas, 7-12.

in it, or that (b) for a system of things, for good to exist in some of its parts, evil must exist in other of its parts. (a) directly entails that an all-good God cannot exist. (b) entails that God does not create the textured universe we experience freely, that he had to create evil. 2 strains moral credulity and addresses only some of the challenging phenomena (for example, are congenital birth defects punishment for the newborn's sins?), and typically requires invocation of commitments dependent on, and more dubious than, the theistic hypothesis itself (for example, original sin). 4 instances denial (strategy (ii)) – if whatever God chooses is, by definition, good, then of course there can be no independently identifiable evil that contests God's standing. 3 and 5, and theodicies which combine both, are efforts at traditional solution (strategy (iii)), and are, I think, the two most serious and revealing proposals. The only thing I want to highlight here are the grounds for saying that freedom is an overriding good (5), or that moral maturation or soul-making are worth suffering and struggle (3), and note that if they are non-empirical, they ought not be invoked by a natural religionist.

6.14   *Dialogues* Part XII: Guides to deciding Hume's overall message

Phase Five: the wonderfully rich Part XII. Some day I'd like to write an entire book on these few pages, so I'd better keep it thankfully brief now. I've said a few things about the section earlier (about Hume's footnote describing the dispute as verbal, and about Hermippus' concluding description). I'll just alert your attention to your need to decide a few key issues:

- Whether Philo reverses himself and abandons his sustained critique of the argument from design. This connects up with whether you read the *Dialogues* as developmental or not. It also connects up with whether Philo is using the distinction between accurate and regular, and irregular arguments, maintaining his criticism of all regular arguments for natural religion, but admitting the force, as if by sensation, of an irregular one. Note at the beginning of XII his shift to passive locutions, such as (my italics) a "sense of religion being *impressed on his mind*," and how purpose or design "*strikes everywhere the most careless*, the most stupid thinker."
- Whether Philo is embracing faith without reason when he says that the realization of natural reason's imperfections will induce a person to "fly to revealed truth with the greatest avidity." Or is the conclusion the conditional one that given the demise of natural religion, if one insists on believing, one had better do so as a matter of undefended faith? Or is the appeal to faith merely ironic?
- Whether Cleanthes converges towards Philo's position by abandoning traditional theism in favor of limited theism. For a while he seems to do so, but then seems to backslide.

- Whether Philo has attenuated his affirmation to the point of evisceration when he concludes:

> If the whole of natural theology ... resolves itself into one simple, though somewhat ambiguous, at least undefined, proposition, *That the cause or causes of order in the universe probably bear some remote analogy to human intelligence*: If this proposition be not capable of extension, variation, or more particular explication: If it affords no inference that affects human life, or can be the source of any action or forbearance: And if the analogy, as imperfect as it is, can be carried no further than to the human intelligence, and cannot be transferred, with any appearance of probability, to the other qualities of the mind: If this really be the case, what can the most inquisitive, contemplative, and religious man do more than give a plain, philosophical assent to the proposition, as often as it occurs, and believe that the arguments on which it is established exceed the objections which lie against it?

Whatever Hume's attitude toward natural religion, he unequivocally opposed what he called *vulgar superstition*, which includes sectarian religions, which promote conflict. We know this from much of Hume's writings, and the testimony of contemporaries. This is another example of the practical side of being a *mitigated* skeptic. Neither believe nor doubt too violently. Since on abstruse matters such as religion no side can make a strong case for its exclusive truth, we should all get along.

Hume died of intestinal cancer. In his final weeks, he remained cheerful and composed a "funeral oration of myself." Concerned for his soul, friends asked him if he would now abandon his agnosticism. He would not. But even his most religious friends could not help but love him. One friend, the famous moral philosopher and political economist, Adam Smith, concluded a memorial to Hume with "Upon the whole, I have always considered him, both in his life-time, and since his death, as approaching as nearly to the idea of a perfectly wise and virtuous man, as perhaps the nature of human frailty will permit."

6.15 Questions about Hume

I present questions in three clusters, first, focusing on the *Dialogues*, then on the *Enquiry*, and then allowing incorporation of material from the *Treatise*. You may want to skim them all, since I use them to introduce some new explanatory material.

1   What's going on in the *Dialogues* overall? There are lots of fascinating data to be interpreted and integrated. In Part I participants seem to introduce strong, conflicting conceptions of and attitudes towards skepticism and educational policy. To what extent are these steadfastly

applied to influence argumentative outcomes? On several occasions Demea and Philo ostensibly agree on some crucial point. Do they really? And Cleanthes and Philo seem to share the same empiricist framework, yet systematically disagree on where positively that framework leads us concerning religion. Here, a central question is whether it is possible to rationally embrace the argument from design without also embracing the inductive or evidential version of the argument from evil, and vice versa, and whether this produces a standoff as regards natural religion, religion approached using empirical, scientific thinking. And Demea typically seems to be a fideist, rejecting rationalizations of religious doctrine. Yet in Part IX he proudly reverts to "that simple and sublime argument *a priori*" to support his theism. Why? And after Demea leaves in frustration, in Part XII Philo affirms his "profound adoration of the Divine Being," seems to acknowledge the force of Cleanthes' argument from (for) design after all, also seems to endorse a flight "to revealed truth with greatest avidity," also seems to insist that the dispute between theists and their opponents is merely verbal, and so on. Are Philo's pronouncements consistent with each other and consistent with his seemingly sustained position leading up to Part XII? When we finish Part XII (even taking into account Pamphilus' and Hermippus' assessments of winners and losers at the beginning and end of the dialogues), what is the message Hume has exemplified? And is this message (and if it is, how is this message) the natural, perhaps inevitable consequence of Hume's recurrent philosophical methodology? So, for example, how is his famous discussion of causality in the *Enquiry* exemplification of his self-proclaimed "academical philosophy" (Section XII of the *Enquiry*)? What is that philosophy, and how is it manifested in the *Dialogues*? Or you can sketch what you take to be Hume's overall position in the *Dialogues* and then defend your account of some component of it in greater detail. Or you can sketch the position and the role of some aspect of it, and then focus on its philosophical merits and/or demerits. Or you can isolate some critical component of the *Dialogues'* dynamic (for example, the use of analogy) and establish how its use is dictated by Hume's argument in the *Enquiry*.

2   Focusing on the *Enquiry*, explain and evaluate Hume's account of matters of fact and the true and false bases of our reasoning concerning them. Or defend or criticize his argument that moral assessment and decision-making, and their presuppositions such as human freedom, are not only compatible with, but fully require, a naturalistic, scientific account of human being, and that only verbal (conceptual) confusion suggests otherwise. Or explain and evaluate his critique of traditional metaphysics and theology implicit in his concept-empiricism and account of meaningful assertion (especially Sections II, IV, and XII of the *Enquiry*). What is the status of that empiricism and that account; are they methodologically irrevisable prescriptions or testable empirical

generalizations? Specifically, what is the meaning and status of the Copy Principle, that all our *simple ideas* in their *first appearance* are *derived from simple impressions* which are *correspondent to* them, and which they *exactly represent?* For example, is it an empirical claim about the causal origin of our ideas in impressions; or another kind of naturalistic thesis; or analytic, that all ideas are defined in terms of impressions, so that to understand an idea is to know its correspondent impression(s); or something else? And how does one's answer to this question influence the way one reads Hume on some crucial, philosophical topic (belief, causality, religion, etc.) or overall? And how does the way one reads Hume on any of these crucial topics – for example, is belief just the vivacity (a detectable manner of conception) of any perception, of ideas only (not impressions), of only a subset of vivacious ideas, namely those produced by association with a present impression, an agency which makes ideas feel more lively, or what – influence one's thinking about some other, philosophical issue? Is Hume's response to the problem of causality the same as his response to the problem of inductive inference (are these the same problem), and what does one's answer to this imply about one's overall understanding of Hume; how, if at all, does Philo's case against natural religion in the *Dialogues* depend on Hume's account of causality and/or inductive inference in the *Enquiry?* Or pursue some aspect of my organizing theme of the kind(s) of empiricist, skeptic, and naturalist Hume is, of your own crafting. Is Hume an intelligibility-skeptic about certain things (what things are nonsense and why), a speculative but not meaning-skeptic about other things (what things are understandable but not knowable, and why), a prescriptive skeptic about other things (knowledge-claims about what things, since unknowable, ought to be withheld, and why), an actional skeptic about other things (what theoretical insights does he actually act on, and why)? And with any of these topics you need not focus exclusively or predominantly on exegesis, but can address the philosophical issues or arguments head on. Another philosophically consequential issue: What does imaginability and possibility amount to in the oft-used principle that whatever is imaginable (*simpliciter?* clearly and distinctly?) is possible, and is that crucial principle defensible? Or discuss how Hume's remarks in Section I on the social, actional, and rational aspects of human beings are to be understood, defended, and subsequently applied.

3   Essentially invoking Book I of the *Treatise*, is Hume's treatment of causality exactly parallel to his treatment of external existence (and what is the relation between external existence and continuous and uninterrupted existence), and if so, what does this show? Is Hume's treatment of personal identity a direct and non-expansive consequence of his previous remarks, or is some new wrinkle required? Does one's reading of the Copy Thesis (perhaps together with some auxiliary attributions to

Hume, such as that judgments are ideas) allow us to understand how Hume treats truth (as a kind of correspondence, as no real property at all but functioning linguistically as a kind of compliment, or what)? Note that Hume, so far as I know, only twice indicates (underdeterminingly) his conception of truth. How does the argument against abstractionism work; does it, for example, ineliminably rely on the Copy Thesis, and if so, does Hume argue in a circle by invoking the impossibility of abstract ideas in defense of Copy-Thesis-empiricism?

If you study the whole *Treatise*, there are lots of questions, interpretational and philosophical, you can ask. If you wish to grapple with Baier's deeply provocative approach, you can bolster, elaborate, further apply, or undermine, amend, restrict some component(s) of the "reflective endorsement" theory of norms and the "sane deep self" view of responsible agency (theoretical and practical) she ascribes to Hume, on which each book of the *Treatise* seeks those mental operations that can "bear their own survey" (i.e. be shown to be neither unstable, nor self-contradictory, nor illusory – and what do "unstable" and "illusory" mean?) upon critical self-examination (i.e. when self-consciously analyzed by the very processes that produced them – and how exactly does this process work?), with causal reasoning, our due sense of pride, and our moral sentiment (etc.?) passing muster but much else (which else exactly, and why?) biting the dust (subverting itself?), and on which the development of adequate norms and a sense of self is progressive, "gathering new force as it [the book] advances," and where exposure of conflict and its stable resolution and the tracing of causal dependencies are pivotal methodologically. This developmental reading of the *Treatise* encourages several specific, often non-standard interpretations: for example, (a) that causality as habituated, subjectively necessitated inference induced by experience of constant conjunctions between kinds of events is defensible in a way that belief in external, enduring reality is not; (b) that the understanding alone can provide no adequate (intelligible? rationally defensible? healthy?) sense of self, so that the account of self in Book I is not the final word; (c) that passions are not non-intentional feelings but cognitively significant perceptions required for an adequate sense of self; further, we are by nature reasonable, sociable and actional beings, and our passions are influenced by *all* aspects of our nature, so that some of the famous claims about the relation between reason and passion early in Book III are in some cases misleading – they are only parts of *ad hominem* arguments against opponents – and in others intended but unremarkable; (d) that moral sentiment is the crucial passion for integrating the potentially self-destructive conflicts among elements of our nature, including the self- and other-centered elements. What about the nature of natural belief in Hume's final scheme, and its alleged distinction from natural illusion? Surveying Hume's writings we discover that the meaning of "natural" varies from "not supernatural," "not rare or unusual," "not artificial" (cultural and/

or by convention or design), "obvious and necessary invention," "common to a species," "inseparable from a species," "proceeding immediately from original principles (versus secondary or tertiary) without thought or reflection," etc. How should we understand the original and the natural as they function systematically? Of course, you may concede something exegetically that you judge blunderous philosophically. For example, you may agree with Baier that the methodological solipsism, and correlative restricted conception of experience, governing much of Book I is abandoned (as the optimistic Introduction to the *Treatise* foreshadowed it would be) by the end of the Conclusion to Book I, and that that concluding section is an exquisitely compressed microcosm of the entire *Treatise*'s "progress of sentiments," but argue that the new liberality and optimistic turn is utterly gratuitous. And how do ways of reading the *Treatise* provide resolving insights into the structure and overall message of the *Dialogues* (*ad hoc* Pyrrhonian educational practice applied through and through? Convergence of unmitigated skepticism (early Philo) and dogmatism (Cleanthes) in mitigated skepticism in the end? Fluctuation of postures depending on sole use of understanding or opening oneself up to felt impressions?).

6.16   Some recommended books

Baier, A. (1999) *A Progress of Sentiments*, Cambridge: Harvard University Press.

A wonderful, eye-opening book that traces Hume's evolving position in the *Treatise*, elegantly making prominent his theory of the passions.

Fogelin, R.J. (1985) *Hume's Skepticism in the Treatise of Human Nature*, Boston: Routledge & Kegan Paul.

A stimulating, general interpretation of the *Treatise* which gives strong prominence to Hume's skepticism, especially in opposition to those who place one-sided emphasis on Hume's naturalism.

Garrett, D. (1997) *Cognition and Commitment in Hume's Philosophy*, New York: Oxford University Press.

A forcible reading of Hume as cognitive scientist, especially excellent in resolving notable, interpretive puzzles.

Gaskin, J.C.A. (1988) *Hume's Philosophy of Religion*, 2nd edn, London: Macmillan; Atlantic Highlands, NJ: Humanities Press.

Restructured, revised, and expanded from the original 1978 edition, this is the best study of Hume's philosophy of religion based on all relevant texts, not just the *Dialogues*.

Livingston, D. (1998) *Philosophical Melancholy and Delirium: Hume's Pathology of Philosophy*, Chicago: University of Chicago Press.

An interpretation organized around the thesis that Hume's persistent, central concern is to explore the nature and worth of philosophy, distinguish true from false forms of philosophical reflection, essentially self-inquiry aspiring to self-knowledge, especially interestingly arguing that the dialectic of Book I of the *Treatise* exemplifies the nature and limits of philosophy.

Loeb, L.E. (2002) *Stability and Justification in Hume's Treatise*, Oxford: Clarendon Press.

Loeb finds in the *Treatise* a naturalistic account of justification in terms of the tendency of belief-forming mechanisms to produce psychological stability, and develops a non-skeptical reading of Hume on induction, carefully criticizing many prominent scholars who treat Hume as a radical skeptic. (Loeb also reads Descartes as centrally seeking psychological stability.)

Millican, P. (ed.) (2002) *Reading Hume on Human Understanding*, Oxford: Clarendon Press.

An especially good collection of essays on the *Enquiry*, with a fine introduction by the editor, and an excellent bibliography.

Norton, D.F. (1984) *David Hume: Common-Sense Moralist, Sceptical Metaphysician*, 2nd edn, Princeton, NJ: Princeton University Press.

Aims to capture the thrust of Hume's philosophy through an interesting account of why Hume is skeptical about metaphysics but not morality.

Norton, D.F. (ed.) (1993) *The Cambridge Companion to Hume*, Cambridge: Cambridge University Press.

A wide-ranging collection that largely portrays Hume as critical, often skeptical, yet building on that criticism a constructive philosophy.

O'Connor, D. (2001) *Hume and the Dialogues Concerning Natural Religion*, London: Routledge.

A clear and engaging, part-by-part discussion of the *Dialogues*.

Penelhum, T. (1992) *David Hume: An Introduction to his Philosophical System*, West Lafayette, IN: Purdue University Press.

A very helpful presentation of Hume as a highly systematic philosopher, especially on the issues of mind, causation, morality, and religion, whose views Penelhum sometimes relates to current concerns. Good bibliography too.

Radcliffe, E. (2000) *On Hume*, Belmont, CA: Wadsworth.

Good, very short, basic outline of Hume's philosophy.

Smith, N.K. (1941) *The Philosophy of David Hume*, London: Macmillan; New York: St. Martin's Press.

Early, influential case for interpreting Hume as constructive naturalist rather than thoroughgoing skeptic.

Stanistreet, P. (2002) *Hume's Scepticism and the Science of Human Nature*, Aldershot, England: Ashgate.

Both offers a guide to much significant recent Hume scholarship and defends a general interpretation (focusing on *Treatise*) on which Hume's skeptical arguments contribute to a constructive effort to provide a science and philosophy which withstand skepticism.

Stroud, B. (1977) *Hume*, London: Routledge & Kegan Paul. Reissued by Routledge in 1999.

Excellent account of Hume's thought, especially his epistemology, and his commitment to a constructive naturalism.

Tweyman, S. (ed.) (1995) *David Hume: Critical Assessments*, 6 vols, London: Routledge.

An especially rich collection of essays on Hume.

Ongoing updates and interesting work can be found in *Hume Studies*.

7 Kant

Immanuel Kant (1724–1804) is certainly one of the most important thinkers of any period, and is the pivotal link between modern philosophy and all major, subsequent movements. He is also very difficult. On the one hand, you come to understand him increasingly deeply when you learn by practiced repetition to speak his technical language. On the other hand, most mortals can only do this haltingly and with great effort, and avidly embrace simplifying assistance. So I propose to present Kant in five stages. First I give a very brief overview of his system, suppressing any hint of controversy. Then I offer a précis of most of the *Critique of Pure Reason*, his tour de force most crucial to themes habitually highlighted in Modern Philosophy courses, with jargon retained but muted. Then I discuss several key components of his argument more expansively, acknowledging some important interpretational disputes. Some parts of the second and third sections, for example the presentations of Kant's transcendntal deduction, are especially difficult. Fourth, I outline his related foundations for moral theory, focusing on the more commonly taught *Groundwork of the Metaphysics of Morals*, but with implications for his *Critique of Practical Reason* and *Critique of Judgment*. Finally, I say a few things about how his *Prolegomena to any Future Metaphysics*, his abridged and so commonly taught rendition of the first *Critique*, differs from its bigger, more daunting sister. I struggle to make Kant's truly profound argument as lucid as possible, but show you respect by giving you what I take to be the real thing, not some facile substitute.

Two editions of the *Critique* were published; as well as first and second editions, they are known by common convention as (A) and (B), and page references are generally prefixed by A or B accordingly.

7.1 The central strand of Kant's argument

Human reason seeks to answer all the important questions that face us: what can I know? What should I do? What may I hope for? And it seeks to answer these questions without contamination from any other source (from sensory information, for example), i.e. to proceed *purely*. When we comprehensively and systematically study its efforts, we discover that both the unrestrained nay-sayers and the unrestrained yea-sayers are wrong, that a carefully circumscribed middle ground is required. The nay-sayers include the skeptics, who deny or doubt we can know; the indifferentists, who think it's unimportant to know; and the strict empiricists, who allow that we have more or less probable outlooks, but nothing that measures up to true knowledge of the world. The unbridled yea-sayers are the rational dogmatists, who are convinced that with proper method pure reason can know all sorts of substantive truths about ourselves, the world, God, and the relations among the three. Theoretical reason, whose interest is knowledge, discovers that there *are* several significant structural facts about the world that we can know with certainty, but precisely given the conditions for the possibility of such knowledge, theoretical reason has strictly definable *limits* too, limits which require that such knowledge apply only to objects of possible experience. Its natural urges to act unanchored in possible experience have to be curbed to avoid all sorts of illusions. But this limiting of theoretical reason uniquely enables practical reason to function defensibly; reason in its practical employment is interested in how we should live, including morally and politically. Such practical thinking presupposes free will, which properly delimited theory can neither establish nor rule out.

The key task for Kant's middle ground is to explain how synthetic *a priori* truths — substantive, universal truths knowable without appeal to particular sensory observations — are possible. Kant thinks that the basic principles of mathematics and natural science are, and the principles of philosophy purport to be, synthetic *a priori*, so by explaining the synthetic *a priori* we can explain why the world is a mathematical and causal order (contra empiricism), but why we can't have dogmatic metaphysical knowledge of it (contra rationalism), and explain how a suitably chastened metaphysics is possible. The explanation contains two main components. First, Kant argues that there are necessary, structural features (forms) of all experience or contentful thinking. Second, he argues that the world must conform to these *a priori* forms of experience. One refutes empiricism. Two refutes rationalism. One and two constitute the core of Kant's theoretical philosophy, which he calls *transcendental* (or *critical*, or *formal*) *idealism*. Transcendental idealism not only supplies the only explanation of non-trivial *a priori* knowledge, but is the only way to be an *empirical realist*, and hold that familiar spatiotemporal objects exist independently of us, and can be known to do so. Hence, transcendental idealism is both a constructive approach to math, science, and philosophy (*Transcendental Analytic*) and a critical tool inhibiting unwarrantable theoretical claims about ultimates such as God, free will, and simple, immortal souls (*Transcendental Dialectic*). And again, although these ultimates can play no legitimate role in our descriptions, they can have a certain practical or normative role.

The central argument for the position developed thus far can be outlined as follows, with Kant's core terminology added:

1   All contentful thinking that could be true or false requires the use of concepts, applied to something that could be made determinate. (There is no direct, unmediated confrontation with reality as it is in itself. Intuitions without concepts are blind.)

2   Contentful, empirical thinking about something (experience) requires the application of concepts to sensibly given data. (Concepts without intuitions are empty.)

3   No sensible data can be given or presented to us (no empirical intuition can occur) unless ordered temporally or spatially (or both); time and space are non-empirical (*a priori*, *pure*) forms of ordering. (*Transcendental Aesthetic*)

4   Using any concepts presupposes the application of certain very general, non-empirical (*a priori*) concepts – categories. And concept-users must have consciousness with a certain kind of unity, and categories are the basic forms of this unity.

5   So experience requires temporal and/or spatial ordering of data which are conceptualized (organized, interpreted, unified) by concepts which guarantee the application of the categories. (*Transcendental Deduction of the Categories*)

6   Experience indubitably occurs.

7   So applicable, spatiotemporal ordering and categorial thinking exist.

8   The fundamentals of thinking (the most basic forms for unifying the barrage of data we confront) can be exhaustively specified and interrelated (but not inter-reduced, that is, not understood in terms of each other). (*Metaphysical Deduction of the Categories*)

9   The principles affirming the universal applicability of these categorial forms constitute the principles of legitimate, critical, scientific metaphysics (proven as necessary conditions for the possibility of experience, or any form of contentful, referential thinking (judgment), including mathematics and foundational physics). (*Analytic of Principles*)

10   Reason has a natural tendency to apply these categories beyond what's experienceable (beyond what's an object of possible experience, beyond appearances, beyond the phenomenal).

11   This tendency, unchecked by critique, leads to old-fashioned, dogmatic (rationalist) metaphysics.

12   Dogmatic metaphysics in principle faces certain devastating problems (rational self-conflicts, fallacious inferences, confusions). (*Transcendental Dialectic*)

13   Dogmatic metaphysics should be abandoned, and replaced by critical metaphysics (transcendental philosophy). More generally, all previous philosophies, which are species of transcendental realism, should be abandoned in favor of transcendental idealism. When doing theoretical philosophy we should use transcendental method, not classical rationalist or empiricist method.

14   But dogmatic concepts (ideas of reason) do have an important, legitimate use outside the realm of theoretical knowledge-claims about determinable objects. (*Appendix to the Transcendental Dialectic*) Through critique, *reason* comes to recognize that to satisfy its theoretical (speculative) interests (answer the question, "What can we know?"), it must

give control to the more sober faculty of *understanding* (make under-standing autonomous, allow it to legislate procedure) and restrain its own, full aspirations. But when it pursues its fundamental, practical interests (addressing the question, "What should I do?"), reason is the legislator, is autonomous, determines itself unfettered by any other faculty (capacity). We have to deny knowledge in order to make room for "faith." These matters are examined through critique of pure, prac-tical reason – our current focus is the nature, scope, and limits of pure, theoretical reason.

I will unpack the details that back up this line of thought in the second and third phases of this chapter. But since rehearsal is so valuable with Kant, I reinforce its first stages in somewhat different terms.

The problems Kant aims to solve are identified in the *Critique*'s prefaces. Contradictions in metaphysics (philosophy), and the oscillations between dogmatists and skeptics, cast doubt on the legitimacy of reason and so threaten common sense and science, and ideas of freedom, God, and the soul, on which morality depend. So reason should self-examine, that is it should critique, to determine whether metaphysics is possible. (The *Aesthetic* and *Analytic* give a general account of human cognition; the *Dialectic* examines metaphysical speculation.) This requires determining conditions under which objects can be known. Transcendental idealism implements a Copernican revolution in philosophy and answers this question. It involves (a) a methodological change, testing whether perhaps objects must conform to our knowledge rather than vice versa, and (b) a substantive claim, that objects of knowledge exist only as appearances, not as things in themselves. An appearance is an object "constituted" by the subject. A thing in itself is an object constituted independently of the subject. Since sense experience is a necessary component of our mode of knowing, appearances are necessarily objects given in sense experience, and so transcendental idealism implies that empirical objects are the only possible objects of knowledge for us, so the limits of knowledge are the limits of possible experience. We can and must *conceive* of a trans-empirical or supersensible realm consisting of things in themselves, but can have no *theoretical knowledge* of it. Therefore, the verdict of critique is that reason can know things within the bounds of expe-rience, an immanent metaphysics of experience is possible, but not know things outside these bounds, so a transcendent or speculative metaphysics is not possible (where reason's use becomes groundless and self-contradictory). The transcendental precedes experience *a priori*, but doesn't go beyond it. Transcendental inquiry requires the method of identifying conditions of possible experience of objects, transcendental conditions. Arguments estab-lishing such conditions are transcendental proofs. So transcendental concepts and principles give us *a priori* knowledge of objects, a legitimate meta-physics of experience, and correlatively of commonsense judgments about the empirical world, and of natural science (Newtonian physics); they also explain the grounds of mathematics, and are essential preparation for a proper grounding of morality, which in turn will provide a rational foundation for religion. (Reason can in the practical sphere of morality fulfill its interest in the transcendent concepts of freedom, God, and the soul, which are affirmable in a restricted sense in that context.)

Kant aims to establish a class of synthetic *a priori* judgments that entail the inadequacy of rationalist and empiricist epistemologies. The *Critique*'s overarching goal is to explain how such judgments are possible. Knowledge of the necessary can't be derived from experience; so necessity entails *a priority*. There is some *a priori* knowledge, for example in mathematics. As for metaphysics, it is not derivable from logic, as in strong rationalists like Spinoza, but it is not rejectable on the grounds that it is not based on logic or sense-experience, as in strong empiricists like Hume.

Kant's argument proceeds from an analysis of cognition (representations), which involves objects being given to us, which yields intuitions, and being thought by us, which involves concepts. An intuition relates immediately to an object (B33, B377) and is a singular representation (B136n) of an individual. A concept relates to an object by means of a feature that several things may have in common (B377) and thus only mediately, via intuitions, and is inherently general. Sensibility is a capacity of receptivity (passivity); understanding is spontaneous. Neither intuitions nor concepts are individually sufficient for knowledge; intuitions without concepts are blind, thoughts without intuitions are empty. They are mutually irreducible and dependent. Rationalism's and empiricism's failure to appreciate this crucial fact is a deep source of their inadequacy (B60–2, 327).

Objects of sense experience, appearances, have a matter and form. The matter (what in appearance corresponds to sensation) is *a posteriori*; its form must be *a priori*. Therefore, there must be intuitions that contain nothing belonging to sensation and provide the form of appearances (i.e. pure intuitions). The forms of appearances are space and time. We can study space and grasp geometric truths independently of experience by mentally constructing lines, triangles, etc., and from our *a priori* knowledge of space derives our *a priori* knowledge of the spatial properties of external objects, which must conform to the principles of geometry. Geometry gives us real information about the world, so is not based on concepts alone, but on the intuition of space; and since its truths are necessary, they can't be based on (finite) experience. So geometry is based on an *a priori* intuition of space. Analogous things can be said about time, and its mathematics, arithmetic.

You can get an excellent picture of transcendental idealism from the *Aesthetic*, §3 and 6–8, the *Phenomena–Noumena* section that concludes the *Transcendental Analytic*, and Section 6 of *The Antinomy of Pure Reason*. Transcendental idealism says that the objects of our *knowledge* are *empirically real* but *transcendentally ideal*, and so are (*mere*) *appearances*, not things *as they are in themselves*. Your central task is to understand the italicized terms as Kant intends them. Here are some questions to keep in mind as we proceed.

How inclusive or restrictive is the concept of knowledge? Are first-person reports of subjective experience knowledge? At the other end of the spectrum, is only objective cognition of the law-governed objects of Newtonian physics knowledge? The anti-skeptical force of Kant's idealism hinges partly on this. And how does Kant draw the empirical–transcendental, real–ideal, and appearance-in itself distinctions? In the *Aesthetic* Kant seems committed to saying that the essential frameworks in which objects can be presented to us, space and time, belong *only* to the subjective constitution of our mind, ruling out that they belong to things in themselves *as well*. But if that's true, things in themselves are knowably not spatiotemporal, as B42–5 suggests. How does this square with Kant's presumptive position that we can't know anything of a positive or contentful kind about things in themselves? Answering questions like these clarifies the relationship between Kant's transcendental idealism and Lockean causal representative realism, Berkeleian idealism, and Humean skepticism, each of which Kant rejects. Indeed, as he makes clear in the *Antinomies* (B519), reaffirming an argument from the *Fourth Paralogism* (A369), all pre-critical philosophies are species of transcendental realism, the denial of transcendental idealism. Indeed, the *Antinomies* present an indirect proof of transcendental idealism to supplement the direct proof of the *Aesthetic* and *Analytic*: either transcendental realism or transcendental idealism. Transcendental realism inevitably leads to absurdities and confusions. So transcendental realism is not true. So transcendental idealism is true.

The *Transcendental Aesthetic* identified space and time as the pure forms of sensibility, by which data are received. The *Transcendental Analytic* examines the capacity to understand data, and specifies the conceptual conditions of human knowledge. It has two main tasks: to identify the fundamental concepts of the understanding (categories) on which all other concepts depend, and to justify the application of the categories to objects by showing they are presuppositions of the very possibility of experience. This last task, the *Transcendental Deduction*, exquisitely elicits profound connections between the concepts of an object, self-consciousness, judgment, concept-application, and experience. Since it is where the argument gets especially perplexing, I conclude my breezier outline; I'll offer a rich account in stage three.

7.2   A précis of the *Critique of Pure Reason*

I now offer a précis of the *Critique*, excluding only its direct analysis and criticism of Leibniz (*The Amphiboly of Concepts of Reflection*) which concludes *Transcendental Analytic*, its discussion of freedom and God in the *Third* and *Fourth Antinomies* and *The Ideal of Pure Reason* – which transition to Kant's practical philosophy – and its concluding division on method (*Transcendental Doctrine of Method*), each of which I outline by different means. You can use the précis as a starting point for your own, more detailed study of passages, but I think it is better to read the original first, and then see how your basic take on things squares with mine.

7.2.1 Prefaces and Introduction: Clarifying the project

PREFACE TO FIRST EDITION

Reason poses certain questions which arise from its very nature yet transcend its power. All true knowledge, which is *a priori*, and distinguished by universality and necessity, rests on pure reason. Science requires employment of pure reason. If pure reason applies to the unconditioned ("the un/conditioned" means that which is not/is conditioned by something else), then constructive metaphysics is possible; if not, not. Hence we see the metaphysicians' need to study pure reason.

The two traditional approaches to metaphysics are dogmatism and skepticism. The former assumes human reason's capacity to transcend the limits of possible experience. The latter challenges any pretension to knowledge. Both methods are abortive. Recently a "physiology of the human understanding" has been offered by Locke, wherein metaphysical conclusions are deduced from empirical evidence, but no such deductions can work. And some indifferentists purport to avoid all concern with metaphysics, but have implicit metaphysical commitments after all. We must critically determine the status of knowledge gained independently of experience by pure reason.

The nature of pure reason can be exhaustively determined, and so all the questions it raises can be answered with finality and certainty. If one difficulty remains unsolved by the common principle, the enterprise is to be rejected. And yet our task is modest: we seek to deal only with that faculty of reason which presents itself to us within our own minds – we need not transcend possible experience. The resulting metaphysics will be the only complete science; it can be complete since it is nothing but the inventory of all our possessions through pure reason, systematically arranged. (Logic is complete, but is not truly science.) And it is certain, since elimination of everything empirical and examination of pure conceptions according to exclusively *a priori* principles guarantees elimination of all hypothesis and opinion. So we are instituting a critical investigation of the sources, scope, and limits of *a priori*, metaphysical knowledge.

PREFACE TO SECOND EDITION

Logic, whose sole concern is giving an exhaustive account and strict proof of the formal rules of all thought, seems to be a secure, closed and completed body of doctrine. Its success is due to its limitations – it abstracts from all particular objects of knowledge. Mathematics achieved security as a science by a methodological revolution. It banished appeal to observation or bare concepts and proceeded by the principle: don't ascribe to a thing anything but what necessarily follows from what you yourself set into it in accordance with your concept. Similarly, physics learned that reason's guide in its investigation of nature is that which it has itself put to nature.

We are going to introduce a Copernican revolution in metaphysics. If we are to have metaphysical knowledge, objects must be viewed as conforming to thought, not thought to independently real objects. Only thus can they be anticipated *a priori* and be objects of science. Just as Copernicus explained the apparent motions of heavenly bodies in terms of the observer's motions, so we shall explain the apparent features of reality in terms of the mind of the knower.

The result of this method, however, is that we can never transcend the limits of possible experience, which seems highly prejudicial to the whole point of metaphysics. Our critique does indeed show that transcendent metaphysics is impossible. Only the unconditioned satisfies speculative reason. But if the empirical world is regarded as true reality, unconditioned-ness (totality) is self-contradictory. By proving that things in themselves are unknowable, we thwart theoretical reason's search for the unconditioned, but open the door for practical reason.

Space and time are merely forms of sensuous intuition; the concepts of understanding can yield knowledge only in connection with them. The concepts alone have a quite general meaning, but are insufficient to constitute knowledge. Yet this fact, that categories, independent of sensibility, have general significance, is revealing. Originating in pure reason the concepts have a wider scope than the forms of sense, and enable us to conceive, though not to gain knowledge of, things in themselves. Thought reveals the existence of things in themselves.

On this view, free will and determinism are reconcilable. The doctrines of morals and nature can be independently developed, without conflict. The problems of the immortality of the soul and the existence of God are similarly resolved. I had to remove knowledge, in order to make room for belief.

INTRODUCTION

I. THE DISTINCTION BETWEEN PURE AND EMPIRICAL KNOWLEDGE

Temporally, all knowledge begins with sensible experience. But it does not follow that it has its sources in experience. Perhaps there is *a priori* knowledge. By "*a priori*" is meant independent of all experience whatsoever, not merely antecedent to or independent of some particular experience (relatively *a priori*). A proposition is purely *a priori* if it is known to be true *a priori* and all the concepts involved in the proposition are non-empirical.

INTRODUCTION II. WE ARE IN POSSESSION OF CERTAIN MODES OF A PRIORI KNOWLEDGE, AND EVEN THE COMMON UNDERSTANDING IS NEVER WITHOUT THEM

There are two sufficient conditions for *a priori* knowledge. A judgment is *a priori* if (i) it is necessarily true or deducible from necessary truths alone, or

(ii) it is strictly universal, that is, true without possible exception. These two marks always accompany each other, though sometimes the presence of one or the other is more readily established.

There are judgments satisfying these conditions. Hence, there are *a priori* judgments. Further, we can show that experience is possible only if there exist *a priori* principles, and thus prove the existence of *a priori* principles, by affirming the actuality (and thus possibility) of experience – experience having certain features such as certainty.

We can also establish the existence of *a priori* concepts such as substance and spatial extension by abstracting from various empirical concepts and noting that the underlying concepts cannot be stripped away in such a thought experiment.

INTRODUCTION III. PHILOSOPHY STANDS IN NEED OF A SCIENCE WHICH SHALL DETERMINE THE POSSIBILITY, THE PRINCIPLES, AND THE EXTENT OF ALL A PRIORI KNOWLEDGE

Pure reason purports to extend the validity of human judgment beyond the limits of possible sensible experience. Such judgment deals with the three compelling problems posed by pure reason itself – God, freedom, and immortality. To solve these problems is the aim of metaphysics, which has typically proceeded dogmatically, that is, without first examining whether or not reason is capable of undertaking this loftiest of enterprises, and uncritically, that is, without determining the sources, extent, and validity of its fundamental principles.

But since experience cannot contradict *a priori* judgments, nothing impedes the fabrication of a metaphysical system so long as its various propositions are mutually consistent. And since much of reason's task is conceptual analysis, which though merely clarificatory, is often regarded as new insight, the dogmatic metaphysician is lulled into complacency as regards the thoroughness and soundness of his system, and unwittingly tends to introduce *a priori* synthetic judgments. Hence, we must not proceed dogmatically, but must carefully consider how the understanding can arrive at metaphysical knowledge which is *a priori synthetic*, and what is the nature of such knowledge.

INTRODUCTION IV. THE DISTINCTION BETWEEN ANALYTIC AND SYNTHETIC JUDGMENTS

There are two mutually exclusive and exhaustive kinds of subject-predicate judgment: analytic and synthetic. Analytic judgments are those in which the concept of the predicate is included in the concept of the subject – the predicate is found by analysis of the subject-concept; they are explicative judgments articulating the elements of the synthesis already conceived, although confusedly; they are judgments reducible to identities, and hence testable by the law of contradiction. Synthetic, ampliative judgments are all those judgments which are not analytic.

All experiential judgments (knowable *a posteriori*) are synthetic. The various concepts of such judgments are contingently connected as parts of a whole, that is, an experience which is itself a synthetic combination of intuitions. Contrapositively, all analytic judgments are non-experiential (knowable *a priori*).

But obviously an appeal to experience cannot support synthetic judgments knowable *a priori*. So how do we know that a predicate-concept is necessarily connected to a subject-concept when the former is not analytically contained in the latter? Again, it cannot be experience, since the judgment in question is universal and necessary, and hence can never be experientially established. The question of how such *a priori* synthetic judgments are possible is crucial, since all genuine, theoretical knowledge is of this kind (analytic judgments are merely elucidatory, and are not genuine extensions of knowledge).

INTRODUCTION V. IN ALL THEORETICAL SCIENCES OF REASON SYNTHETIC A PRIORI JUDGMENTS ARE CONTAINED AS PRINCIPLES

All mathematical judgments are *a priori* synthetic. No analysis of the subject-concept of an arithmetic proposition will establish its truth. For example, no articulation of the concept "the sum of 7 and 5" will reveal the concept "12." We must employ the intuition corresponding to one of the concepts and calculate in order to arrive at the result. Arithmetic propositions involving large numbers reinforce this point.

All fundamental propositions of geometry are synthetic. Again, intuition makes the synthesis possible. Certain transformation rules, identical propositions whose denial is self-contradictory, are analytic, but these are not members of the set of geometric principles. Yet even these are admitted in mathematics because they can be exhibited in intuition.

Also, the principles of physics are *a priori* synthetic. All metaphysical propositions ought to be synthetic, since our intention is to extend knowledge and not merely to clarify concepts by analysis.

INTRODUCTION VI. THE GENERAL PROBLEM OF PURE REASON

The question fundamental to all we have said is this: how are *a priori* synthetic judgments possible? The success or failure of metaphysics rests on the answer. If, for example, the synthetic proposition relating cause and effect is dependent on experience and hence not really necessary (as Hume argues), then all that we call metaphysics is a mere delusion.

There are three sub-questions to which we must address ourselves: (1) How is pure mathematics possible? (2) How is pure physics possible? (3) How is metaphysics possible? Since the sciences of (1) and (2) are actual, they are possible. Hence, we may legitimately ask, "How?" As regards

(3), we must ask both whether and how such a science is possible. This latter task is strictly limited, since we need only deal with reason itself and the problems which naturally arise entirely from within itself.

Pure reason is the faculty which supplies the principles whereby we know anything absolutely *a priori*. A critique of pure reason examines the sources and limits of this faculty and is preparatory to a system of pure reason (all *a priori* knowledge) generated from an organon of pure reason (the totality of principles of *a priori* knowledge).

Transcendental knowledge is concerned with our ways of knowing objects *a priori*. A system of such knowledge might be called "transcendental philosophy." Our task is not to present such a philosophy, but only a transcendental critique from whose principles the entire system will follow. The critique must supply a complete list of all the fundamental *a priori* concepts that go to constitute *a priori* knowledge. But it need not provide an exhaustive analysis of these concepts. We can tell that our enumeration is complete by establishing that the concepts exhaust the principles of synthesis.

By way of introducing the transcendental doctrine of elements we note that there are two stems of human knowledge: sensibility and understanding. Through sensibility, objects are given to us; through understanding, objects are thought. Since the conditions under which objects are given must precede those under which they are thought, the transcendental doctrine of sensibility constitutes the first part of the science of the elements.

7.2.2 Transcendental Aesthetic: How we receive data

TRANSCENDENTAL DOCTRINE OF ELEMENTS: TRANSCENDENTAL AESTHETIC

Intuitions, immediate awarenesses of individuals, are possible only if objects are given to us. Objects are given to us only if the mind is affected by them, and this capacity for affectation is called "sensibility." When sensation occurs, the intuition is empirical, and the object of empirical intuition is called "appearance." The matter of appearance, that in the appearance which corresponds to sensation, is always given to us *a posteriori*. The form of appearance, that which allows the ordering of appearances in certain (to be specified) relations, lies *a priori* in the mind, and is independent of sensation, or pure. The science of all principles of *a priori* or pure sensibility, that is, of the form of appearance or sensible intuition, is called "transcendental aesthetic."

What is space? A real existent or substance? A quality of, or set of relations among, things in themselves? Or does space belong only to the form of intuition, and therefore to the subjective constitution of our mind? First we shall provide an analysis of the concept of space which establishes that space is given *a priori.*

1 Space is not an empirical concept derivable by abstraction from experience of spatial objects since the representation of objects as spatially related presupposes the representation of space as a whole. Sensation is insufficient to account for the experience of objects as spatial. The notion of space as a whole is required.

2 We can never represent to ourselves the absence of space, though we can think it as empty of objects. Therefore, space is a necessary condition of the possibility of appearances, and is an *a priori* representation.

3 Space is not a general concept but a pure intuition. Space is an intuition since particular spaces are parts of one all-embracing space and not instances of space (and concepts essentially have instances while intuitions do not). Further, we must represent space as singular and unique, and this is characteristic of intuitions. Space is *a priori* since notions of particular portions of space arise by imposing limitations on the prior notion of a unitary, unlimited space.

4 Space is an intuition since no quantitative facts about an entity are deducible from a general concept of its qualitative nature, but we know *a priori* that space is infinite. And again, since we think of space as containing an infinite number of representations within itself, that is, as all its parts coexisting (and not under itself, as with concepts), space must be an intuition.

THE TRANSCENDENTAL EXPOSITION OF THE CONCEPT OF SPACE

We shall now show that certain *a priori* synthetic knowledge is possible only on the assumption that our account of space is correct. Succinctly, geometry, the mathematics of space, is possible only if space is merely the form of outer sense. The necessity of geometric propositions shows that they are knowable *a priori.* The fact that such propositions genuinely extend knowledge shows that they require appeal to intuition. Ours is the only theory which satisfies these two demands. Therefore, our theory is justified.

CONCLUSIONS FROM THE ABOVE CONCEPTS

• Space does not represent any quality of or relation among things in themselves since we cannot intuit any such property prior to the existence of the objects having the property, and hence not a priori. But we must intuit space a priori.

• Space is the subjective condition of sensibility necessary for outer intuition: it is the form of all outer appearances. Space is empirically real (in respect of whatever can be presented to us outwardly as object) yet transcendentally ideal – it is nothing when we withdraw the conditions which limit it to possible experience.

SECTION II: TIME: METAPHYSICAL EXPOSITION OF THE CONCEPT OF TIME

- We can represent things as coexisting or existing successively only by presupposing time. Hence, we could not obtain notions of coexistence and succession by abstraction from experience.
- Time is given *a priori*. Time itself cannot be removed though all appearances may vanish.
- Time is a pure form of sensible intuition, not a general concept. Different times are parts of one and the same time, and the representation which can be given only through a single object is intuition.
- Different durations can only be represented as parts of (unlimited) time as a whole, and hence presuppose the latter. Time must therefore be an intuition, not a concept, since for concepts the parts precede the whole.

THE TRANSCENDENTAL EXPOSITION OF THE CONCEPT OF TIME

Certain necessary truths concerning time (that time has only one dimension; that different times are not simultaneous but successive) are possible only if time is an intuition given *a priori*. Certain necessary truths concerning change and motion are possible only if time is an *a priori intuition.* In fact, change itself, which requires the combination of contradictory predicates, could not be rendered intelligible by any concepts. Only by introducing time (intuition) does change become possible.

CONCLUSION FROM THESE CONCEPTS

- Time is neither a substance nor a property of things as they are in themselves. If it were the former, it would be substantial but not objective, which is impossible. If it were the latter, the possibility of certain legitimate *a priori* synthetic propositions would be precluded. Time is nothing but the subjective condition necessary for intuition of our inner state.
- Since we can picture the time-sequence spatially, time itself is an intuition.
- Time is an *a priori* condition of all appearances whatsoever, since all representations, as determinations of the mind, belong to our inner state, and this inner state presupposes self-consciousness and thus time. Time is empirically real; necessarily, all objects of the senses are in time and stand in temporal relations. Yet time is transcendentally ideal. Abstracted from the subjective conditions of sensible intuition, time is nothing.

ELUCIDATION

Objection: changes in states of consciousness are real. Such change is possible only in time. Therefore, time is real. Response: Time is real, as the way of representing myself as object, that is, time is the real form of inner intuition.

- The reality of outer objects and inner states, both of which are appearances, are, as representations, equally real. The subjective idealists are mistaken.
- If space and time were substances with absolute reality, then there would exist two eternal and infinite self-subsistent non-entities. But this is absurd. If space and time were relations of appearances abstracted from experience (imaginative constructs), then mathematical doctrines would lose their necessity. If space and time were forms of things in themselves and hence conditions of all existence in general, then they would be conditions of the existence of God, who is unconditioned. On our view, all these difficulties are removed.
- Since all other concepts belonging to sensibility are empirical or presuppose something empirical, the transcendental aesthetic (being concerned with the *a priori*) cannot contain more than the two elements, space and time.

GENERAL OBSERVATIONS ON TRANSCENDENTAL AESTHETIC

The difference between the sensible and the intelligible is transcendental and not merely logical. It is not a question of sensibility's knowing the nature of things in themselves confusedly, relative to understanding. The difference concerns their origin and content. Sensibility cannot know things in themselves at all.

We are now in a position to contribute something in response to the question, "How can a subject inwardly intuit itself?" The consciousness of self (apperception) is the simple representation of the "I." If all that is manifold in the subject were given by the activity of the self, the inner intuition would be intellectual. But in man this consciousness requires introspection of the manifold already given in the subject. It is given non-spontaneously, and therefore by sensibility. Consequently, we know ourselves only as we appear, and not as a thing as it is in itself.

CONCLUSION OF THE TRANSCENDENTAL AESTHETIC

The *a priori* intuitions, space and time, provide part of the solution to the general problem of transcendental philosophy: how are synthetic *a priori* judgments possible? Inherent in this solution is the discovery that such judgments are valid only for objects of possible experience.

7.2.3　Transcendental Analytic: How we understand data

TRANSCENDENTAL LOGIC:

I. LOGIC IN GENERAL

The mind's capacity to be affected and receive representations is called "sensibility," the mind's capacity to spontaneously produce representations from itself is called "understanding." These two irreducibly distinct capacities cannot exchange their functions. Sensibility and only sensibility yields intuitions; understanding and only understanding thinks via concepts. Only through their union is knowledge possible. Thoughts without (intuitive) content are empty; intuitions without concepts are blind and unintelligible. In the *Aesthetic* we studied the rules of sensibility. We shall now investigate the science of the rules of the understanding in general – logic.

General logic is the methodical exposition of the necessary rules for any employment of the understanding. It abstracts from all content of the knowledge of understanding and from all differences in its objects, and deals with nothing but the mere form of thought. General logic is either pure or applied. Pure logic abstracts from all empirical conditions under which the understanding is exercised and contains only *a priori* principles. Applied logic deals with the rules of understanding's inevitable de facto employment. It depends on empirical and psychological principles.

II. TRANSCENDENTAL LOGIC

There is also a logic in which we do not abstract from the entire content of knowledge, and which deals with the laws of understanding only insofar as it relates *a priori* to objects. Such a science, transcendental logic, determines the origin, the scope, and the objective validity of *a priori* knowledge. More specifically, transcendental logic concerns concepts which relate *a priori* to objects of experience, yet whose origins are neither empirical nor aesthetic, but solely as acts of pure thought.

III. THE DIVISION OF GENERAL LOGIC INTO ANALYTIC AND DIALECTIC

Logic provides a purely formal, necessary condition of truth – the agreement of knowledge with the general and formal laws of understanding. But logic cannot provide a sufficient condition of truth. And whereas the nominal definition of truth as "agreement of knowledge with its object" perhaps gives both necessary and sufficient conditions of truth, it does not provide a criterion or general test of truth. In fact, since objects and content of knowledge vary, no general criterion of truth is possible. That part of general logic whose principles are necessary conditions of legitimate knowledge is called "analytic." When general logic is treated as sufficient for the establishment of objective truths (as if no material conditions were required), it is called "dialectic." We, however, shall use "dialectic" to refer to logic's role as a critique of dialectical illusion.

IV. THE DIVISION OF TRANSCENDENTAL LOGIC INTO TRANSCENDENTAL ANALYTIC AND DIALECTIC

That part of transcendental logic which deals with the elements of the pure knowledge yielded by understanding, and the principles without which no object can be thought, is transcendental analytic. This provides principles for assessing the empirical employment of the understanding. If we put these purely formal principles to material use and try to make synthetic judgments about objects which cannot be given in experience, the employment of pure understanding becomes dialectical. *Transcendental dialectic* will explore critically the false, illusory character of such groundless pretensions.

FIRST DIVISION: TRANSCENDENTAL ANALYTIC

Transcendental analytic completely exposes the fundamental elements, concepts, and then principles of all *a priori* knowledge that pure understanding by itself yields. Since pure understanding is a self-sufficient unity, the sum of its knowledge constitutes a system comprehended and determined by one idea.

BOOK I: ANALYTIC OF CONCEPTS

Analytic of Concepts is an analysis of the faculty of understanding, investigating the possibility of *a priori* concepts by seeking such concepts in the pure use of understanding alone.

CHAPTER I: THE CLUE TO THE DISCOVERY OF ALL CONCEPTS OF THE UNDERSTANDING:

SECTION I: THE LOGICAL EMPLOYMENT OF THE UNDERSTANDING

The human understanding yields discursive knowledge by means of concepts. Concepts rest on functions, where "function" means "the unity of the act of bringing various representations under one common representation," and where this act of thought is spontaneous. But the understanding is a faculty of judgment; the only use the understanding can make of concepts is to judge by means of them. And since all intuitions but no concepts are in immediate relation to an object, judgment is the mediate knowledge of an object, the unifying representation of representations of the object. The functions of the understanding can, therefore, be discovered if we can give an exhaustive statement of the functions of unity in judgments.

The formal functions of thought in judgments may be depicted by the following table:

I
*Quantity of
Judgments*
Universal
Particular
Singular

II	III
Quality	*Relation*
Affirmative	Categorical
Negative	Hypothetical
Infinite	Disjunctive

IV
Modality
Problematic
Assertive
Apodeictic

Essentially, general logic provides us with this list. But note that in general logic, where focus is limited to relations among judgments, singular (with singular term rather than class term as subject) and universal, and infinite and affirmative judgments may be treated alike. But these must be distinguished in transcendental logic, where the judgment's relation to other knowledge, which has varying content, is relevant.

All relations of thought in judgments are (a) of the predicate to the subject, (b) of the ground to its consequence, (c) of the divided knowledge and of the members of the division, taken together, to each other. The constituents of (a) are concepts, of (b) and (c), judgments. (c) is construed such that the disjuncts are mutually exclusive and exhaustive of the given field of knowledge.

Modality contributes nothing to the content of the judgment (quantity, quality, and relation exhaust the content), but rather relates the object to the understanding. Problematic judgments express logical possibility: assertoric judgments express actuality or truth; apodeictic judgments express necessity. The *a priori* truth of apodeictic propositions is a consequence of thinking the truth of assertoric propositions as determined by the laws of the understanding. Finally, the constituents of both hypothetical and disjunctive judgments are problematic.

SECTION III: THE PURE CONCEPTS OF THE UNDERSTANDING, OR CATEGORIES

If a manifold of intuition is to be known, it must first be gone through and connected in a certain way by the understanding, since before we can analyze our representations, the representations must themselves be given in a single consciousness. This spontaneous act of unification is called *synthesis*. Synthesis is a function of imagination. Bringing (the product of) this synthesis to concepts, yielding genuine knowledge, is a function of the understanding. So first a manifold is given; next the imagination must synthesize the manifold; and then the synthesis is unified by concepts of the understanding.

But the completely general concept of pure synthesis of various representations, unification of intuitions in one consciousness, is the concept of the understanding itself – the same understanding which is essentially a faculty of judgment. So the same faculty which produces an analytic unity of representations in a judgment produces a synthetic unity of representations in an intuition. Hence, we can derive the functions of synthesis from the functions of unity in judgment. But these functions of synthesis are just pure concepts of the understanding, or categories.

I
Of Quantity
Unity
Plurality
Totality

II
Of Quality
Reality
Negation
Limitation

III
Of Relation
Inherence & Subsistence
Causality & Dependence
Community (reciprocity between
agent and patient)

IV
Of Modality
Possibility–Impossibility
Existence–Non-Existence
Necessity–Contingency

These are all the fundamental pure concepts of synthesis that the understanding contains within itself *a priori*. Only by these concepts can the understanding think an object of intuition. The enumeration, since non-inductive and developed from a common principle (the faculty of judgment) is systematic and complete.

The four classes of concepts may, by virtue of the nature of the understanding, be divided into two groups: the mathematical categories, concerned with objects of intuition; and the dynamical categories, concerned with the existence of these objects, in their relation either to each other or to the understanding. The third category in each arises from the combination of the second category with the first. Yet these third categories are not derivative since the combination producing them requires a special act of understanding, diverse from that exercised in the case of the first and second.

CHAPTER II: THE DEDUCTION OF THE PURE CONCEPTS OF UNDERSTANDING

SECTION I: THE PRINCIPLES OF ANY TRANSCENDENTAL DEDUCTION

The non-empirical explanation of how pure concepts can relate *a priori* to objects and hence yield knowledge, thus justifying their employment, is called their transcendental deduction. Such a deduction of the pure concepts of the understanding is required since (a) they apply to objects universally, that is, apart from all conditions of sensibility (and hence to things-in-themselves) and cannot be justified by appeal to *a priori* intuition; and (b) unlike space and time, it is not evident that the categories are conditions of the possibility of empirical knowledge.

TRANSITION TO THE TRANSCENDENTAL DEDUCTION OF THE CATEGORIES

Representations and their objects may be necessarily connected only if the representation is *a priori* determinant of the object, and this only if conformity to the representation is a necessary condition of knowing anything as an object. All experience contains both intuition and a concept of an object as appearing. Concepts of objects in general are thus necessary conditions of all empirical knowledge. Therefore, the categories are objectively valid since, so far as the form of thought is concerned, through them alone does experience become possible. The categories relate of necessity and *a priori* to objects of experience since only by means of them can any object of experience be thought.

SECTION II: THE A PRIORI *GROUNDS OF THE POSSIBILITY OF EXPERIENCE*

Pure *a priori* concepts are objectively valid only if they are necessary, *a priori* conditions of a possible experience. If such concepts did not contain the conditions of a possible experience and an empirical object, they would be entirely empty and could never arise in thought. These concepts are the categories. We must first consider the transcendental makeup of the subjective sources of these categories.

Knowledge involves the comparing and connecting of representations; a mere succession of isolated representations is not knowledge. A synopsis of a manifold requires a spontaneous threefold synthesis: the representations must be apprehended, reproduced in imagination, and recognized in a concept.

1   THE SYNTHESIS OF APPREHENSION IN INTUITION – All representations, as modifications of the mind, must conform to the conditions of inner sense, and hence have temporal relations. But though intuition contains a manifold, it cannot be represented *as* a manifold and as contained in a *single* representation without it being run through and held together by the mental act called *synthesis of apprehension*.

2   THE SYNTHESIS OF REPRODUCTION IN IMAGINATION – Empirical laws of association and memory hold only if appearances are

themselves subject to a rule of synthetic unity. This rule is the *synthesis of reproduction in imagination*, enabling reproduction and retention of apprehended representations as I proceed through the temporally ordered manifold. It allows thinking the otherwise disjoint succession of perceptions in one, unified consciousness. All experience requires such reproducibility of appearances. Hence, reproductive synthesis is a transcendental act of the mind.

3   THE SYNTHESIS IS RECOGNITION IN A CONCEPT – Reproductive synthesis is insufficient for knowledge. I must also be conscious of the facts that the reproduced representation is the same as the representation previously apprehended, and that the various representations are members of a unified whole. This mental activity is called *synthesis of recognition in a concept.*

What do we mean in speaking of an object of representations, an object distinct from and corresponding to our knowledge of it? The function of the object is to bind various representations together, to produce synthetic unity in the manifold. But we discovered that ultimately such synthetic unity yields knowledge only if there is the analytic unity of judgment. Hence, the object functions as the ground of the necessary unity of the representations in a judgment. It is by virtue of inter-representational relations and not correspondence to some independently real, unknown x that genuine knowledge is possible.

Knowledge requires unity of the manifold. This unity is not to be found in the object since we can never establish a correspondence between inner states and what those states represent in the object itself. The unity is therefore subjective: it is the formal unity of consciousness in the synthesis of the manifold of representations. It is produced by the mind through the threefold synthesis. Hence, the concept of the object x is the maximally general rule of synthesis, the form of all particular rules of synthesis. It is this formal unity of rule that confers objectivity to a manifold and makes possible knowledge of objects.

Self-consciousness or empirical apperception presents us with a constant flux of appearances and never an abiding self. The identity of the subject can never be established empirically. Hence, if the presumption that introspected inner states belong to the consciousness of a single self is correct, there must be some condition logically prior to this experience itself. This pure, original, unchangeable consciousness is called *transcendental apperception*. Its numerical unity is the *a priori* ground of all concepts.

The transcendental unity of apperception connects successive representations according to rules. It does so only if the mind is conscious that the manifold is being combined according to a unified system of rules. Hence, the original consciousness of self-identity is at the same time a consciousness of the unity of the synthesis of all appearances according to rules. The pure concept of the unintuitable object of appearances, of the transcendental object = x, alone justifies application of empirical concepts in general and is required for knowing any object. So if knowledge is possible, then appearances must conform to the conditions of the necessary unity of apperception, hence, the rules of synthesis. But the categories are the rules of synthesis. Therefore, the categories are the conditions of the possibility of knowledge. They are the conditions of thought in a possible experience, just as space and time are the conditions of intuition for that same experience.

Since they are necessary and universal, these categories cannot be derived from experience. Empirical concepts themselves could not perform their unifying function in experience unless there were such universal and necessary rules (i.e. laws). And empirical rules of association presuppose these necessary laws too; we could not even apprehend experiences as organized, and so as associated, unless these laws applied. Indeed, the very notion of nature (i.e. the aggregate of appearances, the objects of possible experience) implies necessary interconnection. Nature is knowable *a priori* just because its universal unity is given by our thought. The synthetic unity of appearances in accordance with pure concepts is the form of experience.

SECTION III: THE RELATION OF THE UNDERSTANDING TO OBJECTS IN GENERAL, AND THE POSSIBILITY OF KNOWING THEM A PRIORI

There are three sources of human knowledge: sense, imagination, and apperception. Whereas each can be treated empirically in explaining the origin of particular experience, each is also an *a priori* necessary condition of all experience. Consequently, we must distinguish empirical and pure intuition (the latter, the form of inner sense and therefore all consciousness, is a necessary condition of perception), empirical association and pure synthesis of imagination, and empirical consciousness and pure apperception.

The unity of pure apperception is a necessary condition of all knowledge. All my representations must in principle be capable of being connected with each other in a single consciousness. But unity of consciousness presupposes a synthesis by the imagination (a synthesis that is distinct from empirical memory). Hence, imaginative synthesis is a necessary condition of all experience.

But the understanding is the unity of apperception in relation to the synthesis of imagination. To understand is to unify by means of concepts the synthesis that the productive imagination imposes on the manifold of intuition. The concepts involved are the categories. Hence, since the unity of consciousness is necessary for experience, and since the categories are required for this unity, it follows that the categories are necessary conditions of possible experience – all appearances must conform to the categories.

This result is confirmed by arguing backwards from the empirically given to the unity of apperception. We are always conscious of a unified diversity. Sense is insufficient to account for the unity. Hence, a synthesis is required. The categories are the rules of synthesis. Therefore, the facts of empirical consciousness presuppose the categories.

If subjective and empirical association of representations did not have an objective ground (affinity), perceptions might enter consciousness entirely unrelated to each other and my self-consciousness. But we can become aware of our perceptions only if they are bound up in one consciousness, connected according to a rule (the principle of the unity of apperception). So experience requires conformity to this rule. The objective validity of empirical knowledge requires the formal unity of experience. The categories render this formal unity possible. Therefore, the categories are necessary for knowledge. And still more fundamentally, only by means of the categories can appearances enter our consciousness.

In sum, the mind imposes on nature those laws that it then discovers concerning nature, where nature is the sum-total of appearances. All particular empirical laws are only special determinations of the pure laws of understanding, that is, of the categories. The categories, formal conditions of the possibility of experience, are therefore justified.

DEDUCTION OF THE PURE CONCEPTS OF THE UNDERSTANDING (B): THE POSSIBILITY OF COMBINATION IN GENERAL

The senses cannot combine the manifold. Therefore, all combination or synthesis is an act of understanding. One aspect of combination is representation of the synthetic unity of the manifold (synthesis unifies the manifold as well as apprehending and reproducing its elements). Therefore, the representation of such unity cannot arise out of combination. All rules of synthesis presuppose this most general unity. Hence, the act of understanding (judging) is an act of synthesis presupposing conception of the synthetic unity of a manifold given to sense. It should be noted that all analysis presupposes such combination or synthesis, and that all judgments, analytic and synthetic, have synthetic unity.

THE ORIGINAL SYNTHETIC UNITY OF APPERCEPTION

The ultimate ground for all judgment or thought is pure or original apperception. It must be possible for this spontaneous act, the "I think," to accompany all my representations, since diverse sensible intuitions are mine (and are intuitions of some object) only if they can belong to one self-consciousness. So pure apperception involves at least potential self-consciousness, consciousness of the act of thinking. And the unity of apperception is transcendental, being the source of further *a priori* knowledge (and being the ultimate condition of knowledge).

The unity of apperception is itself impossible apart from synthesis of the manifold, and consciousness of this synthesis. All representations given must stand under the original synthetic unity of apperception. Yet the representations must first be synthesized. Drawing these results together, we conclude that the unity of apperception (consciousness of self-identity) and the unity of the manifold (synthesis) mutually entail each other.

This synthetic unity of apperception is presupposed by the analytic unity of apperception. I can unite diverse representations in one consciousness, or under the common characteristic of being mine (an analytic procedure), only if I can unite diverse intuitions into one object (by synthesis). One need not be aware of this act of synthesis, but it is always operative when we employ our understanding. After all, understanding is nothing but the activity of bringing the synthesized manifold under the unity of apperception.

The principle of the synthetic unity of apperception, the most fundamental epistemological principle, is an identical proposition, and hence analytic. Conjoined with the synthetic proposition that the principle provides an analysis of the nature of human understanding, synthetic knowledge may be deduced.

THE PRINCIPLE OF THE SYNTHETIC UNITY IS THE SUPREME PRINCIPLE OF ALL EMPLOYMENT OF THE UNDERSTANDING

It follows from the above that the synthetic unity of apperception constitutes the objective validity of representations. Representations have reference to an object precisely because they are thought together in one consciousness. An object is that in the concept of which the manifold of given intuition is united. But we have shown that unity of manifold requires unity of consciousness. So the same unity is a necessary condition of both consciousness of objects and apperception or understanding. Hence, the principle of the synthetic unity of apperception, "all the manifold of intuition is subject to the conditions of the original synthetic unity of apperception," is the supreme principle of all employment of understanding.

THE OBJECTIVE UNITY OF SELF-CONSCIOUSNESS

The transcendental unity of apperception is an objective unity since it is the source of unity in objects. Such unity should be distinguished from the subjective unity of consciousness, which is an empirical and contingent connection of representations. We do not all share the same contents of consciousness. Subjective unity is a determination of inner sense.

THE LOGICAL FORM OF ALL JUDGMENTS CONSISTS IN THE OBJECTIVE UNITY OF THE APPERCEPTION OF THE CONCEPTS WHICH THEY CONTAIN

The traditional account of judgment as the representation of a relation between two concepts is defective because (a) it applies only to categorical judgments, and (b) the nature of the relation involved is unspecified. Judgment is the act of bringing given modes of knowledge to the objective unity of apperception (where "modes" include judgments as well as concepts). This definition properly distinguishes mere association of ideas through constant conjunction from combination of ideas in an object. The former is not judgment; a judgment holds independently of the particular state of the subject.

ALL SENSIBLE INTUITIONS ARE SUBJECT TO THE CATEGORIES, AS CONDITIONS UNDER WHICH ALONE THEIR MANIFOLD CAN COME TOGETHER IN ONE CONSCIOUSNESS

The principles of synthesis necessary for knowledge of objects, derived from the unity of apperception, are based on the forms of judgment, the ways in which representations are necessarily combined in thought. These principles are the categories. Therefore, the categories necessarily apply to all objects given to sensible intuition. The categories are objectively valid.

The categories are not limited to human experience, as are the forms of space and time, since no kind of intuition could, without thought, possess unity, and so be an intuition of an object, and since thought always has the same forms. Still the categories applied to anything but a manifold given in space and time can give us no knowledge of objects. The categories *are* limited to creatures whose objects are given to sensibility from without. An infinite intelligence would have intellectual intuitions and an intuitive understanding. What is relevant for us is that the categories give *a priori* knowledge only of objects of possible experience.

Imagination, the activity of representing in intuition an object not itself present, belongs to sensibility insofar as all intuition is sensible, but is also spontaneous and determinative of the sensibility with regard to its form, in synthesizing intuitions in conformity with categories. The figurative synthesis of imagination (tied to sense) is distinct from the intellectual synthesis, which is carried out by the understanding alone. The imagination is thus productive and not merely reproductive, that is, not merely subject to laws of association in memory. The crucial point is this: Since our empirical intuitions are given to us under the form of time, they must be subject to a transcendental synthesis of imagination which imposes on them unity in accordance with the categories. Hence we explain *how* the categories apply *a priori* to objects of human intuition, having established *that* they so apply.

The empirical manifold consists in perceptions of outer sense. These perceptions, as modifications of mind, belong to time, the form of inner sense. The self affects itself by bringing its contents to consciousness, which, as has been shown, is equivalent to synthesizing the manifold. But synthesis of the manifold results in knowledge of objects. Hence, the self affects itself, becomes conscious of itself, only through knowledge of objects. Such a synthesis is absolutely required, for whereas we could have impressions of outer sense (though not knowledge) without a synthesis, we could not even have impressions of inner sense without synthesis. So it is impossible to represent time or the phenomenal self without some reference to space.

The consciousness of the self in the transcendental unity of apperception is merely intellectual and without sensible content. It therefore gives me no knowledge of the self as it is in itself (the real self) nor of the phenomenal self apart from inner sense. Thus, I know *that* I am, but not *what* I am.

Space and time as forms of intuition are diversities without unity. Only as pure intuitions do they possess unity, and they possess this unity only because they presuppose a synthesis which does not belong to sense at all. The unity of space and time is an *a priori* condition of the synthesis of apprehension; that is, the manifold must be synthesized so that it can appear in a single spatiotemporal system. But this act of synthesis must conform to the categories (the rules of synthesis). Therefore, the categories are conditions of the possibility of experience. Therefore, the categories are objectively valid for all objects of experience, for all objects of empirical knowledge. Still more fundamentally, the possibility of contents of empirical consciousness at all requires the categories.

TRANSCENDENTAL ANALYTIC: BOOK

II: THE ANALYTIC OF PRINCIPLES

Introduction: judgment is the activity of subsuming cases under rules. General logic cannot provide rules for judgment; to determine whether something falls under its purely formal rules judgment itself is required. Transcendental logic both provides the universal conditions or rules and specifies *a priori* the instance to which the rules apply. First, we shall examine the sensible condition necessary for employment of the categories. Then we shall examine the synthetic *a priori* principles deducible from the schematized categories, which serve as the foundation of all other knowledge.

CHAPTER I: THE SCHEMATISM OF THE PURE CONCEPTS OF UNDERSTANDING

If objects are subsumable under concepts only if the representation of the object has something in common with the concept, and if pure concepts, not abstracted from experience, having nothing in common with sensible intuitions, then how can categories apply to appearances? A mediating third representation, the transcendental schema or transcendental determination of time, is required. Time is both sensible and *a priori*, and hence has something in common with both the manifold of intuition and the categories. And time, the formal condition of inner sense, is a necessary condition of employment of categories. The schema of a concept is a general rule of imagination for providing an image for a concept, a rule of synthesis of pure imagination. Production of the image itself requires employment of the reproductive (empirical) imagination as well. Of course, pure concepts can never issue in sensible images. Hence, the schemata of these pure concepts are general procedures for the temporal ordering of any manifold; they lack reference to particular given manifolds.

The schematized category or transcendental schema of quantity is number, the rule for successive addition of homogeneous units, for generation of the time-series itself. The schema of quality is the rule for the continuous and uniform production of the real filling time (which corresponds to sensation) from a determinate degree of intensity to none, and vice versa. The schema of relation is the rule for connecting the contents of consciousness in a single, unified temporal system. Unlike the above, the schema of modality is not itself a rule of time-consciousness. A thing's modal status, whether and how it exists in time, is a consequence of its conformity to the other schemata.

The schemata of the particular relational categories are especially important. The schema of substance is the rule for representing succession and coexistence of appearances in time as determinations of a perduring reality (substrate of change, what underlies change, and what remains the same through change). The schema of cause is the rule in conformity with which appearances must succeed one another. The schema of reciprocity is the rule in conformity with which the properties of substances coexist.

The categories connect appearances in a unified consciousness. Since the schemata are necessary for the applicability of the categories to objects, and hence required if the categories are to possess more than merely logical significance, knowledge is delimited to objects of possible experience, objects of possible sensible intuition in time.

CHAPTER II: SYSTEM OF ALL PRINCIPLES OF PURE UNDERSTANDING

SECTION I: THE HIGHEST PRINCIPLE OF ALL ANALYTIC JUDGMENTS

The principle of contradiction, that no predicate contradictory of a thing can belong to it, a necessary condition of all truth, is both necessary and sufficient for all analytic knowledge. This principle is sometimes misleadingly formulated: it is impossible that something should at one and the same time both be and not be. By apparently limiting its assertion to time-relations, a synthetic element is added to the principle.

SECTION II: THE HIGHEST PRINCIPLE OF ALL SYNTHETIC JUDGMENTS

How can distinct concepts be compared in judgment? All representations are in time, the form of inner sense. All synthesis of representations rests on imagination. All synthetic unity rests on the unity of apperception. Hence, inner sense, imagination, and apperception are the sources of the possibility of synthetic judgments of knowledge of objects.

The possibility of experience is what gives objective reality to all our *a priori* knowledge-claims. Experience rests on the synthetic unity of appearances (synthesis according to the concept of an object). This synthetic unity is required for the conformity of perceptions to the transcendental unity of apperception. Given these facts, we may state the highest principle of all synthetic judgments as follows: every object stands under the necessary conditions of synthetic unity of the manifold of intuition in a possible experience.

SECTION III: SYSTEMATIC REPRESENTATION OF ALL THE SYNTHETIC PRINCIPLES OF PURE UNDERSTANDING

Among the principles of the pure understanding, we may distinguish the mathematical from the dynamical, or the constitutive from the regulative. Mathematical principles (1) are concerned with the objects of intuitions; (2) account for the possibility of mathematics; (3) deal with the synthesis of homogeneous elements which do not necessarily belong to one another; (4) are intuitively certain (provable by construction in intuition, constitutive); and (5) are unconditionally necessary in relation to a possible experience. Dynamical principles (1) are concerned with the existence of objects in relation either to one another or to the understanding; (2) account for the possibility of physical dynamics; (3) deal with the synthesis of heterogeneous elements which necessarily belong to one another; (4) are discursively certain (provable via concepts); and (5) are conditionally necessary in relation to empirical things. They guide us in discovering the sorts of connections holding among objects, but do not allow construction of the objects themselves; hence they are regulative, not constitutive. The axioms of intuition and anticipations of perception are mathematical; the analogies of experience and postulates of empirical thought are dynamical. We shall proceed to discuss these principles in turn.

AXIOMS OF INTUITION

All intuitions are extensive magnitudes.

Proof 1: An intuition can be apprehended in consciousness only if its manifold is synthesized. In synthesis, representation of the parts precedes and makes possible representation of the whole. But, by definition, a magnitude is extensive if representing the whole is dependent upon first having represented the parts. Therefore, all intuitions are extensive magnitudes.

Proof 2: It is impossible to represent a line or a span of time without drawing it in thought. But all intuition is spatial or temporal. Therefore, by definition of extensive magnitude, all intuitions are extensive magnitudes.

ANTICIPATIONS OF PERCEPTION

In all appearances, the real that is an object of sensation has intensive magnitude, that is, a degree. Objects have sensible qualities in addition to spatial and temporal qualities, and the qualities of objects must have a degree corresponding to the degree of our sensation.

Proof 1: Sense perception, empirical consciousness, must contain sensation; appearances contain matter as well as form. A continuous change from empirical to pure consciousness is possible. Hence, a synthesis producing a quantity of sensation beginning from zero is possible. Thus sensation has a characteristic, non-extensive quantity. Thus sensed qualities have degree.

Proof 2: Intensive quantity, degree, is given as a whole and at once (no synthesis is required). Yet every sensation is capable of diminution to nothing. Hence, between reality and negation there is a continuous sequence of sensations; a quantity is continuous if no part of it is the smallest possible part. Therefore, sensation (and the real corresponding to it) has intensive quantity or degree.

We can ascribe continuity *a priori* to all quantities, both intensive and extensive; all appearances are continuous. In particular, since no part of space or time is the smallest possible, they are continuous magnitudes. Hence, points and moments are limits or boundaries, not parts of space and time. Finally, continuous quantities are the products of continuous (actual or possible) syntheses. If a synthesis is discontinuous, the product is an aggregate.

ANALOGIES OF EXPERIENCE

Experience is possible only through the representation of a necessary connection of perceptions. (All appearances, are, as regards their existence, subject *a priori* to rules determining their relation to one another in one time.)

The Analogies are rules which govern all appearances of objects in one and the same objective time. The unity of time is grounded on the unity of apperception, which presupposes synthesis according to rules. But the nature of these synthetic rules depends in part on the fact that time itself cannot be perceived. If there were a perceptible, absolute time, we could determine temporal position directly by reference to it. But since there is not, temporal position is determined by relating objects to one another in time in accordance with *a priori* rules valid for all times. The specific character of these rules will be established in the sequel.

The proof of the principle of the Analogies concerns only objects of possible experience, and not things-in-themselves. Such a proof may proceed from the unity of apperception or from the unity of objective time-relations, since we have established by the Deduction and the Schematism that the synthetic unity of apperception and the synthetic unity of the time-relations among objects mutually entail each other. Remember that experience is knowledge of objects distinct from mere subjective impressions. To experience is to relate perceptions to objects, wherein the perceptions are ordered in a way independent of my subjective apprehension of them. Now, all objects of experience are encompassed by a single time order. But what is the nature of this order? It must be such that experience is rendered possible, that our *a priori* knowledge of nature is made comprehensible.

Later on, it shall be argued that the schematized categories are the rules for such an order, rules necessary for subjective perceptions to have objective reference.

It should be noted that Analogies of Experience are different from mathematical analogies. In the latter we are given three items of a proportional equation and from these infer the value of the fourth item. But in the former we know only that a relation obtains, not what the specific nature of the unknown item is.

FIRST ANALOGY

All appearances contain the permanent (substance) as the object itself, and the transitory as its mere determination, that is, as a way in which the object exists. (In all change of appearances substance is permanent; its quantum in nature is neither increased nor diminished.)

Proof 1:
1   Only in time, the permanent form of inner intuition, can coexistence or succession of appearances be represented.
2   Time itself does not change but abides permanently (time is singular; there is only one time in which all other items must be placed as successive). If "time" did change, it would require another time in which to change. So the two modes of time can only be represented as determinations of this unchanging something in our experience.
3   But time itself cannot be perceived (perceived ≠ intuited).
4   So the unchanging something of 2 must really be found as some substratum in appearances which somehow manages to represent time itself. We can be cognizant of the modes of time manifested in experience (change and simultaneity) only by relating our appearances to this unchanging background (the substratum).
5   This permanent substratum of the real is substance; consequently, objective appearances must be viewed as determinations of substance.
6   Remaining ever the same, substance is unchangeable in its existence, and so its quantum in nature can be neither increased nor diminished.

Proof 2:
1   Our apprehension of the manifold is always successive.
2   So apprehension is insufficient for determining whether the manifold is objectively successive or simultaneous.
3   For such determination we require an underlying ground which exists at all time, something abiding and permanent, of which all change and coexistence are only so many ways in which the permanent exists.
4   The permanent is the substratum of the empirical representation of time itself, and so there could be no objective time-relations without the existence of the permanent.
5   Change does not affect time itself, but only appearances in time.

6   If we ascribe succession to time itself, we should have to think of another time in which this succession occurs.

7   Bare succession never yields magnitude of existence; only through the permanent can duration of the time-series be acquired. If each perception just came and went and there was no connection (unity) between them, we could not experience magnitude of the real.

8   So again, without the permanent there are no objective time-relations.

9   Time itself cannot be perceived. Events are not presented to us with their dates stamped on them.

10   Therefore, the permanent must be present in appearances, as substratum of their relations (their particular time-determinations). The permanent is a necessary condition of the synthetic unity of appearances.

11   Therefore, all (knowable) existence and all change in time must be viewed as simply a mode of the existence of that which remains and persists.

12   Therefore, in all appearances the permanent is the object itself, substance as phenomenon. Everything which changes or can change belongs only to the way in which substance or substances exist (the determinations of substance or substances).

SECOND ANALOGY

All alterations take place in conformity with the law of the connection of cause and effect. (Everything that happens, that is, begins to be, presupposes something upon which it follows according to a rule.)

Proof 1: All empirical knowledge involves the synthesis of the manifold by the imagination, and this synthesis is always successive. The order of this sequence is not fixed. But there is a difference between subjective fancy and objective knowledge. In objective knowledge, the sequence must be represented as determined. This synthetic unification can only result from a pure concept of understanding, and the relevant concept is that of causality, connection according to a rule. So experience is possible only if the succession of appearances is subject to the law of experience.

Proof 2: The apprehension of the manifold is always successive. But representations are intentional; they are not only contents of consciousness but also representations of objects. The successiveness of perceptions in subjective consciousness does not imply objective succession; consideration of perception of large physical objects such as a house shows this. How then can I determine whether my mental contents have objective reference? As we have demonstrated in the Deduction, objectivity is, by analysis, necessity of connection. And a manifold is so connected only if the imagination reproduces it according to a rule. This rule of synthesis required for a unified, objective time order, is the schematized category of cause.

Proof 3: Suppose there is nothing antecedent to an event, upon which it must follow according to a rule; that is, suppose the principle of causality is false. Then all succession would be merely subjective, relating to no objects.

But then I could make no empirical judgments and have no empirical knowledge. Therefore, whatever happens (is an event) presupposes something upon which it follows according to a rule.

Proof 4: Preceding time necessarily determines subsequent time, since I can only reach subsequent time by passing through precedent. But only in appearances can we empirically apprehend this continuity in the connection of times. Therefore, precedent phenomena determine subsequent phenomena. Note that there must be a necessary succession of appearances in order to represent in experience the necessary succession of the parts of time, just as there must be a permanent substratum of appearances in order to represent the unity of time (as shown in the First Analogy). This is so, again, because absolute time is not an object of perception.

In sum, given the facts that (1) successiveness in subjective apprehension is insufficient to establish succession in the object, (2) an object is a set of (actual or possible) perceptions, (3) time itself cannot be perceived, (4) all succession is successive determinations of permanent substances, (5) to know a succession is objective requires thought as well as sense, and (6) we do possess knowledge of objective successions, we may provide several proofs that objective succession requires necessary succession, that is, succession of appearances according to a rule. And this was the goal of the Second Analogy.

It is objected that in some cases the effect does not follow the cause, but is simultaneous with it. In fact, the beginning of an effect seems always to be simultaneous with its cause (consider the heat of a room and the heated stove which causes it). But our point is that in *order* of time every event is preceded by a cause. This does not imply a passage of time between them. The temporal succession involved is continuous. Change must be continuous, and its continuity is due to the continuity of causal activity.

THIRD ANALOGY

All substances, in so far as they can be perceived to coexist in space, are in thoroughgoing reciprocity.

Proof 1:
1 Two things A and B are coexistent if and only if the order of perceiving them is reversible – this is the criterion for distinguishing objective coexistence from objective succession (not a mark warranting the inference from subjective succession to objective coexistence).
2 We cannot perceive time itself (and so infer reversibility of perceptions from existence at the same time).
3 The synthesis of apprehension is insufficient to warrant the assertion that objects A and B coexist.
4 So a concept of understanding is required to say that the reciprocal succession of perceptions is grounded in the object, that is, to know that

the coexistence is objective. Only such a rule can confer necessity. This is the rule of community. So coexistence in space is experienceable only if objects interact reciprocally.

Proof 2:

1   The criterion of coexistence of things is reversibility in the order of the synthesis of apprehension.
2   Suppose substances exist without interacting.
3   Then their coexistence would not be perceivable; they would be separated by completely empty space.
4   We do distinguish objective coexistence from objective succession.
5   Hence, there must be more in experience than mere apprehension
6   There must be something through which A determines B's position in time and B reciprocally determines A's position in time.
7   One thing can determine another's position in time only by causing it.
8   But substances themselves do not cause each other, since substances are permanent. What are caused are the determinations or states of a substance.
9   So, if their coexisting is to be experienceable, each substance must stand in dynamic interaction with all others.
10 The condition of experience is the condition of objects of experience.
11 Therefore, all appearances coexisting in space interact.

THE POSTULATES OF EMPIRICAL THOUGHT IN GENERAL

The Postulates are regulative (non-constitutive) principles which explain the concepts of possibility, actuality (existence), and necessity as used in making experiential judgments about things (in their empirical employment). Modality expresses the relation of the concept to the faculty of knowledge, the understanding, or, what comes to the same thing, the relation of the object (fully determined) to the knowing subject. The modalities are concerned with the synthetic activity which imposes unity on the sensuously given. They represent how the mind knows, and not what it knows.

Therefore, the content of the concept of an object remains the same regardless of modality. The modalities do not in the least enlarge the concepts to which they are apparently "predicatively" attached; they do not provide additional determination to the set of determinations which constitute a judgment. Hence they are not real (determining) predicates.

Thus, as empirical realists, we recognize that the possible, actual, and necessary are coextensional (coincide). All phenomena, as objectively real, must at one and the same time be possible, actual, and (hypothetically) necessary. The laws of nature (which provide the forms of inference within which we may place particular, factual premises derived from specific experiences) remain fixed. The same laws that make actual perceptions necessary under actual conditions are those that make other perceptions possible (necessary under possible conditions). So everything has a hypothetical or conditioned necessity. Anything currently experienceable must be understood in terms of modal relationships to further (past and future) experience, which is possible under possible conditions. This follows from the empirical realist analysis of objectivity. To occur is to be objectively situated in time, which is to be causally determined. And nothing outside the single, unified objective temporal order is an object of possible experience. Consequently, the actual, necessary, and (really, not logically) possible coincide.

We may also, however, as transcendental idealists, assert that from our subjective viewpoint the three concepts are separable, and that modal status depends on how much we know of a particular empirical thing in a given circumstance. If we know of something only that it can be brought into consistent agreement with the formal conditions of an experience in general (with space and time as the forms of intuition and the categories as the forms of understanding), then we regard it as possible. If we also discover that the something is given in sensation or can be inferred (by the Analogies) from something else so given, then it is actual for us. If, in addition, we are able to explain its existence (or occurrence) by causal laws, then we understand it as necessary.

An object of knowledge, no matter what its modal status, conforms necessarily to causal laws. This is what is meant by the existence of a real object, as opposed to a series of subjective apprehensions. But any particular connection of this sort must be learned empirically. In each case the modality is relative to the immediate conditions of judgment, the conditions in which we, here, now, are placed. That an event E is somehow caused is necessary; how, in particular, E was caused, is not.

We must keep in mind that material or causal necessity holds between states of substances, and not substances themselves. Given this, and what we have established previously, we may assert the following *a priori* principles concerning nature:

- Everything is necessarily determined;
- Each determination is a consequence of some specifiable condition, both of which conform to the synthetic unity of appearances;
- All change is continuous; and
- Empty space is not an object of possible experience.

REFUTATION OF IDEALISM

Dogmatic idealists maintain that objects in space are imaginary (or so Kant wrongly construes Berkeley). Problematic idealism holds that the existence of physical objects in space is uncertain. This latter, skeptical thesis is based on the consideration that physical objects, though existing independently of us if existing at all, are not immediately perceived, and so their existence, causally inferred, is uncertain. We shall now establish the empirical realist thesis that physical objects are immediately perceived and so known with certainty to exist.

1 I am conscious of my own existence as empirically determined in time.
2 To say that my consciousness of myself is empirically determined is to say that it is restricted to an awareness of momentary items which stand in the temporal relations of successiveness and simultaneity.
3 So, to perceive my empirical self is to perceive a succession of momentary items.
4 All determination of time presupposes something permanent in perception.
5 So, consciousness of succession requires awareness of something permanent.
6 So, whatever is permanent cannot be a momentary item among others because it is only by perception of the permanent that I can perceive the succession of these items.
7 So, the permanent I perceive is not part of my mental history.
8 So, I directly perceive objects outside me.
9 If I directly perceive something, then I know with certainty that that something exists.
10 So, I know with certainty that physical objects in space exist.

We have shown that inner experience in general presupposes outer experience in general. Of course it does not follow that every one of our representations has objective reference; some may be the product of imagination. These latter representations are merely the reproduction of previous outer perceptions. The criterion for distinguishing veridical from non-veridical perceptions is a separate matter.

GENERAL NOTE ON THE SYSTEM OF THE PRINCIPLES

The categories are merely forms of thought, ways of organizing given intuitions in order to yield knowledge. So no synthetic proposition can be made from mere categories – connection of distinct concepts requires intuition. In fact, demonstration of the objective validity of the categories requires outer intuitions. For example, the permanent in intuition corresponding to the concept of substance is spatial (matter), since everything in inner sense is constantly changing. Motion, or alteration in space, corresponds to the concept of causality. All alteration presupposes something permanent in intuition, and, again, only outer intuitions can be permanent. Even inner alterations are comprehensible only by representing time figuratively as a line, that is, as spatial. And community of substances is rendered comprehensible if they are represented in space.

CHAPTER III: THE GROUND OF THE DISTINCTION OF ALL OBJECTS IN GENERAL INTO PHENOMENA AND NOUMENA

The transcendent employment of a concept is its application to things in themselves, while its empirical employment is its application merely to appearances (objects of a possible experience). Only the latter application is feasible. The application of the categories is limited to appearances; they never have transcendent employment. So the principles of pure understanding can never apply to things in themselves, things unconditioned by our mode of intuiting them. Hence, an important conclusion of the Analytic is that the most the understanding can achieve *a priori* is to anticipate the form of a possible experience in general. The employment of a concept involves a function of judgment whereby an object (particular) is subsumed under the concept, and so involves at least the formal condition under which something can be given in intuition. If this condition of judgment (the schema) is lacking, all subsumption becomes impossible.

The word "noumenon" has two senses: a negative sense in which it merely means "non-phenomenon;" a positive sense in which it means "object of a non-sensible (intellectual) intuition." We have shown that the categories cannot be used in thinking of noumena. So we must understand "noumena" only in the negative sense.

A concept is problematic if and only if it is self-consistent, serves to limit other concepts involved in knowledge, yet cannot itself be known to have objective reference. The limiting concept of a noumenon, which serves to curb the pretensions of sensibility as regards things in themselves, is problematic. Hence, a noumenon is not for our understanding a special kind of object, namely, an intelligible object. But the understanding limits itself and sensibility with respect to things not regarded as appearances by the negative employment of noumena. As these things cannot be known through the categories, they must be thought of as an unknown something.

7.2.4 *Transcendental Dialectic: How we fundamentally misapply thought*

SECOND DIVISION: TRANSCENDENTAL DIALECTIC:

I. TRANSCENDENTAL ILLUSION

The senses do not err – not because they always judge correctly but because they do not judge at all. The understanding alone, if it acts in accordance with its own laws, is also incapable of error. Truth and error are only to be found in judgment, in the relation of the object to our understanding, where the sensibility has an unobserved influence on the understanding.

Principles whose application is restricted to objects of possible experience are called "immanent;" those which purport to extend beyond the limits of possible experience are called "transcendent." The task of the dialectic is to expose the natural and inevitable illusions of transcendent judgments, which result from regarding fundamental but subjective rules for employment of reason as objective principles.

II. PURE REASON AS THE SEAT OF TRANSCENDENTAL ILLUSION

A. REASON IN GENERAL

Just as understanding is the activity which unifies appearances according to rules, reason is the activity which unifies the rules of understanding under principles (where principles, in their primary sense, are synthetic *a priori* propositions). Consequently, reason never has direct application to experience, but only to understanding. The unity of reason is not the unity of a possible experience; it is not a synthetic unity. The real employment of reason generates concepts and principles; the logical employment is merely the activity of mediate inference. Analogously with the metaphysical deduction of the categories, the logical functions give us the clue to the transcendental.

B.THE LOGICAL EMPLOYMENT OF REASON

The immediate inference of one proposition from another is an inference of understanding. If an additional premise is required for the deduction, the inference is one of reason. Every syllogism has a major premise which represents the relation between what is known and its condition either categorically, hypothetically, or disjunctively. The goal of all such syllogistic reasoning is systematic unity of knowledge.

C.THE PURE EMPLOYMENT OF REASON

The maxim of pure reason is: find, for the conditioned knowledge obtained by the understanding, the unconditioned whereby its unity is brought to completion. The principle corresponding to this maxim is: whenever the conditioned is given, a whole, unconditioned, series of conditions is also given. This principle is synthetic, yet transcendent with respect to all appearances. The status and implications of this principle will be examined in the Dialectic.

BOOK I: THE CONCEPTS OF PURE REASON

Concepts of pure reason or transcendental ideas such as the unconditioned are acquired by inferences from experiences, and never by mere reflection. These ideas function to organize experience in its totality.

SECTION I: THE IDEAS IN GENERAL

Platonic ideas are ideals or archetypes, perfect patterns, objectives of striving which are never fully attained in experience. Value concepts are paradigmatic cases of ideas; normative laws are not derivable from experience. The term "idea" ought to be employed by metaphysicians in this correct, original sense.

SECTION II: THE TRANSCENDENTAL IDEAS

The transcendental idea is the concept of the totality of the conditions for any given conditioned. The three possible forms of idea should be deduced from three kinds of syllogism – the categorical, hypothetical, and disjunctive. More precisely, the ideas are obtained by combining the concept of the unconditioned with the relational categories embodied in the major premise of the three kinds of syllogism. In syllogistic inference, the condition of a possible judgment (the minor premise) is subsumed under the condition of a given judgment (the major premise), which asserts something universally, subject to a specified (further) condition. So the predicate of the conclusions is shown to be connected with its subject in accordance with a condition which is universally asserted in the major premise. The case satisfies the specified condition; hence the rule is valid for the case. If the conclusion is valid, then the totality of premises required for its establishment is given, forming a regressive series. But what corresponds in the synthesis of intuition to the universality of the major premise is totality of conditions. The totality of conditions is equivalent to the unconditioned. Therefore, the unconditioned is the ground of the synthesis of everything conditioned.

So when the conditioned is given, the series of conditions is given. The series is either finite or infinite. If finite, its first term is unconditioned. If infinite or unlimited, then the series itself is unconditioned. Categorical synthesis in one subject corresponds to regressive categorical prosyllogisms to the unconditioned and gives rise to the idea of absolute subject. Hypothetical synthesis of the members of a series corresponds to regressive hypothetical prosyllogisms to the unconditioned, and gives rise to the idea of a presuppositionless presupposition. Disjunctive synthesis of the parts of one system corresponds to regressive disjunctive prosyllogisms to the unconditioned, and gives rise to the idea of a complete aggregate. These ideas regulate the understanding in its empirical pursuit of that systematic unity which it requires for its satisfaction.

Note that if not-p is internally impossible, then not-p is impossible in all respects, and so p is absolutely necessary. The converse, however, is not true. So p is absolute if it is universally valid, and absolute necessity is diverse from inner necessity.

SECTION III: SYSTEM OF THE TRANSCENDENTAL IDEAS

Representations may be related either to (1) the subject, or to (2) the manifold of the phenomenal object, or to (3) all things in general. All pure concepts are concerned with the synthetic unity of representations. The transcendental ideas are concerned with the unconditioned synthetic unity of all conditions in general. Hence, all ideas can be arranged in three classes: (1′) the absolute unity of the thinking subject (the self or soul), (2′) the absolute unity of the series of conditions of appearance (the totality of phenomena or the world), and (3′) the absolute unity of the condition of all objects of thought in general (God). (1″) The thinking subject is the object of psychology; (2″) the sum-total of appearances is the object of cosmology; (3″) the thing which contains the highest condition of the possibility of all that can be thought is theology.

Pure reason is concerned only with the absolute totality of the synthesis on the side of the conditions, not the conditioned. The possibility of the conditioned presupposes the totality of its conditions, but not of its consequences.

BOOK II: THE DIALECTICAL INFERENCES OF PURE REASON

CHAPTER I: THE PARALOGISMS OF PURE REASON (B)

Knowing an object is organizing a diversity given in intuition; knowledge requires intuition. So self-knowledge requires an intuition of myself. But the determining or apperceptive self is not a possible object of knowledge – it is not an object at all. Only the determinable self, the object of inner intuition, is even *prima facie* a possible object of knowledge.

The proposition that the thinking "I" is always subject, never predicate, is analytic. From it, we cannot infer the synthetic proposition that I (as object) am a substance. That the apperceptive "I" is logically simple is analytic. It does not entail the proposition that the thinking "I" is a simple substance, which is synthetic. Similarly, the analytic identity of the subject through time shows nothing about personal identity, where this latter concept involves identity of substance through changes, and where judgments about personal identity require intuition. Finally, that I (as thinker) am not identical with my body (or anything outside me) is analytic. Yet it does not follow that I could exist disembodied, or that self-consciousness is possible without consciousness of outer things.

If the conclusions of the rational psychologists were justified, the possibility of synthetic *a priori* propositions applicable to things in themselves would be established, and the critical teaching overturned. But the fundamental argument of rational psychology is paralogistic:

1　That which cannot be thought otherwise than as subject does not exist otherwise than as subject, and is therefore substance.
2　A thinking being, considered merely as such, cannot be thought otherwise than as subject.
3　So a thinking being exists only as subject, that is, as substance.

The argument is fallacious in that "thought" and "subject" are being used in different senses in the two premises. In premise 1, "subject" is used to signify a permanent object and the objects of thought are phenomena. In premise 2 "subject" is being used in a formal sense (the "I think" can accompany all judgments as subject) and the object of thought is identical with what thinks, which, it is assumed, is not phenomenal. Further, knowledge of substance requires a permanent intuition, but nothing is permanent in inner intuition.

REFUTATION OF MENDELSSOHN'S PROOF OF THE PERMANENCE OF THE SOUL

The argument designed to show that a simple soul, since indissoluble, is indestructible and so everlasting, is defective, since it is possible that it would cease to exist by simply vanishing. Mendelssohn attempts to disprove this possibility as follows: since a simple soul is not composed of parts, it cannot disappear gradually but only all at once. But it is impossible for it to disappear all at once. Hence, the soul persists through time. But we have seen in the Anticipations that all reality has intensive magnitude. So the soul, even if simple, has intensive magnitude, and this may diminish to nothing gradually. Consequently, Mendelssohn's argument is unsound.

Although all theoretical proofs for immortality are spurious, we do have moral grounds to support the belief in personal survival. The moral law sets before us an ideal which cannot be attained in this life. But the moral law is objectively valid. So citizenship in a better world must await those who sacrifice inclination, etc., to abide by the moral law.

CHAPTER I: THE PARALOGISMS OF PURE REASON (A)

Rational psychology is concerned with the proposition "I think" and all its implications. It claims to establish that the soul or self is (1) a substance which is (2) simple and (3) numerically identical through time, and which is (4) in relation to possible objects in space. These theses are indemonstrable; their alleged proofs are paralogisms resulting from conflating apperception with inner sense. Epistemologically at least, the "I" is identical with its activity; the agency and its acts are inseparable. And since the categories presuppose this unity of apperception, the unity of apperception is not itself subject to their application, and hence is not a possible object of experience.

FIRST PARALOGISM: OF SUBSTANTIALITY

- An absolute subject of judgments, that which can serve as subject but never predicate, is substance.
- I, as thinking being, am an absolute subject.
- I, as thinking being, am substance.

Response: the "I think" yields no knowledge of the thinking self; it tells us nothing about the nature of the "I." Knowledge of self-consciousness is distinct from knowledge of the self as substance. To know the self as substance, an intuition of it would be required. But there is no such intuition. Once again, the metaphysician has confounded the nature of the representation with the nature of the object represented.

SECOND PARALOGISM: OF SIMPLICITY

1 That, the action of which can never be regarded as the concurrence of several things acting, is simple, and that which is an aggregate of a plurality is composite.
2 The action of a composite is an aggregate of actions, distributed among the plurality of constituents.
3 A composite thinks (assume).

4   A composite can think only if the totality of parts of the composite contain the whole thought.

5   But representations distributed among different beings can never make up a whole thought.

6   So, 3 is necessarily false: it is impossible that thought inheres in a composite. So, the thinking self is simple.

Response: premise 5 is unjustified. That thought requires a unity of the thinking subject (not merely the formal, apperceptive unity) is not analytic. The negation of the proposition is possible. Nor can the claim be established experientially. The proposition is synthetic *a priori*. But the transcendental argumentation required to support such a proposition can establish only things about the self as condition of the possibility of consciousness, and nothing about the noumenal nature of the thinking self. And as regards the apperceptive self, simplicity is not inferred. "I am simple" just means that "I" is an absolute logical unity. Hence, simplicity is not inferred from apperception, but is a way of expressing that fact.

Proposition: mind is distinct from body. None of the qualities essential to body are discoverable in inner experience. Essentially mental attributes and minds cannot be objects of outer intuition. The mind cannot be an appearance in space. Therefore, the soul cannot be corporeal; it is diverse from body.

Response: the argument fails to distinguish appearances and things in themselves. If material bodies were things in themselves, the argument would succeed. But bodies are appearances, and their noumenal substrata cannot be known through sensible predicates. It remains possible that that which conditions all outer appearances is identical with the subject of our thoughts, the mind (soul).

THIRD PARALOGISM: OF PERSONALITY

- That which is conscious of the numerical identity of itself at different times is a person.
- The soul is so conscious.
- So the soul is a person.

Response: the argument confuses numerical identity of the self in representation and the subject in itself, fallaciously inferring the identity of the underlying self from the identity of representation. The unity of self-consciousness and representation of an identical self is compatible with radical transformations and loss of identity in the noumenal self; the unity of apperception is not a refutation of Heraclitus.

In my individual consciousness, personal identity is ever-present, since identity of self-consciousness is a formal condition of all my thoughts. But an outside observer need not represent me as a persisting thing (the time of his own consciousness is distinct from mine). So the grounds for personal unity are merely formal, and do not justify inferences concerning the objective permanence of the real self.

FOURTH PARALOGISM: OF IDEALITY

- That, the existence of which can only be inferred as a cause of given perceptions, has a merely doubtful existence.
- No outer appearances are immediately perceived; we can only infer their existence as the cause of given perceptions.
- So the existence of all objects of outer sense is doubtful.

The conclusion expresses the doctrine of empirical (skeptical) idealism, a doctrine held by all rational psychologists. The empirical realism and transcendental idealism established in the Analytic provides the refutation of skepticism as follows:

- Physical, external objects are only a species of my representations.
- So I immediately perceive physical objects.
- So I know with certainty that physical objects exist.

Since objects are nothing but representations, empirical consciousness guarantees their existence.

CONSIDERATION OF PURE PSYCHOLOGY AS A WHOLE, IN VIEW OF THESE PARALOGISMS

Nothing synthetic is knowable *a priori* about the thinking being since there is no permanent inner intuition and hence no knowledge of objects. The "I" seems to denote a simple object only because its representation contains no manifold – it is the mere form of consciousness. A positive upshot of our discussion, however, is that materialism is false. Without the thinking self the material world (of appearance) would vanish. Again, the source of all the illusions of rational psychology is confusion of appearances and things in themselves.

Three theories of the relation between mind and body are possible: physical influence (interactionism), predetermined harmony, and supernatural intervention (occasionalism). The first and commonsense view is wrongly dogmatically attacked by counterasserting that the mental and the physical are too radically different to interact. This attack is based on confusing body as appearance and thing-in-itself, and hypostasizing representations. One can, however, critically object to the argument used to support interactionism since all dualisms treat extended substances as existing in themselves, and so are unjustified.

The mind–body problem, then, reduces to this: how in a thinking subject is outer intuition possible? This question is in principle unanswerable. The related question of personal survival after bodily death has the same status.

CHAPTER II: THE ANTINOMY OF PURE REASON

SECTION I: SYSTEM OF COSMOLOGICAL IDEAS

The time-series is necessarily thought to be completed at any given time (is given in completed form). In the series, *a*, *b*, *c*, *d*, I must presuppose, when (say) *c* is given, the regressive synthesis or grounds of *c*, which include *a* and *b*. But the possibility of *c* does not rest on *d*, or any progressive synthesis or consequences. The cosmological ideas thus deal with the totality of the regressive synthesis.

Time is a series, the present moment is conditioned by the past. Space is an aggregate, its parts coexist. Yet the synthesis of space is successive. Each part of space (each space) is limited, hence conditioned, by some other part. And reality in space, that is, matter, is conditioned by its parts — the completed division of matter results either in the simple or nothing at all. Lastly, contingent existence is always conditioned, and reason takes us back to the unconditioned necessity which conditions the whole series of existents. So four cosmological ideas are generated from four categories. Only these categories lead to a series in the synthesis of the manifold.

The unconditioned can be conceived in two ways: as an unconditioned part of the series to which the other parts are subordinated; or such that all parts are conditioned, but the totality is unconditioned. If there is such a totality, it is guaranteed to be unconditioned. And note that on the latter alternative the regress is potentially, but not actually, infinite. Terminologically, the conditioned condition of an appearance is its natural cause. Its unconditioned causality is freedom. The conditioned is contingent. The unconditioned is necessary.

SECTION II: ANTITHETIC OF PURE REASON

Antithetic deals with the conflict of the doctrines of reason and its causes. Since the claims involved purport to extend beyond the field of all possible experiences, they can be neither confirmed nor refuted by experience, nor by their relation to possible experiences. The only test of these assertions of transcendental reason is internal consistency.

FIRST CONFLICT OF THE TRANSCENDENTAL IDEAS

Thesis:
A   The world has a beginning in time and
B   is also limited as regards space.

Proof A:
1   Suppose that the world has no beginning in time.
2   Then an infinite past series has elapsed prior to any given time.
3   But it is impossible that an infinite past series has elapsed.
4   So the world does have a beginning in time.

Proof B:
1   Suppose that the world is an infinite given whole of coexisting parts.
2   An unlimited given quantum is thinkable only through a completed synthesis of its parts – a successive synthesis of infinite items must be completed (which takes an infinite amount of time to run through).
3   It is impossible for a successive synthesis of infinite items to be completed.
4   So the world has limited extension in space.

Observation: the true transcendental concept of infinitude is such that a quantum is infinite if, and only if, the successive synthesis of units required for enumeration of the quantum can never be completed. Hence the notion of an infinite completed series (which leads up to some specified moment) is self-contradictory. Hence the world must have a beginning. The manifold of a world of infinite extension is given as coexisting, and so the contradiction does not arise as above. Yet the concept of infinite extension is impossible since to have the concept of a never to be completed successive synthesis of parts requires completion. So such a totality is not thinkable by means of such a synthesis, and an infinite totality cannot be thought prior to such a synthesis.

Antithesis:
A   The world has no beginning and
B   no limits in space; it is infinite as regards both time and space.

Proof A:
1   Suppose the world has a beginning in time.
2   Then there must have been a time in which the world was not, that is, an empty time.
3   But a thing cannot come to be in an empty time.
4   So the world cannot have a beginning in time.

Proof B:
1   Suppose the world in space is finite.
2   Then it exists in an empty space (which is itself infinite).
3   Then things will be related to space (as well as to each other in space).
4   But empty space is not a possible object of intuition, and so the objects which comprise the world could not be related to it.
5   So the world cannot be limited in space; it has infinite extension.

Observation: space is not an object but only the form of possible objects. Absolute space is nothing real, and so cannot determine the magnitude or shape of real things.

SECOND CONFLICT OF THE TRANSCENDENTAL IDEAS

Thesis:
A   Every composite is made up of simple parts, and

B   the world consists of simple and composite substances.

Proof A:
1   Suppose composite substances are not made up of simple parts.
2   If all composition were removed in thought, there would be either simple parts left or nothing at all left.
3   So either there must be simple parts or not all composition can be removed in thought (since there is something).
4   But composition can only be a contingent and not a necessary relation of substances (by the nature of substance) and so the second disjunct in 3 is false.
5   So composite substances are made up of simple parts.

Proof B follows immediately from the above conclusion. Further, reason must think the simple as prior to all composition.

Observation: the inference from the composite to the simple applies only to substances. It does not apply to space or time (which are not composed of substances) nor to alteration of the states of substances.

Antithesis:
A   No composite thing in the world is made up of simple parts, and
B   there are no simples.

Proof A:
1   Suppose a composite substance is made up of simple parts.
2   Since composition is possible only in space, a space must be made up of as many parts as are contained in the composite which occupies it.
3   Since space is not composed of simple parts, but of spaces, every part of the composite must occupy a space.
4   So the simple occupies a space.
5   But everything real which occupies space is a composite of substances.
6   So the simple is a composite of substances (self-contradiction).
7   So no real composite is made up of simple parts.

Proof B: the world is the sum of all possible appearances. The objective reality of the idea of the absolutely simple can never be established in any possible experience, neither by outer nor inner experience, and from the fact that we cannot apprehend a diversity it does not follow that diversity is really absent. So simplicity cannot be inferred from any perception whatsoever.

SECTION III: THE INTEREST OF REASON IN THESE CONFLICTS

Why do people prefer the dogmatic theses to the skeptical or empiricist antitheses? Our practical interests are better served by the dogmatist – that the world has a beginning, that my thinking self is simple and indestructible, that it is free in its voluntary actions, that all order is due to a primordial being from which everything derives its unity and purposive connection, are fundamental to morals and religion. And reason has a speculative interest since in the theses the entire chain of conditions and the derivation of the conditioned can be grasped *a priori*. Further, human reason is by nature architectonic, that is, it regards all our knowledge as belonging to a possible system. The antitheses render systematic knowledge impossible. Hence, reason favors the theses.

SECTION IV: THE ABSOLUTE NECESSITY OF A SOLUTION TO THE TRANSCENDENTAL PROBLEMS OF PURE REASON

Transcendental philosophy is unique in all speculative inquiries in that no question concerning an object given to pure reason can be insoluble for this same reason. This is so because the object is not to be met with outside its concept, and this because the ideas go beyond possible experience. The cosmological ideas involve the unconditioned totality of the synthesis of appearances. But all possible perceptions are conditioned. Therefore, there can be no object corresponding to these ideas. Mathematics and ethics are also in principle complete and certain for the same reason. Also, in the case of ethics, if we did not know what we ought to do we could not be under an obligation to do it.

SECTION V: SKEPTICAL REPRESENTATION OF THE COSMOLOGICAL QUESTIONS IN THE FOUR TRANSCENDENTAL IDEAS

The theses are too small for the understanding; the antitheses too large. The former claim is true because understanding always demands further conditions, the latter, because we cannot grasp infinity. Since no object can conform to the cosmic concepts, strictly speaking, they are meaningless.

SECTION VI: TRANSCENDENTAL IDEALISM AS THE KEY TO THE SOLUTION OF THE COSMOLOGICAL DIALECTIC

To call an appearance in space and time a real thing prior to our perceiving it can only mean that in the advance of experience we must meet with such a perception. Appearances consist solely of representations given to us. And past events mean nothing but the possibility of extending the chain of experience from the present perception back to the conditions which determine this perception in respect of time. If the event is not locatable in the empirical regress, it is not objective.

SECTION VII: CRITICAL SOLUTION OF THE COSMOLOGICAL CONFLICT OF REASON WITH ITSELF

The dialectical argument of the antinomies is as follows:

1   If the conditioned is given, the entire series of all its conditions is given.
2   Objects of the senses are given as conditioned.
3   The entire series of conditions of these objects is given.

The argument commits the fallacy of equivocation. Premise 1 takes the conditioned in the transcendental sense of a pure category, while premise 2 takes it in the empirical sense of a concept of the understanding applied to appearances. The first sense involves no temporal succession, but just the demand for a sufficient premise-set; the second sense involves the temporal successive synthesis of appearances. Again, in 1 all the members of the series are given in themselves, without any condition of time, but in 2 they are possible only through a successive regress.

We must take care to distinguish contraries (p and non-p) from contradictories (p and not-p). Contraries, or dialectically opposed judgments, may both be false, although not both true. If two contraries presuppose something false, then both are false. Of two contradictory, or analytically opposed, judgments, we may insist that one is true and the other false.

That the world is infinite in magnitude and that it is finite in magnitude are contradictory only if the world is a thing in itself. But the world does not exist in itself. The world-series is always conditioned, and thus can never be given as completed; so the world is not an unconditioned whole, either finite or infinite. Therefore, the two propositions are only dialectically opposed.

The same considerations hold, *mutatis mutandis*, for the other cosmic ideas. These antinomies provide indirect proof of the transcendental ideality of appearances.

SECTION VIII: THE REGULATIVE PRINCIPLE OF PURE REASON IN ITS APPLICATION TO THE COSMOLOGICAL IDEAS

The principle of reason (wrongly formulated in premise 1 above) is properly only a rule, prescribing a regress in the series of the conditions of given appearances, and forbidding it to bring the regress to a close by treating anything at which it may arrive as absolutely unconditioned. It is neither a principle of understanding nor a constitutive principle of reason, but rather a regulative principle of reason. The idea merely serves as a prescriptive rule, and has no objective reality. It tells us how to carry out the empirical regress, not what the object is.

We may distinguish an infinite from an indefinite regress. The former occurs when the whole is given in empirical intuition and we regress to its parts. The latter occurs when only a member of the series is given from which we regress to other members.

SECTION IX: THE EMPIRICAL EMPLOYMENT OF THE REGULATIVE PRINCIPLE OF REASON, IN RESPECT OF ALL COSMOLOGICAL IDEAS: SUBSECTION I: SOLUTION OF THE COSMOLOGICAL IDEA OF THE TOTALITY OF THE COMPOSITION OF THE APPEARANCES OF A COSMIC WHOLE

Since the world is not given in its totality in any intuition its magnitude is not given prior to the empirical regress of conditions. The magnitude of the cosmic series depends on the possible empirical regress (on which its concept rests). Since this regress can yield neither a determinate infinite nor a determinate finite (that is, anything absolutely limited), the magnitude of the world can be taken neither as finite nor as infinite. The regress, through which it is represented, allows of neither alternative. Appearances in the world are conditionally limited, but the world itself is neither conditionally nor unconditionally limited.

SUBSECTION II: SOLUTION OF THE COSMOLOGICAL IDEA OF THE TOTALITY OF DIVISION OF A WHOLE GIVEN IN INTUITION

Division of a given whole into its parts is an infinite regress. If the parts of a continuously progressing decomposition are themselves again divisible (simples are never reached), then since the whole (conditioned) is given, the parts (conditions) are also given. Nevertheless, infinite divisibility does not imply that the given whole consists of infinitely many parts. Although the parts are contained in the intuition of the whole, the whole division arises only through the regress that generates it. Hence both spaces and appearances in space (both given) are infinitely divisible, yet do not consist of infinitely many parts.

The contrary assertions in these first two mathematical antinomies have both been shown to be false. There can be no unconditioned totality in mere appearances; every condition of the series of appearances is itself an appearance, and hence is a member of the series. The crucial point is that all the items of the series are of the same character; the conditioned and the alleged unconditioned are homogeneous. The third and fourth dynamical antinomies, however, admit the possibility of a synthesis of heterogeneous elements. Whereas all conditions of a mathematical synthesis must be sensible it is possible that there is a purely intelligible condition outside the dynamical series. Hence, it is possible that both the thesis and antithesis of the dynamical antinomies are true, and so that both reason and understanding find satisfaction.

SUBSECTION III: SOLUTION OF THE COSMOLOGICAL IDEA OF TOTALITY IN THE DERIVATION OF COSMICAL EVENTS FROM THEIR CAUSES.

Since appearances are only representations, they must have a ground which is not itself an appearance. The effects of this ground or intelligible cause appear, and so are determined through other appearances. But the cause itself is not so conditioned – it lies outside the empirical series, and, not being subject to time, does not require a cause to precede it.

Freedom is a transcendental idea which can be neither derived from nor verified by experience. If appearances were things in themselves, freedom and determinism would be incompatible. But on our account both the thesis and antithesis may be true – they are not mutually exclusive. A given event may be free relative to its intelligible cause, and yet also determined as something objective in space and time.

7.3 Exploration of pivotal stages of Kant's argument

7.3.1 My general orientation to the Critique

Thus concludes my précis. In this third stage of the chapter I take sides on central debates, and try to reinforce key components of Kant's thought as revealingly as I can. Two points of orientation. First, there is long-standing debate concerning Kant's central mission. Some see Kant primarily as *integrator of all our frameworks of knowledge* (everyday common sense, scientific, moral, aesthetic, etc.), showing how they are jointly coherent and acceptable; as *articulator of foundations of science*; as *anti-skeptic*, undermining skepticism on its own terms, without invoking external, potentially question-begging, considerations; as *constructive, systematic metaphysician*, autonomously (without appeal to science, etc.) developing a new, displacing metaphysics. There is *prima facie* evidence for all these readings, but many interpreters dismiss or demote some of them. We should not assume these goals are competing; I am inclined to see Kant as stupendously managing them all.

Second, *heavily* indebted to Henry Allison's work,[1] my organizing theme is that the central route to understanding and appreciating the force of Kant's *Critique of Pure Reason* is to see it as an effort to state, elicit the implications of, and defend the metaphilosophical, for me at bottom methodological, position called *transcendental idealism*, which is allegedly the contradictory of (the two alternatives exclude each other and exhaust all possibilities) the metaphilosophical position called *transcendental realism*. Kant thinks that, whatever their considerable substantive differences, all pre-critical philosophies, all philosophical systems before his, are transcendental realisms, and so takes his proof of transcendental idealism to be a conclusive refutation of alternative philosophies. By and large, Kant gives a direct and an indirect proof of transcendental idealism. The direct proof occurs in the *Transcendental Aesthetic* and *Transcendental Analytic* and aims to show that only transcendental idealism, and its views about the nature of space, time, objects in them and their necessary interconnections, "things" not in space or time, etc., can account for certain data, and that transcendental idealism is deducible from basic, indubitable premises. The indirect proof occurs in the *Transcendental Dialectic* and consists in showing the severe problems that inescapably follow from transcendental realism, the most decisive of which is that, given transcendental realism, reason is in internal conflict with itself (the Antinomies). Since either transcendental idealism or realism, and not-realism (by *reductio*), idealism.

As we shall see, transcendental idealism rests on drawing the appearance–thing itself distinction in the right way, which rests on understanding and properly applying the empirical–transcendental distinction, which rests on there being *epistemic* conditions distinct from *ontological* conditions (which Kant further distinguishes from *psychological* and *logical* conditions). An epistemic condition is a condition necessary for the representation of an object or objective state of affairs, a condition for a representation to have *objective reality*, and Kant will argue that there are forms of sensibility or modes of presentation (space and time) and forms of understanding or modes of interpretation (categories) that are epistemic conditions. Note that epistemic conditions are not just necessary for experience or empirical consciousness of objects, but for non-empirical knowledge as well, such as mathematical knowledge. An ontological condition is a condition of the possibility of things in themselves, in contrast to epistemic conditions that are conditions of things as they appear to us. This of course is not further explanation, since we're trying to distinguish between appearances and things in themselves in terms of epistemic and ontological conditions; it is just pairing of terms. A logical condition is a condition of consistent thinking. A psychological condition is a condition of our human cognitive apparatus designed to account genetically for a belief or empirically explain why we perceive things in a certain way. So, transcendental idealism will rest on the claim that we can and must isolate a set of epistemic conditions distinct from ontological conditions. Transcendental Logic is the articulation of these conditions, just as General Logic is the articulation of logical conditions.

In terms of this central aim, we can understand Kant's criticism of others and his motivations at various otherwise obscure points. For example, Leibniz fails because he confuses "mere logical" with epistemic conditions; Hume fails because he confuses psychological with epistemic conditions (his account in terms of custom or habit can answer the *questio facti*, but not the needed *questio juris*); Newton ("mathematical philosophers") fails because he confuses ontological with epistemic conditions. This framework lets us understand clearly, as many interpretations cannot, how Kant differs from Berkeley – one renowned, wrongheaded view of Kant takes him to be an inconsistent Berkeleian. It lets us see why Kant is not a skeptic (we know only appearances; appearances are representations; inaccessible things in themselves *cause* representations), nor a phenomenalist (objects are just collections of sense data obeying certain laws), nor a Lockean-style representational realist.

As you study Kant, keep in mind that generally, "ideal" means "in the mind" (*in uns*, in us) and "real" means "external to the mind" (*ausser uns*,

---

1   More than any other place in this book I must stress my reliance on the superior work of another. Many of the analyses in this section are Henry Allison's (1983), who twenty years ago transformed my understanding of Kant. Sometimes I merely paraphrase his own presentation. I have not had the opportunity to master Allison's 2004 edition, which expands and in some ways revises his interpretation and defense, but his overarching approach seems retained.

outside us). In the *empirical* sense, "in the mind" means "is a private datum" and "external to the mind" means "is an intersubjectively recognizable object with a determinate spatiotemporal location." Kant calls empirically ideal objects "objects of inner sense," and empirically real objects "objects of outer sense." At the *transcendental* level, to ask whether an object is *in uns* or *ausser uns* is not to ask what kind of object it is (ontologically), but how it is being considered. If through subjective conditions of representation (= *transcendental* = *real* = *epistemic* conditions), as an object of possible experience, then it is *in uns*$_T$, an appearance$_T$, where the subscript T denotes the word is being used in the transcendental sense, not the empirical sense. If independent of such conditions, as an "object in general," then it is *ausser uns*$_T$, and a thing in itself$_T$. Transcendental realism views all objects as *ausser uns*$_T$, therefore as things in themselves. This is the common prejudice of all pre-critical philosophies. But within this group, (1) some fail to recognize any *a priori* or necessary conditions of human experience, and assume the mind is in immediate contact in sense experience with the real$_T$, and that all our knowledge must be based on that contact. This implies the denial of the possibility of any *a priori* knowledge of such objects. This is supposed to include the "empirical idealism" or representative realism of Locke and Descartes' early-stage meditator, and the "phenomenalisms" of Berkeley and Hume. (2) Others recognize there are necessary conditions through which objects are given (and so affirm the possibility of *a priori* knowledge), but fail to recognize these as subjective (but epistemic, not psychological) conditions of human experience, treating them as conditions of reality itself (ontological conditions), so that our purported *a priori* knowledge is of objects as they are in themselves. This is supposed to include Newton and Leibniz. Kant calls (1) *skeptics* and (2) *dogmatists*. *But*, it will evolve, skepticism for Kant is itself dogmatic (i.e. not critical) *and* dogmatism necessarily leads to skepticism (see, for example, A389). Given this division within transcendental realisms, Kant's refutation takes two forms. Against the skeptical version, he must show the possibility of *a priori* knowledge. This is the central task of the *Aesthetic* and *Analytic* (there the main task is to establish the *possibility*, not the *limits* of *a priori* knowledge). The refutation of the dogmatic version most effectively takes an indirect route, showing the disastrous consequences that emerge from a failure to determine the *limits* of human knowledge – and again, at the same time, such a refutation implies the distinction between appearances and things in themselves, which gives a proof of transcendental idealism) – accomplished in the *Dialectic*, especially the *Antinomy*. It's revealing to note that Kant attributes to the discovery of the problem of the Antinomy the same significance he grants to his "recollection of Hume" as awakening him from his "dogmatic slumber" (letter to Garve, 21 September 1778).

At bottom, the appeal to *a priori* conditions of experience (representation of objects) is the decisive feature of Kant's idealism, enabling him to juxtapose it to all varieties of transcendental realism. He affirms (a) the (transcendental) ideality of the conditions themselves and (b) the ideality$_T$ of the objects known in virtue of these conditions (for example, A111). In a narrower sense that Kant sometimes adopts, (b) is transcendental idealism. (a) follows from his theory of the *a priori*. That's why Kant says the fundamental question is how is the synthetic *a priori* is possible. Kant will argue that it is their status as ultimate, epistemic conditions that requires us to locate them in the mind rather than in the objects known (considered in themselves, apart from their relation to mind). The ideality of objects known follows from the ideality of conditions in virtue of which they are known. Because they can only be known insofar as they conform to these conditions, they can only be known as they appear, not as they are in themselves.

I called transcendental idealism a metaphilosophical position. This will be defended as we proceed. For now, suffice it to say that the thesis of transcendental idealism is the thesis that empirical objects are *in uns*$_T$, which reduces to a claim about how objects must be "considered" for the purpose of philosophical reflection. So transcendental idealism ends up coinciding with the transcendental method itself.

Let me put my outlined view in the context of one of the main, long-standing disputes of Kant interpretation. Some think the things in themselves–appearances distinction is an ontological distinction between two types of objects (the *two-object* view), others, that it is a distinction between different perspectives on (ontologically) one set of objects (the *two-aspect* view). Most contemporary interpreters who ascribe the two-object view to Kant saddle him with inconsistency. For example, some argue that while Kant explicitly forbids countenancing distinct things in themselves, his theory of space and time as forms of sensibility or intuition requires such things, since Kant couldn't construe space and time in such a way if we were affected by ultimately real spatiotemporal features rather than transcendent things. Others complain that Kant analyzes objects phenomenalistically as mere collections of sense data, yet is committed to non-phenomenal (noumenal) entities, especially by his practical philosophy and the need for a moral self. Only a few adopt *and endorse* a two-object view across-the-board, or even as applied to the self. (A quick argument one might give for the two-object view is that phenomena are spatial, but noumena are not spatial, therefore, by Leibniz's Law – for all x and all y, and all properties F, if $x = y$, then x has F if and only if y has F – phenomena are really distinct from noumena. Ask yourself why this argument fails to settle the issue.)

There are many proponents of the two-aspect view as correct interpretation, but many of these go on to maintain that Kant saw no distinct and positive sense in even *considering* objects *as* things in themselves, that is, that he criticized any separate *idea* of a thing in itself; others seem to concede that Kant sometimes but not usually *did* adopt a non-empirical perspective on objects, but that he *shouldn't* have; and still others systematically defend a distinct and intelligible use in the idea of considering items as things in themselves rather than as appearances. I'm in this last camp, while stressing that for Kant thinkability does not entail knowability.

7.3.2   Fuller analysis of introductory material

On Allison's view, which I am defending, the success of Kant's whole transcendental approach depends on the defensibility of his claims about epistemic conditions. Kant holds that (1) discursive knowledge has specifiable epistemic conditions, and (2) all possible human knowledge is discursive, so that (3) all possible human knowledge has specificable epistemic conditions. (Hold off from reading "knowledge" in its most common current, truth-entailing sense. Since so much rides on this, you should wait until the *Analytic* to take a firm stand on how to read "knowledge" (*Erkenntnis*). I agree with those who translate *Erkenntnis* as "knowledge-claim" or "judgment," where a knowledge-claim must be either true or false, but need not be true.) Note that while maintaining (2), Kant does hold that (4) non-discursive knowledge is conceivable or *logically* possible, which allows him his critical distinction between conditions of human knowledge and conditions of things in themselves. Such knowledge is characterized by use of the (*problematic* – a notion earlier explicated in the *Phenomena–Noumena* section) conception of an intuitive intellect which would (i) grasp its object immediately, (ii) without need for any conceptualization, and (iii) without being affected by the object. Such an intellect's act of intuition literally produces the object; it is archetypal, not ectypal; divine cognition is the typical model for this. Kant's thesis that human knowledge is discursive is crucial to his overall critique of transcendentally realistic epistemologies – against empiricist versions, it implies that knowledge requires conceptualization; against rationalist versions, it implies that knowledge involves sensible, not intellectual intuition. Underlying (or identical with – this decision is equivalent to the decision about how to read "knowledge," *Erkenntnis*) Kant's account of discursive knowledge is his theory of *judgment*. In the Introduction to the *Critique* Kant draws famous distinctions between analytic and synthetic judgments, and judgments justifiable *a priori* and *a posteriori*. In my view, it is extremely important to appreciate that these are distinctions that relate to his theory of judgment. Judgments are distinguishable from both sentences and propositions. A sentence is a unit of language that requires interpretation to have meaning. It is a grammatically well-formed formula, a string of words formed in accordance with certain rules of sequence. It is a syntactic entity. A proposition is what is expressed by the use of a meaningful sentence by a person at a time. It is what is said when a person uses a declarative sentence at a time to assert something that is either true or false, the content of or truth-assessable thought conveyed by a statement, an historically identifiable speech act (excluding whatever psychological associations, emotive meaning, etc. might be conveyed as well). Judgments are much like mental statings, so are cognitive *activities*.

Kant should have given his account of judgment before he made these introductory distinctions. Let us proceed for him that way.

For Kant, there are two elements in discursive judgment about the world – *concepts* and *sensible intuitions* (for example, A50, or A320 for a full classification). A *concept* is a general representation, a representation of what is potentially common to several items. Concepts function as organizing principles for consciousness (for example, A106), as means for holding a series of representations together in an "analytic unity." To apply a concept is, according to Kant, to form a judgment about the object(s) – concepts are "predicates of possible judgments" (for example, A69). For empirical concepts, content means sensible features that are thought in the concept as its "marks" (derived from experience), form means its universality or generality, which is the same for all concepts. A mere conjunction of sense impressions is not a concept; a concept requires the thought of the applicability of this conjunction to a (potential) plurality of possible objects. The thought itself is not derived from experience, but is produced by acts of understanding (comparison, reflection, abstraction). Concepts combine common features into "analytic unity."

An *intuition* is a singular representation, which refers immediately, hence non-conceptually, to its object. Intuitions don't in fact represent or refer to objects apart from being brought under concepts in a judgment, but they can be brought under concepts, and when they are they do represent particular objects. Kant uses "intuition" (*Anschauung*) ambiguously. In its most common usage, an intuition is a kind of mental *content*. But sometimes (importantly) it designates the *act* of directly representing an individual (*intuiting*); and sometimes (confusedly) it designates the object represented by the content, the *intuited*, in which case it is equivalent to an *appearance*. Keep this in mind as you analyze relevant passages.

So we may portray Kant's main account of judgment as the result of an argument:

1   Every judgment involves an act of conceptualization (i.e. of unification of representations under a concept) and vice versa.
2   No concept is ever related to an object immediately.
3   Therefore judgment is the mediate "knowledge" of an object, the representation of a representation of it (for example, A68–9).

The intuition provides the sensible content for the judgment, while the concept provides the rule in accordance with which the content is determined. The concept is brought in relation with the object by determining the content, so is mediately related, via intuition, to the object. Judgments essentially make reference to an object in a modest sense that entails that they are susceptible to truth-assessment. The mere subjective association among representations or the mere entertaining of concepts is not judgment, does *not* have truth-value.

When Kant calls concepts "predicates of possible judgments" he is *not* limiting their function to grammatical or logical predicates. His main claim is that concepts function to determine the very content to be judged about, by providing a general description under which this content can be thought. Insofar as a concept fulfills this function it is regarded as a "real," not merely "logical" predicate, and is called a *determination*. So consider the analytic judgment, "All puppies are young." "Puppies" is the logical subject, "young" the logical predicate. But "puppies" is a real predicate since it provides the initial description under which subject *x* is to be taken in the judgment, whereas "young" is a merely logical predicate since it doesn't add further determination to the subject, since the judgment is analytic.

Only now that we have a sketch of Kant's theory of judgment can we turn to Kant's *analytic–synthetic* distinction. It should be noted that while Kant thought the *a priori–a posteriori* distinction was a philosophical common-place, he thought that no one had properly drawn his analytic–synthetic distinction, and so would have rejected identifying it with Hume's relations of ideas–matters of fact distinction or Leibniz's truth of reason–truths of fact distinction, as some commentators do.

Kant's conception of analyticity rests on his notion of a concept as a set of marks (themselves concepts) that are thought together in "analytic unity," which can serve as a ground for the recognition of objects. These marks collectively constitute the intension of the concept. C_2 is contained in C_1 if and only if C_2 is either a mark of C_1 or a mark of one of its marks. Analytic judgments add nothing through the predicate to the concept of the subject, merely breaking it up into those constituent concepts that have all along been thought in it, although (perhaps) confusedly (A7); they are merely explicative; they formally extend (whether immediately or mediately) knowledge. In analytic judgments, the predicate B is related to the object *x* (the subject of judgment) by virtue of the fact that it is already contained, as a mark, in the concept of the subject. One could say the predicate is "about" an object, but since the truth or falsity of the judgment can be determined merely by analyzing the *concept* of the subject, the *reference* to the object *x* is otiose. That is why we can form analytic judgments about non-existent, even impossible objects, and why all analytic judgments are knowable *a priori*; appeal to particular experience is unnecessary since recourse to analysis of concept is sufficient. Kant supposes that typically the marks of a concept can be sufficiently determined, even without explicit definition, for the purposes of analysis. The difficulties that arise concerning analytic judgments involving empirical concepts all stem from the difficulty of sufficiently determining such concepts, not with the concept of analyticity itself (see A728).

"Synthetic" is the contradictory of "analytic;" every judgment is analytic or synthetic, but not both. Synthetic judgments are ampliative, not merely explicative; through them we "materially" extend rather than merely clarify our knowledge. This way of putting things suggests that the analytic–synthetic distinction is one of epistemic function concerning the contents of judgments, rather than one concerning the origins or logical form of judgments. This is not to say that analyticity can never be a formal matter. Kant holds that the law of contradiction is the sufficient principle of all analytic knowledge (A151). So the negations of formal contradictions are analytically true, and tautologies, based on the law of identity, the flip-side of the law of contradiction, are analytically true. But formal truths can only have a certain epistemic function, an explicative one, and it is the epistemic function about which Kant is at root concerned.

In synthetic judgments the reference to the subject and, therefore, the reality of the predicate are just the points at issue. That is why the question of how such judgments are possible *a priori* is so perplexing. Kant's view is that a synthetic judgment (of theoretical reason – we'll worry about judgments of practical reason later) can materially extend our knowledge only if the concepts in it are related to intuition.

1   Concepts can never relate immediately to objects, but only to other representations, concepts or intuitions. So discursive knowledge is mediate.
2   If the concept is a real predicate or determination, it must be related to some representation that itself stands in an immediate relation to the object, that is, it must be related to an intuition.
3   Synthetic judgment is real determination.
4   So all synthetic judgments (of theoretical knowledge) relate a concept(s) to an intuition.

Kant thinks the possibility of synthetic *a priori* judgments is seen as the central problem of metaphysics as soon as the analytic–synthetic distinction is properly drawn. The key assumption in his argument is that the truth-value of judgments that lay claim to universality and necessity, his stated criteria of the *a priori* (B4), cannot be grounded empirically. But can synthetic judgments have non-empirical grounds? Since synthetic, the grounding can't be purely conceptual or logical; since *a priori*, the grounding can't be experiential. How is it possible to materially extend one's knowledge beyond a given concept, independent of any experience of the object thought through that concept? Kant says that synthetic *a priori* judgments require *a priori*, or pure, intuitions, and sensibility is the sole source of our intuitions – pure yet sensible! Empirical intuitions are particular – a determinate, or conceptualized, empirical intuition is the representation, under a certain description, of a particular spatiotemporal (or at least temporal) object – and so can't express the universality and necessity that is thought in a pure concept and asserted in a synthetic *a priori* judgment. For example, we need a singular representation of a triangle that can nonetheless attain universality of concept, making it valid for all triangles. Kant's controversial thesis seems to be that the universal and necessary conditions of intuition, the *forms* of intuition (forms of sensibility), *are* pure intuitions. The precise status of such (epistemic) conditions remains to be explored.

We can now explicate with precision the Introduction's other notions. An intuition (*Anschauung*) (i) is a singular representation, a representation of a thing which is one and present (a present individual), as distinguished from a concept or general representation, which can in principle represent many things which may or may not exist; the intuition is empirical if the thing here-now present is a sensory individual; (ii) is a constituent of judgment, and a necessary constituent of all judgments *about* the world, which do not just express connections between our concepts about the world; (iii) *refers* to its object. In a derivative sense, an intuition is *what* is intuited in the (primary) act of intuition. "Intuition" does *not* mean "direct sensory awareness of phenomenal objects," as in directly seeing or feeling a phenomenal object. Non-pictorial, concrete illustrations or examples count as intuitions (for example, Axviii).

In its *central* usage, an experience (*Erfahrung*) is an empirical judgment, *not* what the empirical judgment is based on, the experiential datum. Sometimes, used in the singular, "experience" means "the totality of empirical judgments."

Keeping in mind that the essential features of the objects of an intuition are presence and uniqueness, we can understand the *form* of an intuition as that which makes the thing be present and makes one thing be distinguished from another thing, a common Scholastic usage. A distinct meaning of "form" used by Kant is "that which contributes order or structure to things," a use from the Pythagorean beginnings of philosophy. In these senses, space and time are organizing forms that provide the basis for a system of references. They are co-ordinate systems in Descartes' sense, and are singular, all-embracing frameworks necessary for all interrelation. Kant uses sensation (*Empfindung*) to explain *empirical intuitions* – to affect (*affektieren*) is to confer by the form of a thing. So Kant's claim is that the presence of the object in space or time gives the object its existence, uniqueness, and capacity to affect our knowledge. (So far, no commitment to a causal theory of empirical knowledge has been made.) "Appearances" designates the undetermined objects of empirical intuitions. They are thus far undetermined because "determining a thing" means "ascribing real properties (marks) to the thing," and property-attribution is the result of the use of concepts, general, in principle multiply applicable, representations; put linguistically, the result of predication, not individuation, which uses referring, naming terms.

As far as the special problem of the *Critique* is concerned, that of legitimating the right to use pure concepts and intuitions, to say a representation is empirical is to declare a certain kind of right in the representation, not to describe its factual causes. It is not a right of original possession, something we did on our own, but one dependent on our ability to be able to appeal to the presence of the object. Hence intuition is needed. Sensations are the sensory contents (matter) of our representations – that part of any representation that can be referred to, or validated by appeal to, the objects of the senses. Kant is concerned to distinguish one part of our intuitions and concepts, the empirical part, from another, the *a priori* part, a contrast between parts *justified* in two different ways. The rightful possession and use of the former rests on presence to the senses; the latter can only be validated *indirectly*, since, Kant will argue, ultimately dependent on a proof of our rightful or lawful use of our own capacities. Kant argues that the forms of intuition, which confer upon the objects their capacity to affect us in our empirical representations, cannot themselves be the objects of merely empirical representations.

7.3.3   A fuller analysis of the Aesthetic

With key concepts in tow, try this reading of the overall argument of the *Transcendental Aesthetic*, focusing on space. The central, essential argument is from (1) The representation of space is an *a priori* intuition, to (2) Space itself is a form of the mind's sensibility (receptivity). (1) is fully defended in Metaphysical Exposition, by its Arguments 1–2 (the representation of space is non-empirical, it is not derived from an affection by an object, and every representation is either empirical (*a posteriori*) or *a priori*), and 3–4 (the logical behavior of intuitions and concepts is definitively different, the representation of space exhibits the characteristics of intuition, and all representations are either intuitions or concepts). It is fairly easy to see why (2) entails (1). If the content of a given intuition is a form or formal feature of objects of intuition (the intuition that pertains to these objects only in virtue of the constitution of the mind, its form of intuiting), then that intuition must be *a priori*, because (i) the content of such an intuition would be universal and necessary, at least for all with the same form of intuiting, and universality and necessity are the two criteria of *apriority*, and (ii) its source would not lie in the objects themselves, nor in any sensible data produced by the affection of the mind by these objects, and so it would be pure.

But it is not so easy to see how (1) entails (2), why we can account for the possibility of an *a priori* intuition of space *only if* space is assumed to be a form of sensibility. The argument for this is one by elimination of alternatives – the Leibnizian (relational-type) and Newtonian (absolutist-type) theories. (For the explanation of relational and absolutist theories of space, see Chapter 4.9 on Leibniz.) It's fairly clear how Kant contests Leibniz. Kant offers anti-relational arguments in both the Metaphysical Exposition and Transcendental Exposition (geometry is synthetic *a priori* only if the representation of space is an *a priori* intuition), and elsewhere, including the *Prolegomena*, offers the argument from incongruous counterparts to the same end. This latter argument is an interesting addition, and can be presented straightforwardly: things in themselves are objects completely determined by concepts, objects as a mere understanding, incapable of intuition, might conceive them. The phenomenon of incongruous counterparts (see Question

3 at the end of this chapter for details) entails the falsity of the identity of indiscernibles, Leibniz's principle that necessarily, if *a* and *b* share all properties, then *a* is identical with *b* (exact duplicates cannot exist), which, given the intuition–concept distinction, entails that the representation of global space, in which the incongruous objects need to be oriented, is an intuition, since not a concept, which entails, given the definition of things in themselves, that (a) objects in space aren't things in themselves and that (b) outer *perception* can't be construed as obscure or confused *conception* – focus on (b), since Leibniz didn't really hold (a).

But how is Newton eliminated? Why can't space be transcendentally real and a condition or form of the experience of real things rather than appearances? Indeed, Kant says Newton is superior to Leibniz in that he at least makes conceivable that geometry applies to nature, since Newton regards space as real, not a creature of the imagination, but Kant insists that neither can explain how math, pure or applied, can be both synthetic and *a priori*. And much of the Metaphysical Exposition *seems* compatible with Newton – that space is a condition of objects; that we can conceive space as empty of objects but can't represent the absence of space. And the phenomenon of incongruous counterparts supports Newton as against Leibniz.

We saw that Leibniz holds that space is the order of coexisting phenomena, but that we conceive it as more than and independent of this order since we can't perceive distinctly minute differences between situations, so that in a sort of imaginative gloss we confound resemblance with numerical identity. So for Leibniz the something extra we think of as space is superimposed by the mind on the order of coexisting phenomena; it is a mental construction, an ideal thing. Argument 1 of the Metaphysical Exposition purports to show the something extra is a necessary condition for the awareness of the order in the first place. At the same time it purports to show, against empiricists, that the features of experience to which one appeals in trying to account for the origin of the idea of space or extension already presuppose it.

The argument goes as follows: my referring my sensations to something (a) "outside *me*", and my representing objects as (b) "outside or external to *one another*" presuppose the representation of space, and not vice versa. (a) and (b) shouldn't be read as synonyms for "spatial." That would render Kant's claim trivial, and would invite the objection that Argument 1 could equally prove empirical concepts to be *a priori*, since, for example, you can't represent objects *as red* without presupposing the *concept of red*. Note the further alleged difference between the empirical and the spatial case, that the ability to distinguish things from each other and from us is a necessary condition of the possibility of experience, while the ability to distinguish red from blue is not, so the former ability can't be acquired through experience.

The key issue for your reflection is this. Kant's main aim in the Aesthetic seems to be to prove his critical view of space and time, as against Newtonian and Leibnizian alternatives, which he takes to be a direct proof of transcendental idealism. He wants to establish conclusions about the *nature* of space and time, yet seems here to be analyzing our *representations* of space and time. *Are these separate tasks, and if so, how does Kant get from one to the other?*

Before leaving the Aesthetic, it is worth wondering whether and how Kant's position is utterly unique by placing it in comparative context.[2] A longstanding contest among theories of space- and time-cognition concerns the role of sensory experience. Empiricists say experience must be involved, *nativists* say it cannot be involved. Since Kant repeatedly insists that knowledge of spatial and temporal relations is not based on how we are affected by the objects that interact with our sense organs, he has naturally unequivocally been deemed a nativist. But what form of nativist? The central dispute is this. *Intuitionists* hold that inputs to the cognitive process already contain certain outputs, and all that's required is transmission or attention. *Sensationists* hold that products of the cognitive system are already present in the sensations originally given to the system as input; *non-sensationists* hold that the product is given in input (partly or wholly) other than sensation. *Constructivists* hold that a given output is not already contained in the input to the cognitive system, but only results from some substantive process(es) such as association, inference, comparison, combination, composition, or abstraction (for example, Berkeley's theory of visual spatial depth perception). So neither intuitionism, sensationism, nor constructivism should be identified with nativism or empiricism. For example, though sensationists are a subset of empiricists, you can be a constructivist nativist, or an empiricist intuitionist, *or*, less obviously, a non-sensationist intuitionist who is also an empiricist (if you think sensory experience involves more than having sensations).

This is best exemplified by considering an account on which the input data cannot be described simply as the *reception* of all the bits of data, since the order, at least of succession in time and possibly also disposition in space, in which they are received matters. So even if all the bits of data are sensations (the *matter*), the ordering would be a component in sensory experience (the *form*) in addition to those sensations. Such a view – that sensations are received successively over time, and perhaps also at diverse locations in space – aptly called *formal intuitionism*, seems best to capture Kant, and ought to be distinguished from sensationism (that we have sensations of spatiotemporal determinations), innate-ideas nativism (that knowledge of spatiotemporal relations is already present in the mind prior to all experience) and any form of constructivism (empiricist or innate-mechanisms nativist). Formal intuitionism could be either empiricist or nativist, depending on whether one takes the form in question to be given only through sensory experience or to be grounded on some innate feature that

2   This paragraph follows Falkenstein's excellent 1995 discussion.

determines how the subject is constituted so as to be able to receive sensations. The Aesthetic seems to defend (uniquely) the latter, nativist version of formal intuitionism. That this is Kant's position is supported by the facts that (1) he firmly distinguishes between a receptive faculty of the mind (named *intuition*), through which the data for the cognitive process are first given, and a faculty responsible for processing (*synthesizing*) the data; (2) he describes space and time as *forms of intuition* and *manners in which sensations are ordered*; and (3) synthesizing is wholly combining or unifying the previously given bits of information (the *manifold*) in a judgment. So, the problem of knowledge or representation is just the problem of how, from any array of matters spread out over space and occurring over time in a progressive intuition, the mind is able to produce a unified thought. Space and time are not constructed through synthetic operations performed on matters not themselves spatial or temporal (in which case Kant's problem would have been one of localization or discrimination rather than combination or unification). Kant's position invokes neither innately given ideas nor innate acts of mind processing immediately received data, but rather the existence of an innate structure to the receptor system, determining, not an idea or sensation or concept, but the *manner* in which sensations are received. So the specific locations sensations have in space and time are contingently, empirically given; it is only the structural (such as topological and metrical) features of space and time that are grounded in the subject. Appreciating Kant's position requires beginning with serious commitment to Kant's claim that intuitions are distinct from thought and from the representations generated through (what we'll discuss later to be) intellectual and imaginative synthesis, and as given prior to them.

7.3.4   *A fuller analysis of the Analytic of Concepts*

The plot thickens as we turn to the famous *Analytic of Concepts*. I remark on some of its milestones. First, I think the pivotal texts in "The Clue to the Discovery of All Pure Concepts of the Understanding," the Metaphysical Deduction, are B93–4 and B102–5. The rest of the chapter is secondary for the development of Kant's overall argument. The next stage of that argument, "The Deduction of the Pure Concepts of Understanding," the Transcendental Deduction, aims to show that understanding has a real or transcendental use. The remainder of *Transcendental Analytic* articulates precisely what that use is. *Transcendental Dialectic* exposes its misuse. *The Clue* affirms, and begins to defend, the conditional conclusion that *if* the understanding has a real or transcendental use, then this use must involve the very same unifying functions as is found in its logical use, its use as studied by formal or general logic. Why? Kant here must argue that the understanding, the activity (spontaneity) of thought, the use of concepts, is essentially the activity of judging, that "concepts are predicates of possible judgments."

Next, a representation's transcendental content (i.e. its form of the thought of an object in general, independent of the particular nature of the manifold of intuition) is an extralogical, objective content, what relates the representation to an object. Again, it's not until the Transcendental Deduction that Kant argues that the synthetic unity of the manifold is the form of the thought of an object in general (whatever particular ontological type the object may be), and hence concludes that insofar as the understanding produces such synthetic unity, it introduces a transcendental content into its representations (that is, its judgments). These generic content-introducers are the pure concepts of the understanding or categories. Judgment introduces this synthetic unity, but this aspect of judgment isn't disclosed to general logic or purely syntactical analysis. Again, Kant's view is that the understanding exercises one fundamental activity, which can and must be analyzed on (at least) two levels.

As regards exhaustively deriving the forms of judgment, Kant seems ambivalent. Sometimes he talks of the unity of understanding allowing systematic insight into its operations. Sometimes he speaks as if all the ground-floor necessary conditions of experience – the forms of judgment and categories as well as the forms of sensibility – are inexplicable givens. The important point for now is that abandoning claims that complete lists can be established leaves unscathed the central argument that the activity of judgment presupposes a set of essential, *a priori* concepts.

In the Aesthetic, Kant thinks he can move directly from the premise that space and time are sensible conditions of experience to the conclusion that they are empirically real, given that intuitions are received passively. Here he thinks we cannot validly infer from the premise that certain concepts are indispensable for certain forms of judgment that these concepts actually apply to what's sensibly given. A transcendental deduction is needed to make that connection. To render the Metaphysical Deduction probative, we must forthrightly develop the non-stipulative case for insisting that the exercise of certain judgmental forms requires certain concepts, and conversely.

As regards the Transcendental Deduction of the Categories, perhaps our first question should be, how strong a conclusion is Kant defending? For example, is it one of the following three, increasingly weak conclusions?

1   The categories are conditions of being merely sensibly affected; or
2   The categories are conditions of all consciousness; or
3   The categories are conditions of all consciousness in which the subject can distinguish itself from what it is conscious of.

The following should help. The notion of an object is essentially that of an object of judgment (an object for judgment). The question of how we can judge about what is given is identical to the question of how what is given can be an object for us. That judgment always has its object is familiar. That to be an object is to be an object of judgment is a novel claim. Subject and object are conceptually correlative (object in contrast with and as distinct from subject). This does not entail that subject and object are existentially interdependent. The subject distinguishes itself from what is given to it through making what is given to it into an object of judgment.

The main point of transcendental deduction is that judgment can relate to what is given in experience (what is given in experience can be an object of judgment) only if what is given conforms to certain epistemic categories that set up or define the relation between judgment and what is given sensibly in the first place. Epistemic concepts and only epistemic concepts can bring what is given into necessary relation to the understanding, the faculty of judgment. So the Metaphysical Deduction argues that epistemic concepts are concepts that can apply to what is given only insofar as what's given is brought under a certain judgment form, and the Transcendental Deduction defends the converse, that what is given can be brought under certain forms of judgment only insofar as epistemic concepts apply to what is given. The Metaphysical Deduction shows the *a priority* of epistemic concepts; the Transcendental Deduction shows the objective validity of epistemic concepts. Hence, at least 3 above is true.

Scholars argue about the relation between the Transcendental Deduction in the first and second editions. Many argue that the second edition is superior and self-sufficient. Those who dismiss the entire apparatus of transcendental idealism (pre-experiential mental activities, etc.) and admire Kant for his analysis of the structure of our conceptual scheme especially favor the second edition, and take it to reflect Kant's explicit dissociation with any earlier hint of psychology. I disagree, even to the point of believing that the most unchastened exercise of transcendental psychology from the first edition, its opening account of the threefold synthesis (A97–103), is necessary to support an otherwise inadequately-defended starting point in B.

I propose the following map for discerning the flow of Kant's line of thought. The lead question is, What are the *a priori* conditions on which the possibility of experience (of objects) rests? §13 articulates the profound problem to be addressed. §14 outlines the special method suitable for a solution. There are two aspects to the solution. One is *subjective* transcendental *deduction*, which establishes the cognitive powers and their operations required for experience of objects. The other is *objective* transcendental *deduction*, which establishes the *a priori* preconditions of experience without reference to the subject's cognitive powers. In the Preface Kant says these are two sides of same inquiry, *yet* subjective deduction is inessential. Again, I cannot see how the actually unfolding argument allows the option of bypassing subjective deduction, yet others confidently dismiss such "transcendental psychology" as fanciful speculation. It's a deep divide in approaches to Kant.[3]

Described in the broadest terms, there are three types of pre-categorial conditions Kant purports to establish as necessary for experience.[4] On the side of the subject, what he calls the *transcendental unity of apperception* is required. On the side of the object, what he calls the *transcendental object*, an indeterminate *something in general* = *x*, is required. This is differentiable into maximally generic *determining* concepts, the categories; they are not individually specified in the Deduction, but are individually defended later in the Analytic. The transcendental object is not now to be identified with the thing in itself – the latter is unknowable because it has a constitution inaccessible to our mode of cognition; the former is unknowable because it is, as the *concept* of an object *prior to* any constitution, not a *thing* at all.

The third condition concerns the *relation* between the subject and the object, the fundamental issue of transcendental philosophy, settled by transcendental logic. What makes transcendental self-consciousness (transcendental unity of apperception) and transcendental object, each necessary for experience and so known to be non-empirical, *themselves* possible? Kant's very deep answer is that they explain each other: the conditions under which self-consciousness is possible are the same conditions under which representations can be taken to have objects. But I think he is clear that *explaining* each other does not mean *creating* each other.

Much of the A-edition transcendental deduction is subjective deduction, with focal concern to uncover the cognitive powers and their operations required for synthetic unification of the temporal manifold. The overall argument seems presented twice, first moving from lower to higher powers (98–114), then from higher to lower powers (115–30). *Three* powers are required: receptivity of sensibility (apprehension in intuition (98–100)); combination by imagination (reproduction in imagination (100–2)); conceptualization by understanding (recognition in a concept (104–10)). And as indicated above, on the object side, the transcendental object is required (104–5, 108–10); on the subject side, transcendental unity of apperception is required (106–8). Kant articulates the necessary relations among empirical unities, analytic unities, and synthetic unities. The general result is that every empirical condition has a transcendental presupposition, and that analysis or conceptual discrimination always presupposes a prior synthesis or bringing together.

The B-edition transcendental deduction is overwhelmingly objective deduction. (The previously recurrent notion of synthesis is discussed only at 151–52 and 160.) Its structure is highly debatable, but here is a plausible proposal, which treats the argument/explanatory theory as unfolding in two stages. Stage 1 (15–20 or possibly 15–21) establishes that categories are

---

3   With this as with other interpretational disputes, influential proponents of alternatives are indicated in the annotations to recommended books in section 7.8.

4   My exposition of the transcendental deduction is influenced by dozens of sources studied over many years, but (in addition to Allison) is especially helped by Gardner 1999. Gardner is also the dominant influence later in my presentation of the transition from the Analytic to the Dialectic, and in some components of my treatment of the Dialectic. As I say in my book annotations, his elegant presentation of the entire first *Critique* is, in my judgment, overall the best available to students.

non-empirical, subjective conditions of thought, and concludes that "All the manifold, therefore, so far as it is given in a single empirical intuition . . . is necessarily subject to the categories" (143). Stage 2 (21–26 or 24–26) establishes that these subjective conditions of thought are objectively valid, that the categories are constitutive of everything presented in intuition (161). And the further, critical consequence of deduction is that the categories are restricted to objects of possible intuition (appearances), thus bolstering transcendental idealism.

A caveat concerning the transcendental object: Kant carefully says that an object is "that in the concept of which the manifold of a given intuition is *united*" (B137), not that an object is a unified manifold, or that the concept of an object is the concept of a unified manifold. We shouldn't confuse the concept of an object with its function in synthesis, or objects with the way we realize them in representation. We can represent objects in our experience only by *taking* necessary unities of representations *as* representings of objects. This doesn't mean the concept of an object reduces to that of a necessary unity of representations. Allusion to "a something = x" in addition to necessary unities alerts us to their non-equivalence.

The first stage of the B-edition transcendental deduction, designed to establish the reciprocal connection between the transcendental unity of apperception and the representation of objects, wholly abstracts from our way of receiving data (our form of sensibility). Note that the segment of argument which purports to show that the representation of an object is *necessary* for unity of consciousness, equivalently is purporting to show that unity of consciousness is *sufficient* for representation of an object, thereby addressing the question of how representation is possible at all. The argument goes as follows: to function as a representation, it must be possible for me to be aware of a representation as mine (attach "I think" to it). This principle of the transcendental unity of apperception (i.e. original synthetic unity of apperception) is analytically true (B135, 138). Any representation of a manifold as a manifold is a single, complex thought (involves a synthetic unity of representations, as was shown at the beginning of the A-Deduction). A single, complex thought requires a single, thinking subject. So, a numerically identical "I think" can be reflectively attached to each representation taken individually, and this thinking subject can be aware of the numerical identity of the "I think." If representations X and Y are to be thought together in a single consciousness, which is necessary if they are to constitute a single, complex thought, then the I that thinks X must be identical to the I that thinks Y, and if the subject is to be conscious of the representations as collectively constituting a unity it must also be possible for it to become conscious of its own identity as subject with respect to the thought of each of the representations (B138). To think the thought of the identity of the "I think" *is* to unify the distinct representations in a single consciousness. The (bare) "I" of the "I think," which is the same in all consciousness, has no determinate content, so cannot be characterized apart from its representations, so I must be aware of both representations (X and Y) together to be aware of my identity. The identical "I think" is the form of the analytic unity that pertains to all general concepts; it is analytic unity considered in abstraction from all content. So consciousness of the "I think" is the thought of what is common to all concepts (analytic unities). And the consciousness of the act of synthesis is the consciousness of the form of thinking. So, the doctrine of apperception provides the model for the analysis (dissection) of the understanding in its logical activities, and the theory of synthesis which the doctrine implies is an analytical account of the way the model operates (neither introspective psychology nor idealist ontology). The unity of apperception is an objective unity, is objectively valid, because it is the ultimate condition of the representation of an object. Representing an object X is unifying the manifold of intuition of X by means of concepts, and all non-categorial concepts unify by rules which are governed by the maximally generic, invariant, *a priori* rules associated with the categories.

And we can bolster our understanding of the second stage of the Deduction as follows: the *Aesthetic* showed that awareness of a time requires awareness of it as a portion of a single, all-inclusive time. But the whole time is not itself actually given as an object (but only one moment at a time). To represent the portion of time, and myself as representing it at that time, I must be able to represent past and future time (what's not present), and ultimately the single time, by imagination. So, the determinate representation of time is a product of the transcendental synthesis of imagination. This synthesis is sufficient as well as necessary for such representation – there is a reciprocity between transcendental synthesis of imagination and its "transcendental product" (i.e. the determinate representation of time), which parallels the (earlier) reciprocity between the intellectual synthesis (in judgment) and its "logical product" (the *Objekt*). Kant is arguing from the unity of time (and space) to the unity of consciousness, but does not affirm the converse. The unity of time is a requirement of sensibility, not of understanding, serving to limit or restrict the understanding. The notion of several times (spaces) that are not parts of a single time (space) is not logically incoherent. Remember, the unity of consciousness is an analytic principle. Syntheticity is introduced by introducing our sensibility.

A pivotal segment of the argument occurs at B160–1, and can be sketched as follows:

1   Empirical synthesis of apprehension must conform to space and time.
2   Space and time are not only forms of intuition but are themselves intuitions with a manifold of their own, representable only insofar as their manifold is unified (as was proven in stage 1); they're unified by the transcendental synthesis of the imagination.
3   What is necessary for the representation of space and time is necessary for the apprehension or perception of anything intuited in space and time.

4   The unity required for apprehension is an application to human sensibility of the unity of the manifold of an intuition in general that is required for apperception (and the rules for such unification are the categories). The claim that synthesis of apprehension, like synthetic unity of apperception, is governed by the categories, rests on the (mediating) fact that synthesis of imagination is governed by the categories. The argument goes as follows: the principle of apperception (which is analytic) together with the fact that time is the form of inner sense (which is synthetic) together with the fact that imaginative synthesis is necessary for the representation of time entail that synthesis of imagination is governed by the categories, because the categories are the fundamental modes of apperceptive unity.

5   Therefore all unification, all synthesis (intellectual, figurative (implies extraconceptual), apprehension) is subject to the categories.

To help you hone in on topics of special interest, note the foci of the twelve §16–27:

Now note some highlights of these sections: (§16) the principle of TUA is a logical, not psychological fact (B132) expressing the universal property of all consciousness, defines the nature of an understanding whose fundamental act is the synthesis of a given manifold. (That human understanding is such an understanding is a synthetic proposition.) (17) The epistemological notion of object (i.e. something represented, a correlate of judgment) is explicit here. Knowledge is the "determinate relation of given representations to an object," but an object is a "that which" – "that in the concept of which the manifold of a given intuition is united." So the connection we locate *in the object is* the unity the understanding imposes on the *consciousness* of the representations. So to think representations together in one consciousness *is* to confer on them relation to an object (B138, like A104–6). (18) The empirical unity of my consciousness as a phenomenal object concerns the associations which serve to specify my particular empirical character, and must not be confused with the necessary unity of apperception in the act of synthesis which the understanding performs, which is the condition alike of empirical objects *and* the unity of empirical consciousness. (19–20) Note that only the existence of a table of categories, not a specification of particular categories, is affirmed, and that Kant *criticizes* the view (commonly attributed to him) that all judgment consists of a subject-term and a predicate-term. Unity of consciousness is required for relational as well as subject–predicate judgments. (21) The categories are not valid for an intuitive intellect (B145). "Temporality" of consciousness is presupposed. (22) "Knowledge" is used very strictly here; pure math is the only potential knowledge. Discussion implies that pure space is *not* an individual given *a priori* – if it were, pure math would have its own separate object. (24–25, second half) Read with General Observations II B66–9 in *Aesthetic* and *Refutation of Idealism* to answer charges of idealism. Note that "noumenal" means "object of intelligence."

Kant accepted the fact of consciousness as basic, and wished to certify scientific knowledge of material objects. This required him to deny privileged access to the real self and explain how the self is given to itself as an object of knowledge. He presents a doctrine of an *inner sense* (*outer sense* is the five senses) whereby the self appears to itself as phenomenon. Note (perhaps surprisingly) that the original manifold of sensibility is spatial (composed of perceptions having a spatial form), not spatiotemporal (B49–50 and Bxxxix note). Kant faces these tasks: 1. He must discover a manifold of inner intuition which can serve as the representation of the self. 2. He must explain how, by the affection of inner sense, a temporal form is imposed on the spatial manifold of outer intuition. 3. He must explain how the self manages to project an objective temporal ordering onto outer appearances, distinct from the subjective temporal order of their apprehension in (empirical) consciousness (offered in Second Analogy). In this connection one needs to get fully clear on the nature of and relations between inner sense, outer sense, apperception and self-knowledge. (26) The first three paragraphs complete the deduction. The end of the section stresses that the understanding dictates laws to nature, though particular laws cannot be derived from the categories (B165).

By showing the dependence of transcendental apperception on *a priori* synthesis, the transcendental deduction shows the necessity of there being objects corresponding to and distinct from our representations, but these distinct objects haven't been determinately described yet (for example, as (empirically) outer objects (in space)). Still, Kant already has navigated a path between Hume's radical empiricism and consequent skepticism about the self, and Descartes' substance essentialism about the self. It's already a (partial) refutation of Hume, who self-defeatingly requires that I represent as subjective something that I must contrast with myself in order to be self-conscious. And Descartes is (partially) upset, since it's been shown that self-consciousness shouldn't be viewed as a relation in which a pre-existent object with a unique essence becomes known to itself, but instead as an encompassing ground of the world of objects, but not something included in the world of objects (and that empirical self-knowledge is no different philosophically than empirical knowledge of the other – both are knowledge of objects only as they appear).

The interpretation of the B-edition transcendental deduction is hotly contested. It seems that §15–21 aim to show that *any* sensible content must be subject to the categories if it is to be thought or conceptualized (i.e. brought to unity of consciousness). §24–26 then seem (presupposing results of the Aesthetic) to argue for the necessity of categories with respect to human sensibility and its data. But if 15–21 succeed, 24–26 seem unnecessary. Allison plausibly argues that 15–21 defend the objective validity of the categories (*objektiv Gültigkeit*), show the categories make judgments (objectively valid (i.e. capable of being true or false) syntheses of representations) possible. Since it is only through judgments that we represent objects, the categories are necessary conditions for the representation of objects. And 24–26 defend the objective reality (application to an actual object) of the categories, purporting to show that categories apply to all objects of possible experience (whatever objects are given to us in intuition), connecting the categories with the forms of human sensibility via the transcendental synthesis of imagination. *Objective validity* goes with a judgmental or logical conception of object – very broadly construed as anything that can be the subject of judgment – and is usually 'Objekt' in the deduction. *Objective reality* (*Realität*) goes with a "real" sense of object, an *actual* entity or state of affairs (object of possible experience, as explicitly reinforced in the Postulates of Empirical Thought later), and is usually "*Gegenstand*." And there are two species of *Gegenstand* – objects of outer sense ("objective objects," spatiotemporal entities and states of affairs) and objects of inner sense ("subjective objects," representations) – where this inner–outer distinction is empirical, not transcendental.

§15 argues that all combination is an act (synthesis) of the understanding, and can't be given – it's a unification of a diversity by synthesis. As I see it, Kant needs to explain and justify this premise, which he does elaborate in the A-Deduction, A97–104, part of what he himself describes as the *subjective* deduction of the categories. So at least one part of the subjective deduction does not seem optional to me. The gist of that part is as follows: a succession of items is given in consciousness. To be aware of a succession is to be aware of a plurality as a plurality. Such awareness in turn requires that one hold the items together (*synthesis of apprehension in intuition*). But one could not hold the succession of items together unless one kept in mind or remembered earlier members as one apprehended later members (*reproduction in imagination*). But to be aware of *that* succession (diversity), I must identify the earlier members as the very same items I apprehended earlier, not retrieve them in any old way (*recognition in a concept*). So combination or unification requires this (pre-experiential) threefold synthesis; it's not part of what's given to me.

Even readers who admire the subjective deduction sometimes disagree about how the three syntheses relate to each other. Some think they are three, temporally-orderable stages in a process. I think there is just one process, the process of holding the diversity together, synthesis of apprehension in intuition, and that this logically requires reproduction, which in turn logically requires recognition – it is the beginning of the deduction of further and further necessary conditions. (For example, the next move is that recognition requires the use of concepts.) Results from the Transcendental Deduction will be invoked in Kant's later proofs. The main transition from the Deduction to these later proofs is the *Schematism*.

7.3.5   A fuller analysis of the Analytic of Principles

The *Schematism* concerns the relation between the sensible and conceptual. It shows how the abstract content of the categories (for example, ground–consequent) is transformed into content applicable to the data of our senses (for example, cause–effect) – the Transcendental Deduction didn't tell us what the sensible instantiation of a pure concept amounts to. Schemata are procedures presupposed for the generation of images, which enable subsumption of objects under concepts. A transcendental schema is a way of conceptualizing time, a transcendental determination of time. Categories gain application through realization in thoughts about time. The only thing that has a sensible aspect but is *a priori* is pure intuition, and time is the most general unifying condition of all representations. (But categories allow for thinkability independently of schematism.) I take it that schematism is Kant's acknowledged limit of transcendental explanation, "an art concealed in the depths of the human soul" (B180–1). But it seems necessary to avoid the dreaded transcendental realist (pre-Copernican) model of concept-application, in turn necessary to escape the rationalism–empiricism dichotomy.

In the *Schematism* Kant deals with the products of transcendental synthesis of imagination, which unites pure concepts with pure intuition, explaining how categories can apply to appearances, by providing the "sensible conditions under which alone pure concepts can be employed" (B175). Sensible conditions for use of a concept = empirical meaning conditions of the concept = the specific features of what's sensibly given which reflect or correspond to what is thought in the concept. Apart from such conditions (the schemata) the categories have a logical use (as logical functions of judgment) but not a real use (an application to "real" objects). To specify these conditions is to specify just what is being claimed about the phenomenal world when it is claimed that particular categories apply to it – a body of *synthetic a priori* propositions (*Principles*) in which categorial claims are made about the phenomenal world. If the second part of the Transcendental Deduction succeeds, it shows categories stand in a necessary connection with time, and, therefore, with objects qua temporal. But this by itself does not imply specific metaphysical propositions. Demonstrating an extralogical or real use does not by itself show how and under what specific conditions the particular concepts are to be employed. For example, it doesn't tell us what property or relation of appearances in time is to be taken as the sensible expression or analogue of the logical relation of ground and consequent. This is the task the *Schematism* must perform for each of the categories.

Don't read "subsumption" as the relation between a class concept and the particulars falling under it. The relation between categories and the sensibly given is one of form and matter, structure and content. It's a syllogistic, not judgmental conception of "subsumption" here. Inferring or judging mediately takes place "by the subsumption of the conditions of a possible judgment under the conditions of a given judgment." The given judgment is the universal rule which functions as the major premise. The condition of the rule is the middle term in the syllogism, the "third thing," which connects the universal rules with the particulars to which it is applied in the conclusion. The categories are derived from the nature of the understanding; as such, they have no direct relation to intuition. But the Transcendental Deduction showed they do relate to intuition (and so appearances). Where the categories are the universal rules, there is a need for some analogue of the condition of the rule, or the middle term of the syllogism, under which appearances are to be "subsumed." The analogue is the transcendental schema, the third thing mediating category and appearance. So the question of the *Schematism* is the question of how synthetic judgments are possible *a priori*, since concepts are "predicates of possible judgments." Judgments which apply concepts to appearances are synthetic; those which apply *a priori* concepts are *a priori*. When Kant first posed the organizing question of the possibility of synthetic judgments knowable *a priori* in the Introduction, without specific reference to the pure concepts, he alluded mysteriously to an "unknown = x" (B13) which is needed to ground the connection between the concepts that is asserted in the judgment. When he returns to it in the *Transcendental Analytic*, this unknown = x is more precisely characterized as a transcendental schema.

Kant says in both our *Critique* and the *Critique of Judgment* that a schema is a pure intuition. Recall two senses of pure intuition: (a) form of intuition (sensibility), and (b) formal intuition. The "third thing" seems to be a formal intuition, but space doesn't permit explanation here.

The *Schematism* concretizes the pure concepts of the understanding. Now let's look at schematized principles of the understanding to get a flavor of how Kant's arguments go. *Principles* are judgments which ground the possibility of other judgments but are not deducible from any other, more universal judgments (B188).

Axioms and *Anticipations* are the principles involved in the *a priori* determination of appearances according to the categories of quantity and quality (the formal aspects of quantity and quality, necessary for (universal) applied mathematics), and are intuitively certain. They describe basic conceptual conditions intuitions must meet if empirical knowledge is to be developed from them. Mathematical principles concern only the intuition of an appearance in general; they are necessary but not sufficient for objectivity, which also requires dynamical principles, which concern the conditions for the existence of the objects of a possible empirical intuition and the rules for connecting and unifying empirical intuitions (Postulates and Analogies), whereby objective cognition or experience arises, which involve the *a priori* determination of appearances according to the categories of modality and relation, are discursively certain (which is not a lower grade of certainty), and are necessary for applied physics. Given that the Axioms are necessary conditions for the possibility of experience, we can say that applied math requires cardinality (subjective ordering is not enough). What the dynamical principles will teach us is that physics (dynamics) requires ordinality (objective ordering, not just objective counting) as well.

The *Axioms of Intuition* is not an axiom of arithmetic or geometry, but a condition that must be satisfied if such axioms are to have application to the world. Under what conditions can properties of objects be determinately measured? We must be able to order the objects, that is, place them in correspondence with the number series. But this only suffices for comparative measurement, which falls short of determinate measurement. Let us say a property of an object is additive if there is an empirical operation applicable to it formally analogous to addition in arithmetic (like, paradigmatically, length). If orderable objects have additive properties as well (so that a *precise* correspondence between their properties and numerical relations can be established), their properties can be determinately measured. The space and time of the *Aesthetic* has at that point no fixed metric (precise location of intuited objects in the spatiotemporal framework is not yet possible, and so determinate spatial and temporal magnitude is not yet measurable). Only the necessity of locatability sometime (somewhere) or other was established in the *Aesthetic*. Kant is now arguing that metric is brought to space and time by the understanding, by conceptualizing space and time in certain ways, that is, by acts of synthesis. Kant has argued (in *Aesthetic*) that all objects of intuition have spatial and temporal properties. But, Kant now argues, spatial and temporal properties are additive. (Spatiality implies size, which is clearly additive. And Kant asserts that temporality can be represented only spatially (as a line), and so it too is additive. This currently obscure point is pursued in the Analogies.) But to say an object has an additive property is just to say it is an extensive magnitude (and the representation of the parts necessarily precedes the representation of the whole). Therefore, all objects of intuition are extensive magnitudes. And, as has been argued above, pure mathematics precisely applies to extensive magnitudes (as just defined). Therefore, pure mathematics has universal, empirical application. In Kant's language, the Axioms subsumes all appearances, as objects of intuition in space and time, under the schematized category of quantity, and thus is a principle of the applicability of mathematics.

Note the anti-Newtonian cosmology here. Absolute space (and time) implies a unique set of coordinates defining all positions (an intrinsic metric). In arguing against intrinsic metric, Kant is arguing against absolute space and time. The argument is anchored in the fact that space and time are empirically real – properties of appearances, not things in themselves, and so lack intrinsic metric.

As for the Anticipations, I'll say only that it guarantees that the math of intensive magnitudes applies to the real in space. Since the use of affirmation and negation depends on the presence or absence of sensations that come in continuously varying degrees, the empirical use of the categories of quality is connected with the mathematics of intensive magnitudes.

The *Analogies of Experience* warrant a bit more attention. Underlying all the Analogies is the thesis that experience must form a unity, must conform to the unity of apperception, which entails that it must conform to the unity of time. But connections are not given in sense, so must be determined conceptually. If a realm of objects is to be represented, it must be possible to draw a distinction between subjective (refers to us as their subjects) and objective (taken to refer to a world of objects) aspects of our representations (as per the Transcendental Deduction), and so, first of all, between the temporal order of our representations (subjective succession – I'm in one mode, then another) and the temporal order of objects which exist with a determinate location (an objective time-order). Time itself cannot be perceived, as a fixed, determinate, self-subsistent framework, known independently of events that occur in it (objective re-ordering cannot be given to us directly); time is a form of sensibility, not a thing in itself. So, to think of appearances as being in time, I must think something fixed and unchanging (besides time), something permanent, in (accessible) appearances, use of the concept of substance (First Analogy). Also, the experience of the world as changing is necessary for the experience of an objective time-order, and only by using the concept of causality can we make the distinction between change occurring in our representations and change occurring in an objective world; that distinction is neither intuitable nor analytic. To be thought as objective, the relation of succession must be determined according to a rule, as necessary and irreversible; my experience changes because the (numerically same – retaining the role of substance) object changes (Second Analogy). And things can be determined as coexistent only through being determined as capable of causal interaction in space; objects are determinable as having the same location in time only when I can view the order of my representations as reversible, their time-order as indifferent, in turn only by using the concept of influence such that each substance reciprocally contains the ground of the determination of the other (Third Analogy). The upshot is that all objective empirical facts have a certain form (provided by the categories of substance and causality), and all appearances collectively form one nature. This is not a transcendent claim, but one internal to experience and constitutive of the existence of appearances.

The most familiar objection to the Analogies is that we don't need absolute permanence and necessary connection, only relative permanence and some degree of regularity. The core of the most common reply is that the critic is confusing what's needed for making claims once we're in a world we've legitimated with what conceptual form the given must have in the first place to be a world for us, and specifically, what is necessary and sufficient to express time in general and so make an objective time-order thinkable.

Considering the *First Analogy* in more detail, I read it as presupposed by the rest of the *Analytic of Principles*, so it's especially important to make its logic explicit, as follows:

1   All appearances are in time (it's the "substratum" of all appearances).
2   The constant flux occurs in a single time; the framework of time retains its identity throughout all change (time is unchangeable).
3   Time itself cannot be perceived, is not an object of experience (so we cannot determine the objective temporal relations of appearances by referring them to time itself; instead we must consider appearances themselves and the rules for their connection in consciousness).
4   Some perceptually accessible model (substratum) for time itself is required. (If everything were in constant flux, if nothing endured, we could not be aware of succession (or coexistence) as such.)
5   All changing appearances with determinate positions in time must be regarded (experienced) as states or determinations of substance (all "change" (*Wechsel*) among appearances must be conceived and experienced as alteration (*Veränderung*) of a substance that endures (for Kant, that substance is permanent is tautological)).
6   There is something substantial in things that does not come into or go out of existence (i.e. matter, but the nature of matter is not specified; that is an empirical question). A coming into being or passing out of existence is logically possible, but is not an object of possible experience, since were it to occur, "we should then lose that which can alone represent the unity of time (and so the unity of experience), the identity of the substratum" (A156).
7   Permanence entails conservation of its quantity in the universe. Spatiality is matter's only transcendentally specifiable property. So conceived, matter can only be conceived via the category of quantity. So the permanence of matter must be conceived as the permanence of its quantity.
8   (The permanent must be relevant to the measurement of time, the consciousness of duration, but the Analogy's main aim is more basic, to show that something permanent is required for the unification of all (phenomenal) things and events in a single time.)

The central problem of the *Second Analogy* is to determine how time-consciousness (the representation of any temporal order at all), and specifically consciousness of objective succession, is possible. It is not the more familiar problem of justifying judgments about objective order based on subjectively apprehended data. Kant maintains that if all we had were the indeterminate subjective order – the indeterminate preconceptualized material for sensible representation (what would remain if, per impossible, we could remove the determinate structure imposed on the sensibly given (manifold of inner sense) by the understanding) – we could not represent *any* temporal order at all, either among states of ostensible physical objects or events in one's mental history. Note in this connection, and in support of my ongoing interpretation, how explicitly liberally Kant construes "object" from the very beginning of his discussion (A190–1), as in, "Everything, every representation [empirically construed] even, in so far as we are conscious of it, may be entitled object." And note how he proceeds, shifting to questioning the meaning of the objectivity of representations qua intentional.

Kant thinks the transcendental realist cannot explain, for example, the possibility of distinguishing between an objective and subjective temporal order within the realm of appearances – time itself cannot be perceived; all we have to work with are our representations, so we cannot directly compare our representations with a pre-given temporal order (assuming one exists).

Kant's view is that *causality* requires necessity, meaning strict universality or invariability – for every event there is some (unspecified) antecedent condition which is its cause. *Event* is the coming to be of a state or determination of some object; an event involves an alteration. Kant's argument begins with an account of the essential features of event perception. I cannot be aware that something has happened unless I can contrast the present state of some object with its preceding state (from First Analogy – since all apprehension is successive this is only a necessary, not sufficient condition for event perception). To think event E I must think the order of my perceptions as determined, and so irreversibility characterizes the way in which we connect perceptions in thought (in the objective unity of apperception) if we are to experience through them an objective succession. That is, irreversibility does not refer to a given perceptual order, which we can inspect and then infer that it is somehow determined by the object, but refers to the conceptual ordering by the understanding (by subsumption under a rule) through which the understanding determines the thought of an object (in this case objective succession). Prior to the conceptual determination there is no thought of an object at all, and, therefore, no experience. So the task is to determine the conditions under which we think of the order of perceptions as irreversible. What *a priori* rule; and since the order is temporal, what transcendental schema?

The answer is the schema of causality, rule-governed succession. So it is only by subjecting our perceptions to this rule that we can regard them as containing the representation of an event. But then the event itself, qua object represented (object of possible experience) is likewise subsumed under the schema, that is, it is presupposed that there is something antecedent to the event on which it follows according to a rule. This is true because "the conditions of the possibility of experience in general are likewise conditions of the possibility of the objects of experience" (A158), the key operative principle in Kant's argument (but not because judgments about objects are just reducible to judgments about perceptions of objects). Hume can't doubt we do in fact distinguish between a mere sequence of perceptions and the perception of an objective sequence, because the possibility of event awareness is presupposed in Hume's account of how we come to form the belief that future sequences of events will resemble past sequences. Hume of course would not accept the transcendental perspective from which the problem is approached (the epistemic condition conception of objectivity), but Kant does not beg the question insofar as he *argues* that the transcendental realist cannot explain the acknowledged facts.

Allison stresses that the schema of causality is argued to be necessary for experience of succession of the states in an object, that is, of an event, and not for the ordering of distinct events. The notion of the complete determinability of the location of events in a single time is, for Kant, a regulative Idea (to be explicated in *Transcendental Dialectic*), a requirement of reason, not a transcendental condition of all possible experience.

How much is built into the claim that every event has a cause? There are three possibilities:

1   The initial state (perceptual antecedent) A must be regarded as the cause of the change to state B.
2   The sequence of state A-B must be "lawlike," that is, given some initiating condition (not necessarily A), the transition from A to B is necessarily subsumable under a "covering law."
3   The sequence can (but need not) be "contingent," that is, it's not necessarily 1 or 2, but the event is still subject to the principle of causality as a transcendental condition.

1 implies that the only succession we can experience is that of cause and effect, an absurdity which is not Kant's view. 2 is still too strong. Judgments about objective temporal succession do not presuppose that the elements in the succession are connected by empirical laws. All that is presupposed is that there is some antecedent condition (presumably roughly contemporaneous with x's being in state A at time1), which being given, state B necessarily ensues upon for this particular x at time2. There are no additional assumptions regarding the repeatability of the sequence and its relation to other objects of x's type that are licensed by this presupposition. The fact that one seeks a lawful connection somewhere does not change this. It makes possible the explanation of the event, and the search for such conditions is a requirement of reason in its regulative capacity. This, in turn, requires the assumption of the uniformity of nature or affinity of appearances. But it is not the Second Analogy's task to provide a justification for this requirement of reason.

So, to repeat, Kant never infers the causal relations of ontologically distinct entities that supposedly correspond to perceptions from a feature of the perceptions (their irreversibility). But neither is he a subjectivist or phenomenalist. The argument assumes the Copernican conception of an object as the correlate of a certain mode of representation ("distinct from representations," but not in the way understood by the transcendental realist). The very concept of an (weighty) object must be characterized in terms of the conditions of our possible representation of it.

One culmination of the *Analytic of Principles* is the resolution of a "scandal to philosophy" by proving the existence of outer objects. Retrieving required steps from earlier argument, here is Kant's *Refutation of Idealism*:

1 I am judging.
2 Some act of judging is occurring.
3 Any act of judging is an act of consciousness or awareness.
4 Acts of consciousness or awareness are representative (have a content).
5 Awareness of the instantaneous is impossible.
6 So the content of awareness is non-instantaneous.
7 Any non-instantaneous content is a successive content, that is, a series of items occurring in an order, and not all at a single instant.
8 So judgmental awareness is of a succession of items.
9 Awareness of succession implies awareness of a plurality of items as a plurality – awareness of a diversity or manifold.
10 Awareness of a plurality of items as a plurality requires that the plurality be apprehended as a numerically identical collection over the time during which the awareness is occurring.
11 This identity of the manifold over time requires that the act of awareness of this identical manifold connect up or relate the various elements which comprise it, that is, be aware of all the elements together.
12 Such a connective awareness requires that earlier items in the series be recognized together with the later items, and that all the items be recognized as belonging to this unity over time.
13 Only a persisting, identical subject of awareness can be connective; a series or collection of diverse subjects of consciousness is incapable of such connective activity.
14 So any act of judgment requires a persisting judger.
15 An identical judger must be able to be aware of his unity of consciousness.
16 But awareness of an objectless awareness itself is impossible. I can be aware of consciousness only by being aware of the object of consciousness.
17 So awareness of a persisting consciousness requires awareness of a persisting object of consciousness.
18 So awareness of succession requires awareness of something persisting.
19 This something persisting cannot be an item in the series, or of the succession, since only by being aware of it can I be aware of the series.
20 This series of items (of acts of representation) constitutes my mental life.

21 So the persisting something is not part of my mental life.
22 But if something is not part of my mental life, it is existentially and attributively independent of me.
23 And since it is something which I can perceptually identify and which persists, it is reidentifiable.
24 So the persisting something required for awareness of succession, which in turn is required for judging, is an objective particular.
25 So I am aware of an objective particular.

Remember, the conclusion is the general one that we know that external objects exist. There is no aim to solve the problem of the criterion by discovering a philosophically certain test for distinguishing true from false judgment in each particular case. It is characteristic of transcendental philosophy to establish structural features of the accessible world, and not to overreach and purport to solve local disputes.

7.3.6   The transition from Analytic to Dialectic

The Appendix to the *Transcendental Analytic*, *The Amphiboly of Concepts of Reflection* (amphiboly is ambiguity), defends no new premises, but seems an appropriate transition to *Transcendental Dialectic*, as it (together with the section on the Phenomena–Noumena distinction which precedes it) elicits negative, restrictive implications of the analysis of cognition just completed, here by critiquing Leibniz's unchastened rationalist methodology, and consequent ontology (account of the nature of reality and relations among real things); much of the critique began by implication with Kant's account of the possible, the actual, and the necessary (the alethic modalities) in the Postulates of Empirical Thought, which immediately precedes the Phenomena–Noumena section, and as I see it, concludes the main, constructive argument of the *Critique*. The Amphiboly treats Leibniz as entirely well-motivated and profound (since Kant *shares* Leibniz's view of reason as (dispositionally) essentially metaphysical, revealing its nature in the Ideas of the unconditioned to be examined in the Dialectic), but provably confused, given the just-achieved results of the Aesthetic and Analytic. Indeed, for pure, abstract thought, Kant seems to insist that Leibniz's is the only possible philosophy; were thought capable of determining the nature of things in themselves, Leibniz would be fully correct. But Leibniz's "intellectual system of the world" is based on a transcendental amphiboly, a confounding of an object of pure understanding with appearance.

Two specifics are worth noting. First, the very specific statement of the fallacy occurs at B336: it's true that what belongs to or contradicts a universal concept belongs to or contradicts the particulars that fall under that concept. But Kant alleges that Leibniz argues that what is *not* contained in a universal concept is *not* contained in the particulars to which it applies, fallaciously denying the antecedent. Second, Kant says that Locke's philosophy is equally amphibolous with reverse tendency. Leibniz "intellectualized appearances," Locke "sensualized all concepts of the understanding."

Kant's complaint is sketched as follows: *concepts of reflection* are used in *logical reflection* to compare concepts. Leibniz bases his metaphysics on logical reflection. He only uses general logic, and does not recognize the need for transcendental logic. For example, he determines differences among things wholly in terms of differences among concepts. But logical reflection only factors in the form of concepts, which is insufficient to determine the nature of objects. It confuses logical with real relations, treating all concepts as if they were intellectual, so all objects as if they were noumenal. Metaphysics requires *transcendental reflection*, which always decides whether a representation belongs to sensibility or understanding, hence whether its object is an appearance or thing in itself. Logical reflection suffices to determine the nature of things in themselves, but not of appearances. Ultimately, outer appearances are differentiated spatially, so intuitively rather than conceptually. So Leibniz's metaphysics would apply to noumena, if they exist, but does not apply to any reality that may be given to us. (Detailed criticism of Leibniz occurs at B328–34.)

As Kant presents things, the pivotal oversight of both traditional rationalists (dogmatists) and empiricists is their failure to recognize that understanding and sensibility are irreducibly distinct sources of representations. (Concepts without intuitions are empty; intuitions without concepts are blind.) Anti-Kantians ought to press hard on this decisive component of Kant's system. The Amphiboly applies it along the four dimensions open to logical reflection. Most famously, it argues that Leibniz's identity of indiscernibles (his principle of identity and difference) exemplifies transcendental amphiboly. The principle says that what's identical in conception is identical in all respects. (Note how strongly rationalist it is, guaranteeing that all real differences are in principle apprehensible by discursive thought.) But the principle is not a law of nature, but only an analytic rule for the comparison of things through mere concepts. Equisized spaces are alike for thought, but are distinguishable for sense; difference in spatial location is a matter of intuition, not discoverable in pure concept. (Recall incongruous counterparts here.)

Let's look at one more of the four dimensions to appreciate the thrust of Kant's critique of Leibniz. The second amphiboly has it that realities can never conflict, but always harmonize, since in pure thought the only form of opposition is logical negation (a consequential principle that leads to saying things such as that evil is merely negative, a privation). But, Kant retorts, space, time, and the resulting possibility of dynamical causality allow for real opposition between real, positive existents, and allow for non-logical conflicts. At bottom, Kant's complaint is that Leibniz fails to recognize the difference in kind between sensibility and understanding, and (relatedly) confuses analytic and synthetic judgments, treating them all as ultimately analytic, determinable by thought alone.

As we approach the transition from the Analytic to Dialectic, we must say more concerning things in themselves (including the self in itself). For one thing, we might wonder whether the Dialectic plays an ineliminable role, or is strictly optional, at best reinforcing the Aesthetic and Analytic, which purport to give a sufficient proof of transcendental idealism, and so the impossibility of transcendent metaphysics. The Analytic specified the conditions under which we can rightfully claim that our thoughts have objects (our judgments are capable of truth), namely the conditions of possible experience, which are necessary and sufficient for (theoretical, descriptive) knowledge. So limits of knowledge are limits of experience, so the claims of transcendent metaphysics (about objects beyond possible experience) are (theoretically) unjustifiable *tout court* – presumptuous Ontology must cede to a mere Analytic of pure understanding (B303), an immanent metaphysics of experience.

But I continue to insist that for Kant, *thought* about non-empirical objects is possible (the unschematized categories are thoughts about objects in general, unconditioned by our sensibility). Talk about things in themselves is not nonsense. Such talk does lack sense (*Sinn* and *Bedeutung*), that is, cognitive, objective, determinate meaning, or specifiable content, but "without sense" does not imply "nonsense." The categories require input from sensibility to have application to objects, but not for them to have meaning. Recall that by themselves, the categories are forms of thought or judgment as such, concepts of objects in general. (Think about it: if categories were literally meaningless on their own, why in the world would meaning suddenly arise when they are conjoined with sensibility?) So I think the situation leaving the Analytic is this: we know we can defend immanent metaphysics in a way that we cannot defend transcendent metaphysics. But what if someone still insists that since Kant's theory of theoretical (speculative) knowledge rules out transcendent metaphysics, so much the worse for Kant's theory? After all, Kant himself told us in the Preface that in some sense, we cannot get rid of metaphysics; we need it. And in fact the Analytic hasn't sufficiently pacified our propensity to speculate about transcendent reality, or have the natural beliefs we do. We need a deep diagnosis of these tendencies and beliefs. Why does transcendent metaphysics take the forms it does (we keep talking about God, selves, freedom, the whole universe, etc.)? How can we resolve the conflicts generated by these tendencies? Can we achieve a harmony among our theoretical (What can I know?), practical (What should I do?), and aspirational (What can I hope for?) interests? Further, the issue of the limits of knowledge themselves seems to demand philosophical examination. But the understanding, dissected in the Analytic, cannot form concepts of totalities or wholes (i.e. of the unconditioned), or of objects beyond experience, so if we must investigate bounds, if we must investigate where experience stops (which is not itself a matter of experience – experience doesn't bound itself, but always only leads us from one empirical object to another) then something else must conduct the inquiry, namely reason, using *its* characteristic modes of thinking, namely Ideas. So there remains the need to track the inevitable moves of transcendent metaphysics, systematically document its specific transgressions, in order to authoritatively acquire positive cognition of the bounds of knowledge. The Copernican reversal persists: reason, turning back on itself, discovers that the problems of transcendent metaphysics are generated entirely by ourselves. So, whatever considerable achievements have been made in the Aesthetic and Analytic, (a still frustrated) reason has not been made assuagingly transparent to itself, and shown to be coherent. This is the main, new work of the Dialectic.

Even if one is persuaded by the above, some critics think deep and embarrassing questions remain, from how can we identify or distinguish (so count, etc.) things in themselves, to how should we conceive the synthetic activities of the object-constituting subject. What are appearances, what are things in themselves, how do things in themselves relate to appearances, and (so) what is our proper relation to things in themselves in terms of (descriptive) thought and knowledge? To get things on the table, I'll be fairly baldly assertive. First, appearances are empirically real, not definitively mental states (for which *esse* is *percipi* or *concipi*, i.e. which depend on being perceived or conceived) – though one species of appearances, viewed empirically, namely objects of inner sense, are mental states – not phenomenalistic constructions out of experiences, *not correctly defined in terms of ANY traditional ontology* (again, for example, B303). Transcendental logical explanations are not like any traditional ontological inventories or explanations. (So, for example, being subject to the conditions of experienceability (necessarily relating to intuition) in no way implies being composed of experience; and rule-governed *a priori* synthesis is nothing like the phenomenalist's logical construction of objects). The decisive distinction between transcendental idealism and transcendental realism is that the former affirms and the latter denies that that our mode of cognition determines the (generic, structural) constitution of its objects, so are contradictory views on the possibility of knowing things in themselves (in the sense of things with fully determinate, intrinsic constitutions). Empirical objects are all *appearances* only in the transcendental sense (from the point of view of transcendental logic). We can classify objects into ontological kinds (for example, mental and non-mental) only after the conditions for cognition of an accessible world have been satisfied. So transcendental discourse cannot use concepts of these ontological kinds in seeking these conditions. So calling appearances nothing but representations, or *mere* representations, and thus determinations of the self, is not at all ontological classification. Kant is bypassing as fruitless the debate, if taken as metaphysical, between a causal representative realist like Locke and an idealist like Berkeley – a plague on both your houses, endless, non-adjudicatable opponents!

Concerning things in themselves (at least in one sense (use) – I'll elaborate on my caginess shortly), our knowledge of them (for sure) does not determine any object, does not allow object-individuative thinking, and so they cannot be referred to as either singular or plural. We know of their existence without knowing anything (synthetic) *about* them. Remember, the aboutness-relation is the relation-to-an-object, and Kant has already argued that relation to an object requires satisfaction of transcendental conditions, and what satisfies transcendental conditions are only appearances. But what's the status of the affirmation of the existence of things in themselves? It goes beyond experience, so it's obviously not an empirical claim. If the propositions of transcendental philosophy all specify the structure of experience, and are the results of transcendental proofs, it's not a transcendental proposition. Indeed, it is a striking fact that Kant barely argues for the existence of things in themselves at all, though he's convinced they must exist. It's not a piece of transcendent metaphysics either, since transcendent objects are positively, determinately conceived (are noumena in the positive sense), and the concept of the thing in itself is properly a boundary concept (again, at least usually – when one turns to Kant's practical (moral) concerns, things get messier, especially as regards the self in itself).

So what's the basis for affirming the existence of things in themselves? Again, it plays no role in the constitution of objectivity; that's done by the transcendental object (object in general = x). And even if we unhesitatingly agree that appearances require the concept of the thing in itself, it doesn't follow that there must exist things in themselves (this issue will become prominent when we discuss the relation between the empirical self (character) and moral self, more specifically between practical freedom and transcendental freedom, near the end of the Antinomies). And we can't say that the thing in itself is needed to cause appearances, both because saying so would just beg the question, but more deeply because (as the Second Analogy purports to show) causality is a schematized category, so only applies within the realm of experience. And it's not to be identified with the unconditioned of the Dialectic which is invoked to explain the realm of appearance, which is not self-explanatory, but for which we seek explanation. At best the unconditioned is a regulative idea (of reason), and regulative ideas are not necessary to the account of the possibility of experience in the way constitutive concepts (of the understanding) are.

7.3.7   A fuller analysis of the Transcendental Dialectic

To make further headway, let's plunge directly into the *Transcendental Dialectic*. *Transcendental Dialectic* reintroduces the problem which initiated the critique of reason: unavoidable but illusory metaphysics. The task is to account for this, and provide a constructive solution. The solution depends on distinguishing constitutive and regulative unity. Their conflation yields the unconditioned as object.

There are three types of unconditioned:

1   Absolute thinking subject which is a substance (basis for others), simple, a person, known as external objects aren't, and (corollaries)

immaterial, incorruptible, spiritual, and (real goal of rational or speculative psychology) immortal.

2 The cosmos (totality of things and conditions in space and time).

3 God.

Reason is now used more narrowly in contrast with *understanding*. Reason's
goal is to *regulate* understanding by unifying judgments (supplied by the
understanding) into *scientia* (expounded in a system of syllogisms), but it
naturally adopts a *constitutive* (object-constituting) role, prompted by the need
to posit an *unconditioned* to stop the otherwise endless regress of explanations
(*ascending* conditions), and so achieve systematicity, its goal; that natural shift
generates *dialectical* or *transcendental* illusion. Different illusions have specifically different diagnoses as well, but all judgment-distorting transcendental
illusion stems from *transcendental realism* (claims to (theoretically) know
things as they are in themselves), and can only be deeply diagnosed and defused
by *transcendental idealism* (which correctly makes and properly marshals the
distinction between *things as they are in themselves* and *things as they appear* (and
its correlates within the fleshed-out Copernican framework, such as the
analytic–synthetic distinction). Understanding is the source of its own
concepts, the categories (the fundamental structure of the understanding).
Reason does not have its own concepts. *Ideas* of reason are formed by
extending the categories, shown to apply only to objects which are objects of
possible experience, beyond possible experience, as if they were about *transcendent* objects. As ideas of unconditioned totalities they have a legitimate,
indeed vital, regulative use (minimally, as *methodological* imperatives to unify,
simplify, systematize – mere *ideals*, but influential in how we approach the
empirical world). But as ideas of real and (theoretically) knowable objects,
they are provably illicit. And from the *practical* point of view, an importantly
different story is forthcoming; in that context, ideas do more than order our
thought about the empirical world.

So transcendental illusion stems from the nature of reason itself; a
philosopher can't make it disappear (since reason has a need for something
unconditioned), but can keep us from being tricked. The illusion is generated by ambiguities (for example, between logical subject and real subject as
knowable objects), which lead to reification (hypostatization), and cannot be
exposed by formal logic alone, but requires the lessons of transcendental
logic. Only transcendental (critical) philosophy (transcendental idealism)
enables a critique of pure, theoretical reason.

Regulative unifiers (ideas of pure reason) have methodological, not
constitutive function with respect to knowledge. Experience necessarily
shows us only parts of reality. Reason rightly seeks to put these parts
together into a whole – a goal demanded by reason, but never something
given. (Science is a never-ending search for knowledge.) The limitations of
theoretical reason clear the field for pure practical reason (postulates of practical reason), and for faith (i.e. recognition of pure practical reason, i.e.

morality conceived in terms of freedom (autonomy, agency) and its requirements).

The three purported unconditioneds are the self, the world, and God.
Kant treats them in turn in the *Paralogisms*, the *Antinomies*, and the *Ideal of
Pure Reason*. *Paralogisms* debunks rational psychology, a science of non-empirical apperception (the "I think," its sole object). It fallaciously moves from
truths about the (general) logical role of the representation "I" as subject to
the object-involving (*real*) sense of subject on which the "I" is a substance (so
permanent), which is simple (so indivisible), conscious of its self-identity (so a
person), and distinct from things in space (so that mind–body dualism is
true). So, for example, all "I am simple" (second paralogism) amounts to is that
the representation "I" does not contain any manifold (since it has no content
at all); and (fourth paralogism) that I distinguish myself from things outside
me, including my body, does not entail that my existence is independent of
my body. Rational psychologists invalidly infer the synthetic from the exclusively analytic. As we saw in *Transcendental Analytic*, transcendental
apperception is a precondition for the application of the concept of substance
(along with the other categories), so cannot be a form of the concept of
substance. (So, to address one famously vexing question, at least from the
theoretical point of view, the "I" is not a thing, and so *if* we mean by activity
something that entails change of state of a thing, synthesis is not an
activity.)

Antinomies arise when reason seeks the conditions for everything empirical
(the absolute totality in the synthesis of appearances) – seeks:

1   the totality of appearances in space and time,
2   the complete decomposition of appearances,
3   the totality of causal conditions of appearances, and
4   the totality of existential conditions of (contingent, so not self-explanatory)
    appearances.

(Note that 3 and 4 capture the two possible versions of cosmological
argument to the unexplained explainer). The conundrum we confront here
is that cosmological ideas do seem essentially to express reason itself, but
contradict each other, humiliating reason. This is the continuous vacillation
between dogmatic assertion and counter-assertion, sometimes prompting
skeptical despair, that Kant bemoans in the Preface. Since they loom largest
in the Dialectic, I will devote the most attention to the Antinomies.

To appreciate the pivotal role of the Antinomies, we need to understand
their basic features. The first and the second are *mathematical*, concerned
with magnitude; the third and fourth are *dynamical*, concerned with
causality and existence. In each case, theses treat the world of experience as
a closed, limited whole, and invoke intelligible (non-empirical) objects to
explain appearances, antitheses treat the world of experience as unclosed,
and remain in that world of experience to explain appearances. (Therefore,)

theses always satisfy the interests of practical reason (religion and morality), antitheses always threaten them. In every case the contradictions stem from transcendental realism (here supposing that the cosmos is a determinate object which thus has to have exactly one of every pair of contradictory properties). But the theses always go too far, the antitheses not far enough.

Transcendental idealism exposes the mistakes in rational cosmological reasoning, and brings reason in harmony with itself. It can make plain that two different conceptions of the unconditioned are operative, and that (more deeply) appearances are being confused with things in themselves, such that any defense of theses contradicts the nature of experience, but any defense of antitheses attributes a false self-subsistence to the realm of experience. But the way transcendental idealism solves the antinomies significantly varies. With the mathematical, it shows that thesis and antithesis rest on a false presupposition which renders them both false – thesis and antithesis are contraries, not contradictories. With the dynamical, we cannot reject both as false without destroying the interests of morality and religion, and (only) transcendental idealism shows us how both can be true, such that the transcendental illusion resides in the appearance of incompatibility. I will substantially expand on these features, and in doing so, aim to explain the crucial role of the Antinomies. I will discuss the first antinomy as representative of the mathematical, and the upshot of the third antinomy as representative of the dynamical.

Best understood, the overall argument involving the first two antinomies goes as follows:

1 Transcendental realism implies that the world (the sum of all appearances) is a whole existing in itself.
2 If the world is a whole existing in itself, then it is either finite or infinite (in the relevant respects specified by the various arguments in the first two antinomies).
3 But (the arguments for theses and antitheses show) the world is neither finite nor infinite.
4 So transcendental realism is false.
5 Transcendental idealism is true if and only if transcendental realism is false.
6 So transcendental idealism is true.

Reason's conflict with itself has its roots in reason's demand for an absolute totality of conditions (grounds) for any conditioned, which is a consequence of the principle that if the conditioned is given (*gegeben*), the entire sum of conditions, and consequently the absolutely unconditioned (through which alone the conditioned has been possible) is also given (A409). This principle (A416) reflects the logical principle of sufficient reason (PSR). Application of PSR to the whole spatiotemporal world immediately gives rise to the set of cosmological Ideas – when the categories (those involving the thought of a synthesis of subordinate elements or conditions) are extended to the unconditioned. Kant uses the "skeptical method," examining the presuppositions underlying the dispute, revealing that both sides (thesis (Newton) and antithesis (Leibniz)) share the initially plausible but ultimately incoherent conception of the sensible world (entailed by all transcendental realisms) as a whole existing in itself (which entails that one of two contradictories must be true). Reject the common assumption and the contradiction between thesis and antithesis vanishes, and is replaced by a dialectical opposition between contraries, which are both false.

Before explaining more fully Kant's diagnosis of the mathematical antinomies, let's consider the following sketches of the arguments of the first antinomy, as applied to time.

Thesis: The world has a beginning in time.
1   Suppose that the world has no beginning in time.
2   Then an infinite past series has elapsed prior to any given time t.
3   But it is impossible that an infinite past series has elapsed.
4   So the world does have a beginning in time.

Antithesis: The world has no beginning; it is temporally infinite.
1   Suppose the world has a beginning in time.
2   Then there must have been a time in which the world was not, i.e., an empty time.
3   But a thing cannot come to be in an empty time (would violate PSR).
4   So the world cannot have a beginning in time.

According to Kant, anyone who regards appearances as if they were things in themselves (any transcendental realist) is committed, given PSR (and so the intellectual imperative to seek conditions, an imperative with a wholly legitimate regulative function), to presuppose the presence of sufficient conditions for every given conditioned. But since this applies in turn to every specified condition, it requires that the absolute totality of conditions be presupposed as given. This absolute totality is what is meant by "the world" – "world" is taken to have a referent, in itself, that is, independently of conditions of empirical synthesis (empirical accessibility). The synthesis that generates this conception of the world is a synthesis of mere *understanding*, an intellectual synthesis (B150–1) – distinguished from a figurative synthesis, the transcendental synthesis of imagination – considering things according to their mere concept (as if they were noumena). There would be nothing wrong with this if not for the fact that the objects or states of affairs that the transcendental realist regards in this manner are empirical, and so can't be meaningfully referred to in abstraction from the conditions under which they are given in empirical synthesis. For example, they disregard time order (A500) and so assume a tenseless logic with respect to inherently temporal items. Note that this tenseless view (*sub specie aeternitatis*) is at bottom a God's-eye view of things, which ties in with another broad theme of the *Critique*, namely that transcendental realists are committed to a theocentric model of knowledge, and that what's needed is (a carefully circumscribed) anthropocentric model of knowledge (i.e. the critical, transcendental, or Copernican point of view). Kant's point is that without his transcendental distinction (which factors in epistemic conditions), it is perfectly natural, that is, rational, to assume that the totality of conditions for any conditioned is *gegeben*, even when the conditioned and its conditions are states of affairs (see A497, 409, 307–8, 330–3, 336–7, 416) and not propositions (see A499–500 for diagnosis of fallacy as *sophisma figurae dictionis*).

A few noteworthy features of the *Ideal*: the critique is set up by analyzing the idea of God as a composite of three more basic ideas: of highest being, necessary being, and author of nature. Its genesis is as follows. Reason requires an *absolutely necessary being*. The core concept of God is that of *the highest being* (being with the highest degree of reality). If a highest being exists, it exists necessarily. But reason strives to unify its ideas, so highest being is *identified with* absolutely necessary being (affirming converse too). So the *idea* of the highest being is reified, treated as transcendent *being*. But monotheistic religions require personal deities. So add to highest and necessary being properties such as being personal creator and you get the God of religion. The ontological argument focuses on highest being. The cosmological argument focuses on necessary being. The physico-teleological argument (from design) focuses on author of nature. All theoretical arguments for God's existence reduce to these. But the full success of the design argument rests on the cosmological argument, and the full success of the cosmological argument rests on the ontological argument, hence the success of all of (theoretical) rational theology rests on the ontological argument. Understanding why this is so, and why the ontological argument fails, deepens our mastery of Kant's philosophy.

I omit elaboration of Kant's critique of rational theology because I have provided sustained discussion of the three main theological arguments earlier (the ontological in section 1.8, the cosmological in section 6.12, and *physico-teleological* (design) in section 6.11), and because in this chapter Kant's distinction between analytic and synthetic judgment, and the postulates of empirical thought (on the meaning of possibility, existence, and necessity) provide the basis for his famous objections to the ontological argument. (*The* most famous objection is that *existence* is not a first-order, descriptive (i.e. real, determining) predicate (specifying what object you are talking about), but a second-order predicate, a predicate specifying that an already-specified set of predicates is exemplified, or applies in the world. This squarely foreshadows the Fregean treatment of existence in modern logic.)

7.3.8   The transition from theoretical to practical philosophy

Remember that for me transcendental idealism is at bottom a unique philosophical *method* that entails a new, defensible way of doing epistemology and metaphysics, which has major implications for ethics and religion. The Antinomies support transcendental idealism indirectly (aiming to prove it, or at least show that it is superior to all extant expressions of transcendental realism) by arguing that it uniquely relieves inconsistencies in theoretical reason, and protects ideas needed for morality and religion by finding their proper role in practical, not theoretical contexts. All four do the first by showing that transcendental realism can't explain reason's disposition to contradiction, but that transcendental idealism can (by properly drawing and applying the things in themselves–appearances distinction). The third and fourth (dynamical) antinomies, together with the Paralogisms, Ideal, second Appendix to the Dialectic on The Final Purpose of the Natural Dialectic of Human Reason, and (culminating in the) Canon, do the second, and point squarely forward to the completion of Critical philosophy in the *Critique of Practical Reason* and *Critique of Judgment*.

The most important argument that emerges from Kant's solution to the third antinomy and subsequent analysis of practical freedom concludes that theoretically, human freedom is possible (compatible with determinism), and that practically, we know we're free. I'll explain his account in a moment. But it's helpful to embed it within a larger set of three commitments about reason. First, *all* the ideas of reason are *problematic*, meaning that they cannot be ruled in *or* out by theoretical reason. They are all extensions of concepts of the understanding beyond the accessible (experienceable) driven by the (moral and theological) interests of practical reason. When ruled in, when treated as theoretically constitutive, as necessarily having a determinate object (as in the transcendent metaphysics of God, the immortal soul, and the free agent), they have been proven indefensible. But that doesn't entail the theoretical defensibility of their negations, since they properly behave merely regulatively, as ideals, and the logic of ideals is different from the logic of determinate conditions (general plus transcendental logic). (For example, a fully comprehensive and systematic science (of natural explanation and prediction) is merely an ideal, and so does not rule out new beginnings through causality of freedom.) Replacing dogmatic theoretical metaphysics with Critical theoretical metaphysics removes impediments to a *practical* dogmatic metaphysics deducible from pure practical reason (this is what he means when he famously concludes that he had to deny *knowledge* to make room for *faith*). Well, even if the path for practical dogmatic metaphysics (whose central concept is *will*) is cleared, should we take it? Kant does, thus assuming that, second, the interests of practical reason take precedence over competing interests of theoretical reason, so long as it doesn't bring theoretical reason into conflict with itself (a theme foreshadowed at the start, in the Prefaces).

An interesting aside to consider is whether this means that Kant is ancestor to will-to-believe doctrines, such that when momentous choices are intellectually undecidable, it is not only permissible but necessary for our passional natures to prevail? No, since Kantian will is quite unlike Humean/Pascalian/Jamesean will, but is itself in a strong sense a species of rationality. I instance the famous contrast: whoever wills the end wills the indispensably necessary means to that end; but not: whoever desires (or is otherwise disposed toward) the end desires what's essential to achieving that end.

This obligatory respect by practical reason for theoretical reason is indicative of a more general commitment, also signaled up front by Kant, namely, third, that rationality (by its very nature) requires that theoretical and practical rationality be integrated, form a unity. This is best (exclusively?) understandable in terms of Copernicanism: our rational powers must be answerable only to themselves, not things in themselves. Kant infers from this that our rational powers must carry their ends within themselves; that's how teleology first enters his system. I will not comment on the role of teleology, which becomes increasingly important as the Critical system unfolds – that it is prominent in the *Critique of Judgment* is clear; that it is influential in the *Critique of Practical Reason* too is arguable, despite the acknowledged fact that Kant squarely rejects teleological ethical theories such as utilitarianism (the teleology appears in the conception of agency itself – it's *heteronymous* teleology that's repudiated). And reason's ultimate (highest) end is not to gain knowledge, but to will the highest good, to be morally worthy, and to be happy because we're morally worthy. But in achieving its highest end it *does* gain knowledge – morality accomplishes what rational psychology unsuccessfully sought, namely the possibility of knowing ourselves as legislating completely *a priori* in regard to our own existence. This is one of many examples of how, rerouted by the chastening of critique, pure reason (now in practical employment) attains what it was ineradicably disposed to seek, but could not find (in theoretical employment).

Now we can sketch Kant's account of practical freedom.[5] *Practical freedom* is our (ostensible) capacity to act on the basis of reasons or general principles, the power of rational agency we attribute to humans but not animals (and since humans are not angels, and have non-rational and potentially idiosyncratic wants, these reasons or principles take the form of imperatives). *Spontaneity* is independence of the causality of nature, which includes sensuous motives or inclinations. This is a species of *negative freedom*, freedom from the given. Earlier Kant argued that we can become aware of apperception, the spontaneity of theoretical thinking (though not as a determinate object). The spontaneity of acting involves this same spontaneity of thinking, but also the capacity to set goals and resist the pull of inclinations attracting us away from those goals. It makes sense to talk of degrees of spontaneity. *Transcendental freedom* is the limiting case of spontaneity, complete independence from everything sensible (from all sensible affection), empirically unconditioned, absolute spontaneity, the power of beginning a new, empirical, causal series. *Autonomy* is the capacity to determine oneself sufficiently to act on the basis of considerations independent of one's inclinations as a sensuous being, a form of motivational independence. As self-determination (self-legislation), it is a species of *positive freedom*. *Willkür* is Kant's term for the human will. *Wille* is pure practical reason, the *a priori* structure of *Willkür* (and fully constitutes a holy will). Practical freedom is to transcendental freedom as human freedom is to divine freedom (see, for example, section 9, III of the Antinomy and the Canon, section 1). What does this analogy mean? I believe it does not entail that the reality of practical freedom requires the reality of transcendental freedom. Consciousness of acting establishes our relative spontaneity, but there can be no consciousness of absolute spontaneity. Practical freedom requires the (coherent) *idea* of transcendental freedom; transcendental freedom (intelligent, noumenal causality) serves a regulative function, provides a model for forming the notion of practical freedom, a model which allows us to think of the causes of actions as *normative*, again, as *reasons*. (An equivalent formulation is the distinction between two ways in which the efficacy of the agent's activity can be considered – in its empirical character, and in its intelligible character). If the complete explicability and predictability of human actions and transcendental freedom were theoretically determinate concepts, they would be incompatible, and practical freedom would be impossible. But they are both merely regulative Ideas, which can coexist (just as generalization and specification are simultaneous, legitimate, "contrary" regulative laws of scientific inquiry).

So what does this amount to in familiar terms? Sensuous motives, desires, are causally efficacious, and every action one ever performs is influenced by desires. But as we intuitively think, we can be influenced by desires without those desires being the sole, sufficient explanation of our action – indeed, for our action to be an *action*, and not just a behavior or bodily movement, it must be more than the causal consequence of antecedent, natural states (action is a partly normative concept). Kant seems to argue that desires lack pre-assigned weights. Their relative efficacy depends on our evaluation of them (the invocation of normative principles, judgments and inferences). This appeal to principles is something the subject does (and must do) for itself (a form of spontaneity). This is where all the detail of actions always being conceived under maxims (subjective policy statements), etc. of Kant's famous foundations for ethics comes in. The overarching point

---

5   There are large volumes on this, including for recommendation Allison 1990, so apologies for my starkly truncated rendition.

is that in practical reason, just as in theoretical reason, we must look to the subject for sources of justification – nothing transcendent, like God, or empirical, like human nature, will do, and the fundamental feature of the subject here is its power of willing. Transcendental idealism is required to decouple morality from the speculative use of reason, which has previously inhibited its proper grounding. Critical philosophy does not prove the reality of freedom, but allows it to be thought, and that is all morality requires (given its essentially non-theoretical nature). So, in the theoretical sphere pure reason was right to relinquish autonomy to understanding, and adopt for itself only regulative use. But pure practical reason is constitutive of its principles having objective reality, since when practical reason functions non-empirically, its objects are just the ones the subject creates (and here we do mean "creation," and not just "constitutes in its generic, formal respects"); the concepts of pure practical reason need not await intuitions to acquire meaning since they produce the reality of that to which they refer, namely a morally good determination of the will. We do in the practical sphere what only an intuitive intellect could do in the theoretical sphere, namely create our own objects.

As I've (controversially) said before, though, I think Kant treats rational agency (practical freedom) as broader in scope than moral agency (action according to categorical imperatives, or out of respect for the Moral Law). But we've said enough on this topic to appreciate section 7.4 on Kant's practical philosophy.

7.4 The philosophical foundations for moral theory

This is a perfect segue to Kant's ethical theory, or, more accurately, his philosophical foundations for ethical theory, focusing on the *Groundwork of the Metaphysics of Morals*. Section I of the *Groundwork* tells us that the analysis of the key concept of ordinary moral thinking, the concept of good will, reveals three propositions of morality: (1) describes the kind of motive a person must have to be properly called morally good, namely one inducing action for the sake of, and not just in accordance with, duty, a motive distinct from – neither entails nor is in conflict with – the person's inclinations. A person's striving resolutely to do his duty for duty's sake is not only necessary, but sufficient for being morally good; success in action is inessential. (2) concerns the moral worth or value of the good will, answering the question of the basis of its value for (1) to be true. It must have unconditional worth, so based solely on the principle which it exemplifies, and not dependent on bringing about ends, in which case it would only be means, conditional on ends. (3) describes the kind of emotion or internal attitude that characterizes a person's state of mind when he is motivated by a good will, which is a deep cause of the binding obligation to obey the moral law, respect for the moral law, and not kindness, benevolence, or love, which are inclinations, inappropriate to doing duty just because it's duty. In effect, Kant begins with the datum that it is the resolute intentions of a person that we count in ascribing moral worth (1), and elicits (2) and (3) as immediate implications of this datum. He hasn't yet addressed the question of the criterion of duty, but begins to do so at the end of Section I, arguing that (i) the standard can't be the utility of action, and so must be conformity of action to rule or principle, and that (ii) valid moral rules, which must be universal (applying without exception) and necessary (not contingent on the way the world happens to be at a time), must be justified by their satisfaction of the categorical imperative, which is explicitly or implicitly acknowledged by any person who acknowledges an act to be his moral duty. A rule binding the will independent of inclinations and purposes must be one that demands (since it's all that's left to demand) that the person act on a maxim (policy, principle) which he, as a rational being, could prescribe as a rule for every person to act on.

Section II tells us that for a rule to be a moral rule, validly binding all in the way described in Section I, it must prescribe to us categorically (independently of our ends), not hypothetically (dependent on ends). Different formulations of the categorical imperative follow, highlighting key aspects of morality's supreme principle even if, as I think they are, equivalent. A moral rule must (a) be consistently universalizable, (b) be such that, if all people were to follow it, they would treat each other as ends in themselves, never as means merely, and (c) be capable of being self-imposed by the will of each person when he is universally legislating, that is, deciding to adopt rules for the guidance of his and others' conduct. These need elaboration and defense.

Section III tries to show that there is a moral law whose nature has been analyzed in I and II, that morality is a fact. This is done in three main steps. (1) If men have free will, they are obliged to obey the categorical imperative, since freedom is identical with autonomy ("the property of the will to be a law to itself," self-legislation or self-determination), and as Section II showed, autonomy is just one way of expressing the categorical imperative. (2) One is free, from the practical point of view, as far as moral choice is concerned, if he must conceive himself as being free when he is using his practical reason in deliberating about what he ought to do, and all rational beings must so conceive themselves in that they take their reasons for action to be *their* reasons, and not influences forced from without. (3) To account for freedom in a world which can only be known in terms of cause and effect, we must adopt two standpoints from which to understand humans, one in terms of explanation by appeal to causes of behavior and thought, fitting humans into the order of the empirical world of nature, the other as a rational being confronted with choices yet bound by moral rules. The key question is whether there's a metaphysical underpinning of this dual perspective, or is this just a way of looking at our situation?

Our task is to find an object of the moral will, which, while standing in a necessary relation to the will and serving as a guide to moral action, would not destroy the freedom of the agent. The solution is that the object of the will must be determined by the will itself: free will must be the object of the will, maintained by willing according to universality of law. If the good stands in no relation to the will, then it is not the determining ground of the will; it in no way binds the will. If the good stands in a contingent relation to the will, then it cannot provide an objective maxim or practical law, but is peculiar to persons at times, and is not binding either. If the good is distinct from the will and has the power to determine the will to action, then it destroys the will. The will can't be free and, so, responsible unless it is unconditioned; the will must freely elect the good as its object. Therefore, all practical principles which presuppose an object of desire as the determining ground of the will are without exception empirical and can furnish no practical laws. And note also that if the good were the necessary object of desire, it would always be sought, and virtue would become identical with happiness, which is false. In confronting the good as heterogeneous, the agent confronts the good as object of (multiple) desire and the moral law. The moral law tells him what he ought to do as a self-legislating member of the "intelligible world," not what he must do as a member of the natural world, revealing simultaneously the agent's duty and freedom.

I'll now focus more on Section II of the *Groundwork*, then on Section III and the associated metaphysics from the first *Critique*. I begin with a plausible rendition of Kant's argument for the Categorical Imperative.

1   Let us say that an agent *chooses* a state of affairs S in a situation T if and only if the agent, in situation T, would perform any act he believed he knew to be an indispensable means to actualizing S. (S and T are descriptions of types of states of affairs and situations, and not particular states of affairs or particular situations.)

2   Let us also say that an *imperative* is of the form, "in situation T, (you ought to) actualize state of affairs S."

3   Such an imperative can be *binding* on an agent only if the agent chooses S in T. (premise)

4   An imperative is *categorical* if and only if it is one that is necessarily binding on any rational agent. (definition)

5   Therefore, an imperative is categorical if and only if it commands the actualization of a state of affairs S in situation T that necessarily, any rational agent would choose in T. (3, 4)

6   *To adopt a maxim* that commands the actualization of S in T is to choose S in T. (definition)

7   Therefore, an imperative is categorical if and only if it is a maxim that necessarily would be adopted by any rational agent. (5, 6)

8   An agent adopts an imperative on *inclinational* grounds if and only if he is inclined to strive for a means he believes he knows will actualize the state of affairs whose actualization is commanded by the imperative, and would not strive for it were he not so inclined. (definition)

9   No inclination is necessarily present in all rational agents. (premise)
10   Therefore, an imperative is categorical if and only if it is adopted by no agent only on inclinational grounds. (7, 8, 9)
11   The only grounds besides inclinational are *purely rational* grounds.
12   An imperative is categorical if it is adopted by all rational agents on rational grounds. (7, 10, 11)
13   Every moral law is a categorical imperative. (definition of "moral," from Section I)
14   If there is such a thing as a moral law, one ought never to act in violation of it.
15   There is such a thing as a moral law. (premise, to be pursued in Section III)
16   Therefore, one ought never to act according to a maxim unless it would necessarily be adopted by any rational agent on purely rational grounds. (12, 13, 14, 15)
     (16) is equivalent to:

(c1) Do not adopt a maxim unless necessarily, any rational agent would adopt it on rational grounds alone, which is one central way the Categorical Imperative has been interpreted.

Three other (possibly equivalent) interpretations we should keep in mind as we proceed are these:

(c2) Do not adopt a maxim if you could wish, on rational grounds alone, that it not be adopted by everyone.
(c3) Do not adopt a maxim whose adoption by everyone is (in some sense) an impossibility.
(c4) Do not adopt a maxim whose adoption by everyone is contrary to natural (i.e. teleological) law, whose adoption would inhibit the progress of mankind toward a harmonious coexistence.

To round out the initial outline, note that Kant argues that the validity of the Categorical Imperative (c1) is the condition of the very possibility of action, as follows:

17   To *act* is to act according to a maxim adopted on purely rational grounds (for now a premise, but to be defended on the grounds that genuine agency requires what Kant calls *positive freedom*, which entails 18.) As positive freedom turns out to be autonomy, one begins to see why the universalizability and autonomy formulations are equivalent.
18   Therefore, to act is to act according to a categorical imperative. (12, 17)
19   Every categorical imperative is a moral law. (premise, converse of 13)
20   There is such a thing as action. (premise)
21   Therefore, there is such a thing as action according to a moral law. (18, 19, 20)

22 There is such a thing as a moral law. (21)

The preceding seems to me to provide a logically valid argument for (c1). The question is whether the argument is sound, whether all its premises are true as well. In the process of assessing soundness, and perhaps revising premises in order to achieve soundness, I hope to clarify Kant's *Groundwork* for you. I hope also to relate Kant's ethics and metaphysics in a helpful way.

A few interpretive remarks in a first, partial attempt to understand Kant's argument: a maxim (or principle of volition) is a rule of conduct that has been adopted by reason as a policy of action. Kant holds that in rational action, reason does not will to do this particular act A in this particular situation S, but instead wills that acts of a relevant kind be done in situations of a relevant kind, that acts in a certain respect similar to A always be done in situations in a certain respect similar to S. Remember that reason, unlike sensibility, distinguishes things by general principles only. Since reason cannot distinguish between indiscernible acts and situations, its willings are always of the form "always do an act of type X in a situation of type Y," its willings are always that certain maxims be adopted. (By contrast, irrationalist ethical theory such as existentialism or situationism seems to deny just this claim, or more precisely, the claim that moral agency requires adoption of general policy; presumably such theorists deny that moral agency is rational agency at all.)

Kant then introduces the distinction between a *material maxim*, one that directs us to pursue some particular (type of) end, and a *formal maxim*, which mentions no particular (type of) end. He says that an act's moral worth derives from the formal properties of the maxim it exemplifies. This talk of the formal properties of the maxim is misleading. What Kant is saying is that the value of an act derives from the motivation the agent has; and a motivation that confers moral worth on an act must be one present in all rational agents, and does not depend on the particular inclinations of the agent. The reasoning behind this seems to be the following: morally valuable acts are universally valuable; in particular, moral obligations are universally binding. Now, striving for a particular end can always be rejected, as lacking value, if the agent is not inclined toward the end. So those maxims that mention a particular end cannot be maxims that all rational agents have a motivation to adopt. So the moral value of an act cannot derive from the end whose fulfillment is intended. We might say: if motivation is the basis of moral value, and if moral value is universal, then the motivation for moral action must be universal, and so cannot depend on aiming for certain particular, rejectable ends. Of course, the main point of dispute here is whether motivation is the basis of moral value. Kant has tried to show that this is what we all pre-theoretically believe in his section I discussion of the sole, unconditional value of the good will. But this is precisely what classical act- and rule-utilitarians openly and centrally reject; motivation is irrelevant to obligation in classical consequentialist ethics. (This is something to reflect on yourself.) Minimally, my point is that, even granting the above, Kant should have said that the source of value is the formal characteristics of the motivation for adopting the maxim, not the formal characteristics of the maxim. He makes the mistake because he often conflates the maxim, conditional or "if–then" in form, with its consequent or "then" component. When the antecedent or "if" condition, which specifies motivation (which he sometimes designates "maxim"), is formal, that is, specifies no particular inclinations or ends, he calls the whole thing "formal." Appreciating his tendency to confuse the maxim with its consequent helps appreciate his deep point.

As I have been using "maxim" so far, maxims are conditional, but their antecedents do not include specification for motivation. Instead, I talk of motivation ("reasons") for adopting a maxim (policy for doing A in S). The bottom line here is simply that moral worth lies in the agent's adopting the maxim for some reason other than to fulfill a certain end. The only alternative for Kant seems to be that the morally good agent's reason for acting must be the *rightness* of the action. Whether these are exhaustive alternatives, and what "the action's rightness" means, need to be decided.

A few more terminological points complete the first, partial confrontation with Section II. The way Kant talks, all maxims are *subjective* principles (principles adopted by subjects), but not all are merely subjective; some are *objective* as well; objective is a species of subjective, not its contrary. Objective maxims are binding on all agents. And objective maxims may be called *practical laws*. This last identification is misleading, if we view maxims as policy *prescriptions*, since practical laws are *descriptions* of the way perfectly rational agents necessarily act. Of course they are not descriptions of the way imperfectly rational beings (i.e. moral agents like ourselves) act, but are the bases for prescriptions about how they ought to (try to) act. So we might want to say that objective maxims (prescriptions) "correspond to" practical laws, but are not identical with them. What is really surfacing here is how we are to interpret "agent" throughout Kant's argument. Some things Kant says are true only if he has perfectly rational agents in mind; others are true only if he has imperfectly rational agents in mind. You might think that Kant's fudge is successful in coping with this tension, namely his repeated talk of agents *insofar as* (or qua) they are rational. This is a critical and very interesting issue for Kant's theory and its metaphysical commitments. Related to this is Kant's occasional confusion over *will*. Since will *is* for Kant practical reason (acting according to the dictates of reason), it is impossible that the will "not in itself completely accord with reason," at least if will is *pure* (employed in an *a priori* way) *practical reason*. If one decides this is sloppiness on Kant's part, substitute "the law places an obligation on an imperfect agent" for "the law places an obligation on an imperfect will."

Finally, we can tentatively distinguish *imperatives* as follows: *problematic* – if you were to choose X (where X is something contingent), you ought (then) to Y; *assertoric* – since you choose to be happy, you ought to X; *categorical* – since you choose to act (i.e. be a rational agent), you ought to X. Since, Kant seems to argue, no agent can choose not to act (since to so choose is already to act), the "since" of the categorical covers all rational agents, and is essential to agency. The "since" of the assertoric is only de facto.

Let me round out this sketch of Section II by relating Kant's various formulations of the Categorical Imperative. First, concerning the variants on the universalizability formulation, notice that if "impossibility" in (c3) means "teleological impossibility," then (c3) is tantamount to (c4). Also, if what all rational agents on solely rational grounds would adopt is always what all wishers (see c2), influenced by rational grounds alone, would adopt, then (c1) entails (c2) as well. So if our argument establishes (c1), it also (on the supposition articulated) establishes (c2) and (c3), and if further it can be shown that what is rationally necessary is teleologically necessary, then (c4) is established also. Now according to a teleological conception, nature has purposes that are manifested in the laws of nature. And so we might try to support the (at least *prima facie* plausible) move from (c1) to (c4) as follows: according to Kant, noumenal agency creates phenomenal reality. So no consistent maxim, when adopted by all rational agents, will result in phenomena which obey inconsistent laws of nature. Thus any maxim whose universal acceptance would be contrary to the present laws of nature must be inconsistent with maxims noumenal agents have in fact adopted. So, to adopt a maxim incompatible with the natural law that noumenal agents have in fact helped to establish is to disobey the Imperative's injunction to act only according to non-contradictory maxims (c3), which follows from (c1). (c1) prohibits maxims which conflict with the laws of nature, which are expressions of purpose. So (c1) entails (c4). What do you think of that argument?

Now let's bring in the other formulations of the Imperative, via a general line of thinking. What does it mean to enjoin that one act for the sake of persons? Not to act for their welfare, which would be a subjective end. Rather to act so as to allow *people* to *be* what they are. What are they? Rational agents. Act so as to preserve the autonomy of persons. But to be an autonomous, rational agent is to be able to *act*, so the Imperative commands us to act so as to allow people to act. Since action (unlike mere behavior) is necessarily free, freedom is an end having absolute worth.

A question remains whether freedom is the sole *intrinsic* value. It doesn't seem so. For example, happiness is good for its own sake, and freedom doesn't guarantee happiness. But is freedom the sole *absolute* or *unconditional* good? It would be, if a truly free will is a good will, given that the only thing that has unconditional worth is a good will, and supposing that worth and goodness are interchangeable concepts.

For a categorical imperative to bind an agent is for the agent to adopt it. But an imperative adopted by an agent (on purely rational grounds) is adopted by all (on rational grounds), and so is unconditionally binding on all. Hence, a moral law is a maxim that an agent can transform into a universal law merely by adopting it. That is, the moral law can be legislated by the will. Such a legislative will must be disinterested, in order for single adoption to suffice for universal bindingness. In a kingdom of ends (a society of purely rational agents) all actions by citizens would be out of respect for laws that are independently but unanimously legislated by all agents. There would be no imposition of law, but only freely chosen respect for the common code. In other words, the ideal social contract is the moral law! Finally, if moral laws are those maxims an agent would will to become universal law, then any agent would so will them, so that a law can never direct one to *use* a person as a means alone, for then the agent would will to make a universal law in which he is used, but that is nonsense, for it would undermine his own agency.

What about freedom, moral selves, and their relations to moral action? Kant holds that "ought" implies "can" in two senses – first in the sense of freedom from compulsion (negative freedom), second in the sense of capacity for (autonomous) self-determined action (positive freedom). It is tradition-ally argued that both these kinds of freedom require that moral agents be noumenal. For first, phenomenal beings are governed by natural law and so lack freedom. Since all beings are either phenomenal or noumenal, and moral agency requires negative freedom, moral agents must be noumenal. It follows from this that moral agents are supersensible beings divorced from all sensuous conditions, and so their will can only be determined by the *a priori* moral law in a wholly *a priori* way. (And the converse entailment holds too: so X is noumenal if and only if it is supersensible if and only if it is determined wholly *a priori*.) And second, autonomy, required for moral agency, also requires isolation from all sensuous conditions, and so again the agent's will must be determined in a wholly *a priori* way, and so the agent must be a supersensuous noumenon.

This traditional view can't be an adequate account of our moral agency. For first, agents are obliged only if negatively free to choose rightly or wrongly, but if the will is determined by *a priori* law in a wholly *a priori* way, the agent must (necessarily) will in accordance with the law, and so is compelled. And second, since untempted by sensuous impulses, the noumenal agent can experience no moral struggle and so cannot be obliged, that is, confronted by imperatives. Noumenal agents have *holy wills* – compelled, untempted wills – not the wills of agents obliged by impera-tives.

To preserve Kant's theory, we seem required to hold that, and explain how, an agent's will must be determinable autonomously by the *a priori* moral law in an *a posteriori* way, and that the agent is neither noumenon nor phenomenon, but some third kind of being (talking for simplicity as if noumena were distinguishable kinds of being at all, which I have denied). That is, the two premises above, that autonomy requires isolation from the sensuous, and that all beings are either phenomenal or noumenal, must be rejected. The first is accomplished by arguing that autonomy only requires self-legislation. If the laws governing the occurrence of impulses of the will are laws of nature, the will is *heteronomous*; if they are laws made by the agent himself in accordance with the moral law which is an *a priori* structure of his own will, the will is autonomous. An agent can be conceived as free to choose to allow natural laws to determine his volitional impulses or to (re)order (*synthesize*) them in obedience to the moral law – to passively allow psychological laws of subjective associations to determine impulses or to actively order such impulses in practical *judgments* or maxims that accord with the moral law.

To compare the way empirical cognitive reason legitimately may employ the Ideas of pure reason (totality, unity, universality, system) as *regulative* principles is to begin to understand where this account is heading. Also, more painstaking analysis would do better than uncritically adopt the locution, "passively allow psychological laws of subjective associations to determine impulses," since passively allowing is not the same as sheer passivity. Passively allowing suggests agency too, as when someone agrees to be another's obedient servant for some specified time. But we need not push so far here.

As regards the second premise, persons, as obliged and obliging agents, are neither things in appearance (phenomenal objects) nor things in themselves (noumenal objects, assuming for simplicity that the concepts of thing in itself and noumenon are equivalent) because they are not *objects* at all. They are *subjects*. They are not objects to which representations are referred via the synthetic activity of judgment, but the subjects which so synthesize representations and refer them to objects (of practical or cognitive judgment, depending on the materials for synthesis, that is, the distinctive features of the representations being organized – it is an underlying supposition of this account that all the faculties Kant discusses (except sensibility) are alternative employments of the single power of synthesis (spontaneity), differentiated by materials for synthesis – for the will, the material is sensuous impulses). Nor can they be mere objects of God's intellectual intuition, for then they would be mere things (in themselves) under the compulsion of a deistic determinism, and just as unfree as phenomena governed by naturalistic determinism, so that the notions of moral reform, cultivation of virtue, etc. are ruled out. So, the requirements for moral agency of positive and negative freedom can be satisfied. An agent's will is empirical practical reason (i.e. synthetic activity ordering empirical representations in accordance with *a priori* rules in a causally efficacious way), capable of lawfully ordering sensuous impulses in accordance with the moral law that is its own *a priori* structure. It is capable of self-legislating autonomy in that the rules according to which sensuous impulses are combined can be legislated by it entirely in accordance with a principle derived from itself. Human will is *Willkür*. The *Wille* (pure practical reason) is a holy will, and can be viewed as the *a priori* structure of the human will. So, positive freedom – autonomy as self-determined law which structures sensuous impulses in practical (i.e. efficacious in the phenomenal world) synthesis – can be given an account within Kant's philosophy. But negative freedom – a requirement of moral agency which, as above, implies that agents are neither phenomenal objects under the compulsion of natural law nor noumenal objects under the compulsion of the moral law but rather temporal and sentient subjects – which requires absolute spontaneity, is inscrutable. However, treated as a regulative Idea whose employment occurs at the interface between cognitive and practical empirical reason, it is susceptible to coherent application, serving to delimit the point at which cognitive cognitions come to an end and the responsibility of practical conditions begins. So, in practical judgments that are intentions to act in some way, we alter the ways in which representations are conjoined and this results in the occurrence of actions and their consequences, which would not have occurred if we had judged otherwise or not at all. Such judgments thus initiate a new causal sequence by intervening in the natural realm already ongoing; freedom is compatible with determinism, in that while all objects of cognition in the temporal realm must be determined by causes, there are occurrences in the temporal realm which are not objects of cognition, namely judgments (free and not caused). This is an important insight for the third *Critique*.

7.5   Kant on philosophical method

I conclude my discussion of the *Critique of Pure Reason* conveying the gist of its often-neglected final one hundred pages, its *Transcendental Doctrine of Method*. It allows us to come full circle by seeing that it is framed by the stage-setting skeptical trilemma about attempts to vindicate reason: the attempted vindication is either based on other, rationally arbitrary, starting points, or is circular, or involves an uncompletable regress of considerations.

Kant distinguishes four elements in his methodological discussion of reason: its needed *discipline* ("the compulsion, by which the constant tendency to disobey certain rules is restrained and finally extirpated" (B737)); its *canon* ("the sum-total of the a priori principles of the correct employment" of pure reason (B824)); its *architectonic* (the exhibition of its achievements, systematically related (B860)); and its (previously disappointing, partial) *history* (from the transcendental point of view) (B880).

An understanding of Kant's approach is derivable from analysis of the *Discipline of Pure Reason*. Critique of reason includes criticism of alternative philosophical methods. So (Section 1) the dogmatists (rationalists) doubly wrongly model all rational method on mathematics, construed analytically, with proofs based on axioms and definitions. And (Section 2) the skeptics wrongly treat reason as polemic (war) whose goal is victory. But critique also aims at constructive vindication. Kant alerts us to his own position from the very beginning of the book (for example Bvii and xiii), frames the Doctrine of Method in terms of it (B735), and outlines it subsequently (B736–40). I highlight a main feature of his line of thought.

Recall that Ideas of Reason are precepts for seeking unity of thought and action (for answering the questions reason ultimately has an interest in, namely "What can I know?" "What ought I do?" and "What may I hope for?"), not archetypes that ensure that unity can be found. *The Transcendental Dialectic* showed that the archetypal model leads to contradictions and fallacies, and that completed unification is unachievable. Theoretical inquiry is guided by the Ideas of scientific inquiry (outlined in the Dialectic); practical inquiry is guided by formulations of the Categorical Imperative and their implications; aspirational inquiry is guided by the Postulates of Practical Reason and maxims seeking purposiveness. But that the many Ideas of Reason are all aspects of one definitive striving for unity does not entail reason's vindication, and does not entail such striving has authority for all thought and action. Kant argues that reason is an active capacity that generates, yet may resolve, problems. Guided by the trilemma above, the discipline of reason required for reason's vindication must be a form of self-discipline (without appeal to any unvindicated, outside reality or necessity), must be negative (without controvertible content), and must be law-giving (in order to adjudicate, to enable systematicity, etc.). But any law-giving that is to be both self-imposed and negative can impose no more than the mere form of law. So the discipline of reason can require only that no principle or standard incapable of being a law be relied on as a fundamental principle for governing thought and action. Anything more determinate would subject thought and action to some outside, hence unvindicated, authority. So the fundamental principle of reason proscribes violating the form of law, or obliges governing thought and action by principles others too can adopt and follow. There are no sufficient instructions for all thought and action. Reason offers only a canon, or *necessary* conditions, for thought and action. We face pluralism, and to avoid "nomadism" we must adopt some plan that does not invoke illusory capacities or unsharable authorities. Autonomy, not submitting to groundless authorities, thinking or acting on principles we can freely adopt, on universalizable principles, is the core of reason. Reason is a (provably) demanding system of constraints on thought, action, and hope.

7.6 The *Prolegomena*'s relation to the *Critique*

I very much hope my extensive treatment of the first *Critique* enriches your experience with the *Prolegomena to Any Future Metaphysics*, if that is what you are reading. Let me conclude this chapter with a very few remarks about that work, and its relation to the *Critique*.

The *Critique* was composed in four or five months "as if in flight," after not publishing anything for eleven years. The *Prolegomena* was published two years after the *Critique* as a more popular guide to what Kant himself calls the *Critique*'s "thorny paths." (Seven important works were then published in rapid succession over the next decade.) In lucidly focusing on how synthetic *a priori* truths are possible in mathematics, natural science, and metaphysics, it parallels its older sister. But already in the Preamble he alerts us to an important difference. It uniformly adopts *analytical* or *regressive* method, whereas the *Critique* is a potent mix of analytical and *synthetic* or *progressive* method. Regressive argument begins with an assumed conclusion, and then seeks its only sufficient explanation. That explanation may then be used to discover other things. The *Prolegomena* takes it as given that pure mathematics and pure physics consist in synthetic *a priori* truths, argues that transcendental idealism is the only explanation for those facts, then uses transcendental idealism to show how non-dogmatic metaphysics is possible. But such argument may obviously lack anti-skeptical force, if the skeptic doubts or denies the assumptions. And indeed, Hume would surely deny that mathematics or physics (or anything, for that matter) is synthetic *a priori*.

But progressive argument rests on no contestable fact, and involves reason's self-examination. As we saw, key transcendental arguments begin with data undeniable by the skeptic, such as the fact of consciousness. So insofar as Hume awoke Kant from his "dogmatic slumber," Kant can put Hume decisively to rest only by synthetic argument. (Note that the uses of "analytic" and "synthetic" to distinguish *methods* is unrelated to Kant's way of distinguishing analytic and synthetic *judgments*.)

On the other hand, some think that Kant's distinction in Part II between *judgments of perception* and *judgments of experience* shows that he is not tempted to pursue an anti-skeptical strategy. They read judgments of perception to be subjective or *seems* judgments, and judgments of experience to be objective or *is* (for all persons) judgments. Since Kant argues that the categories are required for judgments of experience but not judgments of perception – indeed, that what converts a judgment of perception into a judgment of experience is the application of categorical thinking – and since a skeptic like Hume doubts objective but not subjective judgments, Kant begs questions of knowledge against such skeptics.

The text invites this reading. Nevertheless, I think it is a misreading, caused largely by Kant's unfortunate use of "judgment" as applied to the perceptual case. "Judgments of perception" are not *judgments* (cognitions with truth-value) at all. They are mere subjective associations. They are not valid claims about a state of one's mind (an object of inner sense), but just some sort of conjunction of states. His comparison to feelings is revealing, since feelings for Kant are not representations, that is, cognitively significant mental states, at all. If my reading is right, then the doctrine of the *Prolegomena* seems to accord with that of the *Critique*. Or so I say. Some disagree.

7.7   Questions about Kant

Here are some paper topics, a few limited and straightforward, some deeply challenging, some in-between.

1   Kant thinks his analytic–synthetic distinction is important and novel. But why is it different from, and if different, superior to, Hume's relations of ideas–matters of fact distinction, or Leibniz's truths of reason–truths of fact distinction?

2   Explicate and evaluate the claim that all experience requires both intuition and conceptualization. Is this already the whole ballgame against his predecessors (e.g. if it is definitive of empiricist philosophy that all experience is based on intuition (in Kant's sense), and that concepts are just confused, or degraded copies of, intuitions)?

3   Can Kant make a case for the synthetic *a priori* character of geometry? Some think the existence of non-Euclidean geometries refutes Kant. Some think the axiomatization of geometry shows that geometry is analytic (the axioms jointly define all the fundamental notions). Are either of these attempted refutations any good? (Or, why can't alternative conceptions of space (and/or time) adequately explain the status of geometry (and/or arithmetic)?)

4   Sometimes, as in the development of his theories of space and time, Kant uses "metaphysical expositions." If such expositions are conceptual maps, specifying relations among key notions (such as "Space" and "a region of Space"), do they show us something essential about the things represented by the notions, or is how we must think no sure guide to how things are?

5   Do we know the nature of space or time by the end of the *Transcendental Aesthetic*, or must we go through the *Transcendental Analytic* to do so? Why or why not?

6   What is (are) the relation(s) between space and time?

7   Some describe Kant's philosophy as at bottom a theory of synthesis, and its fundamental forms. What exactly is synthesis? How does it relate to analysis? How can we understand the key notions of Kant's philosophy (categories, self-consciousness, judgment, ideas of Reason, etc.) in terms of synthesis?

8   Kant wrote a second, revised edition of the *Critique of Pure Reason* largely to address what he took to be the gross misinterpretation of his philosophy as traditionally idealistic (see, for example, B274), and yet he calls his own philosophy "transcendental (or critical, or formal) idealism," and still today many read him as insisting that all (including physical) objects are "mere appearances," which they construe as equivalent to mental representations. But Kant repeats that one must be a transcendental idealist in order to be an empirical realist, a realist about the everyday and scientific objects accessible to us. And yet, to be a transcendental idealist one ostensibly must hold that space and

time are not independent substances, or relations among phenomena, but ways (contributed by the mind) of receiving data. And so on. So how should we understand Kant on this overarching issue of the role of the human mind in constituting nature (and mathematics, etc.)? Or defend or criticize some contributory element to his elaboration of his "critical" idealism (from the Aesthetic's discussion of space or time, to the seemingly innovative conception of what it is to be an "object of representation" in the Transcendental Deduction (innovation tantamount to changing the subject?, begging the question against prior, allegedly "transcendental realist, so empirically idealist" philosophers?), to the Refutation of Idealism (what are the purportedly proven "existing objects in space outside of me," "objects of outer sense,"?)).

9   What precisely is Kant claiming in the Metaphysical Deduction of the Categories? Defend or challenge his claim that his table of categories is complete, that there are no other basic concepts of the understanding, or his claim that each category in the table is ineliminable, that none are reducible to any (combination of) others.

10   I make various claims about the structure of the Transcendental Deduction, for example, that there's a difference for Kant between objective validity (contributing to having truth value, being true or false) and objective reality (applying to the world), and that the first stage of the Deduction establishes objective validity, the latter stage, objective reality of the categories. Bolster or challenge one or more of my claims. Is the whole Deduction outlined in §26, so one can appreciate the force of the argument by reading from 26 to the end of the Deduction, without reading all the earlier material in the Deduction?

11   How do we know that a category can't be used for cognizing things except when it's applied to objects of experience (Deduction, §22)? "Proved by appeal to X" doesn't generally entail "doesn't apply to not-X."

12   Kant describes the unity of apperception (self-consciousness) variously as "transcendental," "original" or "underived," "unchangeable," "synthetic," etc. How do these descriptions collectively convey the full import of such unity? Probe more deeply the meaning and strength of Kant's argument that conscious activity (or awareness of succession) requires a concept-using, "persisting self."

13   In the Axioms of Intuition and Anticipations of Perceptions Kant makes the distinction between extensive and intensive magnitudes (magnitudes resulting from synthesis of pre-existing parts, which couldn't exist unless their parts existed, and magnitudes which are logically prior to their parts, which are limitations on, not really components of, their magnitudes). What is the importance of this distinction for scientific inquiry?

14 What's the relation between the three Analogies of Experience? For example, can the Second Analogy succeed if the First Analogy fails? (For that matter, how detachable are any of the central arguments of the *Critique*? For example, does the Refutation of Idealism depend on the First Analogy, which depends on the Transcendental Deduction of the Categories, etc.?) Why are some Analogies called "mathematical," some "dynamical"? In the Second Analogy, Kant purports to answer Hume's skepticism about causality by proving with apodictic certainty that all alteration occurs according to the law of the connection of cause and effect. What precisely is Kant's conclusion, how precisely does it relate to Hume's position, how does Kant argue for the Analogy, is the argument sound? Or address a similar question about the First Analogy, concerning substance.

15 What recurrent (pattern of) fallacy committed by pure, rational psychologists does Kant expose in the Paralogisms, how does he diagnose the mistake, and is he right? Can you defend Descartes' use of the *Cogito* against Kant's critique in the Paralogisms?

16 Analyze one Antinomy (the third, on freedom, is most famous) and Kant's solution to it. Or criticize the Antinomies as ineffective, for example, as not making equally cogent cases for opposing positions.

17 What's the nature and importance of the distinction between regulative and constitutive uses of Ideas of Reason? In particular, what does their legitimate "regulative" use amount to? Is it merely heuristic, an optimal goad to inquiry, or something stronger?

18 Show that rational theology does not rest on the ontological argument, as Kant says it does.

19 Don't disregard the Canon of Pure Reason, which after nicely recapping reason's plight in its pure, theoretical use, argues for its successful, exclusively practical role (where what's practical is what's possible through freedom). What are the proper roles of pure reason's objects, namely the freedom of the will, the immortality of the soul, and the existence of God? What is to be done if the will is free, if there is a God, and if there is a future world?

20 Explain as fully as you can the nature of and relation between practical freedom (freedom in its practical meaning) and transcendental freedom (freedom in its transcendental signification). Look especially at the Antinomy of Pure Reason, Section 9, subsection III. This is a segue to the *Groundwork of the Metaphysics of Morals*.

21 In sum, Kant influentially defended revolutionary views of time (and space); the subject; the relation between the subject and the objects of knowledge; the relation between the faculties of reason, understanding, and desire; the inadequacies of both empiricism and traditional rationalism as a theory of thought and action, and the nature of legitimate philosophy; the ineliminability but uniquely effective defusion of philosophical illusion, etc. Reflect more deeply and carefully on a theme that grabs you.

22 And finally, getting back to the organizing core of Kant's project, why does Kant take his central task (the central task of philosophy) to be to explain how *a priori* knowable synthetic judgments are possible? Is the re-crowning of philosophy through defense of the synthetic *a priori* a pipe-dream, or an aspiration with promise? Might Kant's case for the synthetic *a priori* be more successful for one class of judgments than another?

7.8   Some recommended books

Allison, H.E. (1983) *Kant's Transcendental Idealism*, New Haven and London: Yale University Press.

A brilliant, historically sensitive and philosophically deep interpretation and defense of Kant's transcendental idealism – a theory about the necessary role of a specifiable set of *a priori* conditions in human judgment – used to organize excellent analyses of the central arguments of the first *Critique*. Best articulation around of the so-called *two-aspect* (versus *two-object*) reading of Kant. My views are often very close to Allison's, and I often rely on his formulations. A revised and enlarged edition of this book was published in 2004. Topically, it notably adds discussion of the metaphysical deduction, the Third Analogy, the relation of the Refutation of Idealism to transcendental idealism, and, to help us better appreciate the Transcendental Dialectic, the Ideal of Pure Reason and the regulative role of reason (with a changed view of dialectical illusion). Thematically, it develops in new ways Allison's understanding of transcendental idealism to counter important critics such as Ameriks, Guyer, and neo-Strawsonians, focusing more on the *discursivity thesis*, that human cognition requires a conjunction of sensible intuition and active, spontaneous conceptualization, than on the notion of *epistemic condition* I highlight as basic.

—— (1990) *Kant's Theory of Freedom*, Cambridge: Cambridge University Press.

A very helpful book on the title topic (especially grappling with spontaneity), naturally exploring texts in addition to the first *Critique*, but innovatively arguing that for Kant the reality, not just possibility, of transcendental freedom is necessary for the possibility of rational agency in general, that is, for the possibility of action in accordance with *any* kind of principle, not just moral agency, *and* that the basis for this view is essentially theoretical, not practical, so already found in the first *Critique*. Allison argues that one needs to interpret transcendental idealism a certain way to make sense of transcendental freedom, namely the way he defends in the book above.

Ameriks, K. (1982) *Kant's Theory of Mind,* New Haven and London: Yale University Press.

A study of the topics contained in the Paralogisms: the mind's immateriality, simplicity, substantiality, relation to embodiment and the external world, identity, freedom, immortality, and ideality. With the help of overlooked materials from Kant's other writings, offers a sympathetic reconstruction of Kant's views, and criticism of several contemporary interpretations. Ameriks uses his rationalist-oriented reading to better understand the transcendental deduction and transcendental idealism (as well as arguments about the self and morality from ethical writings). In the two-object (not two-aspect) camp.

—— (2003) *Interpreting Kant's Critiques*, Oxford: Clarendon Press.

A collection of essays designed to combine historical and contemporary concerns, stressing that main sections of the three *Critiques* share a common, general philosophical position and several very similar argumentative structures, and that recognizing this helps to interpret contentious passages (especially concerning the self and freedom). The basic strategy throughout is supposed to begin with a main kind of human experience – the three main kinds are theoretical, moral (pure practical), and aesthetic (more generally, pure purposive) – develop a transcendental derivation from such experience of various pure forms, categories, or principles; argue that this only makes sense on the basis of a certain metaphysics, transcendental idealism; and then show that the preceding are preconditions for vindicating the ultimate goal of (theoretical, practical, and methodological) human autonomy. So, for example, transcendental idealism is introduced *after* transcendental deductions are completed, and the starting point of all the arguments, experience, is not so minimalist so as to include private representations, but must be as rich as perceptual judgments of common sense. Lots of worthwhile argument, and some valuable review of the literature along the way.

Bennett, J. (1966) *Kant's Analytic*, London: Cambridge University Press.

Generally modest as exegesis, but often quite good, and influential, as contemporary discussion of issues found in the Analytic. Its analytical table of contents allows you to see what Bennett is arguing so you can use the book selectively.

——— (1974) *Kant's Dialectic*, London: Cambridge University Press.

I think this is exegetically and philosophically superior to his commentary on the Analytic, to which it is a sequel, but which it does not presuppose. Ranges over all the main topics of the Dialectic.

Chadwick, R.F. (ed.) (1992) *Immanuel Kant: Critical Assessments*, 4 vols (vols II and IV are co-edited by Clive Cazeaux), London and New York: Routledge.

Especially rich collection of essays on every aspect of Kant's philosophy.

Ewing, A.C. (1938) *A Short Commentary on Kant's Critique of Pure Reason*, Chicago: University of Chicago Press.

Perhaps the best *short* commentary ever written on the whole *Critique*, except for sparse coverage of Doctrine of Method.

Falkenstein, L. (1995) *Kant's Intuitionism: A Commentary on the Transcendental Aesthetic*, Toronto, Buffalo and London: University of Toronto Press.

A serious commentary on the Transcendental Aesthetic, especially its underdiscussed goal of accounting for the basis of our knowledge of the spatiotemporal properties and relations of things (as well as its more familiar goal of explaining how synthetic *a priori* judgments are possible). It covers the distinction between form and matter in intuition, the relation between sensation and the matter of intuition, what it means to say space and time are forms of intuition and the metaphysical and transcendental expositions of this conclusion, and the implications of Kant's theory, some embraced, such as that things in themselves couldn't be in space and time, and some problematic, such as how we are affected by objects, how we accommodate the apparent temporality of the subject, etc., as well as some implications for the Analytic.

Findlay, J.N. (1981) *Kant and the Transcendental Object*, Oxford: Clarendon Press.

A wide-ranging discussion, alluding to many historical predecessors, contemporaries, and successors of Kant's, of Kant's whole philosophy (but mostly on the first *Critique*), organized around the nature of and relation between the thing it itself, noumenon, and transcendental object = x, and their (its?) significance in Kant's system.

Gardner, S. (1999) *Kant and the Critique of Pure Reason*, London: Routledge.

The best medium-length guide to the first *Critique* ever written.

Guyer, P. (1987) *Kant and the Claims of Knowledge*, Cambridge: Cambridge University Press.

A detailed reconstruction of the central argument of the *Critique* which has within analytic circles come to represent the main, contemporary alternative to Allison's, much more sympathetic, interpretation.

—— (ed.) (1992) *The Cambridge Companion to Kant*, Cambridge: Cambridge University Press.

Useful set of essays providing an overview of Kant's thinking.

—— (2006) *The Cambridge Companion to Kant and Modern Philosophy*, New York: Cambridge University Press.

State-of-the-art essays by leading scholars on both central aspects of the *Critique of Pure Reason* and many of Kant's later writings.

Hoffe, O. (1994) *Immanuel Kant*, Albany: State University of New York Press.

A fine, short, overall introduction to Kant's philosophy.

Kemp Smith, N. (1923) *A Commentary to Kant's "Critique of Pure Reason,"* 2nd edn, reprinted in 1962, New York: Humanities Press.

Probably the twentieth century's most widely read English-language commentary on the *Critique*, it combines scholarly attention to the text with sustained philosophical analyses.

Kitcher, P. (1990) *Kant's Transcendental Psychology*, Oxford: Oxford University Press.

Relates Kant's theory to contemporary work in philosophy of mind, arguing that the only way to understand the transcendental deduction is in terms of Kant's attempt to uncover the psychological preconditions of thought, the capacities needed to do what we do cognitively, and what these capacities imply about the structure of our knowledge. The first time I taught a Kant seminar I had Kitcher and then Allison as guest speakers, and the dialectic between them was fantastic!

Lewis, C.I. (1929) *Mind and the World Order*, revised edn, 1956, New York: Dover.

A special entry; a superb, original piece of philosophy by the American pragmatist which can be very helpful in understanding and assessing elements of Kantianism.

Longuenesse, B. (1998) *Kant and the Capacity to Judge*, Princeton, NJ: Princeton University Press.

The Metaphysical Deduction, which purports to generate an exhaustive list of irreducibly distinct, fundamental forms of thinking from a list of judgment-forms provided by logicians, and which immediately precedes the pivotal-by-consensus Transcendental Deduction of the Categories, is widely mocked, and from all traditions, beginning with Hegel, and through the likes of Strawson, and for lots of different, allegedly sufficient reasons. In contrast, Longuenesse carefully argues that the Metaphysical Deduction, in which Kant attempts to elucidate the nature of the understanding, which he identifies with *the capacity to judge*, is the ineliminable key to the argument of the entire Transcendental Analytic, and so to Kant's critical system. So her exquisite treatment of the Metaphysical Deduction is used to clarify and bolster both A- and B-editions of the Transcendental Deduction, Kant's account of the transcendental synthesis of the imagination, the Schematism, Axioms of Intuition, Analogies of Experience, etc., that is, the subsequent results of Transcendental Analytic. Key to her effort is focus on the fact that for Kant, logical forms of judgment are the universal rules of discursive thought, not to be identified with the empty, logical forms of contemporary logic, and that the Table of Logical Forms of Judgment displays forms of mental *activities*. Thence, the transcendental deduction shows that these mental activities are necessary for any representation of an object. Challenging, but worth the effort.

Paton, H.J. (1936) *Kant's Metaphysics of Experience*, 2 vols, London: George Allen & Unwin; New York: The Humanities Press.

One of the classic commentaries on the *Critique*, very helpful in getting the hang of Kant's system in Kant's terms, often paraphrasing more expansively what Kant says tersely, but for the most part doesn't penetrate as deeply as Kemp Smith or Allison.

Pippin, R.B. (1982) *Kant's Theory of Form*, New Haven: Yale University Press.

Offers a systematic interpretation of Kant's theoretical philosophy from the perspective of his theory of form, necessary to distinguish his position from rationalist theories of mind, dogmatic idealisms and empirical psychologies. Discusses lots of secondary literature in making its case, and argues more generally for the limitations of formalism in epistemology so popular since Kant.

Smyth, R. (1978) *Forms of Intuition*, The Hague and Boston: M. Nijhoff.

An insightful, stimulating, knowledgeable, historical introduction to the Transcendental Aesthetic.

Strawson, P.F. (1975) *The Bounds of Sense*, London: Methuen.

A famous attempt to exorcize the allegedly unacceptable "transcendental psychology" (and architectonic) from the true analytical and critical achievement of Kant's work in the *Critique*. An influential, unified, anti-idealist interpretation (not scholarly), which is very much worth studying, even if you strongly disagree with it.

Van Cleve, J. (1999) *Problems in Kant*, New York and Oxford: Oxford University Press.

A clear, rigorous (regularly making arguments fully explicit in standard form) treatment of key arguments in the *Critique* – sometimes clarifying what Kant's problems, positions, and arguments were, sometimes trying to determine whether he's right – organized around Kant's attempt to determine the scope and limits of *a priori* (especially synthetic) knowledge, defending such against skeptics in areas where it is legitimate (such as arithmetic, geometry, and the foundations of natural science), and exposing its lack of credentials in areas where it is not (such as specifying the properties of the soul, the outer limits and inmost nature of the cosmos, and the existence of God), reaching some controversial results (for example, supporting the synthetic *a priori* and things in themselves, but rejecting the transcendental deduction, the condemnation of rational psychology, and idealism overall). Van Cleve judges the two-aspect view as either wrong or unfathomably mysterious, and treats appearances (phenomena) as what he calls *virtual objects*, roughly, mere logical constructions out of mind-dependent entities, so reads Kant as a more robust kind of idealist (phenomenalist).

Wolff, R.P. (1963) *Kant's Theory of Mental Activity*, Cambridge: Harvard University Press.

Focusing on synthesis as rule-governed mental activity, portrays the Transcendental Analytic as a single, connected argument, beginning with the fact of my being conscious, and successfully answering Hume's skeptical doubt by proving the causal maxim and other Analogies. Appealing because its plausible rendition of Kant is something you really feel you fully understand and appreciate.

Bibliography

Aaron, R. (1971) *John Locke*, 3rd edn, Oxford: Clarendon Press. Originally published in 1937.

Adam, C. and Tannery P. (1964–74) *Oeuvres de Descartes*, 2nd edn, Paris: Vrin.

Adams, R.M. (1994) *Leibniz: Determinist, Theist, Idealist*, New York and Oxford: Oxford University Press.

Allison, H.E. (1983) *Kant's Transcendental Idealism*, New Haven and London: Yale University Press. A revised and enlarged edition of this book was published in 2004.

——(1987) *Benedict de Spinoza: An Introduction*, rev. edn, New Haven and London: Yale University Press.

——(1990) *Kant's Theory of Freedom*, Cambridge: Cambridge University Press.

Ameriks, K. (1982) *Kant's Theory of Mind*. New Haven and London: Yale University Press.

——(2003) *Interpreting Kant's Critiques*, Oxford: Clarendon Press.

Ashcraft, R. (ed.) (1991) *John Locke: Critical Assessments*, 4 vols, London: Routledge.

Ayers, M. (1991) *Locke: Epistemology and Ontology*, 2 vols, London and New York: Routledge.

Baier, A. (1999) *A Progress of Sentiments*, Cambridge: Harvard University Press.

Bennett, J. (1966) *Kant's Analytic*, London: Cambridge University Press.

——(1971) *Locke, Berkeley, Hume: Central Themes*, Oxford: Clarendon Press.

——(1974) *Kant's Dialectic*, London: Cambridge University Press.

Boyle, D. (2000) "Descartes on Innate Ideas," *The Modern Schoolman*, 78: 35–50.

Broughton, J. (2002) *Descartes's Method of Doubt*, Princeton: Princeton University Press.

Brown, S. (1984) *Leibniz*, Minneapolis: University of Minnesota Press.

Chadwick, R.F. (ed.) (1992) *Immanuel Kant: Critical Assessments*, 4 vols (vols II and IV are co-edited by C. Cazeaux), London and New York: Routledge.

Chappell, V. (ed.) (1994) *The Cambridge Companion to Locke*, Cambridge: Cambridge University Press.

Chuang Tzu (1968) *The Complete Works of Chuang Tzu*, trans. B. Watson, New York and London: Columbia University Press.

Cole, J.R. (1992) *The Olympian Dreams and Youthful Rebellion of René Descartes*, Urbana and Chicago: University of Illinois Press.

Cottingham, J., Stoothoff, R., and Murdoch, D. (and Kenny, A. for Volume III) trans. (1984–91) *The Philosophical Writings of Descartes*, Cambridge: Cambridge University Press. Abbreviated CSM.

Cover, J.A. and Hawthorne, J. (1999) *Substance and Individuation in Leibniz*, Cambridge: Cambridge University Press.

Creery, W.E. (ed.) (1991) *George Berkeley: Critical Assessments*, 3 vols, London and New York: Routledge.

Curley, E. (1978) *Descartes Against the Skeptics*, Cambridge: Harvard University Press.

——(1988) *Behind the Geometrical Method: A Reading of Spinoza's Ethics*, Princeton: Princeton University Press.

Damasio, A. (2003) *Looking for Spinoza: Joy, Sorrow, and the Feeling Brain*, Orlando: Harcourt.

Dancy, J. (1987) *Berkeley: An Introduction*, Oxford: Blackwell.

Delahunty, R.J. (1985) *Spinoza*, London: Routledge & Kegan Paul.

Deleuze, G. (1988) *Spinoza: Practical Philosophy*, San Francisco: City Lights Books.

Donagan, A. (1988) *Spinoza*, Chicago: University of Chicago Press.

Edelberg, W. (1990) "The Fifth Meditation," *Philosophical Review*, 99: 493–533.

Ewing, A.C. (1938) *A Short Commentary on Kant's Critique of Pure Reason*, Chicago: University of Chicago Press.

Falkenstein, L. (1995) *Kant's Intuitionism: A Commentary on the Transcendental Aesthetic*, Toronto, Buffalo and London: University of Toronto Press.

Findlay, J.N. (1981) *Kant and the Transcendental Object*, Oxford: Clarendon Press.

Fogelin, R. J. (1985) *Hume's Skepticism in the Treatise of Human Nature*, Boston: Routledge & Kegan Paul.

——(2001) *Berkeley and the Principles of Human Knowledge*, London: Routledge.

Foster, J. and Robinson, H. (eds) (1985) *Essays on Berkeley: A Tercentennial Celebration*, Oxford: Clarendon Press.

Frankfurt, H. (1970) *Demons, Dreamers, and Madmen: The Defense of Reason in Descartes's Meditations*, Indianapolis and New York: The Bobbs-Merrill Company.

Garber, D. (1985) "Leibniz and the Foundation of Physics: The Middle Years," in *The Natural Philosophy of Leibniz*, ed. K. Okruhlik and J. R. Brown, Dordrecht: Reidel.

Gardner, S. (1999) *Kant and the Critique of Pure Reason*, London: Routledge.

Garrett, D. (1997) *Cognition and Commitment in Hume's Philosophy*, New York: Oxford University Press.

Gaskin, J. C. A. (1988) *Hume's Philosophy of Religion*, 2nd edn, London: Macmillan; Atlantic Highlands, NJ: Humanities Press.

Gaukroger, S. (1995) *Descartes: An Intellectual Biography*, Oxford: Clarendon Press.

Gilson, E. (1938) *Reason and Revelation in the Middle Ages*, New York: Charles Scribner's Sons.

Grayling, A.C. (1986) *Berkeley: The Central Arguments*, La Salle, Illinois: Open Court.

Gueroult, M. (1984–85) *Descartes' Philosophy Interpreted According to the Order of Reasons*, 2 vols, trans. R. Ariew, Minneapolis: University of Minnesota Press.

Guyer, P. (1987) *Kant and the Claims of Knowledge*, Cambridge: Cambridge University Press.

——(ed.) (1992) *The Cambridge Companion to Kant*, Cambridge: Cambridge University Press.

——(2006) *The Cambridge Companion to Kant and Modern Philosophy*, New York: Cambridge University Press.

Hall, R. and Woolhouse, R. (1983) *Eighty Years of Locke Scholarship*, Edinburgh: Edinburgh University Press.

Hampshire, S. (1987) *Spinoza: An Introduction to His Philosophical Thought* (rev. edn), New York and Middlesex: Penguin Books. Originally published in 1951.

Hatfield, G. (2003) *Descartes and the Meditations*, London: Routledge.

Hoffe, O. (1994) *Immanuel Kant*, Albany: State University of New York Press.

John Paul II, Pope (1994) *Crossing the Threshold of Hope*, London: Jonathan Cape, Random House; New York: Knopf. Knopf edition more readily available.

Jolley, N. (ed.) (1995) *The Cambridge Companion to Leibniz*, Cambridge: Cambridge University Press.

——(1999) *Locke: His Philosophical Thought*, Oxford: Oxford University Press.

Kaufman, D. (2002) "Descartes's Creation Doctrine and Modality", *Australasian Journal of Philosophy*, 80: 24–41.

Keeling, S.V. (1968) *Descartes*, 2nd edn, London: Oxford University Press.

Kenny, A. (1968) *Descartes: A Study of His Philosophy*, New York: Random House.

Kitcher, P. (1990) *Kant's Transcendental Psychology*, Oxford: Oxford University Press.

Lewis, C.I. (1929) *Mind and the World Order*, rev. edn, 1956, New York: Dover.

Livingston, D. (1998) *Philosophical Melancholy and Delirium: Hume's Pathology of Philosophy*, Chicago, University of Chicago Press.

Lloyd, G. (1996) *Spinoza and the Ethics*, London and New York: Routledge.

Loeb, L.E. (2002) *Stability and Justification in Hume's Treatise*, Oxford: Clarendon Press.

Loemker, L.E. (1969) *Gottfried Wilhelm Leibniz: Philosophical Papers and Letters*, 2nd edn, Dordrecht and Boston: D. Reidel.

Longuenesse, B. (1998) *Kant and the Capacity to Judge*, Princeton, NJ: Princeton University Press.

Machamer, P. (ed) (1998) *The Cambridge Companion to Galileo*, Cambridge: Cambridge University Press.

Mackie, J.L. (1976) *Problems from Locke*, Oxford: Clarendon Press.

Madden, E. and Hare, P. (1968) *Evil and the Concept of God*, Springfield, Illinois: Charles C. Thomas.

Mates, B. (1986) *The Philosophy of Leibniz: Metaphysics and Language*, New York and Oxford: Oxford University Press.

Matthews, G.B. (1992) *Thought's Ego in Augustine and Descartes*, Ithaca and London: Cornell University Press.

McRae, R. (1976) *Leibniz: Perception, Apperception & Thought*, Toronto, Buffalo and London: University of Toronto Press.

Miles, M. (1999) *Insight and Inference: Descartes' Founding Principle and Modern Philosophy*, Toronto and Buffalo: University of Toronto Press.

Millican, P. (ed.) (2002) *Reading Hume on Human Understanding*, Oxford: Clarendon Press.

Mondadori, F. (1973) "Reference, Essentialism and Modality in Leibniz's Metaphysics," *Studia Leibnitiana*, 5:73–101.

——(1975) "Leibniz and the Doctrine of Inter-World Identity," *Studia Leibnitiana*, 7: 22–57.

——(1977) "The Leibnizian 'Circle'," in *Essays on the Philosophy of Leibniz*, ed. Kulstad, M., Houston: Rice University Press, 69–96.

Moyal, G.J.D. (ed.) (1991) *Rene Descartes: Critical Assessments*, 4 vols, London and New York: Routledge.

Neiman, S. (2002) *Evil in Modern Thought: An Alternative History of Philosophy*, Princeton and Oxford: Princeton University Press.

Norton, D. F. (1984) *David Hume: Common-Sense Moralist, Sceptical Metaphysician*, 2nd edn, Princeton, NJ: Princeton University Press.

——(ed.) (1993) *The Cambridge Companion to Hume*, Cambridge: Cambridge University Press.

O'Connor, D. (2001) *Hume and the Dialogues Concerning Natural* Religion, London: Routledge.

Pappas, G.S. (2000) *Berkeley's Thought*, Ithaca and London: Cornell University Press.

Paton, H.J. (1936) *Kant's Metaphysics of Experience*, 2 vols, London: George Allen & Unwin Ltd; New York: The Humanities Press.

Peirce, C.S. (1955) *Philosophical Writings of Peirce*, ed. J. Buchler, New York: Dover.

Penelhum, T. (1992) *David Hume: An Introduction to his Philosophical System*, West Lafayette, IN: Purdue University Press.

Pippin, R.B. (1982) *Kant's Theory of Form*, New Haven: Yale University Press.

Pitcher, G. (1977) *Berkeley*, London, Henley and Boston: Routledge & Kegan Paul.

Radcliffe, E. (2000) *On Hume*, Belmont, CA: Wadsworth.

Rée, J. (1975) *Descartes*, New York: Pica Press.

Rescher, N. (1967) *The Philosophy of Leibniz*, New York: Prentice-Hall. Reissued by Ashgate in 1994.

——(1991) *G.W. Leibniz's Mondadology: An Edition for Students*, Pittsburgh: University of Pittsburgh Press.

Rorty, A.O. (ed.) (1986) *Essays on Descartes' Meditations*, Berkeley, Los Angeles and London: University of California Press.

Russell, B. (1900) *A Critical Exposition of the Philosophy of Leibniz*, reprinted 1997, London: Routledge.

——(1945) *A History of Western Philosophy*, New York: Simon and Schuster.

Rutherford, D. (1995) *Leibniz and the Rational Order of Nature*, Cambridge: Cambridge University Press.

Ryle, G. (1949) *The Concept of Mind*, London and New York: Hutchinson's University Library.

Sleigh, Jr., R.C. (1990) *Leibniz & Arnauld: A Commentary on Their Correspondence*, New Haven and London: Yale University Press.

Smith, N.K. (1923) *A Commentary to Kant's "Critique of Pure Reason,"* 2nd edn, reprinted in 1962, New York: Humanities Press.

——(1941) *The Philosophy of David Hume*, London: Macmillan & Co., Ltd.; New York: St. Martin's Press.

Smyth, R. (1978) *Forms of Intuition*, The Hague and Boston: M. Nijhoff.

Stanistreet, P. (2002) *Hume's Scepticism and the Science of Human Nature*, Hants, England: Ashgate.

Steinberg, D. (2000) *On Spinoza*, Belmont, CA: Wadsworth.

Stoneham, T. (2002) *Berkeley's World: an examination of the Three Dialogues*, Oxford: Oxford University Press.

Strawson, P.F. (1975) *The Bounds of Sense*, London: Methuen.

Stroud, B. (1977) *Hume*, London: Routledge & Kegan Paul. Reissued by Routledge in 1999.

——(1984) *The Significance of Philosophical Skepticism*, Oxford: Oxford University Press.

Tarnas, R. (1991) *The Passion of the Western Mind*, New York: Ballantine Books.

Tipton, I. (1974) *Berkeley: The Philosophy of Immaterialism*, London: Methuen.

Tlumak, J. (1978) "Certainty and Cartesian Method," in *Descartes: Critical and Interpretive Essays*, ed. M. Hooker, Baltimore and London: The Johns Hopkins University Press.

——(1982) "Critical Notice of Robert McRae's *Leibniz: Perception, Apperception, and Thought*," *Nous*, 16: 154–60.

——(1983) "Cross-Categorial Priority Arguments," *Metaphilosophy*, 14: 32–39.

Tweyman, S. (ed.) (1995) *David Hume: Critical Assessments*, 6 vols, London: Routledge.

Urmson, J.O. (1982) *Berkeley*, Oxford: Oxford University Press.

Van Cleve, J. (1979) "Foundationalism, Epistemic Principles, and the Cartesian Circle," *Philosophical Review*, 88: 55–91.

——(1999) *Problems in Kant*, New York and Oxford: Oxford University Press.

Wilson, M. (1978) *Descartes*, London, Henley and Boston: Routledge & Kegan Paul.

Winkler, K.P. (1989) *Berkeley: An Interpretation*, Oxford: Clarendon Press.

Wolff, R. P. (1963) *Kant's Theory of Mental Activity*, Cambridge: Harvard University Press.

Wolfson, H.A. (1934) *The Philosophy of Spinoza*, 2 vols, Cambridge: Harvard University Press.

Woolhouse, R.S. (ed.) (1994) *Gottfried Wilhelm Leibniz: Critical Assessments*, 4 vols, London: Routledge.

——(1983) *Philosophers in Context: Locke*, Minneapolis: University of Minnesota Press.

Yolton, J.W. (1970) *Locke and the Compass of Human Understanding*, Cambridge: Cambridge University Press.

Index